FRANCE IN THE AGE OF HENRI IV

STUDIES IN MODERN HISTORY

General editors: John Morrill and David Cannadine

This series, intended primarily for students, will tackle significant historical issues in concise volumes which are both stimulating and scholarly. The authors combine a broad approach, explaining the current state of our knowledge in the area, with their own research and judgements: and the topics chosen range widely in subject, period and place.

Titles already published

FRANCE IN THE AGE OF HENRI IV

the struggle for stability

Second Edition

Mark Greengrass

Longman
London and New York

Longman Group UK LImited,
Longman House, Burnt Mill,
Harlow, Essex CM20 2JE, England
and Associated Companies throughout the world.

*Published in the United States of America
by Longman Publishing, New York*

First published 1984
Second impression 1987
Second edition 1995
ISBN 0 582 08721 X PPR

British Library Cataloguing-in-Publication Data

A catalogue record for this book is available from the British Library

Library of Congress Cataloging-in-Publication Data

Greengrass, Mark, 1949–
France in the age of Henri IV: the struggle for stability / Mark Greengrass – 2nd ed.
    p.   cm.
  Includes bibliographical references and index.
  ISBN 0 582 08721 X
  1. France – Politics and government – 1589–1610. I. Title.
DC122.G73 1995
944' .031–dc20

94-6451
CIP

Set by 7 in Bembo
Printed in Malaysia

CONTENTS

LIST OF FIGURES AND MAPS

FIGURES

MAPS

Preface to the Second Edition

'It is a thing to be wondered at', reflected Edmund Burke in 1790, 'to see how very soon France, when she had a moment to respire, recovered and emerged from the longest and most dreadful civil war that ever was known in any nation.' With the drama of the French Revolution evolving before his eyes, he had a good vantage point from outside to look back to the remarkable recovery of France from the wars of religion 200 years previously. Less partisan presenters of modern history textbooks approach the period of France's wars of religion with sinking hearts. How can they readily make sense of the sordid, squalid successions of ambitious aristocrats, abetted by foreign powers, who, under the pretext of religion, organised endless coups and nearly destroyed the monarchy? Perceptibly relieved by the accession of the Bourbons, they explain the swift return to order in France, which had so impressed Burke, by referring to the anarchy of the civil wars which so wearied the country that it naturally turned to a strong and absolute monarchy.

When this book was first published in 1984, it presented some of the interim conclusions of recent research into the French civil wars which had begun to emerge from a group of American scholars and the notable research of French historians such as Emmanuel Le Roy Ladurie, Denis Richet, Janine Garrisson and their pupils. Now, a decade later, historians are much better informed about the nature of the propaganda, of sectarian conflict, of the operations of aristocratic patronage and the working of provincial and municipal politics during the civil wars. The old-fashioned 'anarchy' is gradually being rendered intelligible. In this new edition, the text and bibliography have been completely revised, corrected and expanded to take account of this research. A new chapter has been added to the text and new figures included in the appendix.

This study was never intended to be a biography of Henri IV. In the same year as the first edition of this book appeared, Janine Garrisson and David Buisseret published their interpretations of the king and his reign.[1] These followed the thorough and perspicacious biography by Jean-Pierre Babelon, whose book had been published in 1982.[2] This book was intended to provide a revision of historical perspective, and its basic propositions seem to have been upheld in the decade since the first edition appeared. It argues that Henri IV had consciously to create the stability of his rule after the wars. There was nothing natural or automatic about it. It was a deliberate, in some senses artificial creation, which could have been easily overturned and which was constantly being tested, but which became stronger the longer it lasted. Many elements of this proposition lay behind a national exhibition to commemorate the quatercentenary of Henri IV's accession to power. First displayed in Pau, and then later in 1989 in Paris, the exhibition brought together a remarkable and exciting collection of surviving artefacts under the title: 'Henri IV and the Reconstruction of the Realm'.[3]

The perspective of this study was already suggested in Roland Mousnier's *Assassination of Henry IV*, an investigation into the background to the king's assassination in 1610, first published in French in 1964 at the time of the attempted assassinations of the first president of the fifth republic, Charles de Gaulle. As Mousnier suggested, the assassination crystallised a myth about the personality and achievement of the king which turned Henri IV into the man for all seasons, 'blessed of all ages' as Voltaire put it in his epic poem, the *Henriade*. To pious catholics in the seventeenth century, he was a truly catholic statesman; to Louis XIV, he was presented as a model of kingship, of the *métier du roi*. For the peasants of the Normandy rising in 1639, his epoch represented a golden age. In the Fronde, Parisians met under the shadow of the great equestrian statue of the king, the *Roy en bronze*, placed at one end of the Ile de la Cité, and, in Fronde pamphlets, dialogues between this statue and *la Samaritaine*, a statue on the right bank of the river, reminded Parisians of the first Bourbon's concern for their welfare. The legend reached its height in the next

---

1. J. Garrisson, 1984; D. Buisseret, 1984.
2. J-P. Babelon, 1982.
3. *Henri IV et la reconstruction du royaume* (1989), a beautifully illustrated catalogue of the exhibition. This is also the point to record the significant impact of the 'Association Henri IV, 1989', whose conferences from 1987 onwards have regularly brought together a range of specialists and whose publications have materially helped to change our perspectives of the period.

century when Voltaire praised the king as the champion of enlightened toleration while the Physiocrats saw in his reign the beginnings of a true respect for both agriculture and free trade. Louis XVI presented himself as 'another Henri' while Marie Antoinette was pleased to regard herself as a romantic version of Gabrielle d'Estrées. If the legend of Henri IV became a focal point of uniting people in the *ancien régime*, this was because the whole emphasis of his rule was placed on the struggle for stability.

It is important, therefore, to penetrate beyond this myth and arrive at an assessment of the political stability of France which does not depend on the legend and its inevitable stress on the undoubtedly considerable magnetism and personal charms of the monarch. The term 'political stability' has been chosen with some care. Stability does not exclude the possibility of continuing tensions of different sorts; the simple example comes to mind of a bridge which requires structural stress to keep it upright. It would be wrong to imagine that France was, at any stage in the lifetime of Henri IV, politically apathetic or lacking a vigorous political debate about sectarianism, government weakness, the dangers of civil war and the possible social upheavals that followed periods of prolonged civil wars. The precise historical problem is to assess the reality of these tensions and the potential damage they could do to the polity of France. To those tempted to suggest that 'political stability' is an anachronism or variety of historical impressionism, the reply would be that contemporaries were both precise and articulate in presenting stability, harmony and order, as one of their clearest and most deep-rooted political aspirations.

I have kept manuscript references to a minimum, preferring to concentrate on referring to the rich amount of material which has appeared in print since 1945. When a primary source is used, the reference utilises the date of the printed edition and this is indicated by the use of square brackets. To the many debts of gratitude recorded in the preface to the first edition of the work, I should add those owed to various reviewers and to my colleague Joe Bergin for spotting errors in the first edition. My wife, Andrea Greengrass, has been magnificent in assisting this wayward author to prepare the revised text for publication.

MARK GREENGRASS
Sheffield
December 1993

Abbreviations

Arch. cur. de l'hist. de France	*Archives curieuses de l'histoire de France depuis Louis XI jusqu'à Louis XVIII* (1st Series), (15 vols, Paris-Beauvais, 1834–37).
AD	*Archives Départementales.*
AN	*Archives Nationales*, Paris.
ANG	*Acta Nuntiaturae Gallicae* (Correspondance du nonce en France, vols i–xvi appeared, Rome, Université pontificale grégorienne).
d'Aubigné	Agrippa d'Aubigné, *l'Histoire universelle* (ed. A. de Ruble, 9 vols, Paris, 1886–97).
Bèze	*Histoire ecclésiastique des églises réformées au royaume de France* (3 vols, 1883–89 – reprinted Niewkoop, B. de Graaf, 1974).
Bib. Mazarine	*Bibliothèque Mazarine*, Paris.
BN	*Bibliothèque Nationale*, Paris.
BL	*British Library*, London.
Bib. Prot.	*Bibliothèque de la société d'histoire du protestantisme français*, Paris.
Cal SP For	*Calendar of State Papers Foreign.*

Cayet	Palma Cayet, *Chronologie novenaire* (ed. Michaud and Poujoulat, *Nouvelle collection des mémoires*, vol. xii, 1881).
DBF	*Dictionnaire de biographie française* (Paris, 1954–).
Fontanon	A. Fontanon, *Les édits et ordonnances des rois de France* (4 vols, Paris, 1611).
Haag/Bordier	E. Haag and H. Bordier, *La France protestante*, (10 vols, Paris, 1846–59 – reprinted Geneva 1966).
Isambert	François Isambert, *Recueil général des anciennes lois françaises* (29 vols, Paris, 1829–33; reprinted Burt Franklin, New York, 1964).
LN	Robert Lindsay and John Neu, *French Political Pamphlets* (Univ. of Wisconsin, Madison, 1969). This is an inventory of pamphlets held in the Newbery Library, Chicago, many of which have been microfilmed and are available from UPI (Ref: Fr. 3041). Individual titles have not been cited in the text but references are to the inventory number of the pamphlet.
MC	*Mémoires de Louis I, prince de Condé* (6 vols, London, 1743).
ML	*Mémoires de la Ligue, contenans les événements les plus remarquables depuis 1576 . . .* (6 vols, Amsterdam, 1758–63).
de Thou	Jacques-Auguste de Thou, *Histoire universelle depuis 1543 jusqu'en 1607* (16 vols, London, 1734).

Valois

Noël Valois, *Inventaire des arrêts du conseil d'Etat (règne d'Henri IV)* (2 vols, Paris, 1886-93). Reference is made to *arrêts* by their inventory number.

CHAPTER ONE
The French Civil Wars

SECTARIAN MEMORIES

During the French civil wars, Louis Le Roy (c.1510-77), professor of Greek at the Collège Royale in Paris, published his world history. Among the notable changes in his own civilisation he was impressed by the invention of printing, gunpowder and the compass and alarmed by the lamentable spread of venereal disease. But the real disease of his own time, he wrote, was the 'sects [*which have*] sprung up in all nations, greatly disturbed the public order and withered the well-being of humans one to another . . . Everywhere, states have been attacked, disturbed or overturned: everywhere, religions have been plagued with heresies. Everything is out of place and in confusion and nothing is as it should be.'[1] To this author it was evident that the decisive event of his century had been the protestant reformation. For the first time, Christendom had been irreparably divided. Families, cities and states were split, not just along the lines of private convictions or theological beliefs, but by rival attitudes, values, political ideas, assumptions and shared experiences.

France could not have expected to escape from the evangelism of persuasive protestant preachers. Yet, in comparison with Martin Luther's first decade of explosive and liberating influence in Germany, the impact of his message in French-speaking Europe appears initially to have been muted.[2] More went on than was apparent since French Lutheranism intermingled with a less than strident reforming

---

1. L. Le Roy, *De la vicissitude ou variété des choses en l'univers* (Paris, 1576), ch. xi. Cf. W. Gundersheimer, 1966.
2. M. Greengrass, 1987b.

1

evangelism and did not wear its convictions on its sleeve. This was, at least in part, because (unlike in Germany) there were tolerably effective royal and ecclesiastical instruments for the repression of heresy in France. Repression of religious unorthodoxy was the stronger, too, because France was a huge country and, for the most part, a very traditional society. Change was particularly threatening and there were strong traditions to identify religious change with heresy.

It has recently been argued that the sudden prominence of eschatalogical beliefs in the popular and almanac literature in France from the 1520s was the sign of a common anxiety, a panic reaction within traditional catholic France to the frightening and novel prospect of religious pluralism.[3] The notion that the world would shortly come to an end was part of a belief system in which holy power was immanent in the forces of nature and the world at large. God was engaged mystically and prophetically in a mighty struggle against the forces of evil. Every natural event therefore carried sacral significance. Monstrous births, comets in the sky, plagues and famines were all capable of being mobilised to indicate God's imminent vengeance upon a society which allowed heresy to flourish in its midst. Heretics were identified as the harbingers of the Last Days. Contemporaries were urged to join in the ultimate battle against the forces of evil, mustering in the reformation.

Historians are still debating how precisely to interpret the significance of this 'panic literature'.[4] Was it a reflection of a series of stock responses, well-rehearsed and well-known but more prominent from the 1520s because of changes to the patterns in the surviving corpus of printed material? How seriously did contemporaries take the frequent expressions from the pulpit and in print of their living in the Last Days and under an imminent Judgement? Were such expressions part of an accepted means by which some of those in the privileged bodies of corporate France sought to protect society from change and ruination? For the most part, however, historians accept that one of the most striking features about the reformation in France was the divisive and hostile responses to the prospects for change which were manifested from an early date. These provided the motive power for the gradual harnessing of the forces of repression which took place in the 1540s and 1550s. The failure of persecution to eradicate (as in the past) the roots of heresy contributed still further, we may imagine, to a greater sense of discomfiture. This frustration found its outlet in the

3. D. Crouzet, 1990, I, pt 1.
4. M. Greengrass, 1991.

violence which has been identified on the printed page as well as on the streets in the later 1550s. This constituted the prelude to the sectarian divisions of the civil wars. However historians interpret these early phases of the religious troubles in sixteenth-century France, the anxiety, frustration and disorientation which greeted the prospect of religious change would have a long history through the sixteenth century and into the reign of Henri IV. It is a central theme of this book that he took the irrational fears which were engendered by it seriously and that he ministered a healing balm to them.

One consequence of the gathering forces of repression, both institutional and more generally rooted in society at large, was the emergence of a brand of protestantism at once less tolerant, more convinced of its righteousness and ultimately more committed than in German-speaking lands. This 'second-generation' reformation – Calvinism – spread among exiles from France in the French-speaking parts of Europe, especially in the Imperial Free City of Strasbourg and the newly independent Geneva. Relatively free from constraint, reformers like Jean Calvin (1509–64) were able to develop a strong sense of community within a new model church and to preach the pure kingdom of Christ. The pastors and elders of the Calvinist church organised consistories to enforce a hard, clear moral code on believers. Refugees from catholic persecution in France joined them in increasing numbers after 1545. They were encouraged to see themselves as the precious few, the leaven in the lump, the Elect from whom true reformation would eventually flow. Some of them became permanent exiles. But others were sent out again as an élite – the Saints – to conquer and destroy the 'great worldly Babylon' in their native country. Nicodemites, temporisers, those who refused to subscribe to the new faith, were to be cast aside. In 1559, the Huguenots (as the Calvinists became known in France) held their first National Synod in Paris and established their Confession of Faith and Ecclesiastical Discipline. A year later, in March 1560, an edict was issued in the king's name granting an amnesty for heretics who agreed to abjure, an implicit recognition that repression was failing. The text admitted that 'great numbers of people of all sexes, ages, qualities and conditions' had become heretics. The licence of the times, the preachers and pamphlets spreading from outside the realm, especially Geneva, were to blame for leading astray 'the people of our realm who, lacking in judgement and knowledge, have no discernment in matters of doctrine'.[5]

5. N.M. Sutherland, 1980, pp. 104–5, 347–8. Cf. D. Kelley, 1981.

How many Huguenots were there in France on the eve of the religious wars and how were they socially and geographically distributed? These questions confronted contemporaries as much as they have perplexed historians. Answers depend on whom one asks and where one looks. Gaspard de Saulx-Tavannes (1509–73), a marshal of France and a royal councillor, knew without a doubt that it was the townsmen, the lesser people (*paisans bourgeois, menu peuple*), women, children and vagabonds who were most infected in his native Burgundy.[6] Well-informed spy and smooth Venetian diplomat, Jean Michieli, reported that the nobility was the most contaminated – especially those 'under forty years of age'.[7] His successor, Suriano, estimated that nine-tenths of the kingdom were infected, early in 1562.[8] Elderly battle-hardened catholic lieutenant of Gascony, Blaise de Monluc (c.1501–77), blamed heresy on his enemies among the royal officers and financiers of Bordeaux.[9] One of those magistrates, Florimond de Raemond (1540–1601), reflected from the comparative quiescence of his old age how schoolmasters when he was young had made his contemporaries vulnerable to heresy by teaching them to read, think and, eventually, to act for themselves.[10] In the small catholic *bastide* town of Gaillac, a hostile witness thought the rich merchants carried heresy with them as it were the plague. In Toulouse, another judge believed that the richer young men and the more beautiful young women were mostly to be blamed for the spreading spores of heresy.[11]

For the Huguenots, a sense of imminent victory is the hallmark of those pages in the great protestant compilation, the *Ecclesiastical History of the Reformed Churches of France* which relate to the years 1561–2.[12] Calvin could not believe what was taking place in France and lamented that there were not enough well-trained ministers to fulfil the demand.[13] A report from the church in Paris to the protestants in Zurich said that 'the harvest for Christ' had been excellent. Providence had protected them. 'We have confidence . . . there is an extraordinary desire to see the Kingdom of God increase.' They talked of their congregation changing from being *petits gens* to becoming 'the élite of France' with 'many nobles and magistrates . . . women and

6. G. de Saulx-Tavannes, [1881], VIII, 368.
7. N. Tommaseo, [1838], I, 413.
8. Ibid., 541. Cited in I. Cloulas, 1979, p. 137.
9. B. de Monluc, [1964], p. 472.
10. F. de Raemond, [1605], I, 261.
11. M. Blouyn, [1976] p. 74. G. Bosquet, [1862], pp. 47–8.
12. Bèze, I, Bks IV and V.
13. R. Kingdon, 1956, ch. viii.

honourable young ladies and from the best families' attending the sermons.[14] With an edict of toleration granting them a basic civil liberty (as in January 1562), they flaunted their respectability. A Paris merchant tailor spoke out in public against the cardinal of Lorraine. Leading members of the Paris congregation dressed up in their best clothes so that they could be seen by the queen mother on their way to a Huguenot church service.[15] To those who had been so recently persecuted, this sudden degree of recognition was, in itself, a sign of the Lord at work. In provincial cities, public meetings were held in markets, main streets and even town halls, demonstrating that protestantism had become part of the social fabric of French city life. Communal singing, marriages between the faithful, public burials, organised rallies of the new sect were not just moments when the Huguenots called on the Lord, but ways of demonstrating to those who took part that He really was on their side.[16]

Attempts to quantify this consciousness within a statistic are unlikely to be accurate. It is frequently said, for instance, that there were 2,150 Calvinist churches established by May 1562.[17] It is evident that some kind of review was carried out then to establish how many troops the Huguenots could muster in the imminent event of war. But this figure was also inflated in order to impress the queen mother and her advisors of the overwhelming strength of Huguenot numbers. Attempts to reconstitute a list of those churches which had a minister or a deacon at around this date arrive at nowhere near this figure and the best estimate is of about 1,400 communities running right across France with 800 of them concentrated in a broad crescent sweeping across western France and down through the Midi to the Alps.[18] The size of congregations varied enormously, so that any estimate of the numbers of believers is nothing more than an educated guess. Suriano, the Venetian ambassador, was clearly exaggerating their strength when he spoke of nine-tenths of the kingdom; it may have been only as many as 2 million. From these churches came many of the 20,000 who assembled at Orléans under the prince of Condé to fight for the cause in the first civil war.[19]

14.   F. Aubert, 1947, p. 97.
15.   D. Richet, 1991, pp. 17–19. For the Paris congregation see also B. Diefendorf, 1991, ch. vii.
16.   Bèze, II, 432–5, 712–18, III, 1–14, 249–55. N.H. Galpern, 1976, pp. 155–6. P. Benedict, 1981, ch. ii. D. Kelley, 1981, pp. 96–118. M. Lamet, 1979, ch. iv.
17.   R. Kingdon, 1956, p. 79. L. Romier, 1925, II, 180.
18.   J. Garrisson-Estèbe, 1980, pp. 63–4.
19.   D. Kelley, 1981, p. 225.

The impressions of contemporaries were all, in their way, correct. Modern, more sophisticated analysis has been directed towards discovering the social status and religious experience of the Huguenots in various cities, provinces and individual social groups. The research confirms the diverse and profound effect of protestantism within the French polity.[20] But the Huguenots paid an enormous price for this success. Far from the approaching victory of the New Jerusalem of their dreams, they faced bitter and entrenched catholic hostilities. This swiftly erased their naive optimism which, while it returned to parts of the Huguenot world again in 1566 and 1571–72 and shortly after the peace of Monsieur in 1576, was to be repeatedly crushed by catholic reaction and civil war. France was, in fact, officially at war for most of the periods 1562–63, 1567–70 and 1572–77. Sectarian tension in these years has a distinctive rhythm and ritual which provides a kind of seismograph to these religious tremors.[21] Massacres occurred towards the beginning of formal periods of warfare, when passions were at their height. They were long past by the time the military campaigns reached their stalemates. Cities where the two religions existed in close proximity were most at risk. Moments when official catholic leaders tried to control or proscribe protestants were the most dangerous ones. Advent and Lent were the seasons of greatest fear, partly because these were traditionally times of great catholic preaching. Sermons by preachers openly criticised royal policy and even invited their congregations to take the law into their own hands. Royal and municipal authorities were almost powerless to restrain them since the arrest of a catholic preacher could produce the rising which the authorities were trying to avoid.

The resulting massacres were frequently extremely bloody. One protestant pamphleteer with a happy knack of endowing his work with a spurious certainty estimated that 765,000 people had been killed in the wars to 1581 of whom 36,300 had been massacred, 4,500 of whose bodies (according to his estimates) had washed down the Seine.[22] His figures were based on no more than guesswork, but it is

---

20. See M. Greengrass, 1987b.

21. D. Richet, 1991, pp. 21–4; B. Diefendorf, 1991, provides the most thorough case-study; D. Crouzet, 1990, gives the most shockingly vivid evocation of the rituals of sectarian killing.

22. N. Froumenteau (ascribed to Nicolas Barnaud or Jean Frotté) *Le secret des thrésors* (*finances* in the second edition) (n.p., 1581). He provides a survey, diocese by diocese, of the effects of the civil wars. J.B. Wood, 1984, takes this source as providing 'detailed and comparable information on contemporary perceptions and claims about the consequences for all of France of two decades of civil war'. The claim, and the extrapolated statistics which result from it, should be treated with scepticism.

clear that the massacres of this period were of a scale and intensity which was unmatched anywhere else in Europe. In one sectarian battle in the streets of Toulouse in May 1562, the battle raged for days and between 3,000 and 4,000 people have been claimed as dying inside and outside the city walls.[23] The Huguenot defeat was remembered in an annual procession in the city which Voltaire later described as a commemoration 'to thank God for four thousand murders'. The massacre of St Bartholomew was the most notorious and marked a turning-point of the civil wars for many of the Huguenot communities in France. Beginning in Paris in the early morning of 24 August 1572, it lasted for some days there before spreading to several provincial towns like Lyon (31 August), Orléans (25 August), Bordeaux (3 October) and Toulouse (4 October).[24] The death-toll was doubtless large. The Huguenot pamphlet *Le Reveille-Matin* (*The Morning Reveille*) of early 1573 – one of the first in French to create the protestant legend of a premeditated attempt by the authorities to annihilate every protestant in the kingdom and the most influential pamphlet on the subject in protestant Europe – spoke of 100,000 put to death during that period.[25] The estimate was an evident exaggeration but other estimates are of little value and incapable of verification. Perhaps 3,000 died in Paris and a further 7,000 in the provinces.[26] It was frequently the case that the authorities could not control the killing, once it had started, and sometimes they did not try. The *parlement* of Toulouse legalised the pillage and slaughter of any heretic by any individual in May 1562.[27] 'Kill them all, the king commanded it', the duke of Guise was reported to have told catholics in Paris in August 1572.[28] The *parlement* of Paris, it has recently been argued, may have had a part to play in the events leading up to St Bartholomew; a stronger case can be made for a faction within the city militia of Paris exploiting the violence once it had begun.[29] Priests as well as ministers of the reformed religion legitimised violence and bloodshed, albeit often only implicitly. Massacres involved both rich and poor and could, unless checked, manifest a sense of class hostility with the indiscriminate pillaging of rich people's property on the

23.   M. Greengrass, 1983.
24.   J. Garrisson-Estèbe, 1968, chs viii–ix.
25.   Q. Skinner, 1978, II, 304–5. R. Kingdon, 1988, ch. vii.
26.   Estimates in P. Joutard *et al.*, 1976, p. 68. I. Cloulas, 1979, p. 297, puts the figures substantially higher.
27.   Bèze, III, 17.
28.   D. Richet, 1991, p. 24. N.Z. Davis, 1975, pp. 152–87.
29.   J-L. Bourgeon, 1992; but see especially the judicious analysis in B. Diefendorf, 1991, ch. vi.

assumption that it belonged to protestants or sheltered suspects.[30] Private scores were settled as well. The hangman of the city of Carcassonne took the opportunity of the religious riot there in 1562 to kill five of his personal enemies, 'eating the liver of one of them' and then 'knifing another'.[31] Women and children played their part in the disturbances, convinced (or so it has been powerfully argued) that they were acting in accordance with God's wishes as revealed to them in the sermons and panic literature which spoke of the imminence of God's judgement and the Last Days.[32] Protestants, too, engaged in violent acts of destruction, especially in the smashing of images, crosses, stained glass and relics.[33] To the cry of 'the Gospel' they went about their work with a sense that they were undertaking God's purpose and created in the minds of many contemporaries the impression that, by destroying such symbols of authority and removing a priesthood, they were, in fact, creating a new and dangerous equality. This was particularly the case in rural areas and among the nobility, although the expressions of equality were also heard in those towns where protestantism had taken root at the lower level of the social scale.[34]

The bloody and gruesome elements of the French civil wars were incomprehensible to contemporary onlookers from outside. 'These French tragedies . . . cannot be expressed with tongue to declare the cruelties' said Lord Burghley in 1572 after reading the first reports about the latest round of massacres. 'That cruelty that I think no Christian since the heathen tyme hath hard of the lyke' commented the Earl of Leicester, implying perhaps that the 'lyke' could not possibly occur in the England of Elizabeth. The gratuitous violence of the civil wars would become equally incomprehensible to the generation after it occurred, an embarrassment which was not to be discussed openly in polite company. It was glossed in euphemistic references to 'the troubles' or the 'past wars', explained away as the mindless and self-defeating brutality of the crowd. To comprehend the violence of the French civil wars is to confront the way in which religious belief and experience gave pattern and purpose to individual actions in dramatic and unpredictable ways.

At its heart, it has been argued, Calvinism offered a very different

---

30. N.Z. Davis, 1975, pp. 175–6. J. Garrisson-Estèbe, 1968, p. 196. Bèze, III, 17.

31. Bèze, I, 963–4.

32. D. Crouzet, 1990, I, pt 1.

33. N.Z. Davis, 1975, p. 174. J. Garrisson-Estèbe, 1980, pp. 163–5. D. Crouzet, 1990, I, pt 2, ch. vii.

34. Ibid., ch. x.

belief system from that which underpinned the traditional church. Calvin rejected judicial astrology, prognostication, divination and aggressive millenarianism. Holy power was not immanent in the world, fighting the 'mother of battles' against the forces of darkness. World order came about through the laws of nature, imposed by God the Creator directing a Providence which predestined its shape and our salvation in ways that we could not hope to, and did not need to, comprehend. World time and space became desacralised. Holiness lay in the Word of God alone. Through its promises, working their effects upon the consciences of individual hearers, believers were assured of their salvation. The French civil wars were a Theatre of Cruelties because they were the cockpit of two conflicting visions of world order.

So, to Calvin's adherents, every aspect of catholic ritual was polluted with idolatry. Its ridicule, total destruction and obliteration were essential prerequisites for a total reformation. Those who frustrated God's purposes were 'fools', 'dogs', 'beasts', 'ravening wolves'. The irreverence of carnival and the purifying effects of parody were harnessed by Huguenots to desacralise the traditional religion and liberate people from its ruses. The animal lusts of the priests were publicly mocked and they were made to suffer accordingly.

When catholics found the sacred Host thrown to the dogs, the statue of the Virgin Mary covered in mud, the crucifix roasted on a spit, holy oil used to smarten up soldiers' boots and human excrement filling the fonts and holy water basins, their hostility inevitably took the form of demanding the cleansing of a city or locality from the taint of protestant impurity. Religious cleansing in the sixteenth century took on as ugly a disposition as 'ethnic cleansing' in our own. Huguenot victims were thrown into the river Garonne in Toulouse in May 1562 and part of the city burnt to the ground as ways of 'cleansing' an impure city, or so it has been suggested. Why else were children employed in 1572 to castrate and disembowel the body of the Huguenot leader, Admiral Gaspard de Coligny (1519–72) and then drag the remnants around the city of Paris if not to imply that their innocence would transcend his heretical filth? But the desire to purify the world around them from the pollution of heresy was only one aspect of a more fundamental drive to be the conduit of God's wrath, to feel part of God's immanence in the Last Days. The Old Testament provided a lexicon of language, symbols and gestures. Far from reflecting a 'natural' violence to be expected in the sixteenth century, the dreadful events of France's religious troubles took place at moments when individuals were engaged in a sacral act, acting sometimes in a kind of trance or inspired by a form of mental vision. The particularly gruesome cruelty meted out towards protestants, the perverted mutilation of their bodies after their death and the exaltation that apparently accompanied such acts cannot simply be explained as sadism. Rather, the heretics were seen as non-humans, agents of the devil, while their pursuants were God's secret, avenging angels.

After such sectarian moments, catholics held processions and undertook pilgrimages in expiation. Commemorative crosses were constructed to purify particular quarters – the most famous of which was the Gâtines cross in the *rue* Saint-Denis of Paris, constructed in August 1571 on the site of a house inhabited by a Huguenot family which had been host to secret meetings of the Paris congregation. The house was pulled down by order of the *parlement* of Paris and the cross itself was later removed on 20 December 1571 by the king following protestant protests. The act of removal provoked further orchestrated popular unrest. There were reported miracles too. A hawthorn bush in the cemetery of the Holy Innocents in Paris, for example, spontaneously burst into flower at the beginning of the massacre of Saint Bartholomew.[35] In Troyes, eleven years previously, a copper cross, the healing powers of which had apparently lapsed at the turn of the century, changed its colour and began to cure people again after the first public sectarian disturbances in the city.[36] Even the 'happy day' of the massacre of Saint Bartholomew was treated as a kind of miracle in some catholic circles.[37] Such reactions became the first steps by which the catholic majority in France created a common memory of the sectarian tensions in the civil wars.

Acting together in a common cause also left its imprint on the collective consciousness. Confraternities, traditional institutions for catholic laymen, acted (sometimes with municipal or other encouragement from the local urban notability) like vigilante groups in some localities.[38] In May 1568, for example, over 400 people gathered in the ruined cathedral at Mâcon to swear an oath to the newly re-formed confraternity of the Holy Ghost in which the city's catholics agreed to protect each other by force of arms if necessary to expiate the invasion of the city by the protestants in 1562 and 1567, and to rebuild the churches (every one of which had been destroyed). Two months later a Calvinist nobleman from the cavalry company of Coligny's brother was killed by six masked men outside his house in

35. J. Garrisson-Estèbe, 1968, pp. 133–4.
36. N.H. Galpern, 1976, pp. 159–60.
37. P. Joutard *et al.*, 1976, pp. 55–6. D. Crouzet, 1990, II, chs xi and xii.
38. M. Orlea, 1980, pp. 33–4. R. Harding, 1980, 85–107.

Mâcon. This was the first fruits of the confraternity's malevolence, asserted his brother, the admiral.[39] Other confraternities along the Saône valley acted in concert with one another and the pattern was repeated elsewhere. In towns with sovereign courts in the south of France, confraternities united with syndicates of judges to maintain order and municipal traditions in the face of protestant attack.[40] Distinctive clothing and badges identified the participants – red bonnets in the *Bande cardinale* in Bordeaux of 1562, the crucifix in Toulouse at the same time, rosaries and special feathered hats with white crosses on them in Aix-en-Provence.[41] The band in Aix, led by the first consul and a Franciscan, was particularly violent; in towns like Troyes, too, Huguenot-hunting was treated as something akin to a sport.[42] Royal efforts to disband these confraternities were only partially successful. Thus the group in Bordeaux reappeared and Catherine de Médicis had once more to order its disbandment.[43]

By 1577, however, the violence of sectarian massacres was, to a degree, past history. In some provinces such as Champagne and Burgundy, protestants were an attentuated and demoralised minority after 1572. In some northern cities like Amiens, protestantism was restricted to certain social groups like the textile workers and deprived of support and encouragement from the city notability.[44] In others, such as Rouen, it began a period of numerical decline, assisted by emigration to the Channel Islands, England or the Netherlands.[45] South of the Loire, the Huguenots concentrated their forces in fortified towns like La Rochelle, Sancerre, Montauban, Nîmes and Gap where they predominated and began a period of stubborn military resistance. Only towns like Montpellier with large populations of mixed religious persuasion found themselves a prey to religious tensions of the old style as late as 1577.[46] To some extent, the two religious communities were like two boxers, separated after a bruising confrontation. Trying not to show the hurt which had been done, bloodied but conscious, they struggled to come to terms with what had happened in the recent past. The result has been described as an 'internalisation' of sectarian violence. It had been more barbaric, Montaigne mused, than the supposed excesses of the unchristian

39. Catherine de Médicis, [1880–1909], III, 163.
40. Bèze, I, 871–4. F. Hauchecorne, 1950.
41. M. Orlea, 1980, p. 34.
42. N.H. Galpern, 1976, p. 178. D. Kelley, 1973, p. 250.
43. I. Cloulas, 1979, p. 419.
44. D.L. Rosenberg, 1978, p. 52.
45. P. Benedict, 1981, ch. 5.
46. E.g. J. Philippi, [1918], p. 183.

savages in the New World. Where had such barbarism come from if not from within ourselves? In the theatre of the mind rather than on the streets, in poetry, paintings, drama and pamphlets the sectarian violence was relived within and across the confessional divide, almost as a necessary but painful expiation.[47]

For the protestant community, the civil wars were relived through the pages of Jean Crespin's famous *History of the Persecuted Martyrs*. Calvin had taught that the seed of the true church lay in the blood of martyrs and the respect accorded to martyrdom became a vital part of the Huguenot tradition. Jean Crespin (1520–72) was a lawyer who had practised in Paris and fled from persecution to become a printer in Geneva. His *History* was first published in 1554 but it was revised during the civil wars to keep it up to date.[48] It stressed the continuity between earlier heresies in the life of the church and the Calvinist reformation and attempted to demonstrate that God had inspired martyrs to be constant so that their deaths proved the Calvinist Church to be the true one.[49] But Crespin's book was only one in a world of propaganda through which the memories of sectarian tension were channelled, relived and rationalised.

The growth of the printing press in regional centres in France had been little short of prodigious in the first half of the sixteenth century and its significance during the civil wars should not be underestimated. As one Venetian ambassador in France remarked: 'It is necessary to beware of these little books that are being spread abroad . . . . People are by nature curious and, although without intending any evil, they open these books, they read them as though they had the authority of Scripture and cannot imagine that passages may be falsified, altered, and they are thereby confused.'[50] They were widely read amongst those whose political voices counted; the king had even to rebuke the duke of Guise from reading broadsheets whilst at Mass.[51] The pamphleteering wars which had begun in earnest after the

47. For introductions to the pamphlets of the civil war period, see F. Charbonnier, 1919 and 1923. J. Pineaux, 1973. Coligny (Actes du colloque, 1972), 1974, pp. 390–405. D. Kelley, 1981, pp. 276–87. For 'internalisation' see the subtle chapters of D. Crouzet, 1990, II, chs xiii and xiv.

48. J-F. Gilmont, 1981.

49. D. Kelley, 1981, pp. 118–24. A. Soman, 1974, pp. 181–202.

50. N. Tommaseo, [1838], II, 138. Cf *Advertissement sur la fausseté de plusieurs mensonges* (n.p., 1562, LN, No. 258): 'We now see a stock of defamatory libels by which the most excellent persons – princes and seigneurs – are outrageously attacked'.

51. Cayet, p. 103. Estoile, who avidly read and collected pamphlets and broadsheets, said that they were produced 'as much by one party as by another so that nothing was talked of at Paris and at court except new libels containing reasons and defences and the accusations of each party'. Estoile, [1943], pp. 189–93.

conspiracy of Amboise in March 1560 continued throughout the civil wars. That conspiracy was an attempt by some protestants to capture the king and rescue him from what they regarded as the illegal domination of his court by the House of Guise. The plot failed ignominiously and catholics launched a diatribe against the 'detestable conspiracy and fiendish enterprise' of the protestants. Protestants replied with pamphlets which slandered the cardinal of Lorraine (of the House of Guise), accusing him of atheism, corruption and cruelty.[52] Perhaps the most savage attack came from François Hotman's *Letter addressed to the Tiger of France*, in which it was suggested that the cardinal should be removed from public life by force.

This was just the beginning of the kind of vilification in print which led to public vendetta during the civil wars and was interwoven into the bitterness of the period. François, duke of Guise, was assassinated towards the end of the first civil war on 18 February 1563. His murder became the subject of many pamphlets and created a feud between the House of Guise and some of the protestant leaders, especially Gaspard de Coligny, Admiral of France, who had been implicated in the duke's assassination. Coligny's assassination in August 1572 (following several abortive attempts) was the prelude to the massacre of Saint Bartholomew. Similar blood feuds divided many of the provincial noble families and fractured royalist support where it was most needed. Although there were pacifist sentiments also expressed in the civil wars, these were part of the way in which the country came to grips with its sectarian experience. In general, it was (as Estoile remarked in April 1587) the 'discourses, replies, advertisements, alarums and apologies' which 'started the braziers of rebellion'.[53]

We have only scratched the surface of the sectarian tensions which divided French society in the civil wars. It was difficult for its political leaders to stand aside from them. When they tried, they were accused by one side or the other (and sometimes by both) of being '*politiques*'. The historian Jacques-Auguste de Thou recorded of the Guise clan in 1568:[54]

> For those who opposed their ambitions, there was no end to the calumnies which they invented to disgrace their enemies. They called them *politiques*, a name which they invented to designate their enemies.

52. D. Kelley, 1981, pp. 266–7. G. Guilleminot, 1977, 77–83.
53. Estoile, [1943], p. 490.
54. De Thou, V, 524. Cf. G. de Saulx-Tavannes, [1881], VIII, 118.

Those *politiques*, if they were to be believed, were more dangerous even than heretics. They included catholics who were against factions and disturbances and thus unfavourable to their side, such as the cardinal of Bourbon, the chancellor l'Hôpital and the marshals [*François and Henri de*] Montmorency.

Cardinal Granvelle wrote from Brussels in 1564 that Coligny was 'more *politique* (as they say in France) than *dévot*'.[55] The term became exploited by catholic preachers to attack 'all statesmen who worked for peace' and, in their political careers, every major figure in the civil wars with the exception of the Guises was accused of '*politique*' sympathies at some point or other. There used to be a prevalent view among historians that there was a '*politique*' political group active during the civil wars and congregated around the Montmorency family and its allies.[56] The historian de Thou wrote his great work of history (with one eye, perhaps, on the old Constable, Henri de Montmorency-Damville who was in high favour at the time) around the '*politiques*' who appear as the heroes of the hour. Nineteenth-century historians were very sympathetic towards these kindred spirits to whom the state was more important than religion, and who had apparently saved France from the worst excesses of the civil wars.[57]

It must be said, however, that the Montmorency family did not regularly espouse a recognisably '*politique*' cause. On the eve of the civil wars, the elderly Constable of France, Anne de Montmorency, who died in the second civil war in 1567, made common cause with the Guises against the heretics. After his death, his family split in several directions. In 1577, the eldest of his sons was in retirement on his estates, having been imprisoned by the king for his part in a coup d'état in 1574. Meanwhile, his second son, Henri de Montmorency-Damville (1534–1614), was fighting the protestants around Montpellier for the king and against his younger brother, Thoré who was a committed protestant commander. Montmorency-Damville's allies were malcontents who were as interested in dismembering royal authority as they were concerned to appeal to religious sympathies when it seemed politically advantageous to them to do so. In a general sense, almost everyone in royal service was a '*politique*' because prudent trimming to political circumstance was

55. Granvelle, [1841–52], VIII, 118.
56. J.E. Neale, 1943, pp. 84–5. L. Romier, 1925, pp. 215–16. D. Buisseret, 1972, p. 64. Q. Skinner, 1978, II, 249, however, refers to the 'so-called party of *politiques*'.
57. F. Decrue de Stoutz, 1890.

essential to the survival of the French monarchy during the civil wars. Many of the provincial governors, even when faced with the contradictory orders coming from the king in the aftermath of the massacres of Paris in 1572, refused to eliminate prominent protestants in their localities. Instead they prevaricated in the face of clearly erratic royal decisions which would damage royal authority.[58] City councillors and urban magistrates, too, often tried to pursue their own civic agendas in opposition to the sectarian tensions coming from below and without. Although it made their terms of office extremely uncomfortable, their efforts may have shown fruit in those cities where the cycle of suspicion and hatred was less evident.[59]

The most notorious '*politique*' was undoubtedly Catherine de Médicis, queen mother to the three kings who ruled France from 1559 to 1589.[60] Her enemies branded her as a malevolent influence on her sons, corrupt, cruel, treacherous, Machiavellian, immoral and '*politique*'. She avidly read and annotated the broadsheets and scurrilous pamphlets, apparently unperturbed by the 'hate and imputations which are piled on her'.[61] Her attempts to woo the protestants to her support were endless and ingenious. She organised the colloquy of Poissy in 1561, drafted the edict of toleration of January 1562, was the architect of the first pacification of 1563 and ensured its enforcement in a spectacular 'progress' or royal visitation around the kingdom where she took the young king to many of the sensitive localities most disturbed by heresy and attempted to mediate upon local disputes.[62] She played a leading part in the pacification of St Germain-en-Laye in 1570 and the edict of peace at Bergerac in 1577 was enforced through her tremendous efforts of diplomacy in 1578–79, again involving extensive journeying through the southern provinces. She energetically recruited historians, painters, lawyers and astrologers to the task, engaging them to search history, mythology, legal precedent and every agreed wisdom to show that female rule was beneficent, that two religions could be tolerated within one society and that repression of one by the other was rarely successful. Even Louis Le Roy was persuaded to turn his pen to the task.[63] But few people in public life had the queen

58. P. Benedict, 1978, pp. 205–25.
59. M. Konnert, 1989.
60. Among the biographies currently available, that of I. Cloulas, 1979, is the best; but there is no substitute for reading the magnificent edition of Catherine de Medicis' correspondence in order to grasp the measure of her contribution during the civil wars.
61. N. Tommaseo, [1838], II, 245. Also Brantôme, [1864–82], VII, 373.
62. V.W. Graham and W.M. Johnson, 1979. Also J. Boutier, A. Dewerpe and D. Nordman, 1984.
63. W.L. Gundersheimer, 1966, ch. 6.

mother's staying-power or determination. Michel de l'Hôpital (1507–73), her chancellor, was forced to surrender the seals and to retire prematurely. Clerical servants in her entourage found their positions particularly vulnerable.

The case for toleration as a matter of principle was rarely heard in France during this period. The word 'toleration' was synonymous with permitting an immorality which you were powerless to prevent.[64] Those who supported pacification with the protestants did so on purely prudential grounds.[65] Etienne Pasquier (1529–1615) for instance, wrote a poem in defence of the pacification of St Germain-en-Laye in 1570.[66] His views were those of an *habitué* to a refined salon world of Paris lawyers, and he reflected their opinions that peace in the kingdom ensured law and order whereas civil war destroyed religion. The force of the argument (to the author as well as to others) depended on how well or how badly the wars were going.[67] For nobles in the provinces, a more personalised conception of fidelity was interwoven with faith in a religious cause and often used to justify a prudential approach to the religious divisions of the period. La Popelinière cited the example of the sieur de Passac, client of the count of Lude, who followed the count in military engagements for the protestants in the first religious war. However he eventually died in September 1569 still fighting for Lude but on the catholic side, having (as La Popelinière said) sacrificed 'the greatest part of his wealth and in the end his own life'.[68] The notoriety of Lude's change of heart can be judged from a message attached to a maypole in front of what had been his lodgings in 1576:

> The nobles are the only ones to be protected in these civil wars . . .
> they know all too well how to maintain and look after themselves so that,
> neither in their wealth nor their person do they receive any
> inconvenience but, on the contrary, they profit from the troubles. By
> their behaviour, it is easy to judge that these wars are no longer a matter
> of religion. 20,000 catholics and Huguenots, no longer able to tolerate
> such behaviour, are willing to rise up and do away with them.[69]

64. W.H. Huseman, 1984.
65. E.M. Beame, 1966, 250–65.
66. *Congratulation au Roy Charles IX sur l'Edict de Pacification* in E. Pasquier, [1723], II, cols 913–20.
67. E.M. Beame, 1966, 256–8. D. Thickett, 1979, pp. 95–115.
68. La Popelinière, II, f. 478.
69. Cited by Y-M. Bercé, 1974, I, 284. For a claim that nobles married across the religious divide to protect their fortunes, see C. Pradel, [1894], pp. 41–2.

Yet the count of Lude was by means alone in being unclear where his loyalties should lie.[70] In the wider French polity, conformity and confusion played a large part in people's individual choices. La Popelinière, the protestant historian of the civil wars, thought that more than two-thirds of France had remained neutral in the first decade of the civil wars – the 'friends of fortune and the good life' as he calls them.[71] He also recalled that the wars were fought substantially with foreign troops (the protestant army in 1569 spoke six languages; the royal forces included Italians, Germans, Swiss and Albanians as well as French).[72] He added that, for a 'million members of armed bands under the *fleur de lys*', the religious focus of the wars was less important than the opportunities that political disorder provided to form a *bandonil* – or irregular armed band – and live off the countryside.[73] Increasingly the problem of disorder in the countryside came to the fore in the course of the hostilities.

HUGUENOTS IN REVOLT

The year 1572 was a watershed for the protestants. It also led to the most remarkable hostilities undertaken by the Huguenots in the course of the civil wars. As de Thou recalled in his history:

> After the murder of so many generals and the dispersal of what remained of the protestant nobility, and the fright of the people in every town, there was no one who did not regard this cause as absolutely defeated. However, against the opinion of those who took up arms and without premeditated design, a war which began feebly, restored the affairs of the protestants in the space of a year without the help of a foreign prince and despite the lack of resources.[74]

The classic works of protestant political thought all appeared during this period and the institutions which have been christened the 'United Provinces of the Midi' became as mature as they ever would during the civil wars in France.[75] But it is unhelpful to draw too clear a divide at this point. Although the works of political theory appeared

70. K. Neuschel, 1989, ch. ii.
71. La Popelinière, II, f. 478.
72. Ibid., f. 304.
73. Ibid., ff. 39 and 392–3.
74. De Thou, VII, 61.
75. J. Delumeau, 1968, p. 181. J. Garrisson-Estèbe, 1980, p. 185.

after 1572, many of the ideas were formulated beforehand. François Hotman's *Francogallia* (1573) was composed in the period 1567–69 and the three volumes published by the Genevan Simon Goulart and entitled *Memoirs of the State of France* (1576–77) – a compendium of pamphlets produced in the civil wars – included many writings from the first decade of civil war as well as the famous reactions of the Huguenots to the massacre of St Bartholomew, the *Political Discourses* and Beza's *Right of Magistrates*.[76] Elective protestant political assemblies, attended by lay and ecclesiastical representatives from particular regions, can also be traced back to the beginning of the civil wars, exercising the authority with which they were formally endowed after 1572.[77] Catholic commentators were already willing to read a radical and subversive message into protestant endeavours, before the publications in the wake of the massacre of St Bartholomew proved such suspicions (as they saw it) amply justified.[78]

In a society which equated obedience with good order and stability, the belief that in certain circumstances it was right to resist lawful authority was one of the most perceptible signs of the instability of the civil wars. Protestant theorists only espoused such a view circumspectly. In April 1562, the prince of Condé claimed that the young king, Charles IX, had been captured and that the lawful government was usurped by an aristocratic faction.[79] The Huguenot rebellion was thus portrayed as a loyalist uprising to free the king. This view received very cautious support from Calvin in Geneva for princes of the royal family ('of the blood') had a limited authority (in the view of some) to resist manifest tyranny and be a part of the regency government during a minority. In 1567, however, Condé's manifesto reflected a more uncomfortable reality since it was the protestants who, at that particular moment, attempted to capture the king by force in a coup d'état which was foiled at the last moment. This time, the manifesto for rebellion spoke of a fundamental 'ancient constitution' of the realm which was being perverted. Charles IX, although no longer a minor, was still a king 'in tutelage' and would remain so until he was 21 years old and able to assume absolute authority. He needed guidance, argued the protestants, from (among others) a prince of the blood and an estates general.[80]

76. R.M. Kingdon, 1988, provides an analysis of this publication and its background.
77. J. Loutchizky, [1873–96]. A. Dussert, 1929, 110–18.
78. D. Crouzet, 1990, II, ch. xi.
79. Q. Skinner, 1978, II, 302.
80. Q. Skinner, 1978, II, 303–4.

The appeal to a fundamental constitution was taken to theoretical conclusions in François Hotman's *Francogallia*.[81] This long, highly persuasive book had a powerful effect on contemporaries. Hotman was, in many ways, the perfect ideologue. A scholar and lawyer by training, he was a natural propagandist, a fast worker and capable of writing with the right mixture of evidence, argument, anger and wit to suit the occasion. Exiled early in his career (in Geneva and Strasbourg from 1548), he learned to make friends among many different groups. He had a knack of anticipating events and was used by protestant princes as a negotiator and diplomat. He relished his reputation as a 'seditious and tumultuous person' even though it twice cost him his belongings in escaping the sudden tensions of civil war.[82] The *Francogallia* was intended by its author to be 'the work of history, the history of a fact'.[83] That fact – or rather, myth – was that France had once been a free country – free Gaul – whose fundamental liberty had been gradually eroded, first by the Roman empire and, latterly, by the 'great beast of Rome', the papacy. France's lawyer-historians had uncovered the complex laws and precedents of France's feudal past and, with the aid of the Renaissance tools of philology and the study of Roman law, were in the process of codifying and classifying them.[84] Hotman subordinated this legal antiquarianism within a wider picture which appealed to a certain French patriotism, a mythical view of the past.[85] At the same time, he revealed the rich complexity and variety of French institutions beyond the French monarchy.

His conclusions were unambiguous. Kings were, he said, in origin elected by the people.[86] They were magistrates, responsible to the people for the exercise of power. 'The supreme power of deposing kings was also', he wrote, 'that of the people.'[87] Valois monarchs had become 'Roman' in their attitudes – imperial, catholic and absolutist – 'bloody tyrants' as he does not hesitate to describe them at one point. It was essential that France recover the institutions of its 'mixed constitution' which enshrined their former freedom.[88] These were not the *parlements*, law-courts which could be relied on to ratify the king's worst 'Roman' pretensions.[89] (They had even usurped the term

81. F. Hotman, [1972].
82. D. Kelley, 1973.
83. Ibid., p. 253.
84. D. Kelley, 1970, pts 2 and 3 and 1973, pp. 240–1.
85. M. Yardeni, 1971. D. Kelley, 1970, pt 3. D. Kelley, 1973, pp. 241–2.
86. F. Hotman, [1972], pp. 220–33. R.A. Jackson, 1972, pp. 155–71.
87. Ibid., p. 235.
88. Ibid., pp. 287–331.
89. Ibid., pp. 496–505.

'*parlementum*' which had originally and properly applied only to the elected estates of the realm.) The principal institution for Hotman was the estates general, which had once had extensive powers to deliberate on general welfare and which had been 'held as something sacrosanct' in France's feudal past.[90] Provincial estates, town councils, elected clergy, provincial and municipal privileges were all cited as evidence of former Gallic freedoms which it was essential to recover in order to return to a properly constituted order.

Hotman, like other protestant political theorists, was concerned at the damage the civil wars were doing to France and the massacre of St Bartholomew had genuinely shocked him.[91] He regarded the work as 'throwing a bucket of water' on the flames of civil war, hoping that it would contribute to 'the recuperation, and even the restoration, of our French state'.[92] His book had a widespread readership, as Hotman was the first to acknowledge. Even in Paris it was 'well-received by all men of good sense and all good Frenchmen'.[93] It wore its Calvinist protestantism lightly and it did not sneer at '*politiques*' like more intemperate Huguenot writings of the period. The appeal to a national identity, threatened by foreigners, was widely supported by those of every religious persuasion who believed that in the Italianate atheism and Machiavellianism attributed to the queen mother, her entourage and the Italians of the royal service lay the true source of the instability in France.[94] Hotman presented the reality of complex, non-royal institutions operating in a mixed government within a royal context. This was precisely what the deputies to the various political assemblies in the Midi wanted to hear. He gave them legal, historical and political reasons for a limited right of revolt which, in a more inchoate way, those assemblies were struggling for in 1572–73.[95]

The king, Henri III, and the queen mother read *Francogallia* and it horrified them. They tried to have it banned and commissioned various refutations of its arguments from the Italian lawyer, Matteo Zampini, and Louis Le Roy among others.[96] The criticisms which were eventually levelled at Hotman's work cast serious doubts on its

90. Ibid., pp. 332–49.
91. D. Kelley, 1973, pp. 218–26.
92. Ibid., p. 247.
93. Ibid., p. 252.
94. M. Yardeni, 1971, pp. 163–81.
95. See, for example, the opening remarks of the *procès-verbal* of the assembly at Anduze in February 1573, edited in J. Garrisson-Estèbe, 1980, pp. 339–41.
96. D. Kelley, 1973, pp. 253–60. Q. Skinner, 1978, II, 318. W.L. Gundersheimer, 1966, pp. 81–3. G. Bontemps *et al.*, 1965, pp. 155–71.

historical veracity.[97] This is amongst the reasons why the last great work of Huguenot resistance theory, published towards the end of the 1570s, rested its case less on specifically legal, historical or French grounds and more on a thoroughly scholastic argument.[98] It stipulated that there were two essential bonds of society. These were the pact, or treaty, between king and people and the more sacred covenant or bond linking God, king and people. The *Vindiciae contra tyrannos* (or *Revenges against tyrants*) became the starting point for a discussion of the nature of political obedience towards the end of the civil wars.[99] It was an indication of the way in which the internal hostilities had destroyed the common assumptions about automatic obedience to the powers that be, which had been generally taken as the theoretical basis for the French polity.

Meanwhile, the protestant political assemblies and councils which de Thou called 'a raw kind of republic' demonstrated their own, more practical independence. They negotiated with French kings as with a distant respected foreign power in 1575–76 and displayed a boldness and canny persistence that exasperated royal councillors.[100] 'Shopkeepers', 'inexperienced in affairs' scorned the governor of Languedoc, Henri de Montmorency-Damville, but they were a match for his mercurial politics.[101] They put together the credit which sustained the foreign mercenary armies which were the leading edge of their military campaigns. They ran their affairs with a minimum degree of deference to noble authority and a pronounced leaning towards the commons. Montmorency-Damville is supposed to have said that he had learnt 'that they were enemies to all the nobility and wanted popular and communal dominance'.[102] La Popelinière, protestant gentleman and historian, had personal experience of the protestant assemblies to which he had been deputed in the 1570s. He remarked that the 'merchant spirit' at these gatherings was not readily reconcilable with that of the soldiers and that noble liberties 'were incompatible with the equality of the Third Estate'.[103] The protestants provided councils to advise and control the actions of their protector

97. Q. Skinner, 1978, II, 318–19.

98. Etienne Junius Brutus [pseud.], *Vindiciae contra Tyrannos*, [1979]. Cf Q. Skinner, 1978, II, 319–38. The work is frequently ascribed to Philippe Du Plessis Mornay, but the important distinction between 'writing' and 'publishing' is drawn by H. Weber in the 1979 edition, pp. i–v.

99. R. Schnur, 1962.

100. J. Garrisson-Estèbe, 1980, pp. 184–5. d'Aubigné, IV, 183.

101. J. Loutchizky, [1875], p. 83.

102. J. Gassot, [1934], p. 142.

103. La Popelinière, [1581], Bk 37, ff. 101, 225 etc.

and his lieutenants. They tried to reconcile differences of opinions between their military lieutenants, and imposed oaths of allegiance on them all. Their concern for order and upright government under a civil constitution reflected the morality they sought to impose even during the civil wars on their cities through the consistory courts and on their church officials through their colloquies and synods. Both the civil and ecclesiastical protestant constitutions provided avenues for status, power and a sense of achievement for the protestant men of business with the necessary fortitude to make use of them.

REFORM OF THE REALM AND ITS FAILURE

Civil war created a demand for a reform of the French polity from those of both religious persuasions. Catherine de Médicis recognised this fact during her tour through the provinces in 1564–65 and she organised an assembly of notables at Moulins in January 1566. The results included the great reforming statute of eighty-six articles promising, among other things, major changes in the procedures of the *parlements*, the establishment of *grands jours* (or assizes) to deal with endemic crime and disorder, and the appointment of better judges and royal officials (where venality was believed to have rendered them corrupt and partial).[104] It promised to limit the authority of provincial governors (to prevent their appropriating royal revenues as they had done in the civil wars), to stamp out the pillage of property, and to protect civilians from the royal cavalry companies. Hospitals, confraternities, sumptuary and blasphemy laws, the regulation of printing, all appeared within it. Finance was also involved and Catherine was acutely aware of the considerable royal debts (600,000 *livres* was necessary at that moment to keep the royal creditors prepared to enter future loans).[105] Financial pressure and royal attempts at reform were never separable during the civil wars.

Renewed hostilities prevented the Moulins ordinances from taking effect and in due course rendered the financial position of the French monarchy still worse. Further loans were signed up with Italian bankers, mortgaging the customs at Lyon. Loans upon future receipts were made by the city of Paris and a further 2 million *livres* of

---

104. Isambert, XIV, 189–212 (Feb. 1566), summarised in J.H.M. Salmon, 1975, pp. 154–6.
105. I. Cloulas, 1979, p. 221.

ecclesiastical wealth were alienated, beginning in November 1568. There were the first signs of a serious collapse of the currency.[106] The same expedients were used when war began again in 1572–74, but this period coincided with poor harvests, shortages of salt and a more evident monetary crisis. Preparations for a further assembly of notables in 1573 to address the problem of reform were shelved with the king's illness which led to his death in 1574; but the eloquence of the printed polemics in 1574 from all sides, arguing the case for reform, is evidence of the extent of the malaise.[107] The new king was reminded that 'the ruin of his people is the ruination of his state'. He was told that offices, sold to the low-born, damaged the social structure of the country. It was suggested that royal treasurers were pocketing public revenues and that the catholic church was subsidising royal extravagance. 'People are being fleeced, the gendarmerie go unpaid, all piety, religion and discipline are despised and have been let slip.'[108] The remedy for such abuses lay in the holding of a 'free meeting' of the estates general, it was suggested, in which protestants and catholics could remonstrate to the king on the defects in the administration of the state, church and judiciary. From the petitions put before the king by the people of Champagne in 1575 and the independent report of the Venetian ambassador who passed through the province that year, it was clear that conditions were desperate. Villagers sheltered in churches, once-prosperous towns were half tumbled down and the bourgeois were forced to ransom themselves from ravaging troops if they left the comparative security of town walls. In November 1575, it was reported in Paris 'that the nobles and people of Brittany, Normandy, Burgundy and the Auvergne are in league, one with another, and have decided to pay no more imposts, aids, subsidies, loans, taxes, increases and charges over and above what was levied in the reign of Louis XII'. In December 1575, the leading figure of the municipality of Paris, the *prévôt des marchands*, laid before the king a remonstrance which left little to the imagination. The 'wrath of God' visited on France during the civil wars was the consequence of the 'universal corruption in all the estates and order of the realm'.[109] Some royal response was urgently required. The duke of Anjou (the king's

---

106. Ibid., p. 257. Coligny (Actes du colloque. 1972), 1974, pp. 651–705. Cf. H. Hauser, 1932.

107. Some memoirs for the assembly were compiled before news of the cancellation was received. They survive for some of the Languedoc localities, e.g. C. Douais, [1890], 473–80. Devic and Vaissète, [1872–1904], XII, cols 1065–71.

108. LN, No. 760.

109. *Registres de Paris* [1866], VII, 313–17.

brother) also pressed for the holding of an estates general and the king promised to undertake this in the peace of Monsieur (the edict of Beaulieu) in 1576.[110]

That promise was fulfilled by the summoning of the estates general to Blois towards the end of the year. The previous history of estates general as agents for the reform of the kingdom was scarcely encouraging, however. Their cumbersome elective procedures, the methods by which the petitions of grievance were sorted together and sifted, the debating arrangements of the chambers of the estates all stood in the way of a constructive solution. Clearly, royal finances were parlous in the wake of the pressures of war and the enormous burdens of paying for the removal of the German mercenary troops that the protestants had hired and the king had undertaken to reimburse.[111] Figures presented to the estates (and doubtless exaggerated for impact) suggested that the overall royal debt was of the order of 101 million *livres* and the annual deficit stood at about 4 million *livres*.[112] A serious attempt at government reform would have been worth seeking in return for a grant of substantial taxation. But the estates general began, instead, to question the royal accounts and to propose the dismantling of royal authority in justice and finance. The estates were in due course dissolved with no clear reform initiative agreed with the king.

The initiative lay next with the provincial estates to whom the king turned for assistance in dealing with the enormous burdens of royal debts. Some piecemeal reforms were successfully accomplished in the meantime, particularly for the stabilising of the coinage.[113] From the estates of Burgundy came the demand in October 1578 that 'the reformation of the kingdom be attended to' before they would grant further assistance to the king. Normandy's estates threw the royal treasurers out of their assembly in the following month and a clerical representative there, after insulting the *premier président* (a senior judge in the *parlement* of Normandy and a royal nominee) turned to the provincial governor and asked rhetorically: 'When, Monseigneur, when will our afflictions cease? When shall we see an end to the violent seizure of our goods and belongings by the tax sergeants?' They proceeded to follow the example of Burgundy and refused to

110. A. Stegmann, [1979], pp. 116–17.

111. As yet, however, is there is no satisfactory study of the estates general of Blois. *Cahiers*, debates and organisation of the estates are discussed in E. Charleville, 1901; M. Orlea, 1980, pp. 87–96; G. de Taix, [1625]; J. Bodin, [1789].

112. I. Cloulas, 1979, p. 401. M. Wolfe, 1972, pp. 158–68.

113. F.C. Spooner, 1972, pp. 90–2. Summary in J.H.M. Salmon, 1975, pp. 226–7.

grant further taxation to the king. Instead, at a specially convened meeting in March 1579, they demanded that their grievances be met before they satisfy the king's request for more taxes. They wanted reform in many institutions including the church, schools, hospitals and the council of state. They suggested the establishment of a temporary commission of impartial judges to replace the venal *parlement* at Rouen, the establishment of a chamber to investigate and punish corrupt financial officials and the suppression of the provincial treasurers and the *élus* (local royal tax officials) as the first step towards the return of the provincial estates to their former significance.[114] The king gave his consent to their demands verbally in reply to their deputies in April 1579. When they asked him to put his assent into writing, he replied icily 'that they ought to content themselves that the king had given them his word concerning that assembly, which is more to be valued than any written guarantee which might be given to them.' When their deputies were later arrested and imprisoned, the estates of Normandy were given good cause to doubt the king's good faith.

Senior catholic clergy also spent most of the year 1579 haggling with the king over his proposals for substantial new taxes on the clergy.[115] They compared the church to the 'good Joseph who, being forced to obey the squalid wishes of his mistress, would rather emerge naked, leaving his coat behind him, rather than soil his soul with such a grave adultery.' They also demanded reform in the form of the publication of the decrees of the Council of Trent in France by the king and royal cooperation in removing corruption and potential heresy from within the clergy. Their demands were either ignored or rejected. When they seemed on the point of agreement in December 1579, the king (concerned not to arouse the Gallican wrath of the law officers in the *parlement* who had substantial objections to a number of the Tridentine decrees) abruptly increased his demands. The senior clergy were amongst many groups in the realm who came to doubt his good faith.

In order to dispel the growing suspicions, the king had signed the ordinances of Blois.[116] These reflected the demands of the estates of Blois in their final *cahiers* to the king. Yet, like the reforms announced in the edict of Moulins in 1566, these too were a promise of better things to come which was hardly put into practice. The conditions of

114. J.R.L. Highfield and R.M. Jeffs, 1981, pp. 166–7. J. Russell Major, 1980, pp. 208–101, 213–16.
115. L. Serbat, 1906, pp. 89–108. Pamphlets in LN, Nos 958 and 1002.
116. Isambert, XIV, 380–463 (May 1579).

a half-made and half-obeyed peace made it difficult to do so. There was renewed Huguenot disaffection in some provinces, peasant insurrections, disruptive seigneurs and town riots which made any enforcement of law difficult.[117] Pressures for reform, however, led to the final attempt by the last Valois to produce a coherent and successful recovery. A string of reforming measures appeared in royal ordinances in the early summer of 1582. The English ambassador reported that Henri III was closeted with his secretaries for several days, dictating to them his plans for reform, the copies of which he then locked away in a desk to which he alone kept the key. Then, in early August 1582, he announced that he would hold an assembly of notables which was to be properly informed of all the problems in the localities.[118] To this end, commissioners were despatched to tour the provinces in the autumn and winter of 1582 with detailed instructions to visit all the main towns and listen to complaints, and also to stop every seven leagues and hear villagers' laments.[119] Many examples of local corruption were thus unearthed.[120] After several delays, the assembly of notables met in December 1583 and sat for two months. It was attended by the king's closest advisors and by the masters of requests who possessed specialist knowledge about trade, currency and law. Senior prelates were also present and they established a special commission on ecclesiastical reform. Some former ambassadors and provincial governors and lieutenants also took part.[121] The debates, proposals, schemes and resolutions of the assembly were well-informed, extremely wide-ranging and imaginative. Some of the most accurate information on the state of royal debts in the course of the civil war was prepared by this assembly. The breadth and seriousness of their discussions are a sign of the deep-rooted instabilities which they discovered within the French polity and the difficulties of doing much to eradicate them.

They were not entirely pessimistic. If the series of measures which they proposed were to be adopted in full, then, with the assistance of a decade of peace, the kingdom could, they believed, expect to see real recovery. There was to be no mass repurchase of offices; but some *bureaux* of offices were to be disbanded among the *trésoriers* and *élus*.[122]

---

117. S.H. Ehrman, 1936, II, 600–41. M. Foisil, 1976, 25–40. L. Scott Van Doren, 1974, 71–100. A. Dussert, 1931, 123–89. J.H.M. Salmon, 1979, 1–28.

118. A. Karcher, 1956, 115–62. The decision was made in the wake of an Eastertide of intense devotions.

119. The commission is published in G. Hanotaux, 1884, pp. 187–8.

120. See BN MS Fr 16228 and Cal SP For, XVII, 239.

121. Karcher, 1956.

122. Evidence in Fontanon, II, 88, 591–601, 603–4.

Royal offices were gradually to fall vacant on the death of their occupants so that this part of the royal debt would gradually amortise itself without immediate and painful repercussions. Reform of the domain had already begun in 1578. It was to be pushed forward and inquiries would root out fraud while other parts of the domain which had been mortgaged would be repurchased over a number of years. Forest enquiries were also to be undertaken. A chamber of justice would investigate corrupt financiers and tax-farmers.[123] Commissioners would also be sent to provinces to investigate tax registers, render the tax equitable and eradicate corruption and fraud. Investigations of falsely claimed nobility were to be continued.[124] Tax-farms of salt and customs duties would be renegotiated and consolidated to ensure that the king was gaining an economic return.[125] Customs were to be so rated as to protect native manufacture without damaging (by total prohibition of the importation of certain goods such as cloth from England) France's reciprocal trade abroad.[126] Reform of hospitals would, among other measures, strengthen the hand of the royal almoner over their accounts. The muster, review and payment of cavalry companies were considered and a series of reforms produced.[127] The policing of towns was also considered and roving assizes despatched to deal with provincial criminality.[128] Reforms already set in hand at court in the numbers, provisioning, discipline and routine of those attending the king were strengthened with controls designed to limit pensions, the soliciting of favours and the recording of the decisions of the councils of state. The reforms put together at the assembly of notables at St Germain-en-Laye constitute the most thoroughly conceived measure of reforming endeavour undertaken during the period of the civil wars.

Why was it that so many attempts had achieved so little? Was it not the case that the failure to reform the state was the cause of provincial dissension and the frustrations which led to the catholic League? To

123. BN MS Fr 4352 (established in May 1584 and suppressed a year later).
124. See the reports to the council in BN MS Fr 16231-2.
125. This was a slow process, but it led eventually to the engrossed tax-farm, the *cinq grosses fermes*, in 1585.
126. Bib Mazarine, 2635 ff. 67 *et seq*. General background in R. Gascon, 1971, II, 698–727.
127. The assembly envisaged a small, well-equipped, well-paid standing army of 2,400 men serving and training in garrisons for four months each year. Attempts to reduce the size of the army are in Fontanon, IV, 129–39. The admiralty was also reorganised in March 1584.
128. The assizes established at Troyes were extended in November 1582. Others had already been held in Poitou and Guyenne. The English ambassador recorded: 'Truly justice is done in them marvellously severely.' (Cal SP For, XVI, 252).

many knowledgeable contemporaries like Pierre de l'Estoile, Cobham (the English ambassador), Moro (the Venetian ambassador), Busbecq and de Thou, the assembly of notables of 1583 was a kind of propaganda exercise, a way of buying more time in the struggle against disorder in the state.[129] There was plenty of evidence for their view that reform was so intimately connected with the imperious demands of royal debts and that the need for more revenue and the desire for reform were so incompatible, that reform was never going to succeed. Their pessimism was shared by some reactions in the provinces to the appearance of the commissioners in 1582. Lyon was uncooperative and the commissioners spent two months in the city trying to elicit the necessary information. The estates of Picardy greeted them by saying that they were delighted that the king wanted to remedy abuses 'although very late'. For, during the years of civil wars, they had seen: 'So many fine assemblies, so many fine ordinances, the estates (general) so solemnly convoked and held at Orléans and then at Blois, the colloquies and assemblies at Poissy, Moulins, Paris and elsewhere, all of them full of great hopes for the relief of the people: we see, however, that all this has achieved nothing.'[130] There was a widespread doubt as to whether the means, will and confidence existed to achieve any measure of reform, a real pessimism that France was ungovernable on the terms that pre-war France would have understood and that political stability was not an achievable goal but an unrealisable ideal belonging to the golden age of Henri II.

Who was to blame for this? Italians? Financiers? Favourites? Quarrels in the royal family, rival clans of nobles, the size, luxury and morality of the court in general? Henri III himself? All received some share of the resulting acrimony. Every explanation contained a degree of truth among a great deal of misinformation and prejudice. For the court and its members were not completely apart, cut off from the rest of France, but a reflection of the strains and tensions in it. The Italians, for instance, were not the malevolent force that some French xenophobes imagined. It is true that, politically speaking, their influence was to be felt in the councils of state. It is also the case that Italians occupied some of the French episcopal benefices and had gained entry into French noble orders.[131] But their political advice was, to a degree, independent of the factions among the French nobility and they were good soldiers whose companies attracted ambitious Frenchmen and Italians alike. The painters, architects,

129. Estoile, [1943], pp. 350–1. Busbecq, [1845], p. 68. De Thou, IX, 81–2.
130. A. Karcher, 1956, 121.
131. F.J. Baumgartner, 1986, pp. 40, 45. J–P. Labatut, 1972, pp. 57–65.

musicians, dancing masters and fencing teachers who became part of royal and princely retinues were a reflection of Italian pre-eminence in these spheres. The influence of Italian merchants and banking houses at court was less visible and yet at times more pervasive during the civil wars.[132] But their presence was necessary to provide the king and other courtiers with essential short-term liquidity. Their participation in army funding, tax contracts and the mortgaging of various resources was not a sign of their malevolent influence in court but an indication of the extensiveness of the royal debts which they funded. Inevitably, they used their credit to secure power at court and positions as gentlemen of the chamber.[133] Doubtless this led them to some favourable financial deals. Naturally this attracted adverse comment. Sebastiano Zametti (Zamet) was reputedly arrogant and difficult to deal with. Luigi d'Adjaceto was found to have secured favourable contracts on tax-farming by the *chambre des comptes*. Scipio Sardini even published an edict in 1587 on his own authority increasing a tax on certain products, for which he was imprisoned by the *cour des aides* before the king ordered his release. Some Italian financiers became extremely wealthy from their time at the royal court and attracted resentment for the overt, liberal display that they made of it. When Orazio Rucellai left the French court to return to Italy in 1586 (finding the antipathy towards him intolerable) he took with him 1.6 million *livres*.[134] But one tends to forget those Italian financiers who, like Mario Bandini, were bankrupted and broken by their activities in France. At all events, the native intendants of finance were probably as susceptible to corruption. Few at the court of the last Valois enjoyed the reputation for honesty accorded to Claude Marcel, a former *prévôt des marchands* in Paris. Benoît Milon, sieur de Videville, the son of a locksmith from Blois, who rose (as Estoile put it) 'like the mushrooms, overnight' was dismissed from the royal chamber by an irate king for his peculations and took flight to the Netherlands.[135] Perhaps the major distinction was that the Italians could less easily have an ignoble stigma attached to them and, therefore, could insinuate themselves the more easily into high court positions.

The *mignons* (as the royal favourites were called from about 1574) were as easy a target to blame for the failure of reform as the Italians.

132. D. Richet, 1991, pp. 17–19.
133. J. Boucher, 1986, pp. 97–102.
134. E. Picot, 1901, p. 133.
135. Milon rose through military provisioning and salt-tax farming. He eventually became a secretary to the royal chamber. When he went to Spa to be cured of the stone (*calcul*) there were jokes about his 'art des calculs' amidst jibes about his ignoble

They were believed to be the epitome of luxury at court, a force for evil around the king.[136] In fact, the king did not (except for a brief period after 1586) restrict his favours to one favourite for any appreciable length of time. The ease with which disgrace befell the favourites of Henri III was one of the reasons for their intense mutual jealousies. Henri III wrote inside the leaf of the prayer book of Epernon (the most subtle and able of the *mignons* and the one who was able to manipulate the king's confidence after 1586):[137] 'I beg you, my friend, to remember me when you pray as I love no one else in the world more than you.' But, five years later, in 1588, Epernon was banished from the court by royal command. It is clear that the existence of the *mignons* performed a useful political function. As Catherine de Médicis acknowledged, able young men were being trained for future service to the king.[138] Also, the court contained many gentlemen of modest fortune and the rise of a favourite from their ranks gave them hopes of social ascension. Henri III needed men on whose loyalty he could depend. The problem was that, after 1586, Epernon established a measure of control of the privy purse, the *comptants à la main du roi*. At the same time, he tried to dominate access to the king. But in this respect he was unusual and attracted the singular vilification of other courtiers. More generally, the *mignons* were attacked for their extravagance which was occasionally tactless and excessive. But in some ways they were little different from the court in which they had been educated. The evidence for their being the homosexual companions of the king, as hostile pamphlets insinuated (particularly at the beginning and end of the reign) is ambiguous. Many knowledgeable contemporaries gave the rumours no credence. Among foreign diplomats, only the Savoyard ambassadors was disposed to accept the malicious gossip.[139] They were *camarades*, military companions, to whom Henri's liberality was undoubtedly excessive. But Henri II, his father, had behaved in a similar fashion towards his favourites, without attracting any allegations of homosexuality. That the slander existed, that it was given credence, is a sign of the gap between the court and the rest of France in this period.

136. Estoile, [1943], pp. 72–3, 134, 154–5, 235, etc. For the 'Gaveston' literature, comparing Epernon with Edward II's favourite, see F. Baumgartner, 1976, pp. 86–8.

137. Cal SP For, XVII, 256–8.

138. I. Cloulas, 1979, p. 427; as Catherine de Médicis wrote in October 1579: '. . . les vieulx s'an vont et il fault dreser les jeunes.' But Epernon, for instance, was only four years younger than the duke of Guise.

139. R. de Lucinge, [1954–5], pp. 104–5; [1964], p. 92. Lucinge was irritated at the king's obstruction of the proposed marriage of the duke of Nemours and Christine, duchess of Lorraine.

The contrast between the lavishness at court and the conditions in the provinces struck deputies to the king forcibly and did little to strengthen confidence in royal ability to undertake fundamental reforms and spend resources wisely. A further paradox was that poets and writers owing their livelihood to the liberality of the Valois court developed hostile attitudes to the institution of the court. Inspired by Virgil and Horace, they made nature a virtue and dwelt on the servility, ambitions, flattery and false attitudes that were the defining characteristics (as they saw it) of an obsequious courtier. The Italianate forms of the Valois court – particularly its studied artificiality – enabled its critics to present it as a flamboyant and unreal world which protestants were correct to denounce as corrupt and vicious.

More unfortunate were the legacies of family quarrels and noble hostilities which Henri III inherited and which he could periodically control but seemingly never eradicate. There was a sad contrast between the loyalty and fidelity he enjoyed from the illegimate members of the Valois on the one hand, and the resentments and hatreds manifested by his brother and sister. His stepbrother and namesake, Henri d'Angoulême, was a companion from youth who enjoyed similar tastes to those of the king and served him loyally until his assassination at the hands of local factions in Provence in 1586. His stepsister, Madame Diane, ten years his elder, became a trusted councillor. Even the illegitimate son of his brother, Charles d'Angoulême, received favour from Henri III after 1586. To Epernon's scarcely concealed dismay, the king toyed with the possibility of legitimizing him and thus making him the heir to the throne.

Little of the same confidence and trust could be said to have existed between the king and his sister, Marguerite, married in an evidently ill-suited match to Henri of Navarre; or between the king and his brother, François Hercules, duke of Alençon (later, duke of Anjou), who was the heir to the throne from 1574 until his death a decade later in 1584. Morally, emotionally and sexually, François and Marguerite both displayed signs of instability and there was little the king could do except to contain and divert their destructive energies. The comedies of feigned reconciliations, engineered by the queen mother or members of the royal and ducal entourage, or by the mediation of Henri of Navarre with his wife, could not disguise the underlying, lasting and sustained tensions. There is no doubt that many hostile pamphlets, writings and accusations against Henri III originated from close members of his own divided family. They remained either indifferent or actively hostile towards reform. Anjou refused to attend the assembly of notables in 1583 and the queen mother had to be despatched to persuade him to participate in its deliberations.

The destructive tensions and animus between noble clans were also beyond the ability of the king and his court to dissipate. Henri III had inherited the kingdom with the king of Navarre in close confinement and the duke of Montmorency in prison. Navarre escaped from court in 1576 and never returned to the French court again before his accession in 1589. The duke of Montmorency was eventually released too, but he was a broken man and he lived thereafter largely on his estates until his death in 1579. His brother, Henri de Montmorency-Damville, narrowly escaped assassination in 1574, and blamed the attempted murder on the king. He swore a solemn oath that he would never see the king again, except in effigy, and so it was. Removed from the exercise of his powers as governor of Languedoc in the same year, he joined the protestants and only signed a formal reconciliation with Henri III in 1577. He did nothing to help the reform initiative in the years thereafter and, still suspicious of the king's attitude towards him, refused to leave his province, believing that his continued presence there was the best guarantee of his survival. In 1582 he began to resent the growing authority of one of the royal *mignons*, Anne de Joyeuse, whose father was his lieutenant in Languedoc. His response was to negotiate with the king of Spain for a permanent alliance and subsidy, negotiations about which the king learnt as the assembly of notables of 1583 began its debates.[140] In 1585 Montmorency-Damville was declared deposed from his government of Languedoc and his family's property in northern France was confiscated by the king in 1586. He responded with an open revolt and renewed alliance with the protestants and the king of Navarre. Henri III's influence in the Midi was severely curtailed.

Things went little better with the powerful family of Guise. They began the reign in high favour. At the royal coronation in Reims in 1575 (where the king married into their house) the cardinal of Guise took the service; his brothers, nephews and cousins, the duke of Guise, Mayenne, Aumale and Elboeuf, were the chief lay peers and chamberlain to officiate at the ceremony. The council of state even met from time to time in the *hôtel* of Guise in Paris in 1575 and the queen mother feared their predominance.[141] In the following year, the king signed the edict of Beaulieu, a peace agreement with the protestants which gave them large concessions as well as granting huge privileges to the duke of Alençon. By way of reprisal, the Guise clan

---

140. J.M. Davies, 1991, esp. pp. 544–7.
141. Cal SP For, XI, 20–1, 44, 67.

ostentatiously left the court. By the end of 1577 the Guise found that peace with the protestants had strengthened royal authority and rendered the king more independent of them. So they returned to court, fanned the quarrels between royal favourites and supporters of the duke of Alençon (pitched battles at court reduced the king to tears), and then staged a new, menacing departure. Perhaps the refusal of the estates of Normandy and Burgundy to grant taxation before redress of grievances owed something to stimulus from Guise and Alençon.[142] In May 1579 another feigned reconciliation between Henri III and the Guise family was followed by four tiresome years in which the king tried, through the *mignons*, to exclude them from the powerful offices of the kingdom while winning over some members of the family (Elboeuf, Mayenne) with pensions, promises and lavish entertainments.[143] Even so, Guise barely cooperated at the assembly of notables in 1583 and actively resisted reform in the church at the assembly. The king's tactics were astute, desperately clever – a tribute to his political skills – but the Guise were not fooled. In 1584, 'they say privately to their friends that they well understand the mortal hatred in which the king holds them'.[144] As champions of catholicism to the bitter end in France, at least in the public eye, they would not pass over the opportunity created for them by the death of the heir to the throne and the threat of a Huguenot accession. They also signed an alliance for a subsidy from Spain, gathered support from their kinsman the duke of Lorraine, and accompanied a declaration from Péronne on 28 March 1585 with a premature insurrection in several parts of the kingdom. They received the active cooperation of former members of Alençon's disruptive entourage, while Marguerite de Valois established a small sovereignty in Agen to support them. The king was forced to bend before the menacing threats and to cancel protestant privileges. Then began another superficial reconciliation with the Guise clan: more tense encounters at court where mutual suspicions and antagonisms were only just beneath the surface, to be followed by yet another threatened departure from court in 1587. The stage was set for the Day of Barricades in May 1588.

The failures of a generation were blamed on its king. No other sixteenth-century monarch was quite so vilified by his subjects: none

---

142. Ibid., XII, 655–60; XIII, 264–5, 300–3.

143. With the exception of the duke of Mayenne, they were all heavily indebted and in no position to refuse the king's gifts (see below, Chapter 8). For example, 100,000 *écus* to d'Aumale for his wedding; 100,000 *livres* to Mayenne for his; 500,000 *écus* to the duke of Guise on salt receipts in 1582.

144. ML, I, 567.

has received such opprobrium from historians.[145] It was symptomatic of the collapse of political stability that its traditional bulwark was so excoriated in public. The attacks on the court and Henri III can be followed in the pamphlets and engravings collected by the contemporary Estoile, or in the large pamphlet collection in the *Bibliothèque Nationale*. Their volume and abrasiveness varied in direct relation to the confidence or pessimism attached to the king's reforming endeavours. The themes of the criticism of the king are well-known and need little rehearsal here. They would be summarised and repeated by pamphleteers and preachers in the League. Contemporaries like Estoile did not take all they read at face value.[146] Their views altered and changed in the face of political circumstances. Many were aware of the king's abilities: his oratory, his learning, his historical awareness, his knowledge of politics. They knew of his periodic, assiduous attention to the business of state, punctuated by moments of profound, paralysing depression. He sometimes attended to all his own correspondence; he even arranged for a glass window to be cut into the cabinet rooms of his châteaux so that he could watch over their deliberations. Even in the early months of 1589 he sat in council all afternoon examining the *cahiers* from the estates of Blois – a 'miracle' according to one contemporary observer 'amidst such tumult and perturbation'.[147] Those who served him and knew him well were impressed by his abilities: his superintendent of finances, Bellièvre, when asked by Henri IV to tell him frankly about his predecessor, refused to say anything against the memory of his previous master.

The king's strengths and weaknesses, and the extent to which he was misunderstood, appear readily from an examination of the public reactions to his religious convictions. Nothing struck more deeply than the charge that Henri III was a '*politique*' and, worse, an 'atheist'. It reached to the heart of the divinity of the French monarchy to which he had been educated and in which he believed. Ominously, catholics recalled that the crown had slipped twice from Henri III's head during

---

145. Among the more ignorant: A.J. Grant, 1951, 'The historian wishing to understand the strange creature [*Henri III*] should probably have to seek the help of an expert in brain disease' (p. 427). V.H.H. Green, 1969, 'Clearly a psychological case' (p. 247).

146. It is sometimes implied that Estoile's views were those of the pamphlets he collected. But he was evidently outraged by some of them and said that only foolish people believed what they read in them. His support for the king after 1584 was less equivocal.

147. E. Halphen, [1880], pp. 69–75.

his coronation at Reims in 1575 and that the liturgy of the service had been in various respects improper – both signs, perhaps, of God's disfavour.[148] In reality, the king held strong religious convictions which were expressed in public and private. He touched for scrofula with apparently genuine zeal, regarding this as one of the means by which he might contribute to curing his commonwealth's afflictions. At Blois in 1576, and again in the following year at Poitiers, the centre of one of the most devastated regions, he applied his thaumaturgical powers. Catholic preachers scurrilously intimated later that Henri III had rendered his healing powers inefficacious by his compromise peace with the protestants.[149] The king kept a catholic court, employing few, if any protestants directly. Services in his chapels were immaculately presented in accordance with Tridentine liturgical forms. He avidly collected relics and religious pictures, cutting the latter from medieval manuscripts. The most important relics of the royal collection were those of the Passion held in the Sainte Chapelle in Paris. When a fragment of the Holy Cross disappeared in 1575 (its theft was blamed on the queen mother and the Italian financiers) the king ensured that the remaining fragment was given a special reliquary and attended in person the processions to venerate it.[150] Other processions were regularly organised by the king to sustain the realm in times of greatest danger. He required them to be impeccably organised, with no women taking part: 'for there is no devotion to be found when they are around'.

He conceived of reform in religious terms, expending enormous personal effort to create a new noble Order, the Order of the Holy Spirit. That of St Michael had become debased in the civil wars (entitlement had been given to those serving in the cavalry companies instead of arrears of pay).[151] The new Order was to surround the sovereign with a group of nobles of high birth, sworn by a special bond of fidelity to sustain royal authority and the catholic church and restore the natural leadership of the nobility in the kingdom. The scheme provoked years of bitter controversy with the papacy over the ecclesiastical revenues that the king required to sustain it. When it was finally established in December 1578, it was criticised by some as too lavish, by others because they had not been appointed to it and then by Alençon because he feared its success.[152] In fact, it probably did

148. Estoile, [1943], p. 67. K. Cameron, 1974, 152–63.
149. M. Bloch, 1973, pp. 177, 193.
150. Estoile, [1943], pp. 71, 112.
151. R. Harding, 1978, pp. 81–2.
152. J. Boucher, 1972. ANG, VIII, 176–7, 258–60.

encourage some members of the upper nobility to convert from protestantism back to catholicism and those appointed to the order were carefully chosen to be political supporters of the Valois monarchy.

The king also perceived in religious terms reform on a personal plane. He founded private chapels and retreats in the *bois* at Vincennes and the *faubourg* St Honoré where he could undertake retreats for penance, mortification and contemplation. These retreats were criticised by contemporaries as ill becoming the king. But they only lasted for fifteen to twenty days each year and, to those close to the king, it was the severity of his devotions and their effect on the king's fragile health which gave cause for concern. Other monastic orders in France mistrusted the Jeronimites and (later) Minims of Vincennes for precisely this austerity.[153] But these periods of retreat were important: from that of 1582 sprang the royal initiatives for reform in 1583. They were essential for maintaining a royal sense of purpose amidst a hostile climate.

The popular counterpart to the Order of the Holy Spirit and the Jeronimites in Vincennes was the penitent movement. The king was introduced to the penitents at Avignon in 1574 by his confessor, the Jesuit, Edmund Auger. Impressed by their ritual of processions, pilgrimages and confessions, he envisaged that they might stimulate moral and religious revival in catholic France without the political dangers of the local fraternities. He helped to establish the penitents in Lyon in 1582 and introduced them in the following year to the capital itself.[154] Cardinal Joyeuse and bishop Gondi, prominent clerical courtiers, introduced other branches of the penitent movement to the capital city. The penitents were ridiculed by the Parisian notables and called, contemptuously, the *battus* and the 'flagellants', although it seems that the scourges hanging from their belts were purely penitential symbols.

Above all, contemporaries were not able to comprehend the royal attitude to heresy. How was it that the young prince who had seemingly played a prominent part at the massacre of Saint Bartholomew in 1572 could sign and sustain the edict of pacification

---

153. The Oratory in Vincennes was reportedly ready for use in 1584 (A. Desjardins, [1859–65], IV, 485–7) and that of St Honoré in around 1585 (Ibid., 600, 631). François Hotman's view of the king's activity was that he had gone mad with superstition and remorse for his tyranny (R. Dareste, 1850, p. 88). Estoile reported Parisian views of 'le roi se faisant moine'. See Estoile [1943], pp. 417, 498.

154. A. Lynn Martin, 1973; Cal SP For, XVII, 184–6. Statutes of the congregation in Arch. cur. de l'hist. de France, X (1st Series), 437–9.

at Bergerac (1577) which had granted the protestants substantial rights in his kingdom? They ignored the massacre's profound effect on him (he was reportedly taciturn for days after the slaughter). His later political experience taught him that force against an ideological opposition was useless. As he wrote to the French ambassador in Venice, the prudent Arnaud du Ferrier (c.1508–85): 'I have learnt by experience that the evils so long afflicting this realm cannot be healed by force of arms. Softer and more gentle means are needed and these I am resolved to use.'[155] Many of the king's contemporaries understood the realism of this conclusion. Arnaud Sorbin, the king's chaplain, also believed that force would not win back the heretics and the Jesuit, Edmund Auger, preached the same message. But beyond the court there were even more catholic clergy for whom the panic responses to heresy had a greater appeal. They would have agreed with the Italian friar, Panigarola. He was removed from Henri III's court for saying that, with heretics, 'it was pious to be cruel'.[156]

THE DISPUTED SUCCESSION

On 10 June 1584, the direct heir to the throne, François, duke of Anjou, died. François had been a political menace to his brother whilst alive. His death was a disaster, however, for the lack of a clear legal succession to the throne further eroded royal authority. As the Savoyard ambassador reported, 'Every day he [*the king*] has the sound of death in his ears, whether from the letters of his friends or the mouths of his servants and subjects. Everything in France comes down to this question: "If your majesty dies, this might happen . . . "'.[157] Succession disputes had a habit of festering and poisoning sixteenth-century states unless they were quickly resolved. According to royal apologists, the custom in France was that 'la mort saisit le vif' and that therefore a king was declared by dynastic right and not by coronation and, to that extent, disputed successions were automatically avoided.

155. *Henri III, Lettres* [1965–], III, 409. For Arnaud du Ferrier, *DBF*, XI, col. 1393. He was Henri de Navarre's chancellor for a period and died of 'chagrin' at the renewed civil wars of the League.
156. Fr Panigarola, *Leçons catholiques. . .* (Lyon, 1586), pp. 591–2.
157. R. de Lucinge, [1954–5], p.106, [1964], pp. 171–3.

The problems facing the kingdom in 1584, however, could not be so quickly or painlessly despatched. Not only was Henri III legally bound not to make a will or declare his successor but, as contemporaries well understood, he was under powerful pressures not to announce his own political demise by naming his successor.[158]

Claims of the most speculative kind against the legitimacy of Valois rule in France had been made since the beginning of the century. In 1510, Symphorien Champier, physician and historian to Antoine, duke of Lorraine (d.1544) had asserted on the basis of a charter of 1070 that the dukes of Lorraine were directly descended from Charlemagne. The assertion received support in the reign of Henri II, partly from elaborately forged documents. During the wars of religion, its importance grew as other authors such as François Hotman attempted to prove that the Capetians (and, therefore, the Valois) were usurpers to the throne of Charlemagne. The duke of Lorraine was, in 1584, one of the candidates in a position to assert his right to the French throne.[159]

The kingdom of France was not, however, without fundamental laws governing the royal succession. The problem was that they were difficult to apply to the particular case. The principal law was the Salic Law, an invention of French lawyers in the Hundred Years' War to exclude Plantagenet claims to the French throne (but believed towards the close of the sixteenth century to have a more venerable antiquity). According to the Salic law, the French crown was hereditary only through the male line. Were it to apply strictly, the claim of the duke of Lorraine would fall away (since the succession from Charlemagne passed through two females). However the Salic law was not accepted entirely without question. It did not conform to the general principles of Roman law and also conflicted with private customary law in some regions (for instance, Lorraine, where territories 'devolved' through the female line).[160] It also did not hold good for the kingdom of Navarre where queens could rule as of right and where Henri de Navarre might hold his throne through succession in the female line.

However, the Salic law was imprecise on the law of inheritance. If the inheritance passed into a collateral line, whose was the better case? By strict primogeniture, the first in line of succession was Henri de

---

158. F. Hotman, [1972], pp. 463–4. Cf. *Discours sur les calomnies* (Paris, 1588, LN, No. 1245) – 'To declare a successor is almost . . . to condemn a prince'.

159. L. Davillé, 1909, pp. 2–22. The argument was refuted by Philippe Du Plessis Mornay in his *Discours sur le droit pretendu par ceux de Guise sur la Couronne de France* (n.p. 1583, LN, No. 1054).

160. L. Davillé, 1909. The queen mother apparently also had doubts about the Salic law (Brantôme, [1864–82], VIII, 45).

Navarre, followed by his uncle Charles, cardinal de Bourbon. (see Fig. 2) But by consanguinity (the principle used in Roman law to decide an intestate inheritance) the first in line was the cardinal of Bourbon, since the cardinal was only twenty degrees removed from the Valois king as opposed to Henri's twenty-one.[161] The case for strict primogeniture was argued by François Hotman whom Henri of Navarre aproached in August 1584 to sustain him in 'this huge and complex question, so vital for the future, and which needs to be enlightened'.[162] No one, Navarre told Hotman, could do it better – 'Work with diligence and attention . . . and I assure you I will reward your useful service.' By April 1585 Hotman's *Disputes on the Succession Controversy* had appeared. It was a theoretical work of legal sophistication, arguing the case for the *suitas regiae* or the *ius filiationis vel sanguinis*, the royal birthright or succession not as governed by blood or degree but by declared, public law, solemnly enacted in the estates general of the kingdom as the Salic law had been in the previous century. He used extensively a work of a fifteenth-century jurist, Jean de Terre Rouge, an edition of whose treatise he appended to his publication. At the same time, he hastened to amend the fourth edition of *Francogallia* by adding a chapter on the laws of succession in the French monarchy.[163]

The case for consanguinity was argued by the Italian, Matteo Zampini, with whom Hotman had already crossed swords. He produced a treatise *On the Law of Succession* which circulated widely in manuscript before appearing in print in 1588.[164] Zampini criticised Hotman's case for primogeniture. The birthright of the succession always lay with the dauphin, the heir apparent. Antoine de Bourbon, king of Navarre and Henri's father (1518–62) had never been the first prince of the blood royal because he was from a collateral line' and the Valois had always denied the possibility of his *ever* being the dauphin. Therefore there was no *suitas regiae* to Navarre. When there was no direct birthright then, by historical precedent, the succession passed to the next proximate kin by consanguinity. The chief historical precedent was the succession of Louis the Pious as against Bernard, son of Pepin (*c.* 754). Zampini's case was a strong one, although later he was lampooned by those of a Navarrist persuasion as a 'senseless and scurrilous' foreign lawyer. There were, however, residual problems

161. F.J. Baumgartner, 1973, 87–93.
162. D. Kelley, 1973, p. 292.
163. F. Hotman, [1972], pp. 452–72.
164. C. Bontemps *et al.*, 1965, pp. 171–86. It was published in Latin and French in 1588 as *De la Succession du Droict et Prérogative du premier Prince du sang de France* (Paris, 1588).

attached to the way in which precise consanguinity was to be calculated.

In any case, catholics argued the case for another fundamental law in favour of the cardinal Charles de Bourbon: that of 'catholicity'. The case was, once again, an imposing one. The French king was 'the Most Christian King' in Europe, a title accorded the monarchy by the papacy. The monarch had powers to heal scrofula, acquired at his anointment with holy unction at the coronation, to nominate bishops and enjoy in certain circumstances the revenues of the catholic church. The mystique of monarchy, the symbolism of the crown, the coronation and all the rituals which gave the institution its social significance and wider political justification, relied on catholicism. But the case for 'catholicity' was made more complex by the famous papal bull announced by Sixtus V to the consistory in Rome on 9 September 1585, which excommunicated both Henri of Navarre and Henri, prince of Condé and further declared Navarre ineligible to succeed to the French throne. This turned the issue of catholicity into part of a much older question, that of papal rights and authority in France. Hotman was again responsible for the famous reply to the papal bull, the *Brutum Fulmen* (translated into English by a contemporary as the *Brutish Thunderbolt or Rather Feeble Fire Flash*). In his most cavalier fashion, Hotman accused Sixtus V, the 'stupid cuckoo', the 'purple whore', of the seven cardinal sins and pointed out the dangers of papal interference in the law of catholicity. The pamphlet went through four editions in two years and the papal court announced a reward of 2,000 crowns for Hotman's assassination.[165] Nevertheless, the pressure on Henri de Navarre to convert to catholicism was very great. It is doubtful, if he had, whether he would have had an undisputed succession, for his basic dynastic right was still in doubt. It is certain that he would not have carried the protestants with him and he would have placed his own authority in Béarn, the only territory which he ruled as a sovereign prince, in jeopardy. Had he converted at this stage, it is possible that he would have become the prisoner of the catholic League. This was, in a way, what happened to Navarre's uncle, the cardinal of Bourbon. The 'red ass' (as Hotman spitefully called him), the 'old dotard, drunk with ambition' (as de Thou dismissively referred to him) was aware that his age and clerical condition told against his candidature. Although Henri III eventually declared (and registered in *parlement*) that the cardinal was his dauphin (on 17 August 1588) the cardinal knew that this had

165. D. Kelley, 1973. pp. 300–6.

been in response to pressure from the Guise. He eventually was moved to acknowledge that 'the Guise, fatal enemies to his name and his house, had used him to advance themselves'.[166]

166.   De Thou, VIII, 255; *Mémoires de Condé*, IV, 3.

CHAPTER TWO

The Catholic League

The catholic League was the apotheosis of the sectarian struggle and the culmination of the wars of religion. It had its roots in sectarian memory. It drew its energies from the frustrations of the failure of reform in the French state and seized the opportunity created by the succession problem after the duke of Anjou's death. Formally speaking, the League took shape in complicated negotiations which arose in north-east France between September 1584 and March 1585.[1] The venues were Nancy, capital of the duchy of Lorraine; Joinville, principal château of the House of Guise in catholic Champagne; and Reims, the great cathedral city, symbol of catholic France where its kings were traditionally crowned. Those present at various times included Charles III, duke of Lorraine (1543–1606) and every member of the House of Guise who could attend. François de Roncherolles, sieur de Maineville, acted as an agent for the cardinal of Bourbon. Philip II, King of Spain, was represented by Jean-Baptiste de Tassis (c. 1530–1610) who had just been replaced as Spain's ambassador in Paris; also by Philip's chief agent in France, Juan Moreo. Claude Mathieu, a Jesuit from the duke of Lorraine's new Jesuit university, attended in order to carry news of the discussions to Rome. Each party had its own interests to pursue, but the issue of the succession to the French crown and the possibility of exploiting the lively hatred of the Valois court united them all. The results were an agreement at Joinville on 31 December 1584 to support Cardinal Charles de Bourbon's claim to the throne, by war if necessary, underwritten by promises of substantial sums of money from Spain and guaranteed by the duke of Lorraine. Three months later, in the so-called Declaration of Péronne, the

1. L. Davillé, 1909, pp. 41–82.

League for the reform of the state and the defence of the catholic faith was publicly proclaimed.[2]

As with the Huguenots, the most lively and committed part of the catholic League lay in major cities where, following the example of Paris, groups of men, dedicated to the preservation of the catholic faith, seized power in 1589. In Paris, they were known as the *Sixteen* (*Seize*) after the number of quarters (*quartiers*) of the capital from which the members of its organising committees were elected. Many features of the League in the cities – its apparent spontaneity, oath, secrecy and vigilante attitudes – reflected the catholic confraternities of earlier civil wars. They certainly inspired genuine fears and social conflict among catholic city notables: 'This is true anarchy' reported Etienne Pasquier in Paris.[3] The *Sixteen* plotted against the king and expelled him from his capital in 1588. They remained a powerful force for over three years in the capital and their popularity and organisation were such that, in 1589, they seemed to be invincible. Yet, by 1594, the League had collapsed in many traditionally catholic localities. How did the *Sixteen* acquire such influence and how was it so quickly lost? To what extent did their defeat assist France's struggle for political stability? The confused history of the catholic League is that of its own internal quarrels, but from them, something can be learned of the instabilities in France towards the end of the sixteenth century.

THE *SIXTEEN* AND THE DAY OF BARRICADES IN PARIS (12 MAY 1588)

Two documents, written in very different circumstances, supply all our information about the 'prehistory' of the *Sixteen*. One was the passionately written *Dialogue between the Noble and the Townsman* (1593) probably composed by the ardent League supporter, François of Morin, sieur de Cromé.[4] The other was a dossier, compiled by Nicolas Poulain, lieutenant of police in Paris and a double agent in the *Sixteen*

---

2. The declaration of Péronne because this was where the catholic League of 1576 had been proclaimed. In fact, the declaration in 1585 was made from Reims and then published in another version from Lyon in June 1585 (ML, I, 56–62). LN, No. 1089. Cf. LN, No. 1100.

3. E. Pasquier, [1966], p. 396.

4. F. Morin, [1977]. Morin's biography is given on pp. 24–7. This authorship, based on testimony by Estoile and Cayet, is now widely accepted.

for the king almost from its inception until the Day of Barricades.[5] Both accept that the *Sixteen* began to meet in 1584. Charles Hotman de la Rocheblond, younger brother to the Huguenot author and a treasurer to the bishop of Paris, was to be their 'Moses'. He consulted three clerical colleagues about 'the misery of the times, the ambition of the nobles, the insolence of the people, and, above all, the loss of the Roman Catholic religion'.[6] They all agreed on the necessity for action and Hotman and his three friends, Jean Prévost (*curé* of the prestigious Paris church of St Séverin), Jean Boucher (*curé* of St Benoît and a former rector of the university of Paris) and Mathieu de Launoy (canon in Soissons cathedral and a former Huguenot), nominated further catholic zealots and figures of respect within the city to join the group. Nearly all the notables who were later to play a leading part in the history of the *Sixteen* joined at this early stage. They included Etienne de Neuilly (d. 1598); Michel Marteau, sieur de la Chapelle (d. 1605); Louis Dorléans (1540-1627), the prominent League controversialist; Jean Guincestre, their theologian, and Jean ('le Bussy') Leclerc, later the *Sixteen*'s governor of the Bastille.[7] In many ways, therefore, the movement was originally clerical, respectable and thoroughly well integrated into the professional cadres of Paris urban life. Several of these notables had already been involved in past associations to defend the catholic faith so that, to some extent, the spontaneity of the *Sixteen* was more apparent than real.[8]

Their growth was, nonetheless, remarkable. They recruited with care and required a strict oath of secrecy and loyalty to other members.[9] The council of the *Sixteen* – initially a large informal meeting – was transformed (probably in 1587) into a small inner council more suited to the large membership.[10] Members reported daily on the activities of their *quartier*, just as they would have done if they had been serving on the watch committees. Resources were apparently plentiful, collected, it was said, by voluntary donations.[11] They managed to penetrate all the important groups in Parisian public life. By 1587, the *Sixteen* had adherents among the printers, the royal mint, the treasury, the *parlement*, the royal messenger service, the clerks

---

5. 'Le procès verbal d'un nommé Nicolas Poulain, lieutenant de la prévosté de l'Isle de France', Arch. cur. de l'hist. de France, XI, 289–323 (cited as Poulain).

6. F. Morin, [1977], p. 95.

7. E. Barnavi, 1980, pp. 20–1 *et seq.* for further biographical details.

8. Ibid.

9. Poulain, 289–90.

10. F. Morin, [1977], p. 65. C. Valois, [1914], p. 125.

11. Poulain, 294–5, 306.

and attorneys as well as the horse-traders, the Seine lightermen and the retail butchers. For Hotman's funeral in 1587 (he was the 'chief and leader of its affairs') the *Sixteen* provided an impressive cortège.[12]

It is not difficult to explain why the League should have been pre-eminent in Paris. It was a large city with a substantial population. It had a well-established urban political consciousness with corporate institutions which looked to orthodox catholicism to provide them with their rituals and respectability. They were capable of finding ways of presenting their own grievances to good effect and speaking also for those of a wider French polity. When threatened by an apparently common enemy, even if it was the king, it was only natural that some of them should have thought to create a 'syndicate' to react in unison.

Paris was also a city where the earlier bitter sectarianism of the civil wars had created catholic heroes, martyrs and enemies but provided, despite the massacre of St Bartholomew, no final solution. Catholic preachers had anticipated the imminent onset of the 'mother of all battles' in which the forces of Antichrist would shortly be vanquished for good by the violence of the just. Yet the final battle had not happened. Worse, the French monarchy – which by tradition and common expectation was expected to lead these forces into battle – seemed only interested in appeasing the enemy, taxing the wealth and good will of its *bonnes villes* (loyal towns) and its catholic subjects. Such sentiments, however, were difficult to express roundly. What would it achieve to attack the king directly? The preachers in Paris reminded their congregations of the verse from Proverbs: 'The wrath of a king is as messengers of death: but a wise man will pacify it.'

The Paris League began, above all, as an incarnation of a public mood, reflected from, and fostered by the press, pulpit and university. Paris was a major printing centre in Europe and its printers (about 120 of them joined the League) exploited the profitable markets in works of catholic casuistry and piety.[13] For them the League was an immense business opportunity. As Estoile noted; 'There is not a single, small, poor printer who does not have the means to roll off his press some new stupidity or scandalous libel against His Majesty . . . I have collected more than 300 examples, all printed in Paris and sold publicly in the streets.'[14] League pamphlets were seized by the ton on their way from Paris to Senlis and other *bonnes villes* in the provinces. Yet it would be wrong to imagine that this was a propaganda

---

12. Poulain, 293–5; C. Valois, [1914], pp. 123–5.
13. D. Pallier, 1976, ch. ii.
14. Estoile, [1943], p. 626.

campaign cunningly orchestrated by the organism of the *Sixteen*. Rather, it was a reflection of a public mood which was profound but which could not easily express itself. The embryo *Sixteen* drew at least as much in terms of authority and confidence *from* such expression as they were able to contribute *to* it and manipulate it.

The tone of the catholic pamphlets of this period was intrusive, invasive and designed to shock. They put into words what decent *bons bourgeois* of the capital had thought in the privacy of their own hearts and homes, but had not thought it proper to express. The *Sixteen* legitimized the unthinkable – that there was treason within. The *'politiques'* frustrated God's purposes and prolonged the agony of France's good catholics. The *'politiques'* were 'atheists', *'maheustres'* (n'er-do-well noblemen), wicked 'Jezebels'. Worse, they were installed in the highest offices of the land. By their duplicity, the *'politiques'* were still more dangerous than the heretic Huguenots, dissimulating under a 'mask' of devotion to the catholic cause. They were prepared to seize any opportunity which came their way to sacrifice the interests and legitimate aspirations of good catholics to a fraudulent peace. The *'politiques'* were nothing more than a creation of League imaginings – but, in the hands of the *Sixteen*, it was nonetheless a powerful construct.[15]

Initially, the *Sixteen* exploited their clandestine state, publishing the papal bull excommunicating Henri of Navarre and the prince of Condé (it was banned by the king) and distributing copies only to their supporters.[16] Other sonnets and pasquinades developed hidden anagrams and *double entendres*. One fine example was the verse which could be read in a Royalist/Bourbon or Lorraine/Guise direction:

	(Royalist)		(Royalist)
(Guisard)	Plus ne fault endurer		La race de Bourbon
	La Ligue de Lorraine		Est la paix de la France
(Guisard)	Ils tiennent en leurs mains		De l'estat la defense
	Le fer pour nous tuer.		c'est la Religion.[17]

They then began a remarkable series of propaganda exercises which presented the League as the only logical political option for French

---

15. P. Papin, 1991.
16. D. Pallier, 1976, p. 62; Cayet, p. 22.
17. Beyond endurance is   The Bourbon race
    The Lorraine League   Gives peace to France
    Their hands encompass   The defence of the state
    The weapon which kills us   Is the Protestant religion

catholics. In 1585, the issue was the Declaration of Péronne; the following year it was the necessity for war against the Huguenots. This was when Louis Dorléans produced his famous *Advertisement of the English Catholics to the French Catholics*, which the historian, de Thou, later described as the 'general call to arms' of the League.[18] The moderate Huguenot, Palma Cayet, was shocked by its crudity.[19] It painted the heretics as ravaging wolves with whom there could be no peace or security. They should all be burned, beginning with the author of *Francogallia*. The courage and bravery of the duke of Guise was praised. Heresy was a contagion and the lesson of the English catholics and their miseries under the wicked 'Jezebel' queen, Elizabeth I, should be learned before it was too late.[20] The attacks on the king multiplied and 'corroded the hearts of the people' so that, by the end of 1587, he was spoken of as a puppet prince.[21] Royalist printers were liable to find their copies seized and burnt by preachers.[22] The Sorbonne refused to censor works with which it was in fundamental agreement. On 16 December 1587, the doctors of the Sorbonne accepted the proposition that 'if a prince did not do as he should, then he could be dismissed in the same way as dismissing a child's guardian for improper behaviour'.[23] The growth of League propaganda in Paris and in major provincial cities during this period is crudely demonstrated in Fig. 1.

The press appealed to the literate. Engravings, billboards and paintings reached the illiterate. In July 1587, for instance, Henri III ordered the removal of a painted poster erected in the cemetery of St Séverin (the church of the Latin quarter) which depicted the cruelties and tortures suffered by the English catholics while men stood by with pointers to emphasise that this was what Parisian catholics could expect from a heretic king.[24] Organised processions were also employed, leaving the historian, de Thou, with a powerful impression of their popular appeal:

---

18. D. Pallier, 1976, pp. 63–9. De Thou, IX, 69–70. F.J. Baumgartner, 1976, pp. 71–4. Dorléans' diary reveals his interests in, if not his accurate knowledge of, English catholic affairs. I have used the abridged edition in Arch. cur. de l'hist. de France, XI, 11, etc.

19. Cayet, p. 22.

20. Arch. cur. de l'hist. de France, XI, 112–212, esp. 156–76. This volume also includes the reply to the work by Du Plessis Mornay.

21. Estoile, [1943], pp. 507–8, 511–12.

22. D. Pallier, 1976, pp. 66–7. C. Valois, [1914], pp. 147–8.

23. Estoile, [1943], p. 508.

24. De Thou, IX, 270. Estoile, [1943], pp. 497–8, 500, 514–17.

Processions were ordered in all the churches of the city; altars full of gold, silver and jewels were set up to attract the people . . . peasants also took part, and the duke of Guise sent a party of men and women dressed in white robes ornamented with crosses from Champagne . . . These devout ones forming long lines and crossing Paris while mumbling prayers that could scarcely be heard attracted everyone's attention.[25]

The king could scarcely forbid an activity which he himself had encouraged.

From the pulpit, League preachers delivered the same message at Advent and Lent. Contemporaries were impressed with their liberty and the extent to which they were believed by their congregations.[26] In September 1587, Estoile complained (with some exaggeration) that it was difficult to find a preacher who was not a League supporter.[27] His contemporary, Etienne Pasquier, recognised the power of the pulpit in one of his letters from the capital in 1587:

> [*Preachers*] are dangerous tools in a civil war, whether they lend their tongues to one side or the other . . . They say that, when they preach, the Holy Ghost is directing their lips and that, from the pulpit of truth, they are allowed to speak as it moves them . . . their enemies, however, say that they are only men and that, in a civil war, they sell their tongues to the highest bidder.[28]

The king tried to curb their enthusiasms by inviting them to private audiences to admonish them, but with little effect. Jean Boucher (1548–1644) (called 'the butcher' and about whom Estoile cruelly remarked that 'in the kingdom of the blind, the one-eyed are kings' – Boucher was blind in one eye) apparently harangued the king on the evils of his court and royal weaknesses when he was invited to the Louvre.[29] Attempts to arrest three League clergy at St Séverin on 2 September 1587 produced a riot in the Latin quarter.[30] Others were accused of preaching 'democracy, or popular government', of refusing to have the 'peace of God' in the Mass lest it tempered people's ardour against 'closet' heretics in their neighbourhood, and of even

25. De Thou, IX, 654–5; Estoile, [1943], pp. 499, 508–9. F. Yates, 1954.

26. Estoile, [1943], p. 508. A. Lebigre, 1980. The influence of the *curés* was remarked on by Pigafetta and Cornejo during the siege of 1590. Cf. C. Valois, [1914], pp. 134–8.

27. Estoile, [1943], pp. 502–3.

28. E. Pasquier, [1966], p. 283.

29. Estoile, [1943], pp. 509–10. For Boucher, see DBF, VI, col. 1207. Cf. C. Valois, [1914], pp. 151–72.

30. Estoile, [1943], pp. 502–3.

refusing the sacraments to prominent judges of the *parlement* because they were reputed to be hypocrites and dissembling heretics.[31] Popularism – the underlying theme of the civil wars – was again in the ascendant.

While Paris became a crucible for catholic aspirations and ideals, the 'good town' of Paris was called on to make particular sacrifices by its Valois monarch. The demands for forced loans and 'gracious gifts' (*dons gratuits*) came with a monotonous regularity, and although the king could rely on the city provost and councillors (whom he either appointed or nominated) to agree to such additional taxation, he could be less confident of the urban militia, with its colonels and watch committees appointed in each *quartier*. He attempted to appoint his own militia captains in 1585, but this only increased the suspicion of the monarch's interference in Parisian liberties and many came to view the *Sixteen* as a kind of alternative or provisional municipal defence corps.[32] Traditionally, too, war meant the creation of new royal offices and these affected Paris more than any other city in France because of the number of tribunals in the capital and the size of its legal and professional groups. Creations came in job lots and their prices were very high.[33] Among those on the foothills of the world of the office holders – attorneys, *procureurs* and, to a certain extent, clerks – this kind of excessive office creation was badly received. The sovereign courts in Paris issued strong remonstrances in 1586 and refused to register these new edicts.[34] When the king resorted to a formal *lit de justice*, the legal staff of the royal courts went on strike.[35] It is not surprising that many of the *Sixteen*'s most active supporters would come from the legal world of France, and particularly in Paris.

A mutiny of royal servants was engendered by other aspects of fiscal policy which affected the *officiers*. These included periodic failures to pay their salaries and the seizure of the revenue assigned to pay the interest on the government bonds issued through the *hôtel de ville* in

31. *Revue rétrospective*, [1834], 267–77. Cf. C. Labitte, 1849.

32. For the taxation of Paris, P. Robiquet, 1886, p. 47 *et seq*. The registers of the town of Paris (IX, 16–17, 53–4, etc.) provide a full conspectus of the fiscal demands on the city. Cf. F.J. Baumgartner, 1976, pp. 32–3. ML, I, 199–201. For the city militia, G. Picot, 1874, pp. 132–66, esp. pp. 142–3. Estoile, [1943], pp. 376–7, 396, 489.

33. E. Barnavi, 1980, p. 15. Cf. Cayet, p. 30 – 'This innovation of creating offices served as a pretext for the League and the *Sixteen* to turn an infinite number of lesser people from obedience to the King.' Estoile, [1943], pp. 389–90 for the creations of June 1586.

34. Estoile, [1943], pp. 449–50.

35. Ibid., pp. 452–3, 467. They had also gone on strike in May 1580 over a similar issue.

Paris (*rentes*), in which they had invested heavily.[36] The *parlement* told the king bluntly in May 1587 that, by failing to honour his commitments to the *rentiers*, he was attacking 'poor widows and orphans' and that he had received more in revenue in 10 years than his predecessors had in 200 years.[37] Senior judges were particularly incensed by an interview which the king held in the Louvre earlier in 1587. The king had begun the meeting with a heartfelt declaration of his intention to fight heresy until he won. Pausing to allow the judges to express their enthusiastic support, the king then turned to the city provost to demand 600,000 *écus* from Paris by means of a levy on the wealthiest of its citizens. The judges came away murmuring that the king was like a scorpion whose sting lay in its tail.[38]

Beyond the official world of law and government lay the Paris of the Halles, the merchants who, through their guilds, corporations, confraternities and parochial activities, played a vigorous part in civic life. A devalued currency, new indirect taxes on imports to the city and adverse trading conditions in wartime all affected them, but it was the sermons and the pamphlets which influenced them most. They were apparently afraid of losing *their* religion, the traditional catholicism which guaranteed their status, rendered their notability honourable, blessed the substantial dowries they endowed upon their daughters and made sense of the corporate life in which they played such an important part.[39] They were more aware than most of the desperate conditions in the French countryside created by the poor harvests of 1586-87. Louis Dorléans' *Advertisement* went out of its way to prove that heresy was the cause of these natural disasters.[40] Merchants probably experienced at close hand the conditions that deputies came to Paris to describe to the king in May 1586:

> One from Zaintonge and the other from Périgord, who, on their knees have humbly desired the King to make a peace and to have pity upon his poor people, whose want was such that they were forced to eat bread made of *ardoise* [tiles] and of nut-shells which they brought and showed to the King. They told him also that the famine was so great as a woman in Périgord had already eaten two of her children and the like had been done in Zaintonge. The King, at the hearing of this, changed countenance . . .[41]

36. B. Schnapper, 1957, pp. 151–72.
37. Estoile, [1943], pp. 491–2.
38. Ibid., pp. 482–3.
39. R. Descimon, 1983.
40. Arch. cur. de l'hist. de France, XI, 141.
41. Cal SP For, XX, 603.

Two weeks later, the English ambassador reported that the news in Paris was that there were 'many thousand' in the Auvergne 'already dead for hunger, and that, in that extremity . . . they feed upon grass . . . like horses and die with grass in their mouths.'[42]

Paris was unique among French cities in that it saw the king and court more often than any other city. When the preachers and printers retailed scurrilous gossip, it was frequently from courtiers themselves that it had been learned. Estoile often remarked on the inappropriateness of royal lavishness at a time of municipal stringency and he was reacting to the sharp contrast, more easily seen in Paris than elsewhere, between city and court. It was unfortunate, too, that the less secure the king felt in Parisian loyalty, the longer he felt obliged to stay there, and the more exposed he became to rumour and sedition. It was reported in 1585 that he no longer trusted its citizens and, the following year, he hastily returned to his capital when it was feared that a rising in Troyes might spread to Paris.[43] He only left the city on occasions of absolute necessity from then until he was forced from it in May 1588.[44] The proximity of the court led the *Sixteen* towards planning a coup d'état at a relatively early stage.[45] Details of their plots remain vague and, while it would seem that they were well timed it is also true that they were too complicated and ambitious. Most is known about that of March 1587 when, it seems, the *Sixteen* planned to capture the Bastille, assassinate the governor, murder many prominent judges, overwhelm royal institutions of the capital and starve the palace guards from the Louvre. The king was to become a puppet ruler while a massacre would take care of the *'politiques'*. Barricades were envisaged, partly to keep the populace under control and partly to divide the city into sections for guerilla warfare.[46] The duke of Mayenne, for whom the plot was prepared, was notably uncommitted, doubtless aware of the overwhelming difficulties of an

---

42. Ibid., XXI, 6.

43. E. Pasquier, [1966], pp. 252–3. Estoile, [1943], pp. 451–2.

44. A rough sketch of court itinerary is as follows:

1585: most of the court at Paris all year until 15 Nov.

1586: court in Paris from Jan-June and Sep-Nov.

1587: court in Paris from Jan-June and Aug-Dec.

1588: court in Paris from Jan-May. The king left on the Day of Barricades, but queen and queen mother stayed in the capital.

45. Poulain, 292–9. The first plot may have taken place on 7 July 1586, but the evidence is not incontrovertible. First definite plot is from October 1586 (BN MS It 1735, pp. 305–7).

46. The duke of Mayenne had returned from an indifferent campaign in Gascony and was expected to support it. Poulain, 298–9. LN, No. 1097. Estoile, [1943]. p. 485.

operation on this scale; the preparations were leaked to the king by Nicolas Poulain and a member of the *Sixteen* was arrested.[47] As a result of this, and other, failures in the eighteen months before May 1588, the *Sixteen* became nervous that their position was compromised and that they were in danger of arrest and trial for treason.[48]

On Saturday 7 May 1588, the king ordered house-to-house searches to be made throughout the capital city and replaced suspect members of the civic militia with individuals of proven loyalty, an indication that the *Sixteen* had little time left. Two days later, at 1 p.m., the duke of Guise entered Paris with a small retinue, ignoring repeated orders from the king not to do so. The king became terrified by the explosion of popular support for the duke among Parisians and took some necessary precautions. On Thursday 12 May, at about 4 a.m., eleven Swiss and four French detachments of troops entered Paris and took up positions on the bridges, at the Louvre and in the Latin quarter. The city woke to find itself a garrisoned stronghold. In response to the military presence, and with a degree of coordination which is surprising, barricades of barrels and chains began to be erected at 50-yard intervals in streets in the Latin quarter, on the Ile and around the Louvre. The royal troops were thus enveloped in a city revolt; balconies bristled with muskets, arquebuses pointed at them and awnings had been removed to clear the line of fire. Every street in Paris was like a town to be besieged, commented the king's military advisor. The duke of Guise offered to mediate, but the king preferred to withdraw rather than admit to a military defeat in his capital. He hastily left the Louvre by the Tuileries (the only exit left to him) at about 6 p.m. on Friday 13 May.

It is ironical that the timing of the Day of Barricades was not, therefore, the result of a plot by the *Sixteen*, but the result of a series of panic measures by the king. It was not the arrival of the duke of Guise in Paris, nor the activities of his troops to the east of the capital, nor yet the advanced military preparations of the *Sixteen* which determined the timing of the erection of the barricades, although they undoubtedly contributed to the city's tensions. Rather, it resulted from the house-to-house searches and the introduction of the Swiss guards to take possession of key points of the capital so that, as one League

47. Poulain, 298–9. BN MS It 1736, pp. 20–1 (16 Mar. 1587).
48. Other plots were to have taken place in July 1587, September 1587 and February 1588. The fears of the *Sixteen* are clear in Poulain, 304–5 and 310–19. The names of many of the *Sixteen* were revealed in the publication, *La bibliothèque de madame de Montpensier* in *c.* Dec. 1587 (Estoile, [1943], pp. 534–8).

commentator said, it gave the League 50,000 volunteers.[49] The threat to city liberties produced a popular and spontaneous uprising which resulted in Henri III's prudent and hasty retreat from the capital.

The precise part of the duke of Guise and his brothers in the events leading to the Day of Barricades remains a matter for conjecture. The Guises were certainly the heroes of the catholic cause in Paris and some historians have seen the *Sixteen* as a Guisard conspiracy, the product of Guise ambitions to overthrow the Valois. But the evidence points to a more delicate and tenuous involvement than that. The duke of Guise and his brothers and cousins clearly had a substantial clientele of purveyors, debtors and servants in the city.[50] The duke had his agent, Maineville, keep him informed of their activities.[51] His assistance was sought for supplying arms and he could be relied on to offer some protection.[52] But the duke was compromised in one of the plots of 1587 and the *Sixteen* had to placate him with a suitably generous gold chain for the embarrassment they had caused him.[53] When he finally arrived in Paris, in May 1588, it was not to raise a popular revolt against the king but, so he said, to justify himself against his critics and impose his will on the king's council.[54] There is a report that the duke was taken unawares by the sound of the tocsin in the city on 12 May. Realising that he was unarmed, he hastily rummaged through the armoury of the *hôtel* de Guise to find his father's old pike, convinced that the commotion was the signal for his own assassination.[55] If the Day of Barricades had been intended to impose the duke's will on the king by popular revolt, then it failed. For it had driven the king into the hands of Henri of Navarre and committed him to a popular movement which might not be successful and which would certainly leave him open to a charge of inciting sedition and treason.

For the Spanish ambassador in Paris, Bernadino de Mendoza, the Day of Barricades must have been very satisfying news, for it prevented

49. Events of the Day of Barricades are carefully reported in the various accounts of *Revue retrospective*, [1834], IV; Arch cur de l'hist. de France, XI. C. Valois, [1914], p. 205. Also H.C. Davila, [1647], pp. 685 *et seq.* Cf. D. Richet, 1991, pp. 51–67.

50. There is no study of the clientèle of members of the House of Guise. The *rentes* and debts of the duke of Guise in BN MS Fr 8180 give the only impression easily available to date. For the view that the duke of Guise instigated the Day of Barricades, see P. Robiquet, 1886, ch. ix, who echoes the views of Michelet's *Histoire de France*.

51. Poulain, 290–91, 307. Further details on Maineville in E. Barnavi, 1980, pp. 90–92. Cf. de Thou, IX, 65.

52. Poulain, 291–2.

53. Ibid., 307.

54. H.C. Davila, [1647], pp. 680–2. C. Valois, [1914], pp. 199–207.

55. C. Valois, [1914], p. 203.

the French king from interfering with the Spanish Armada which was due to sail up the English Channel shortly. This has led some historians to suggest that the *Sixteen* were in concert with Philip II.[56] The Spanish king certainly knew of their existence and it would have been untypical of the high quality of Spanish intelligence if they had not made some contact. But there is no incontrovertible proof of it and there is an impression that Mendoza was more concerned about activities round the French Channel ports than with what was going on in Paris.[57] Mendoza and Philip II counselled the duke of Guise to keep away from Paris in the crucial weeks before the Day of Barricades. Mendoza appeared surprised by the rising when it finally took place, although it is difficult to read very much into his dry diplomatic despatches.[58] Even if one admits that the ambitions of the duke of Guise and the strategems of Spain did play a part in what happened before May 1588 (and they clearly did afterwards), it was still the case that the explosion in Paris owed more to the popular resentments of the capital and the autonomous activities of the *Sixteen*.

A 'HOLY UNION'

Between the Day of Barricades and the assassination of Henri III on 1 August of the following year, the *Sixteen* became more like a national movement with distinctive and radical solutions to the nation's problems. At an early stage they had sought support in the provinces. Nicolas Ameline, an attorney in the Châtelet (the Parisian law court) was despatched to tour (in disguise) the cities of northern and central France.[59] His message was that Paris had collected large sums of money to rid France of heresy in three years and required the support of every catholic. In some cities, he clearly enjoyed an encouraging response.[60] In 1587, Paris suggested an elaborate federal structure for these provincial contacts. Each town was to be responsible for raising

56. D. Lamar Jensen, 1964, pp. 109–14; 1968, pp. 205–21. E.H. Dickerman, 1976, pp. 19–24. The only direct reference to a meeting between the *Sixteen* and the Spanish ambassador before May 1588 is in a despatch of 1 July 1587, but this reference is ambiguous and other evidence cited by Jensen is misleading.

57. Poulain, 295, and E.H. Dickerman, 1976, n. 55.

58. G. Mattingly, 1959, pp. 218–44. Cf. A. Viñas, 1939.

59. Estoile, [1948], pp. 147–8, describes Ameline as an 'homme de menée et d'entendement'. He disguised himself as a Jesuit, a merchant or a courtier, to suit the people he was trying to attract.

60. In Rouen, P. Benedict, 1981, pp. 169 *et seq.*

its own money and troops within an overall defensive union – 'a Holy Union' – with Paris at its head. This was to be the catholic answer to the 'United Provinces of the South' – the 'catholic cities of the Holy Union'.[61] Whether they developed governing councils like that in Paris is not clear.[62] So much documentation was destroyed afterwards in the rush to conform to Henri IV (he ordered this in order to erase the memories of past sedition) that sometimes only fragments survive now. By the Day of Barricades, there were perhaps 300 towns supporting Paris – most of them towns of secondary importance in the provinces. St Malo, for instance, became the League counterpoint to Huguenot La Rochelle. Abbeville, centre of the collapsed Picardy cloth industry, became an enthusiastic League stronghold in the north.

The months between May and October 1588 were especially favourable to the growth of the 'Holy Union'. The atmosphere was one of dangerous whisperings behind a façade of normality. The revolt against the king was healed with a truce in July 1588 – the edict of Union. The *Sixteen* did not formally overturn the Paris municipal constitution but worked with it to organise elections of suitably minded delegates to the estates general which the king had agreed to summon to Blois in October 1588. At the same time, however, there were renewed plots to assassinate the king and the word on the streets of Paris and many provincial cities was not complimentary towards the king. The *Sixteen*'s agents secured the election of delegates favourable to its cause in numerous places, despite royal efforts to influence the elections against them.[63] Of the 181 delegates to the third estate, 150 were reputed to be supporters of the League. Even before the official opening of the estates, the Paris delegates (La Chapelle Marteau and

---

61. Cayet, pp. 34–8. Cf. another project in BN MS Clairambault 357, f. 146. The curious book *Remonstrance aux Trois Estats de la France* (Paris, 1586) by the lawyer, François le Breton (1549–86) also contains what might be seen as political ideas of the League. Le Breton, who was executed in Paris for the 'sedition' in the book, became a hero to the *Sixteen*: F.J. Baumgartner, 1976, pp. 76–9. D. Pallier, 1975, p. 64. De Thou, IX, 624. Le Breton's fate has been seen as the effect of increasing efforts by the king to control the press.

62. H. Drouot, 1937a, I, 134–6.

63. Henri III complained to the Paris municipality on 10 September 1588 of their activities in circulating hostile pamphlets. He mentioned the despatch of Antoine Hotman to Brittany to the estates (*Mémoires de Nevers*, [1665], I, 744–5; BN MS Fr nouv. acq. 2745, f. 235). The historian, J-A. de Thou was sent to Normandy by the king (de Thou, IX, 305–22; P. Benedict, 1981, pp. 174–5). Among the pamphlets, Palma Cayet (p. 63) thought that N. Rolland's *Remonstrance très humble* was very important for provincial delegates (D. Pallier, 1976, p. 269). Another pamphlet, the *Discours sur la procédure . . .* (n.p., 1588, in LN, No. 1295) gives details of the 'monopolies and gerrymandering' of elections to the estates.

Neuilly were among them) held meetings among the newly arriving delegates to the third estate to coordinate their demands and strategy. The duke and cardinal of Guise organised the members of the other two orders.[64]

The estates of Blois enabled the Holy Union to articulate its political ideas and to gain support for them. These appear in the magnificent *cahier des doléances* of the city of Paris, drawn up under League auspices, to present to the estates in October.[65] Behind its highly specific and wide-ranging clauses runs the general theme of the purification of the state. An excessive liberality had fractured religion and divided the state. The king had listened to the demands for reform but little had been achieved. It was 'difficult, even impossible' to expect any more from either his, or his council's, efforts. Only the estates general could succeed. Heresy was a 'cancer . . . filled with filth and infectious putrefaction'. It must be removed by force. 'All heretics, whatever their quality, condition or estate, must be imprisoned and punished by being burned alive.' The same fate was to await the sorcerers and magicians whose activities had, they claimed, become so prolific during the civil disorders. The law courts should swear to keep, and to publish, the act of Holy Union with the king in July 1588. This was to be treated as a kind of 'fundamental law', guarded by the estates general, the 'corps' of France, which would be reconvened every three years to undertake the necessary purification of the state. Epernon and his brother should present themselves before the estates to answer the charges laid by the delegates and 'purge' themselves. Greedy tax-farmers and grasping foreign bankers should be investigated by a powerful commission from the estates general which would be reconvened automatically every five years and be responsible to the delegates alone. Superfluous noble titles acquired by sordid means were to be abolished. All taxation, apart from revenues of the royal domain, was to be approved by the estates. The royal domain was also to be the subject of the estates' investigations. The royal court was to be cleansed, the pensions cut. Nobles who were apprehended in the act of duelling were to be hanged '*les vivants et les morts ensemble*'. No games of dice, darts, cards or chequers were permissible for 'they rendered youth useless to the republic'. Senior clergymen were to be elected and royal influence in the appointments to the church curtailed.

64. There is no modern study of the estates of 1588. See G. Picot, 1888, III, 370 *et seq.* E. Pasquier, [1966], p. 331. M. Orlea, 1980, p. 102 refers to the delegates coming with copies of the Paris *cahier*.

65. E. Barnavi, [1976–7], 81–154. Elections from Paris in A. Taillandier, 1845–46, 422–59.

Looking back from this *cahier* to the clandestine pamphlets produced in Paris in the years before 1588, the source for many of these notions becomes clear. Looking further back, they bear some resemblance to demands made at the estates general of 1576 and, beyond that, to the alternative conceptions of the French state which had gained currency in the aftermath of the massacre of St Bartholomew, especially among protestants. A recourse to the estates general and the sovereignty of the people; a renewed insistence on a fundamental law that the estates general guarded; a belief in the restorative power of elections in both church and state; an underlying puritanism and suspicion of the old nobility – these notions would soon be joined by another shared notion, that of the right to revolt against a tyrant.

Henri III knew how to deal with an estates general. He would take the League over and declare any other association in the kingdom treasonable. At the same time, he would make promises and concessions, and buy time, just as he had done in 1576. He would reform his household, cut the pension list, establish a commission to flush out corruption and provide deputies with a list of his councillors 'so that they could identify those who were most suspect'. 'I accept your requests' was the king's reply.

In his opening speech to the assembled estates, the king accepted the edict of Union but warned: 'Some grandees in my realm have created leagues and associations; as a sign of my accustomed beneficence I put all the past behind me but, as I am obliged . . . to safeguard royal dignity, I declare that from now on, those amongst my subjects who do not desist, or who persist in so doing without my permission will be guilty of high treason and punished accordingly.' At these words, the duke of Guise reportedly went pale. But shortly afterwards the Guises decided to press the king to disavow the impression that they were being criticised. In the first of a sequence of humiliations for the king, he was obliged to swear (on 18 October) to maintain the Edict of Union as a fundamental law of the kingdom. On 4 November, following the proposition of the clergy, the delegates agreed that the king of Navarre, having taken up arms against the kingdom, was guilty of treason. Navarre's claim to the throne, and that of his successors, was explicitly disavowed. Henri III, unable to muster countervailing voices in the estates, was obliged to accept the proposition, whilst reminding delegates that no one should be condemned for treason without being offered a chance to defend themselves. An embassy should be despatched at once to Navarre to 'remind him of his duty'. The archbishop of Embrun replied, however, that the estates could have nothing to do with an excommunicate. Henri III's perception that he was dealing with an orchestrated campaign to block the succession to the throne of even a catholic Bourbon, was strengthened. The invasion of the French principality of Saluzzo by the duke of Savoy, a Spanish client, was one more sign that the integrity of his kingdom was in the balance. 'We shall see in a few days' time', wrote the Florentine ambassador at Blois, Cavriana, 'who will prevail, the king or the duke of Guise.'

By the time Cavriana wrote, Henri III had probably already instituted some urgent modifications to the royal presence chamber at Blois. These blocked off two points of access to it, leaving only the door to the council chamber.[66] The assassination of the duke of Guise by members of the king's bodyguard as he entered the king's chamber from the council, responding to a royal summons, on the morning of 23 December 1588 had thus been meticulously prepared under the king's personal direction. All the other members of the House of Guise in Blois at the time were arrested, along with their known supporters, including the cardinal of Bourbon. The cardinal of Guise was assassinated the following day. The king explained his actions to his mother whom he visited shortly after the event. Cavriana, who was present during the exchange, recorded more or less what he said:

> 'Madam, good morning. Please forgive me. M. de Guise is dead, and will not be spoken of again. I have had him killed. I have forestalled him in the plot which he had conceived against me. I could no longer tolerate his insolence although I tried hard enough to do so for I did not want the stain of his blood on my hands. I had forgiven the offence which I had received on Friday 13 May, the day when I was constrained to flee Paris. I had also obliterated from my memory his attempt on my life, on my honour and my realm. Nevertheless, as I was aware of, and had at every moment evidence that he was sapping and menacing my authority, my life and my State, I resolved upon this deed which I have long contemplated in myself . . . I want to be a king and not a prisoner or a slave as I have been since 13 May and now I begin again to be king and master.'

Catherine de Médicis' immediate reply was not recorded. But on Boxing Day she wrote to the Capuchin, Bernardino d'Osimo: 'Oh! The poor thing, what has he done? Pray for him – he has more need of it now than ever. I see him on the brink of his ruination and I fear that he will lose body, soul and kingdom.' Already seriously ill, she did not live to see the fulfilment of her prophecy; she died a fortnight later on 5 January 1589.

66. P. Chevallier, 1985, pp. 665–71.

The massacres at Blois provoked an explosion of popular outrage in the major cities of France, turning them into League centres almost overnight. Henri III ensured that the bodies of the victims were burned in quicklime so there would be no relics to venerate. He distributed his justification for his actions around the kingdom. The Guises had planned, he said, 'pernicious enterprises against the state and the king's person'. But this had little effect and Rouen, Blois, Amiens, Reims, Dijon, Orléans, Toulouse and Marseille all joined the Paris League in a matter of weeks.[67] The catholic Union had eventually been achieved not round a common purpose but against a common, royal enemy.

It is difficult to recapture the language and mood of violence in catholic circles in the early months of 1589. In Paris, the preachers went on to the streets crying: *'Au meurtre! Au feu! Au sang! A la vengeance!'* against the king.[68] An extraordinary account of the emotion raised in Rouen has been preserved for us by a refugee English nun. She attended a sermon by the Jesuit, Jacques Commolet, on December 29:

> When he came into the pulpytt, all eyis and mowthes gapying upon hym, the good man was in such a passyon that he seemyed lyke to burst and could scars brying out hys words for weepyng, the passyon of that tyme had so alteryd hys voyce. Hys matter was of blessed St Thomas (of Canterbury), declarying to the people the cause of hys martirdome in the behalfe of Chrystes churche, and of the quarrel betwyxt hym and the kyng, and how hys braynes were stroke out uppon the pavement before ye altar. Thys thyng was so apt for hys purpose that the people could by and by apply ytt that the preacher had no soner named the slaughter of theyr 2 prynces but thatt all fell out into weepyng, and the preacher ther sobying allowde could saye no more. Butt after a preatty space, stryving with himself to speake, he, clappying of hys hands cryed aloude, o pover eglese galicane . . .[69]

This passion — calculated or sincere — was accompanied by the formalities of funeral processions and masses for the royal victims. The number of extant titles of pamphlets produced reached its peak in this year in Toulouse and Lyon (see Fig. 1) and the engravings in them illustrate their intensity.[70] Many people were also influenced by the

67. *Revue rétrospective*, [1834], III, 433–55.

68. Estoile, [1943], pp. 582–3.

69. P. Benedict, 1981, p. 178. For Jacques Commolet, see C. Sommervögel and Bäcker, 1892–1919, II, 1351–2.

70. D. Pallier, 1976, pp. 69–83, F.J. Baumgartner, 1976, ch. v. C. Reure, 1897–98. K. Cameron, 1978. Examples in LN, Nos 1540, 1557, 1597, 1611, etc.

decision of the Sorbonne on 7 January 1589 to release France from the obedience it owed its king and to justify the taking up of arms against a nefarious tyrant. In one procession on 10 January 1589, little children in Paris were assembled from the various parishes to march from the cemetery of the Innocents to the church of the abbey of Ste Geneviève. Each child carried a lighted candle and, at the entrance to the church, trampled it underfoot, 'as a sign that the cursed tyrant [*Henri III*] was excommunicated'.[71] Wall posters emphasised the same message.[72] Tyrannicide was not openly advocated but it was talked of, discussed in private, whispered in secret. Estoile reported a conversation between the radical preacher, Guincestre, and one of his parishioners, an adherent of the *Sixteen* who had declined to make his Easter observance in 1589 because he had such feelings of vengeance against the king. To this, Guincestre replied 'that this was to have a bad conscience over nothing, seeing that everyone, himself amongst the first (and he celebrated Mass every day) had in conscience thought of killing the king'.[73]

The fatal attractions of such private discourse were to be demonstrated by a twenty-four-year-old monk from the convent of the Jacobins in Paris. Jacques Clément told his fellow monks of his mystic visions in which he dreamt of an angel, brandishing an unsheathed sword, coming to him, saying: 'I am a messenger of the all-powerful God who comes to tell you that, by your hand, the Tyrant of France must be put to death'. At the refectory table, Clément once said that the king of France would die by his hand. His fellow monks apparently teased him: 'Go on then, do it.' Before he set out from Paris to kill Henri III, he fasted for twelve days and, once on his way, was impelled 'by the special and providential will of God'. The deed itself, even down to the size and type of the dagger used, seems to have been modelled on the regicidal murder of King Eglon in the Old Testament. Jean Boucher hastily revised his pedantic treatise on *The Just abdication of Henri III* and hailed Clément as a 'new David' who had killed Goliath, a new 'Judith' who had exterminated Holofernes.[74]

The massacres at Blois created a powerful sense of unity but there

---

71. E. Saulnier, [1913], p. 25. Estoile, [1943], pp. 611–12, 614–15. Cf. D. Richet, (1991), pp. 69–82.

72. Estoile, [1943], pp. 610–11.

73. M. Greengrass, 1989.

74. *De juste Henrici Tertii abdicationi* . . . (Paris, 1589). F.J. Baumgartner, 1976, pp. 126–44. C. Labitte, (1849), pp. 137–8. There are detectable passages taken from the *Francogallia* and the *Vindicae contra Tyrannos*.

was no accompanying political mechanism to direct it. The League had lost its king (excommunicated), their aristocratic leaders (massacred), and many of the municipal leaders from Paris (imprisoned with several other delegates to the third estate at Blois). Necessity drove them, as it had driven the protestants after 1572, to form an alternative government. They did so by drawing on their political experience and developing elective councils to fill their needs. In Paris, special ward committees in each quarter elected representatives to a council of the Union which then, in February 1589, constituted another council, the General Council of the Union.[75] This General Council of about forty members had as wide and as representative a membership as possible and it appointed the duke of Mayenne (the duke of Guise's surviving brother) as its military commander. He took his oath before it on 13 March 1589.[76]

In its first few months, the General Council was very active. It corresponded with cities elsewhere in France. It organised purges of known royalists from the great institutions of the capital and forty judges were led away from the Palais de Justice to the Bastille on 15 January 1589. Many were replaced in their posts by nominees of the General Council. Barnabé Brisson, for example, the Union's leading *parlementaire*, replaced Achille de Harlay as president on 26 January 1589, whilst Edouard Molé became its *procureur*. As Palma Cayet remarked, 'the leaders of the *Sixteen* all have some post now'.[77] Yet the active ingredients of the *Sixteen* and the Paris League were, as the latest research confirms, emphatically not (as royalist pamphleteers tried to make out) men from the gutter, inspired by greed, avarice and ambition. (See Appendix.) They bent their energies to protecting the city and raising revenues for the cause. Voluntary donations were sought. Those who wanted to leave the city were fined before they were allowed to go. Their property and wealth was pillaged. Pierre Molan, the treasurer of the king, left 36,000 *écus* in his house and this was appropriated to Union coffers.[78] The Council became responsible for the security of Paris and the reimposition of order. This was a period of great exhilaration for them. Enjoying widespread support, the Union appeared to be a reality and the death of the king was a fitting climax, their first real success. Madame de Montpensier, the duke of Guise's sister, distributed green scarves (green was the colour

75. E. Barnavi, 1980, pp. 132–6. Estoile, [1943], pp. 616–17. F. Morin, [1977], p. 99. A. Bernard, [1842], preface. LN, No. 1544.

76. LN, No. 1569. Estoile, [1943], pp. 619–20. H. Drouot, 1937a, I, 246–92.

77. Cayet, p. 46.

78. Estoile, [1943], pp. 618–19. *Infra*, p. 90.

of fools) to the public in celebration of it. Only one thing, she said, disappointed her and that was that the tyrant had not known that she had played a part in his assassination. She rode round the streets crying '*Bonnes nouvelles! Bonnes nouvelles!*'[79]

In the longer term, however, the king's assassination was not good for the League, for it opened up the contradictions within the Union which their unity against the tyrant had masked. Some of the behaviour of those nominated to their posts by the Union gave offence. The social tensions in the capital and other provincial cities grew more marked. Another rift occurred between the *Sixteen* and their military commander, the duke of Mayenne, who was suspicious of the independence of the General Council. He appointed his own clients to it and then ignored its decisions. Finally, he disbanded it altogether. Already on the horizon was the difficult relationship between capital and provinces in an ill-defined federation at a time of war when communications were disrupted. Everywhere, suspicions of 'royalists' and '*politiques*' divided catholics from each other and were at the root of the waning of the Holy Union.

FROM UNION TO PARTY

In the catholic cities of the Union, the coming to power of a new political group brought with it the threats of social revolution. Royalist propaganda stressed that the one led ineluctably to the other. 'Consider', exhorted the *Manifesto of France to the Parisians*:

> the state of your town . . . into whose hands has it now fallen? . . .
> You will find that it is in the grip of those who went from door to door
> collecting refuse, butchers' and slaughterhouse boys, the filth and
> excrement of your town . . . Are you not ashamed, solid bourgeois and
> good merchants whose wealth has been acquired by just means . . .?[80]

Those judges who escaped to the royalist *parlement* of Tours reported their fears of indiscriminate arrests, and of arbitrary pillage. They explained how they had escaped and spoke of their fears of popular

---

79. Estoile, [1948], p. 19. Arch. cur. de l'hist. de France, Vol. XII (1834), pp. 384–95. Cf. LN, Nos 1386 and 1664. O. Ranum, 1980, pp. 63–82.

80. *Le Manifeste de la France aux Parisiens* . . . (n.p. 1589). Also quoted in E. Barnavi, 1980, p. 144.

violence and 'the clamour of the people'.[81] Some had seen the bodies of '*politiques*' floating down the Seine; others had been threatened with elimination unless they conformed.

To a great extent, it was the behaviour of the members of the Union as much as their social inferiority which alarmed contemporaries. The pages of the diarist, Estoile, and the *Dialogue* give many instances of their arrogance and enjoyment of their new-found status and power. Bussy le Clerc, governor of the Bastille and a former solicitor, was the most notorious. He was a masterly demagogue and one of his first acts was to celebrate with a procession the discovery of a piece of the true cross in the Bastille. Solicitor turned gaoler and judge, he presided over the imprisonment of judges in January 1589.[82] Later, he dined with the archbishop of Lyon and had meetings with the duke of Nemours. But he had a violent streak as well. When an aunt of one of the '*politiques*' in the Bastille came to visit her relation, she was told that he had died in custody and that his body had been thrown to the dogs 'because he was a dog'.[83] Another important figure in the Union was the council's secretary, Pierre Senault. Estoile provided a vivid description of his behaviour at its meetings:

> For a clerk, i.e. a "valet" of the council (for such he calls himself), he has an extraordinary degree of authority . . . He calls them "his masters" but when he finds something proposed in council meetings which is not to his liking . . . he rises to his feet and loudly says: "I forbid and oppose it in the name of 40,000 men." At the sound of his voice, they lower their heads like dogs and not another word is heard about it.[84]

The *Dialogue*'s ironic epithets for the leaders of the *Sixteen* reveal something of the same resentments − Jean Louchard 'the swaggerer', M. de La Rue 'formerly draper on the pont St Michel and now one of the 100 gentlemen and councillors of the Union'. La Bruyère is described as the 'saffron seigneur', a common expression for the socially ambitious.[85]

The bullying swagger and aggression of the Unionists were partly their response to the real fears of a royalist conspiracy in the capital. The *Sixteen* recognised that they were weak in certain quarters and their

81. BN MS Fr nouv. acq. 8299, ff. 7, 40, 205, 227v, 240v, etc.

82. Estoile, [1943], pp. 606–8, 636–7.

83. Estoile, [1948], pp. 68, 101. R. Descimon, 1983, pp. 169–70 for Bussy's family background.

84. Estoile, [1943], pp. 616–17. E. Barnavi, 1980, pp. 46, etc.

85. Ibid., pp. 141–4.

fears were given considerable encouragement by a series of royalist plots. In fact, the failure of the Potier de Blancmesnil conspiracy in August 1589, the 'Bread or Peace' rising of 8 August 1590, and the 'Day of Flour' in January 1591 demonstrated that, in the business of conspiracy, the '*politiques*' were even less competent than the *Sixteen* had proved to be before 1588. The problem was that the fears about royalist sedition were self-justifying. It was impossible to be sure of everyone's loyalties. Oaths were sworn, of course, but this meant little. As one pamphleteer said, it was easy to pretend to be a supporter of the *Sixteen*:

> As soon as two or three of us are together, I take up the subject of the death of M. de Guise. I praise the list of his good deeds to the skies and then I begin to insult the king . . . thus I am respected as the best man in the world and a good catholic. Of course, I do not believe what I say. I only do it to avoid going to prison, and consequently having my goods seized and my house ransacked.[86]

Suspects who were detained, fined or imprisoned, came from among the wealthy Parisians in the royal administration. The League, almost in spite of itself, came to attack those with status and authority in the community whose natural clannishness and desire to protect each other merely heightened the suspicions of the *Sixteen*. Friends, relatives, those who were strangers in the capital, all became vulnerable to the charge of being a '*politique*'. The local watch committees ceased to include office holders in several quarters and removed their influence towards moderation from within the Union.

In some respects, too, the *Sixteen* were the victims of their own propaganda. The violence of the preachers' language encouraged members of the League's committees to violent action. In March 1591, Boucher preached 'nothing but killing', according to Estoile. He excited his congregation 'in words and gestures' to do away with the '*politiques*', and Estoile feared that he would descend from his pulpit and dismember someone before their eyes.[87] The incumbent of the parish of St André wanted to be the first one to 'cut the throats of these '*politiques*' and he knew who they were'.[88] The suspects had only the weapons of the impotent against such hostility – the anonymous

---

86. *Coppie de la responce faite par un polytique de ceste ville de Paris* (Paris, 1589), p. 3. Cf. LN, No. 1547 for a pamphlet which tries to give a description of salient '*politique*' characteristics – shifty eyes, flattery, inconsistent actions, etc!

87. Estoile, [1948], p. 96.

88. Ibid., p. 97.

wall-poster, the hand-written flysheet pushed under doors and the satirical drawing. Estoile used the privacy of his diary to express his moral revulsion at, for instance, a preacher saying that it was better to kill your own children than to accept a heretic king. The thinking heads of the *Sixteen*, men such as Louis Dorléans, eventually reacted against Unionist thuggery. In 1590, he wrote a brave pamphlet called the *Second Advertisement from an English Catholic* in which he warned his confederates that:

> Paris is no longer Paris but Babylon . . . Several have been thrown into your Union who have brought it neither clean hands nor clear consciences. They have taken gold and silver, clothes and other precious things to their own homes . . . They have grown very rich and the city very poor . . . Who wishes to be associated with the crimes of such robbers and brigands?[89]

The siege of Paris from May to August 1590 contributed to the waning of the Union in an indirect way. The economic life of the city became seriously damaged by the most crippling siege in the history of any major European city since that of Constantinople in the fifteenth century. Bread disappeared from the diet. The numbers estimated by contemporaries to have died from malnutrition and associated diseases varies from 5,000 to 12,000.[90] Estoile reported one man to be eating candlewax. Madame de Montpensier encouraged experiments in the milling of cemetery bones for flour. There were reports of cannibalism and some extraordinary fantasies gripped the minds of those whose stomachs had been empty for too long.[91] The siege was only partially lifted on 27 August 1590 by the arrival of the duke of Parma and an army from Flanders. Paris remained completely surrounded with all its major routes blocked by royal garrisons. Grain was allowed through only after the payment of extortionate levies. Royalist pamphlets argued that conditions in every royalist city were better than those in Paris and the *Sixteen* began to criticise their military leader, the duke of Mayenne, whose defeat at Ivry (14 March 1590) had led to the blockage of the capital. By the spring of 1591, Mayenne chose to reside in the city's suburbs rather than endure the preachers' hostility.

89. *Premier et second advertissement des Catholiques anglois* (n.p., 1590), pp. 95–105. Cf. F.J. Baumgartner, 1976, pp. 167–8.

90. Most observers expected Paris to fall. A. Franklin, [1876], p. 133. F. Pigafetta, [1876], p. 22 for estimates of deaths. Latest estimates of population before the siege, A. Lozinski, 1973.

91. *ML* IV, 276–314. Estoile, [1948], pp. 68–72.

'In private', Estoile noted, 'when they retired with the *Sixteen* they said that he was only a big pig who slept with his whore . . . and that he could only fight a war with [*wine*] flagons'.[92]

THE SIXTEEN AND THE EXECUTION OF JUSTICE

Anxious to reinforce their waning authority and to eliminate the malign influence of the '*politiques*' around the duke of Mayenne, whom they blamed for their succession of defeats, the *Sixteen* pressed him to re-establish the General Council of the Union.[93] Their petitions in the early months of 1591 blamed the 'tyranny of the nobility and the injustice of senior magistrates' for their plight. The 'heretic-mongers' must be expelled from the city – by force if necessary. Already a sequence of *billets* of proscription, or hit-lists of suspected '*politiques*', were circulating around the *Sixteen*. On 1 April 1591, the rump *parlement* of Paris was itself subjected to further proscriptions by order of the duke of Mayenne, excluding from its chambers fifteen suspected '*politiques*'. François Brigard, one of the most loyal supporters of the League, an *avocat* in the *parlement* who had rendered loyal service to Mayenne, was accused of treason. He had tried to negotiate the release of his brother, imprisoned by the royalists, but some of his letters were open to almost any interpretation. In May 1591, it was the turn of the governor of the Bastille, Bussy Leclerc, to be suspected, after the escape of a Huguenot from its cells.

The *parlement* took charge of the case against Brigard. He had friends in the sovereign court and they saw to it that the trial was frustrated and delayed. At the head of its judges was the president of the court, Barnabé Brisson. It was not the only case of its sort before the court in the summer of 1591. Another involved a judge at the Châtelet court named Jean Tardif, who was reported to have criticised the *Sixteen* in a public meeting and written a memorandum on the French civil wars, blaming the divisions in France on the princes of the House of Lorraine. He was let off on 19 October with a censure and the seizure of his books.

92. The disaffection with Mayenne began in November 1589 (LN, No. 1659). It became more evident during the siege – F. Pigafetta, [1876], 16. Estoile, [1948], pp. 60, 106 (April 1591).

93. For the events of 1591, see (above all) E. Barnavi and R. Descimon, 1985.

In September, the *Sixteen* (or rather, some prominent individuals from amongst their number) openly began to criticise the *parlement* for its *'politique'* sympathies. François Morin de Crômé, who was also a Parisian magistrate, attempted to publish an exposé of the court's double standards. He was himself rewarded with an injunction from the court which, in the last week of October 1591, gave a light sentence of banishment to Brigard. The anger and frustration amongst the *Sixteen* was thereby concentrated and heightened around a limited series of names and faces in their midst upon whom they could direct it. An intensive series of meetings of the *Sixteen* was organised in which a secret committee of ten was elected on 6 November comprising its most committed and most active individuals. Three members of this committee persuaded the others to sign a blank piece of paper which was soon to become the death warrant for three prominent suspected *'politiques'*.

The arrests took place on the morning of Friday 15 November. Barnabé Brisson, the first president of the *parlement* and leading judge of the Brigard case, was seized by a contingent of the bourgeois militia on his way to the law courts. He was taken to the *Petit-Châtelet* (a tribunal for the Paris region) and, after a brief show-trial, hanged from one of the beams in the court. A second victim, Claude Larcher, one of the veteran magistrates at the *parlement* was taken from the law-courts and hanged alongside him. Jean Tardif was rounded up at his house by a troop under the direction of Jean Hamilton, the parish priest of Saint-Côme, and given the same treatment. A grocer from one of the League militias wrote the following in large letters under each of them: 'Barnabé Brisson: one of the leading traitors and heretics', 'Claude Larcher, one who encouraged traitors and *politiques*', 'Tardif, one of the enemies of God and the catholic princes'.

Much has been written of the significance of these tragic events in Paris. The historiography of the League in its decline has been distorted by a royalist gloss which it acquired in Henri IV's reign. Such an affront to justice was only to be expected, it was argued, when there was no king to sustain it and when thugs, inspired by social envy and spoiled ambition, were dressed in a little brief authority. The events were, in reality, more complex. Brisson was an undeniably erudite judge with a scholarly reputation. He also had gained a reputation, as an advocate, for taking large fees and had risen to high office in Paris from the provinces by a single-minded application of family, favour and fortune. To many at the time within the legal profession, Brisson's career demonstrated, and his death highlighted, much that was wrong with the legal system in sixteenth-century France: the 'crisis of justice, a reflection of the total crisis of a society where reform had failed'.[94] Any account of Brisson's political activities has to include the fact that, after some prudent hesitation, he had lent his support to the League. It was Brisson who had received (and who may even have drafted) the duke of Mayenne's curious title and oath of office as 'Lieutenant General of the Kingdom' for the League and who had enregistered the bulls of excommunication of Henri IV in the *parlement*. These were actions of a senior magistrate who had become involved in a dangerous political arena where he had much to lose and little power to wield. Even the active minority of the *Sixteen* was not, as we have seen, to be dismissed as a bunch of thugs with radical politics. Neither the city authorities nor the garrisoned troops of the duke of Mayenne moved a finger to prevent the deaths of Brisson, Larcher and Tardif. Others in Paris doubtless reacted to the news of what had happened like the parish priest, Aubin Blondel, who began to laugh and say, 'that all these *'politiques'* would have to be put to death'.[95]

These deaths were intended to be the first in a series of show trials of *'politiques'* whose names were already inscribed on a register (known as the PDC register because, after each name, there was an initial indicating the victim's fate – *pendu, dagué, chassé*).[96] The council of ten proposed to create a special legal tribunal to deal with these cases, staffed with young graduates rather than established judges at law. It was to be a calculated extension of the authority of the *Sixteen*.[97] In fact, within a month, the duke of Mayenne had arrived in Paris, determined to amputate the political power of the *Sixteen*. He came with 1,000 loyal troops, forced the surrender of the Bastille, and, on 4 December, murdered four of the council of ten and imprisoned most of the rest. By the time the duke left Paris on 11 December 1591, the *parlement* had approved his actions and the *Sixteen* had been dismantled.

For Mayenne, this was a victory, but not one that he dared to exploit. Members of the *Sixteen* continued to criticise his leadership with increasing vehemence until the fall of Paris in 1594. Whatever their faults, the propaganda and organisation of the *Sixteen* had acted as a unifying force among catholics, capable of encouraging devotion and inspiring zeal. Without the *Sixteen*, Mayenne possessed no alternative

94. Ibid., p. 173.
95. Ibid., p. 26.
96. Ibid., pp. 127–47. Analysis of the list and the *Sixteen*'s position in E. Barnavi, 1980, pp. 205–14.
97. Ibid., pp. 212–14.

in governing Paris but to turn to those '*politiques*' who became increasingly convinced of the necessity of a negotiated settlement with Henri IV.

The history of the Union in Paris is well known; that of its provincial counterparts in Amiens, Rouen, Nantes, Toulouse and the other catholic cities of France remains to be properly investigated.[98] They all established councils which, in their infancy at least, were supposed to reflect the various social groups in these cities. As in Paris, they were vigorous in defence, tax-raising, and the organisation of municipal militias. In some cases, colourful local politicians became popular demagogues – Charles de Casaulx in Marseille, Nicolas Godin in Bayeux, Etienne Tournier in Toulouse. Some of them were as socially divisive as the *Sixteen* in Paris; in Troyes, the Mayennist Philippe de Ver complained bitterly to the provincial governor of the libels and plots against him by the 'zealous Catholics' and the meeting was disrupted by a riot outside the governor's lodging.[99] Some cities like Marseille and St Malo exploited their maritime position to become truly independent republics, conducting their own foreign policy and recognising no superior authority from Paris or from the duke of Mayenne.[100] In other cities, the provincial military governors appointed by the duke of Mayenne suppressed the provincial councils when they became a menace to their authority. In Dijon, Toulouse and Rouen the provincial councils were relatively short-lived; elsewhere they were resurrected, as in Lyon, when the absence of the governor or a lively hatred of military rule provided renewed support for their activity.[101] The confused politics of these provincial cities, many of them under siege from royalist forces, is a true reflection of the Holy Union's transformation into a series of factions and parties.

98. Provincial councils in H. Drouot, 1951, 415–33. H. Hours, 1952, 401–20. R.R. Harding, 1978, p. 93. For Rouen, P. Benedict, 1981, pp. 179–84; Toulouse, M. Greengrass, 1979, ch. ix. The cities in Burgundy are discussed in H. Drouot, 1937a. For a preliminary sketch of possible lines of enquiry, P. Ascoli, 1977, pp. 15–37.

99. Philippe de Ver in BN MS Fr 4019, f. 47. See also the events in Orléans in 1591 in F. Hauchecorne, 1970, pp. 267–78.

100. St Malo, F. Juon des Longrais, *Inventaire sommaire des archives municipales de St Malo* (1914), pp. 110–20. F. Braudel, 1973, I, 1205–17.

101. H. Hours, 1952, 401–20. J–H. Mariéjol, 1947, chs iv and v. F. Rolle, 1865, inventory of registers BB 122–32. Royalist pamphlets did not hesitate to mention the *petits souverains* among the cities and provinces – e.g. de Thou, XI, 614. LN, No. 1711 – 'combien de petites tyrannies y naistront, combien de petites Républiques s'y formeront, & combien de villes se cantonneront?'

ELECTIVE KINGSHIP

The issue of the succession, which initially gave the League its impetus and *raison d'être*, became the one which divided it and hastened its dissolution. In 1589 and 1590, the candidate of the League for the kingship of France was clear; it was Charles, cardinal of Bourbon. If, in theory, his claims to the throne were as good as, or better, than those of Henri IV, in practice he was less eligible. The League preachers vaunted him as a new Melchisedech, a mighty warrior and priest-king but, in fact, he cut a less impressive figure. He was an octogenarian, already known for his vacillation and love of the quiet life. He was also a closely guarded prisoner of Henri IV. League forces never attempted to release him and he died in his bed on 8 May 1591.

League lawyers had, in fact, before his death, already begun to investigate the precedents for electing a new king. They were not as scarce as proponents of the absolute French monarchy presumed, especially in the early history of the Frankish monarchy, as François Hotman had shown.[102] The problems in electing a king were not, therefore, theoretical, but practical ones. Firstly, the suggestion of an election enhanced the fears among catholics that the League would establish a permanently elective monarchy or even a republic. As a Parisian attorney (and a friend of Estoile) lamented in public in October 1589: 'Our civil disorder and factions have opened the door to a crowd of corrupt little men who, with effrontery, have attacked authority with such licence and audacity that those who have not seen it would not believe it. In so doing, they have wanted to jump from a monarchy to a democracy.'

There was an additional problem: the Spanish demands made of the League. Spanish influence strengthened during the siege of Paris. A new Spanish ambassador in Paris, Don Diego de Ibarra, arrived in January 1591 with instructions on how to exert it.[103] Spain must sustain Paris and the *Sixteen* and assist the catholic princes to elect a catholic king. Spanish agents should 'insinuate cleverly' the rights of the Infanta to the French throne and suggest that troops and cash from Spain were contingent on the marriage of the Spanish Infanta to whoever was chosen as king. The Salic law, the ambassador's instructions continued, 'was a pure invention . . . as the most learned and discerning of their lawyers recognise.' Election should take

102. See above, p. 12.
103. BN MS Fr 3982, ff. 222 *et seq.*

place in the *parlement* of Paris which would also ratify the marriage, for it would be too lengthy and disruptive to hold an estates general in the midst of war. Spain's compensation for the 'great expense' she had undertaken would consist of the city of Cambrai, the repayment of all her expenses, some guarantee ports and strongholds on the Channel coast and in Flanders. In a famous letter written by the *Sixteen* to Philip II on 2 September 1591, they offered him the kingdom: 'We can certainly assure Your Catholic Majesty that the oaths and aspirations of all catholics are to see Your Catholic Majesty hold the sceptre of this crown and reign over us, and we would most willingly be held in his embrace as that of our father . . .'.[104] The letter was despatched to Philip II via the Jesuit Claude Mathieu but fell into the hands of the duke of Mayenne.

The possibility of marriage to the Spanish Infanta eliminated many candidates immediately from the election since they were, like the duke of Mayenne, already married. Others, such as the duke of Savoy, were ruled out as too unpopular. This left only two serious candidates – the son of the duke of Lorraine, count of Zweibrücken (Deux-Ponts); and Charles, son of Henri, duke of Guise. Charles had been imprisoned ever since his father's murder at Blois but he managed to evade his captors in August 1591. He swiftly became the darling of the *Sixteen* and the candidate with Spanish support. Philip II sent a Franciscan friar round the towns of the League and the resulting reports of the popularity of the young duke were most encouraging.[105] But Mayenne remained implacably hostile to his nephew's candidature. The removal of the *Sixteen* from Paris was certainly one of his attempts to prevent them from supporting the aspirations of the young duke of Guise and the Spanish Infanta in any forthcoming election or estates general.

The issue paralysed the League and this was a discernible fact at a meeting of its leaders in Picardy at Christmas, 1591. Their discussions had an undeniable element of pantomime to them.[106] The duke of Mayenne, an old dame, equivocated on everything except his debts, his rights, those of his house, his province and his kingdom (in that order). The young prince charming, Charles de Guise, refused to talk to his uncle and complained of his obstructiveness. The duke of Parma could scarcely comprehend the 'great jealousies' of Mayenne, let alone satisfy his importunate demands for money. The Spanish ambassador

104. Estoile, [1948], pp. 124–5. E. Barnavi and R. Descimon, 1985, p. 187.
105. Arch. Simancas K 1579, f. 76.
106. BN MS Fr 3982, ff. 224v, 228, 230. L. Van der Essen, 1933, ch. x.

wanted Charles de Guise elected as king without any delay. Mayenne's advisor, *président* Jeannin from the *parlement* of Dijon, told him that it had to be done with the consent of the princes. This would, he added, be expensive in terms of 'gratifications' to them. The meeting turned into a dialogue of the deaf. Worse, its divisions were quickly known in the Navarre camp. From the moment when Mendoza's diplomatic baggage was captured in January 1591, diplomatic correspondence between the cities, princes and foreign powers behind the League was regularly known to Navarre.[107] His cryptographer, Choirin, was unequalled in Europe for his powers to crack codes and the most intimate details of League politics were quickly open to Navarre for his exploitation.[108]

Mayenne spent the whole of 1592 trying to hold 'what remains of our party' together, at least until the moment when he had extracted favourable terms from Spain in return for his support for Guise's candidature. The problem was that Mayenne's demands were massive and, the longer he delayed the estates general, the less time lay on the side of the League and the more unpopular he became. In October 1592, the bishop of Senlis wrote from Paris that their protector was 'held in derision' and that his timidity and 'nonchalance' had lost the war.[109] The people were 'miserable, full of rumour, discontent and impatient' for peace. When the estates general opened on 26 January 1593 this dissatisfaction turned to open criticism. Mayenne's opening speech was a poor performance, inaudible to many delegates.[110] Others missed his speech because the royalists frustrated their passage to the estates general.[111] It was a rump assembly which finally opened indirect negotiations at Suresnes near Paris with the forces of Henri IV on 21 April 1593 and which produced the truce enabling the king to enter Paris the following year on 23 March 1594.

---

107. D. Lamar Jensen, 1964, p. 212. Sully's capture of diplomatic papers, Sully [1970], I, 330–5.
108. d'Aubigné, VIII, 202.
109. BN MS Fr 3983, ff. 140–44; 3646, ff. 133, 210v.
110. A. Bernard, [1842], pp. 18, 377, 558.
111. Ibid., pp. 45, 378, 559, 650.

CHAPTER THREE
The Pursuit of the Kingdom

'ALWAYS ON HORSEBACK'

Henri IV was in no doubt that his army was essential in the early days of his rule. It was 'the sole basis for my authority and the conservation of my State' he told Du Plessis Mornay in the weeks after his accession to the French throne. By then he was an experienced and an accomplished military commander of protestant forces which had not been slow to adapt to some of the military changes which were gradually transforming Europe's arts of war.[1] Partly because of the strategic circumstances in which they had been obliged to fight (where the advantages of mobility and surprise had been of particular importance), they had probably developed a better field artillery than that enjoyed by the French crown. Their hardened cavalry certainly knew how to use a pistol to good effect, as Henri's victory at Coutras over the forces of the duke of Joyeuse in 1587 had demonstrated. To maintain his armies in the field, and to ensure this mobility, Henri also appreciated well enough the importance of ensuring adequate supplies and payments to the troops. His letters to the secretaries of state sometimes consisted of little else during the wars of the League.[2]

Of his abilities as a strategist, however, there have always been doubts. 'I had expected to find a general; but I encountered no more than a commander of light cavalry' wrote the duke of Parma to the duke d'Aumale in 1592 on his return from the second campaign in

1. D.J. Buisseret, 'Henri IV et l'art militaire' in *Avènement d'Henri IV* (1990), pp. 333–5.
2. C. Desplat, 'Henri IV le soldat et le capitaine' in *Avènement d'Henri IV* (1989), pp. 105–7.

France in support of Mayenne and the League.[3] Yet to be engaged in
a war against Parma – an accomplished strategist with the most
experienced and largest army of his day – was the sternest military test
the sixteenth century had to offer and the king's experience stood him
in good stead. At the battle of Arques, outside Dieppe, (in reality, it
was a series of engagements from 15 to 27 September 1589) the
protestant artillery proved critical in securing the field against the
superior numbers of cavalry and infantry in Mayenne's army. The
victory prevented the king from being driven out of Normandy and
reinforced the royalist lines of communication with his English allies.
It also made the duke of Mayenne wary, even more so than his
natural prudence dictated to him, of attempting any major military
confrontation with the king. During the siege of Paris in the following
year Henri IV inveigled Mayenne into another fixed battle at Ivry, on
the river Eure, on 14 March 1590. Although, once again, Mayenne's
forces were superior in number, this time it was the king's cavalry
which won the day.[4] The victory had a considerable psychological
impact, not least in besieged Paris. Henri IV's capabilities as a field
commander were not in doubt among contemporaries.

Among military historians, however, he is sometimes charged with
not exploiting the fruits of military success because (as Parma's
comment implies) he had no broader strategic sense. He never
confronted Parma's troops directly. He gained no major military
victories in 1593–94. All the major cities of France would be secured
by negotiations, rather than by force of arms. In 1595, his military
campaigns in Burgundy were among the most successful in the wars of
the League (especially the victory at Fontaine-Française) but the cities
of Marseille and Toulouse as well as the provinces of Provence and
Brittany still remained to be subjected. Yet the military constraints on
Henri IV's freedom of action were huge, and his achievements should
be judged in that context. In common with his contemporaries, he
had a rooted fear of lengthy sieges, 'the entire ruination of armies' as
he said.[5] It was with frustration that he was forced to accept the
inevitable inadequacies of his supplies and the unpredictable support of
his allies. He had to work within an inevitably provincial spread of
campaigns where the large aspirations and even larger egos of royalist
captains required a light but sure touch to ensure a degree of
coordination. Within these constraints, there was, nevertheless, an

3. Cited by R. S. Love, 1991.
4. Ibid.
5. E. Halphen, [1872] p. 180.

overall strategic sense to Henri IV's military campaigning. He understood that the kingdom would be won or lost in the north of France. He recognised that the war would turn around the securing of certain key points on the frontiers, the Loire bridgeheads and some key defensible sites in the provinces, not necessarily the major provincial capitals. He had a shrewd sense of the importance of sustaining a military initiative and keeping the enemy insecure and nervous. The king showed enormous energy and stamina, putting himself about, whether at the sieges of Noyon (the vital stronghold for Picardy in 1591), Rouen or Paris. He was to be seen in the trenches, surveying the enemy, mixing with the troops. According to Palma Cayet, this ubiquity and energetic commitment was what was most feared by the League; 'he was always on horseback, ready in pursuit'. Finally, Henri IV understood that, in order to gain the psychological advantage from his military endeavours, he had to demonstrate magnanimity. The quality was much vaunted by the king's publicists but there is enough independent confirmation of it during these years to indicate that this was not merely propaganda. In his pursuit of the kingdom he needed his subjects' hearts as well as their minds. At the battlefield of Ivry he gave prisoners their liberty. The civilian suffering from warfare was recognised and, to the limited degree possible, contained. After Louviers was surprised and overrun in 1591, for example, his armies began to pillage the place but the king put a stop to it. In the short term, this was not the way that armies were kept in the field in the sixteenth century. But it was not in the battlefield that the kingdom would be won or lost.

THE KING'S CONVERSION

The period from the king's accession in August 1589 until July 1593 was politically dominated by the issue of the king's conversion to catholicism. Some contemporaries preferred to call it (and the distinction was an important one to them) his 'abjuration' from the protestant faith. It was a matter which went to the heart of delicate questions such as the nature of French kingship, the relationship between clergy and kingship in the French polity and the importance of mutual, binding and accountable loyalties in the maintenance of that polity. It was the kind of issue where a charge of 'bad faith' could do enormous damage to Henri IV's pursuit of the kingdom and one where there were all too many contemporaries for whom the opportunities to make mischief were almost irresistible. Both were good grounds for the king's hesitancy.

Until recently, the historical commentary on the abjuration has tended to be limited to the rather narrow debates over the precise moment at which Henri IV decided to convert and whether he was sincere.[6] Neither of these, however, are answerable questions. In the case of the former, the evidence is fragmentary and for good reason; from the moment of his accession onwards, the king intended to keep people guessing. In the case of the latter, it begs the key question since the whole point about confessional changes in the sixteenth century is that nobody could know whether they were sincere or not. In a period of intense confessional hostility the relevant question is: how did people, especially the all-important catholic loyalists, expect to be able to measure sincerity?

Catholic scholastic theologians had very clear ideas on the process of conversion.[7] These had been reinforced by the canons of the Council of Trent. They were developed in the penitential manuals and homilies of catholic clergy and formed a bedrock of attitudes which were widely shared among the catholic laity of France. They began with the concept of contrition, the vital change of heart which started the process of conversion and which was stimulated by true humility. To what extent, however, was true humility possible in this world? Were other emotions such as fear or prudence legitimate in the process? Some scholastic theologians distinguished between 'contrition' and 'attrition', the latter being based on a human fear of the consequences of not being humble, a second-best but often the beginning of true contrition. All agreed, however, that contrition was invalid when based upon purely pragmatic or prudential grounds – knowledge of the world or fear of the consequences in this world, rather than knowledge of the world to come or fear of the hereafter. In a famous League critique of the sincerity of Henri IV's abjuration, published by Louis Dorléans in 1594 under the title *The Banquet and Evening of the Count d'Arète (Le Banquet et Apresdisnee du Conte d'Arète)*, the distinction was developed between prudence as knowledge of God and prudence as knowledge of the affairs of the world, the latter breeding '*politique*', or forced, conversions, which were universally agreed to be undermining of an individual's conscience and of the social order as well. One of a famous set of sermons against Henri IV's

6. See the argument presented in M. Greengrass, 'The public context of the abjuration of Henri IV' in K. Cameron, 1989, and, at greater length, the excellent study of Michael Wolfe, 1993.

7. Michael Wolfe, 1993, ch. 1. K. Cameron, 1989, pp. 117–20.

conversion in the summer of 1593 concentrated on it as an act forced upon the king by political circumstances – the estates general of the League and their threat to elect a king to the French crown.[8] Because it was a prudential act, argued the League theologian and preacher, Jean Boucher, the king's abjuration was therefore invalid and could not be accepted as even the first stage towards acceptance back into the catholic church.

Contrition was followed by confession, the change of mind in which a confessor would play a crucial role, leading to the final penance or 'satisfaction' by way of atonement. Contrition was a private, psychological transmutation but, at least to orthodox catholic commentators, penance and satisfaction were the public face of that transmutation, the proclamation of that change before society as well as a public recognition of fault. In a society where oath-taking and oath-keeping were so fundamental a part of social discipline and the accountability of the individual to society at large, a 'confession' of faith should be, had to be, a public affair and not a matter of individual conscience. It was the sense that the king's conversion had to be a matter of public accountability, including a confession of guilt and an acceptance of penance which made it such a delicate and controversial act in an absolute monarchy.

Related to the general attitudes towards conversion lay specific question marks over whether the king's promises could ever be fully trusted. There was the matter of his first conversion, well publicised by League preachers and much discussed in these years.[9] This first 'abjuration' of protestantism had taken place in the aftermath of the massacre of St Bartholomew, following his marriage to the catholic Marguerite de Valois, when Henri of Navarre had been under close confinement at the Valois court and in fear, so his publicists claimed, for his safety. It was, thus, a 'forced conversion' and, furthermore, illegitimate because there had been no public ceremony, no demonstration of a change of heart. The issue of the first conversion was additionally important because it was argued that, as in the case of heretics before the Inquisition, one relapse was a dangerous accident, capable of redemption, whereas two constituted deliberate carelessness which put one outside the realm of civil society and the grace of the church. This was still formally the position of the Roman Curia up to July 1593, the date of the king's announcement of his intention to convert.

8. J. Boucher, *Sermons de la simulacrée conversion* (Paris, 1594).
9. P. Hurtubise, 1976. K. Cameron, 1989, pp. 120–1.

Another doubt occurred as a result of a declaration which Henri IV had made at St Cloud on 4 August 1589 immediately after his accession to power.[10] The declaration was delivered orally to the assembled catholic officers of the crown and grandees who had served Henri III. They included some of the leading figures in the royal army as well as vital individuals in the council and court such as the chancellor, the keeper of the seals, the superintendent of finances and the secretaries of state. Their loyalty was essential to the credibility of Navarre's candidature to the French throne and to the continuity of the state. The declaration promised 'upon the king's faith and oath' to maintain the catholic church, to fill offices vacated by Huguenots with catholics, and to seek religious instruction at the earliest opportunity that a national council of the church could be convened – within six months at the latest. This was a dangerous hostage to fortune and, when the senior clergy came together in general assemblies – as in Tours in May 1590 or again in 1592 – they reminded the king forcibly of his broken promise. The king was aware of it too for, on the eve of the conversion of St Denis, he blamed the delay which had occurred in its fulfilment upon the 'continual wars, impediments and difficulties' in the meantime.

Such a matter was of greater importance than is often imagined. Beyond the Parisian clergy or the senior ecclesiastics in the French polity, there were catholic loyalist nobles in the provinces and in Henri IV's army who had consciences to salve and whose loyalty would depend on whether they believed that they could trust the king. The duke of Nevers, for example, was a senior aristocrat of Italian origin whose power-base incorporated important regions of central France. For him, the point of conscience was as determinant a matter of principle as the point of honour to any nobleman.[11] How the king behaved in regard to the catholic religion, and whether he lived up to his promises, would be vital in securing his continuing loyalty. In letters exchanged with his erstwhile noble client and League military commander, Claude de La Châtre, we encounter something of the prudent waiting and watching which went on amongst the French catholic nobility, wooed by both sides, growing more restive as the war gradually went the king's way, both as to the material rewards which they might expect to receive and as to whether they could trust the king to keep to what he promised to give them.[12]

---

10. Ibid., pp. 121–2. Michael Wolfe, 1993, pp. 56–8.
11. Michael Wolfe, 1989.
12. N. Le Roux, 1994.

Catholic loyalism inevitably found a forum at Henri IV's court. It was bound to do so if the king fulfilled his oath at St Cloud to appoint only catholics to court offices. In 1590, in fact, the king made Cheverny his chancellor in order to put an end to a rather unseemly wrangle over the keepership of the seals. Cheverny was someone of experience, well-respected, of undoubted catholicity, and he was given the task of reorganising what was left of the royal court.[13] He reinstituted the royal chapel with catholic services, the important post of king's almoner going to Renaud de Beaune, archbishop of Bourges. But until the king converted, there was still a possibility that the uneasy religious coalition of protestants and catholics which the king was trying to hold together in these vital years, might fragment and collapse. In such circumstances, the catholic loyalist nobility would look to a '*tiers parti*' (a 'third party' as contemporaries almost unanimously referred to it) for their salvation.

The possibility of an alternative royalist cause should not be dismissed. Although it would turn out to have been more shadow than substance, this was not how it looked in the difficult years of 1590 to 1592.[14] The potential scenario it afforded exercised a significant influence upon Henri IV and his advisors. The period of its greatest effectiveness came after the death of Charles, cardinal de Bourbon, the League claimant to the throne by inheritance, in May 1590. It was then that Navarre's uncle, the cardinal Charles de Bourbon-Vendôme became of significance. He had a blood claim to the throne. (See Fig. 2.) He was politically ambitious and certainly no Navarre sympathiser. But neither was he an adherent of the League for he despised its Spanish protector. Since he had not taken full clerical vows, he was marriageable and (since Henri IV's marriage was itself currently in tatters with no prospect of a dissolution) in some respects a more attractive proposition upon which to refound the fortunes of the dynasty and the realm. An contemporary engraving by Thomas de Leu of Vendôme carried a caption which conveys some of the possibilities associated with Vendôme: 'This cardinal appears as the other Bourbon hope'. Nearly every one of the rumours behind a conspiracy of the '*tiers parti*' in the years 1591–92 had Vendôme located close to its epicentre.

There are many reasons why the '*tiers parti*' remained closet conspirators. They disliked a Spanish-dominated catholic League and distrusted Mayenne even more than they were suspicious of Henri IV. Nor did they want to force Henri IV into a conversion of political

13. Cheverny, [1881], pp. 503–6.
14. Michael Wolfe, 1993, pp. 100–14. K. Cameron, 1989, pp. 123–5.

necessity which would defeat their purpose. For similar reasons, as well as the aristocratic bias of their support, they had no desire to act the demagogue, even supposing that they would have gained a following. So long as there was a hope of a negotiated settlement between Navarre and the League, and so long as the door was never closed upon his abjuration, they were always liable to be wrong-footed, never clear as to their objectives.

In any case, Vendôme was not cut out to be a conspirator. The king had reliable informants in the cardinal's entourage who kept him abreast of all that was going on. Every time he attempted to make a political move in support of his candidature, either the king or the League were on hand to neutralise it. The possible aristocratic backers of the '*tiers parti*' – the English ambassador's reports mention, among others, François d'O, Biron, Longueville, La Guiche, Epernon and others – were therefore never convinced that it would come to anything and they thus held back. But the politicking, the stockpiling of arms in the provinces, the rumours and plots associated with the '*tiers parti*', were all part of the shadow-boxing and complex negotiations with the duke of Mayenne and the League which occupied so much of people's energies in 1592 and early 1593.

Those negotiations resolved themselves into a fairly basic set of issues. Would the king convert before the League submitted to his authority? Or would the League renounce its Spanish pay-masters and accept Navarre's right to the succession before he converted? These matters of timetable were vital to the credibility of the proposed settlement on both sides. At one stage, in Pomponne de Bellièvre's country house at Grignon in April 1592, the negotiators came very close to an agreement.[15] But then Mayenne prevaricated and Navarre pulled back, concerned, perhaps, at Mayenne's Spanish support. He was worried, perhaps, too that the catholic royalists might make common cause against him and to his disadvantage, aware of the possibilities for trouble-making from the French cardinals, Epinac and Vendôme. Yet the more the king delayed his abjuration, the more it would look as though force of circumstance, worldly prudence rather than God-fearing humility, had made him change his mind. And what circumstances could one imagine stronger than an empty treasury, a catholic estates general on the verge of electing an alternative king of France with active Spanish participation and negotiations between the two sides stalled because neither could agree on a timetable for submission and conversion?

15. These negotiations are discussed in Michael Wolfe, 1993, pp. 110–11.

Elaborate and carefully planned stage-management was therefore required for the events at the abbey of St Denis, the mausoleum of the kings of France, on Sunday 25 July 1593. It was there that the king proclaimed his intention to convert to the catholic faith in a well-publicised ceremony. Those most involved – clergy like Renaud de Beaune, Jacques Davy Du Perron and Claude d'Angennes as well as the king's negotiators with representatives of the League estates general at Suresnes – cultivated a political climate in which powerful but undirected desires for peace and reconciliation in France might be channelled to the king's benefit through the royal act of volition at the centre of the abjuration ritual. Invitations to attend were issued en bloc to certain groups such as the clergy. Personal letters were also despatched to catholic aristocrats and magistrates of proven loyalty to the Navarrist cause. It was vital to its political purpose that the ceremony should be manifestly public, engaging representatives from a wide spectrum of corporate France. The collaboration of wavering Parisian *curés* was also secured, thereby further declaring the corporate validity of the abjuration and the disunity within the Parisian League.

At the heart of the events of Sunday 25 July lay a fundamental and intentional ambiguity as to the degree of accountability which the king was to render, both to the Almighty and to catholic France. The penitent king arrived at the door of the abbey dressed in white doublet and hose. Only a sword of majesty might indicate to the casual observer that here was the king of France, always supposing that he had overlooked the presence of the archers of the royal guard, the 800 gentlemen of the body in full accoutrement, the royal trumpeters and the *Vivats* from a crowd variously estimated at 10,000, 50,000 and 70,000. It was more like a royal entry (albeit prior to a coronation) and the brief ceremony of penitence before the king entered the nave was both symbolic and perfunctory. The king knelt in supplication but was not ceremonially struck by the bishop's mitre. A brief summary of the king's act of submission was handed by the king to Renaud de Beaune, who had largely composed it, but it said nothing of any acts of penance or even contrition. And so the king was led towards the high altar, where Henri IV vowed obedience to the catholic church (in under 200 words) and took Mass in both kinds. At that moment, a flock of doves flew from the church roof, the cue for the inevitable claim of a miraculous sign from God of his blessing upon the king and the imminence of peace.

Although carefully contrived, the abjuration still raised awkward questions. The likelihood of a false conversion and the dangers which sprang from it were eagerly pointed out by the League preachers. No papal absolution had been pronounced and none was likely to be forthcoming in the immediate future. Even royalist and Gallican catholics accepted that this ceremony was a kind of 'preliminary affair' one which would require fuller confirmation from the papacy at some future date. The sermons by Jean Boucher against the 'pretended conversion', preached in the first week of August 1593, expressed all these doubts. The abjuration had involved an oath of obedience without any sign of the king's intention to uphold it. There had been no public catechism of the king, no public penance, and no evidence to support the king's change of heart adduced before the world at large. What sort of abjuration was it, Boucher argued, when the catholic capital of France, and most of the catholic provinces and cities of France refused to have anything to do with it?

So the significance of the abjuration was not, as often stated, that it led to the fall of Paris. The king only entered his capital city eight months later on 22 March 1594. It did, however, remove the ground from under the estates general of the League and revive the stalled negotiations with Mayenne. A general truce with Mayenne was concluded on 1 August 1593, itself a further opportunity for royalist propaganda to press home the advantages of royal peace. The stage was also set for the royal coronation at Chartres on 27 February 1594, where (summoning a carefully selected number of the compliant French bishops and using regalia specially commissioned for the occasion as well as a holy unction conveniently found in the monastery at Marmoutier, close to Tours) the king made his coronation vows. Amongst them was one where he promised 'with all my power and in good faith to chase from my Jurisdiction and lands under my rule, all heretics condemned by the Church'. Once more there was a question-mark over Henri IV's good faith. Henri IV never said that 'Paris is well worth a Mass' although he came close to expressing the underlying sentiments at various different times. The prudential kingship which the phrase implies was, however, given force, shape and coherence in the propaganda on behalf of the king.

'KING OF REASON'?

In a famous contemporary engraving which proclaimed the fall of the capital city in 1594, Paris, son of Priam, is portrayed stepping off a ship which has been tossed by the waves. Before him stand the three contrasting beauties of Venus (Lorraine), Juno (Spain) and Pallas

(Henri IV). The third, dressed in the *fleur de lys* and offering Paris an olive branch is Paris' preferred choice whilst behind him, ready to disembark from the boat are his warriors, representing the traditional three orders of the realm. The title of the engraving was 'Paris returning to her senses' (*Paris retournant à son bon sens*).[16] The theme more generally was of a France returning to its 'good senses' after the 'frenzy' of the wars of religion by renewed obedience to a king whose authority was compatible with godliness and reason. The League had allowed individuals to give free vent to their 'frenzied passions and the affections which hurt our souls' and spoil our 'judgement'. It had been a 'labyrinth' of vices, impurities and impieties in which its supporters were ensnared and trapped and from which a monarch, unswayed by passion, would rescue them. It is on the basis of these themes, and other evocations of the nature of order in society and the role of kingship within it, that Denis Crouzet has recently argued that this period marked a 'veritable revolution in political ideology' which involved a 'rethinking or rationalisation of the concept of monarchy'.[17]

It was undoubtedly the case that Henri IV was well-served by a variety of publishers, engravers and propagandists. From his accession to power, the royalist presses at Tours, under the king's master-printer (*libraire-imprimeur du roi*), Jamet Mettayer, ran off editions which announced the king's victories to the royalist corporations throughout France.[18] Some pamphleteers expounded (on traditional lines) the absolute powers of the king. More frequently, they stressed his personal qualities: his chivalry, concern for the poor, his patriotism and his courage. Had not a 'surge of loyalty' inspired the troops to victory at Ivry? Did not that victory (they said) demonstrate that the king had God's blessing? Had he not prevented the sack of Chartres to spare the poor? Had he not (they argued) raised the siege of Paris to avoid unnecessary suffering? For the first time, images of the king were used with an overt political aim and to a wide audience.[19] To the skills of Mettayer as a publisher were added those of the Parisian engraver, Jean Leclerc, who took up refuge in Tours and worked for the king. In 1593, Leclerc was joined by the former League engraver Thomas de Leu. Together they were responsible for creating the definitive image

16. Reproduced in *Henri IV et la reconstruction du royaume* (1989), p. 119.

17. D. Crouzet, 'Les fondements idéologiques de la royauté d'Henri IV' in *Avènement d'Henri IV* (1990), pp. 165–94; partially translated in 'Henri IV, King of Reason?' in K. Cameron, 1989, pp. 73–106.

18. D. Pallier, 1976, pp. 83–96.

19. F. Bardon, 1974.

of the king to emerge from this period – Henri IV on a leaping charger, baton in hand, a white scarf flowing behind him, in pursuit of his kingdom.

The abjuration, the general truce, the coronation and the successive royal entries to Paris, Amiens, Lyon, Rouen and other provincial capitals as they accepted his authority provided a range of opportunities for impressive and shrewd demonstrations of the nature and significance of royal authority. As the king entered Paris on 22 March 1594, the presses of Jamet Mettayer, temporarily established at St Denis, were producing broadsheets which played on the hearts and minds of the Parisians rallying to the king's cause.[20] Meanwhile, Jean Leclerc issued a famous set of engravings of the king's entry into Paris which depicted the king amidst his people.

The propaganda often drew on old, well-established themes in French literature and history, endowing the king with the attributes of a Gallic Hercules in a display of elementary patriotism.[21] As Henri IV entered Abbeville, for example, he found himself in front of a large oval painting of himself as Hercules in triumph over violence and war, standing at the summit of a rocky and inhospitable mountain. Below him and at his feet lay the trophies of war and the bodies of the ravening beasts of the League. A similar image appeared on an obelisk erected in his honour on his entry to Rouen in 1596.

It is important not to become too esoteric in our evaluation of royalist propaganda. It was mainly written to serve the needs of the moment and to have a full emotional impact within a particular political context. In royalist intellectual circles and especially amongst the catholic royalist office-holders, however, there was a distinctive and, in some respects, rather bleak and unadorned picture of social and political obligation which emerged during this period. It runs, for example, through the pages of the neo-Stoic treatise 'On Constancy and Consolation in Public Calamities' (*De la constance et consolation ès calamitez publiques*), written by the League *parlementaire*, Guillaume du Vair, during the siege of Paris in 1590 and published a few years later. Du Vair is a good example of a senior magistrate who had experienced the effects of the civil wars and the uncomfortable political choices which had been their inevitable result. He had been amongst a group of magistrates who had proposed a resolution (*arrêt*) to the parlement of Paris at the time of the king's abjuration requiring the duke of Mayenne to uphold the Salic law in the kingdom. He was also

20. J-P. Babelon, 1982, pp. 587–8.
21. F. Bardon, 1974 (esp. illustrations). C. Vivanti, 1967, 167–97. M–R. Jung, 1966.

amongst those office-holders who busily organised support for Henri IV as he entered Paris in March 1594. Du Vair's treatise is a dialogue about how anxieties about the world can make an individual irrational, obstinate and mad. He advocates a kind of stoic wisdom, accepting the reality of, yet detached from, the wickedness of the world around. Du Vair's treatise suggests that such passive obedience to destiny is the only sensible and prudent way to proceed in a world where God's providence ultimately dictates what will transpire but in ways unknown and unfathomable to man.

From such a perspective, it was not difficult for Guillaume du Vair to accept and justify the kingship of Henri IV, despite the broken promises and veneer of cynicism. With bruised consciences and lively memories of the recent past, senior magistrates of France like du Vair were more than prepared to accept a world-picture and the view of political authority which went with it where surviving in a sea of troubles meant containing the passions and mastering the contrary and partial spirits of religious extremism wherever it was to be found. The justification for kingship was that it provided a 'severe master', a power predestined by God and a force which would put things to rights. This is why the image of Hercules was such a powerful one in the France of the 1590s. It was suggestive of a God-figure who would 'cleanse' the kingdom of its foolishness and reward the sanity of all good men and true. Embedded in this picture of kingship were some of the characteristic components of absolutist political perceptions as they would emerge more fully in later seventeenth-century France.

More immediately, however, Henri IV's propagandists played on the simple desire for peace. They tempted their readers with the image of a day when Henri IV would be recognised everywhere as king and the 'hideous face of France's desolation would be changed to joy and laughter, and all these storms dispersed by a beautiful sun which will bring us a day of contentment and liberty'.[22] The benefits of peace held out to each estate of the realm were quite specific. For the peasant it was the prospect of a safe harvest, for the merchant a profitable trade and for the scholar a renaissance of the arts. All this was contrasted with the antagonisms of the League which were quickly exploited by the royalists. Nowhere is this better demonstrated than in the pamphlet which has been already been referred to in the last chapter. Described as the 'last will and testament of the League', the *Dialogue between the Noble and the Townsman (Dialogue d'entre le maheustre et le manant)* is generally considered to have been written in

---

22. F. Pithou, *Extraict d'un traicté* (n.p., 1594). LN, No. 1929.

the aftermath of Henri IV's conversion. It has the intense and sometimes desperate clarity of defeat and disillusionment.[23] By the end of 1593, it was republished with a few amendments by the royalists to emphasise their adversaries' low morale. It was even reproduced in verse form with a coloured engraving on the front which advertised the royal cause.[24] In the original pamphlet, the *manant* (the Parisian inhabitant, a zealot League adherent) meets the *maheustre* (the *'politique'* nobleman) outside the walls of Paris. The *manant* berates the nobleman and all the other grandees for abandoning the cause of justice, piety and purity. The nobility have lost their privileged position, he argues, by their treachery to the faith. In return, the *maheustre* exposes the divisions of the League, through which France is being dismembered to satisfy individual ambitions. The works ends with a stark series of questions which pull away the comfortable idealism of the zealot: 'Where is your popular support? Who are your allies? Who is your king? How do you know you can trust him?' To each of these questions, the *manant* can only whimper, pathetically, 'Dieu, dieu, dieu . . . .'[25]

All these themes in Henri IV's propaganda appear in a work produced at about the same time and which has become the most famous political satire in the history of France. Called the *Pleasant Satire or the Efficacy of Catholicon* (the *Satyre Ménippée*), it was a composite work by several *'politique'* Parisians.[26] Manuscripts of an early version circulated in March 1593. It was a brilliant work – biting, merciless, humorous and astute. In it, the differences between public and private motives of the League supporters were brutally exposed. The scene was the estates general of the League. Each of the speakers before the estates was fed a Spanish wonder-drug called 'Catholicon', composed of tablets like doubloons, which made them speak the truth rather than mouth the platitudes of the catholic cause. One by one in the satire, the duke of Mayenne, the Spanish ambassador, the League zealot from Lyon, the papal legate and the swaggering nobleman stood on the rostrum, larger than life, and revealed their real and sordid motives for supporting the League. Each both betrayed and ridiculed the ideals that he was supposed to have

23.   P. Ascoli, 1974, pp. 6–22. J.H.M. Salmon, 1975, 57–88. F. Morin, [1977], pp. 9–41.

24.   Estoile, [1888], IV, 300–4.

25.   Morin, [1977] pp. 210–11.

26.   The provenance of the *Satyre Ménippée* was finally elucidated by Charles Read in the 1876 edition (pp. i–xxiii). The notes to the 1726 Ratisbon edition render it still fundamental.

fought for. Only one delegate, the '*politique*' d'Aubray, presented the sober cause: that of peace, justice, the realm and the king. Delighted with the work, Henri IV hastened to sponsor its publication by Jamet Mettayer.

The defeat of the League was completed by the various treaties of pacification with League towns and princes negotiated by the king's councillors and masters of requests in the years from 1594 to 1598. These treaties displayed the skills of Sully, Villeroy, Bellièvre as well as Méric de Vic and other commissioners.[27] They deserve closer scrutiny than they have generally received.[28] Towns were offered the confirmation of their privileges, the exclusion of Calvinist worship, an amnesty for all seditious offences, the accommodation of rivals for municipal offices and the writing-off of their huge debts. Nobles and provincial governors were offered sizeable pensions, gratifications for their close servants and clientèles, and the promise of offices and posts. Not all their demands could be satisfied. Mayenne originally demanded a full and embracing pardon for himself and all his servants and also the exclusion of Calvinism from his province of Burgundy, the heredity *in perpetuum* of the provincial governorship there, six *places de sûreté* garrisoned with three companies of cavalry at the king's expense and the rights to nominate to all the ecclesiastical and royal posts of the province.[29] Not surprisingly, Henri IV's reply was that these demands were 'so extraordinary and without precedent' that they would render Mayenne 'absolute seigneur' in Burgundy at the expense of loyal servants to the king.[30] Eventually, the private demands of the treaty of Folembray, agreed on 24 January 1596, accepted rather less than this, but very substantial concessions were granted to him.[31] The costs of these treaties were enormous – 900,000 *écus* to the duke of Lorraine, 250,000 *écus* to Marshal La Châtre for the strongholds at Orléans and Bourges, 492,800 écus to Marshal de Brissac in Paris . . . as Henri IV ruefully said to one of his secretaries, he had purchased, rather than procured their loyalties (*pas rendu, vendu* . . .).[32]

27. See Map 1 for dates of major towns' capitulations. For Sully's negotiations with Villars see P. Benedict, 1981, pp. 227–8; Sully, [1970], I, 454–7. For Méric de Vic, see M. Greengrass, 1979, pp. 289–95; also E.H. Dickerman, 1968 and R. Kierstead, 1968.

28. They were collected together and published in 1606. The secret treaties were not included. Copies of these are to be found in Devic and Vaissète [1872–1904], XII, cols 1533–64 (for Joyeuse); BN MS Fr 4019, f. 360 (Mayenne), 399 (Mercoeur); BN MS Fr 3646, f. 77 (Guise).

29. BN MS Fr 4019 ff. 265v–270, n.d.

30. Ibid., f. 271v.

31. H. Drouot, 1937a, II, 458–62.

32. Estoile [1948], p. 393.

Yet, in this way, Henri IV had demonstrated that every catholic had his price. His propaganda had proved that, while the aims of the League were laudable in themselves, they were not worth the cost of establishing a new tyranny. He had proved that political stability was, in some sense, a worthy objective and could be gained on the basis of established institutions and laws. Elective monarchy, representative institutions, provincial separatism and noble factions had been proved doubly wanting by *both* catholics *and* protestants. The rest of the reign would be devoted to attempting to confirm the benefits which could accompany stability.

CHAPTER FOUR
Huguenots under the Law

The protestant experience of civil war was a sobering one. At the beginning, in 1562, there had been an air of triumphalism amongst the protestant minority, confident that the conversion of France's governing groups, if not of the country at large, was at hand. Yet, despite many years of intermittent fighting, the protestants had only succeeded in becoming an even smaller minority in the kingdom. War had brought less. At the national synod of Montpellier in 1598, it was calculated that, excluding the principality of Béarn and some remnants of the kingdom of Navarre on the French side of the Pyrenees, there were only 847 fully established churches in France (257 of which were attached to particular estates of protestant gentlemen), served by a total of about 800 ministers.[1] Latest estimates suggest that, by about the same date, protestantism was the religion of not more than a million people in France, or, perhaps, around six per cent of its population.[2]

Everywhere, even in the Midi, there were protestant communities whose churches did not, for one reason or another, survive the civil wars. (See Fig. 3.) Yet the fundamental geography of French protestantism had been reinforced, rather than altered. Edwin Sandys, an English foreign traveller in the 1590s, remarked on its regional concentration as the basis for its enduring political and military strength: 'Neither is it very easy to proportion the parties, by reason

1. J. Quick, [1692], I, 198.
2. An estimate of around 1.25 million protestants living in France in 1598 is often cited. It purports to come from a census of protestants carried out by Henri IV at the time of the edict of Nantes. No reference to the estimate is, however, known before 1692 and its authenticity is in doubt. The estimate of just under 100,000 in France (excluding Béarn) has been extrapolated from the evidence of surviving baptismal records in P. Benedict, 1991, 76.

they of the Religion are so scattered in all places. Yet in POICTOU they have almost all; in GASCOIGNIE one halfe; in LANGUEDOC, NORMANDY and other West maritime Provinces, a reasonable strong part; as likewise in sundry mediterran, of which DELFINAT the chief. But whatsoever be the proportion of their number to their opposite, which is manifoldly superiour, not one to twenty; their strength is such as their warres have witnessed.'[3] In addition, other enclaves within or close to France had become strongholds for protestantism, affording temporary shelter and more enduring links for those seeking refuge from the civil wars. Orange, Béarn, the Channel Islands, Sedan, Metz, Gex and Geneva all became integral parts of the geo-political strengths of French protestantism during the civil wars. In any case, Henri IV's co-religionists had helped to put the king on his French throne and, despite being a small minority, they expected some rewards.

Amidst the triumphalism of the early years of the civil wars it would have been surprising if some French protestants had not occasionally allowed themselves the luxury of dreaming of a different ordering of society, of a real protestant revolution. The smashing of images and popular religious violence of the first decade of civil war had, in some localities, been accompanied by popular intimidation of notables and suggestions that inaugurating a new Jerusalem should not wait upon the decision of the magistrate. But, under the influence of the increasingly dominant components of French protestantism, its grandees and consistorial leaders, such dreams did not last long. The more immediate threats to their continued existence helped to concentrate protestant minds on a stoic determination to provide for their basic security and recognition.[4] They relied on a common cause, a '*parti*' which would be led by an aristocrat responsible to the cause, a '*chef du parti*' who would be the 'protector' of their united front ('*protecteur de l'union des églises*'). They believed that a written document, guaranteed by God, Providence and a powerful protector, would best provide for their ultimate security within the French state. Despite their frequent internal disagreements, the Huguenots were united in the belief that their salvation as a minority lay in some form of royal edict declaring their rights and guaranteeing their freedoms.

To some extent, French protestantism during the civil wars was a 'prisoner of the [*aristocratic*] leaders who it was forced to accept in

---

3. E. Sandys, *Europae Speculae* (2nd edn, 1632), pp. 176–7.
4. N.M. Sutherland, 1980, ch. v.

order to ensure its survival'.[5] Certainly, the relations between the Huguenot political movement and the princes of the blood who served as its protectors were frequently strained and uneasy. Henri de Navarre had been their leader for twelve years before he came to the throne in 1589. Yet he was still not entirely trusted, despite the fact that he was a major figure in French politics whose seigneurial authority was coterminous with Huguenot influence in several regions.(See Map 2.) South of the Loire he owned numerous counties in addition to the important duchy of Albret, in each of which protestantism was overwhelmingly dominant. In the county of Armagnac alone, 1,800 fiefs owed him homage, and that was a part of the world where religious affiliation closely combined with seigneurial loyalty. Even north of the Loire, his seigneurial authority blended into more discreet zones of protestant influence. In addition, as we have already seen, he ruled as sovereign prince of Béarn, an important protestant redoubt in the Pyrenees; he had also inherited the provincial governorship of the province of Guyenne which, in peacetime, entitled him to a royal company of cavalry and a natural precedence over both catholic and protestant in a substantial region of south-west France. Little by little, amongst the deputies at the general assemblies of the protestant movement held at Montauban (1581 and 1584), St Jean d'Angély (1582) and La Rochelle (1588), the proportion of deputies from the south-west in attendance grew, almost as a measure of Henri de Navarre's growing influence within the movement as a whole.[6]

Yet many French protestants felt that they had good grounds to distrust their protector. It was not for nothing had his father been dubbed the 'great undecider' ('*le grand tergivisateur*') for his vacillations towards the protestant cause in 1561–62. Promised a putative kingdom of Sardinia by Philip II 'if he would only remain neutral and make his son once attend Mass', he had, in fact, entrusted the education of his son prior to 1561 to a succession of tutors of a variety of religious persuasions.[7] And although Henri de Navarre spent much of the succeeding decade under the tutelage of his mother, Jeanne d'Albret, who was a committed protestant, there were contrary currents circulating round the young prince. The last letters she wrote to her son urged him anxiously to keep the faith, reminding him of the

5. H. Zuber, 'La noblesse protestante (1584–1598). Histoire politique des rapports entre Henri IV et les grands réformés', *Avènement d'Henri IV*, 1989, p. 76.

6. Janine Garrisson-Estèbe, 1980, p. 204.

7. Christian Desplat, 'La religion d'Henri IV', *Avènement d'Henri IV*, 1989, pp. 238–9. Jean-Pierre Babelon, 1982, ch. v.

tenacity of his sister. Yet, within three months of her death and firm testament entreating him to remain true to his protestantism, he had married a catholic and abjured his protestant faith.[8]

When he escaped from court in 1576, he promptly renounced this abjuration as a recantation extracted by force, and therefore null. But he then proceeded to give some grounds for believing that his protestant sympathies lacked some commitment. He accepted the edict of pacification of 1577 and tried to enforce it in his government of Guyenne and elsewhere in the Midi.[9] Although his court was a protestant one, his entourage and friendships were composed on the basis of personal affinities and proven talents rather than confessional rigidity. 'You would hardly believe how they [*catholics*] are in agreement with those of the Religion who have also come here to find me' Henri de Navarre had written to Damville from Agen in August 1576. As king of Navarre, his chancellor would be Arnaud du Ferrier, nominally a catholic whose protestant sympathies he kept prudently to himself. Antoine de Roquelaure, the king's childhood companion and a close confidant, was catholic. Jean de Beaumanoir, seigneur (later marquis) de Lavardin, another of Navarre's oldest and most trusted advisors, would change his religious persuasion several times, like his master. The king's wider affinities in Guyenne included many catholics like Michel de Montaigne, the moderate catholic judge from Bordeaux.[10] Navarre was married to Marguerite de Valois and the appearance of her catholic court in the south-west in 1583 provoked consternation amongst the protestants of the region until the very public and terminal rupture between the two courts in 1585. And all the world knew the political pressure he was under to change his religion after the death of Anjou.[11] His proposals to hold a national council to settle the question of religion also did little to endear him to his protestant co-religionists. They were part of a plan he had considered for his ancestral lands in Béarn. They were also the subject of discussions with Henri III's envoy, Epernon, in 1584. He returned to the call for a 'free and legitimate' council to settle the religious wars

8.   Ibid., p. 241; N. Roelker, 1968, pp. 395–410.

9.   *Catherine de Médicis*, [1880–1909], VI, 249, 260, etc.

10.   F.S. Brown, *Religious and political conservatism in the Essais of Montaigne* (Droz, Geneva, 1963).

11.   The framework of the secret discussions between Henri III's favourite, Epernon, and the king of Navarre's cabinet in July 1584 was the subject of a famous organised leak by Du Plessis Mornay. His anonymous letter on the subject quickly found its way to Paris and was immediately published at Frankfurt under the title: *Double d'une lettre envoyée à un certain personnage . . . contentant le discours de ce qui se passa au cabinet du roi de Navarre.*

in France in March 1585. He repeated his suggestion to the estates general at Blois in March 1589. Force, he told them, had achieved nothing. He had himself abjured, 'a dagger at his throat', and his subsequent recantation had proved how fruitless it had been. He and his followers had endured the assaults of ten armies in the preceding four years but they had stood firm. There was, however, a peaceful course to be pursued, namely, the convening of a free council. 'Instruct me', he invited the estates general, 'You will not find me ideologically motivated.' His education may well have been defective in matters of religion. He would embrace truth wherever it was to be found. In the meantime, he offered the widest possible toleration in religious matters in the regions under his authority.[12]

Some of these suspicions and the internal dissensions within the Huguenot movement at large were aired in public at the large political assembly summoned to La Rochelle and which took place from 14 November to 17 December 1588. In his opening remarks, Navarre complained of the suspicions that his actions attracted from his co-religionists. But this did not deter the delegates from engaging in a detailed critique of his diplomacy and military strategy (especially following the battle of Coutras), as well as the financial administration of the cause. Navarre had to swear to observe the confession of faith, accept a larger *conseil de surveillance* of ten members, nominated by the national and provincial assemblies of the movement in equal measure. He agreed to receive nominations for all financial posts in the Huguenot administration from the movement and only appoint those whom they had put forward. The authority of the men of business in the movement, particularly at the regional level, was thus recognised and enhanced.[13] In return, the assembly promised him its full military support against the catholic League and accepted different arrangements for elections to the political assemblies. In future, each province would be represented by two deputies each, one chosen from the nobility and the other from the towns. Voting in future debates would be undertaken by province rather than by individual representatives. This was an important, even vital, change which limited the representation of the less amenable provinces (from Navarre's point of view), guaranteed a stronger presence for his *fidèles* amongst the nobility, and restricted the abilities of protestant pastors to foster confessional rigidities in the more frequent and difficult

12. W.B. Patterson, 1972, pp. 247–52. *Lettre du roy de Navarre aux Trois Estats de ce royaume* . . . Châtellerault, 4 Mar. 1589 (n.p., 1589: LN, No. 1537).

13. L. Anquez, 1859, pp. 38–51. The 'procès-verbal' of the assembly is to be found in BN MS Fr nouv. acq., 7191 ff. 112–64.

assemblies held in the wake of the king's second abjuration.[14] But Madame de Mornay overheard one of the deputies say: 'Now is the time to make kings into serfs and slaves' and the comparisons between the estates general at Blois and the assembly at La Rochelle were evident to all contemporaries. Once the assembly was over, Henri de Navarre confided in Madame de Gramont: 'If they hold another assembly I shall go mad.'[15] Even the opportunity to put a king on the throne had not, therefore, united the Huguenots behind his leadership.

Navarre could count, of course, on the support of his councillors and close servants amongst the protestant movement – men such as Sully, the king's secretary Raymond de Viçose, or the pastors who served as his household chaplains.[16] Claude Sommain Clairville, a minister from the western Loire, provides a striking example of pastoral loyalty to the king through the political assemblies of the 1590s, service which would in due course be well rewarded.[17] Aware of the need to win catholics over to the royal cause, they thought that the edict of pacification in 1577 provided a sufficient guarantee of Huguenot freedoms, providing that it was adequately enforced. They ignored the demands for protestant separatism as being, to use Sully's phrase, 'a kind of popular and republican state like the Low Countries'.[18] Yet, despite Henri IV's attempts to influence delegates from the south-west, these sentiments were mostly to be found amongst the contingent of protestant judges and lawyers in these assemblies who, at the most, only made up about a third of their membership.[19] This still left a phalanx of pastors and convinced lay protestants who concentrated on religious demands and the well-being of the protestant churches (the '*bien des églises*'). They tended to regard the latter as automatically consonant with the interests of the monarchy and France as a whole. They regarded peace as an essential prerequisite to the rebuilding of the protestant churches, the re-education of their clergy and the re-establishment of a proper church fabric. They looked to a protestant king to protect their cause. Philippe Du Plessis Mornay, the distinguished Calvinist theologian, scholar and political advisor to Navarre since 1581, exercised a considerable influence over this wing of the protestant movement,

14. J. Garrisson, 1988, pp. 319–20.
15. *Lettres d'Henri IV*, 1843–60, II, 411–12.
16. D.J. Buisseret, 1966, 28–31.
17. He was named a *conseiller* and *maître des requêtes* as well as being granted exemption from the *taille*. Haag Bordier, IV, 381.
18. Sully, [1970–88], I, 493.
19. J. Airo-Farulla, 1975, p. 504.

particularly in the 1590s. He had a vision of a kind of protestant Gallicanism, at the heart of which was a 'good and solid union between all the churches for their just preservation, under the dominance and protection of the king, to whom they owe and swear all obedience'. The dissension and hostilities of the assembly at La Rochelle were just an example of the inevitable dangers of 'particular' interests taking precedence over the common interests of the protestant churches and their protector. 'All the fools are not on one side only' he reminded the king.[20] In the wake of the king's accession to the French throne, he wrote to prominent individuals opposing Navarre to try to persuade them to 'set their hand to this crown of thorns and turn it into a crown of lilies'.[21]

The more dangerous and volatile opposition came from the Huguenot aristocrats.[22] They led seasoned troops in numbers which were vital to Henri IV's army in the 1590s. One estimate is that the 3,500 protestant gentlemen between them were still capable of mustering some 25,000 men at a time when the royal armies on their own were less than half that size.[23] Claude de La Trémoille, duke of Thouars, was the protestant satrap of the Poitevin marshes and southern Brittany, the most powerful and the least predictable amongst their higher nobility. The death of Henri, prince of Condé, in 1588 (some said as a result of being poisoned by his own wife, Charlotte-Catherine de La Trémoille, who was Claude's sister) had opened the way for La Trémoille to play a larger role as broker in the protestant cause. At the critical moment of Henri's accession to the French throne, La Trémoille had withdrawn his battalions from the royal army because of the king's promises to the catholics in the Declaration of St Cloud. Thereafter, he showed himself at best semi-detached from the royal cause, absenting himself from the important campaigns around La Fère and Amiens. By his marriage to Charlotte-Brabatine, daughter of William the Silent, he joined the international network of protestant grandees; thereby he also laid claim to the accumulated resentments towards autocratic usages of power by monarchs and emperors which that network periodically harboured. Several of the protestant political assemblies in the 1590s were held close by regions where La Trémoille had his greatest authority. In 1597, he served briefly as president of the assembly; in all he had his

20. Cited L. Anquez, 1859, p. 48.

21. Du Plessis Mornay, [1824–5], IV, 402 (18 Aug. 1589).

22. H. Zuber, 'La noblesse protestante (1584–1598). Histoire politique des rapports entre Henri IV et les grands réformés', *Avènement d'Henri IV*, 1989, pp. 73–91.

23. J. Mariéjol, 1904.

noble clients, mainly amongst the politically active protestant gentry of western France. One of them was (according to Sully) the poet and soldier, Agrippa d'Aubigné.[24] In his speech delivered to the assembly, probably at Châtellerault in 1597, he reminded delegates that the 'parti' was without a 'chef' and that the choice lay in their hands, either to elect a new protector or to let the assembly itself be the leader of the movement. At the same time he warned that probably no single French nobleman was in a position to bear the costs of being protector on his own, leaving the delegates to work out for themselves that an alternative might be sought abroad, perhaps amongst his Nassau relatives.[25] So Sully was not perhaps paranoid when he suggested in his *Oeconomies Royales* that there were some who resented Navarre's *tyrannie protectorale* sufficiently to want to replace him with another. It would have been a development fraught with danger for the longer-term future of the Henrician regime.

The degree to which that danger came close to reality in the 1590s depended on the extent to which La Trémoille could count on the support of other leading protestant nobles. That would remain something of an open question. Henri, vicomte de Turenne (from 1591, duke of Bouillon) was la Trémoille's close kinsman following his marriage to Elizabeth, another daughter of William the Silent. Turenne, the seigneur of a large part of the upper Limousin, needed no lessons in the serpentine politics of the upper nobility, or in how to advance his own interests through those of the Huguenot cause. 'In serving the public, I serve my own interests', he once boldly declared.[26] Bouillon has recently been exonerated from fishing in the dark waters of alternative protectorship.[27] Certainly Henri IV treated Bouillon and La Trémoille with great tact and displays of generosity; a less diplomatic hand might have led them to reveal more of their ultimate intentions. But their support for the zealots in the political assemblies from the summer of 1596 to secure a strong deal from the king is not in doubt. The pacification of Nantes was not the reward of a grateful king to his former co-religionists in return for their

24. Sully, [1970–88], I, 493. Other Huguenot gentry mentioned as among the zealots lending support to La Trémoille and Bouillon were Augustin de Constant, seigneur de Rebecque, a frequent delegate from northern France to the assemblies; Odet de La Noue, sieur de Téligny, who negotiated Turenne's marriage to the duchess of Bouillon in 1591; and Georges II Clermont d'Amboise, who expressed himself willing to endorse the opinions of the zealots in the assemblies 'with his blood'.

25. Bib. Prot. MS 708 ff. 159–161.

26. Cited N.M. Sutherland, 1980, p. 288.

27. H. Zuber (cited n. 22 above), p. 83 modifies the views expressed in the earlier edition of this book.

continued support. It was a concession, wrung out of him by astute protestant aristocrats who knew just how to exploit a political opportunity to its best advantage.

THE LETTERS PATENT OF MANTES, JULY 1591

Huguenot suspicions had, in fact, begun to increase from the moment of the king's accession. On 4 August 1589, Henri IV was forced to make the declaration of St Cloud, preserving catholics in their posts, offering to sustain the catholic religion and to be instructed in the catholic faith within six months. The king wrote to Du Plessis Mornay shortly thereafter to try to dispel the mounting alarm amongst the protestants:

> They say that I have dismissed officers of the religion . . . that the ministers are no longer paid; that the officials who are in charge of the enforcement of the truce [*made with the royalists*] have reinstated royal officers and the Roman Catholic religion . . . in brief, that in matters of religion, justice and finance, conditions are worse now than they were when the deceased King was alive . . . These are the rumours which are being sown with the intention that they will lead to the naming of a new protector.[28]

In the following two years, Henri IV did his best to curtail the political assemblies of the Huguenot movement at both regional and national level. At the same time, he cosseted La Trémoille and Turenne. He consented to their marriage alliances. In 1592 he made Bouillon (formerly the vicomte de Turenne) a marshal of France and thus an officer of the crown in return for his assistance at the siege of Paris. He then despatched him on delicate missions to protestant powers abroad, perhaps in order to reduce his potentially meddlesome influence at home.[29]

But this did not remove the legitimate and widespread fears of the more moderate protestants like Du Plessis Mornay or the royalist-minded Huguenot lawyers in the organising échelons of the movement. For it was undoubtedly the case that the legal position of the protestant in France was ill-defined and almost non-existent. The

---

28. Du Plessis Mornay, [1824–5], IV, 427. N.M. Sutherland, 1980, pp. 294–5.

29. N.M. Sutherland, 1980, pp. 295–6. H. Lloyd, *The Rouen Campaign 1590–2* (Oxford U.P., 1973), pp. 30–48.

edicts against the Huguenots enacted in 1585 and 1588 were, technically, still in force. The protestants could look to no law-court in the realm for the redress of their grievances. It was to try to meet the most pressing demands of the Huguenot moderates that the king reluctantly issued new guidelines in the letters patent of Mantes on 4 July 1591 in which he revoked the edicts of 1585 and 1588.[30] The letters were drafted by Du Plessis Mornay. In effect, they re-established the terms of the edict of pacification of 1577. Protestants were given rights to worship in one place in each locality (*bailliage*), on the estates of protestant gentlemen, and in eight garrison towns. It was further agreed that the pastors would be paid by the king and that protestants should be free to enter all offices. Bipartisan courts (*chambres de l'édit*) of the kind previously established in 1577 were to be reconvened to deal with cases involving protestants. There was also a reference to a 'Holy and free council or some notable assembly' of an unspecified kind which might, in the future, achieve a final settlement of all outstanding sectarian problems and instruct the king on the true religion.

The concessions of Mantes were only a palliative. They were not an edict and they were never registered in the *parlements*. They were therefore ignored by the catholics. The royalist *parlement* at Tours still required protestants to convert to catholicism before taking up their offices. It did not permit the establishment of any bipartisan court. Protestant pastors were not paid from royal revenues. It is a measure of Henri IV's unwillingness to alienate any potential support from moderate catholics by appearing to favour the Huguenots, his wariness towards the formation of a possible '*tiers parti*' ('third party'), that this was the only substantial measure he was prepared to grant the protestants before 1598.

HENRI IV'S CONVERSION AND THE HUGUENOTS

The abjuration of the Huguenot faith by the king occurred without any consultation of the movement and in a manner which was almost calculated to cause them offence. As the pace of events quickened in the late spring of 1593, Bouillon and La Trémoille were brushed to one side. In haste, Bouillon wrote warning letters to Elizabeth I in England: 'Believe me, unless you come to our aid soon we are lost and an ill-fate shall befall us such as pen cannot write'. Soon, on the eve of the declaration of 25 July 1593, Henri IV was taking an

30. A. Stegmann, 1979, pp. 224–6. N.M. Sutherland, 1980, pp. 295–6.

emotional farewell of his protestant chaplains. His protestant councillors had advised him of the dangers but understood the necessities behind his decision. Maximilien de Béthune (later duke of Sully), provides an account of a conversation with the king in May 1593 which ran through the advantages and disadvantages of the move.[31] Sully's best advice was that the bulk of Huguenot opinion would remain behind the king. The only opposition would come, he said, from the zealots among the consistories and their ministers.

As it was, however, the manner of the conversion and its timing were such as to alienate even moderate Huguenot opinion from the king. Du Plessis Mornay had been detailed to convene a political assembly of the movement at Mantes in late July 1593, the first national assembly of the movement since 1588. He set about the task with some skill, inviting distinguished foreign observers to the deliberations and arranging for the king to nominate some of the delegates (to save time rather than to offend privileges, as he told the churches disingenuously).[32] As events turned out, the king announced his conversion before the assembly had convened. He thus denied Du Plessis Mornay the opportunity of creating a pliable protestant assembly, able to accept what the king would propose for the future of the movement. In disgust, Du Plessis Mornay departed the court and Henri IV, in alarm, tried to use all his personal charm, mixed with remembrances of past fidelity to try to persuade him to return and once again be the king's honest broker with the protestants: 'I have loved you more than any other gentleman in my realm; I have spoken freely to you . . . If you have some complaint against me you should let me hear it . . . I write only this once to see if you are obedient to me. Come; come. You shall not tarry. Come.'[33] Du Plessis Mornay's reply indicated that he felt he had been betrayed. He feared the influence of other advisors around the king:

> The people are saying that it was more tolerable to live under Henri III than it is to live under Your Majesty. It is no wonder that they are looking for a 'protector'. Patience and hope are on the wane. The people look for relief. If you wish to eliminate the desire for a 'protector' you must diminish its necessity. Listen to their demands; you know what they need and what they want.[34]

31. Sully, [1970–88], I, 335–9.
32. Du Plessis Mornay, [1824–5], V, 451, etc. d'Aubigné, IX, 85. See also J. Faurey, 1903, ch. i.
33. *Henri IV*, 1843–60 IV, 5 (7 Aug. 1593).
34. Du Plessis Mornay, [1824–5], V, 510–12.

In November 1593, the assembly summoned to Mantes finally took place. It expressed its final demands in a long petition of 109 clauses.[35] These demanded extensive guarantees of the rights to worship for protestants, regular payments for their garrisons and rights to hold regular public assemblies. They wanted certain royal offices of justice open to nomination by protestants, rather than just available for purchase by individual protestants. Henri IV treated the assembly with humiliating contempt, refused to visit it, denied an audience to its deputies and (when they were finally allowed to see him) declined to give them either written replies or even verbal promises. The assembly at Mantes retired after two months in session, having achieved nothing.[36]

The reasons for this obstinacy are evident. The negotiations with the Pope over the precise terms for his conversion were still being conducted. No major catholic city had yet succumbed to him. The king could therefore offer the protestants his goodwill alone. The failure to extract more from him hurt the moderates in the movement most and opened the door to their more committed brethren. More ominously, there were fewer protestants in Henri IV's close entourage after his conversion to provide the necessary channels of communication between the king and the movement at large. The scene was set for the increasing wrangling and bitterness of the years to 1598.

HENRI IV AND THE EDICT OF NANTES

Between 1594 and 1598 the protestants strengthened their provincial organisation. At the national assembly of Sainte Foy in June 1594, they arranged their provinces, councils and assemblies along with the representation of their orders of the protestant church within them.[37] Some elaborate contingency plans for mutual military protection were discussed and even Du Plessis Mornay was moved to remark that the Huguenots were wasting their time in discussing *religion* in isolation from the wider issues of security and recognition.[38] The legal position of the protestants became even more complicated as well. Several treaties made with individual League cities contravened the letters patent of Mantes and the king did nothing to lessen the confusion by

35. This magnificent *cahier* still remains unpublished in BN Dupuy MS 213.
36. L. Anquez, 1859, pp. 61, etc.
37. Ibid. and d'Aubigné, IX, 85.
38. Du Plessis Mornay, [1824–5], V, 510–12.

asking everyone to obey the edicts of pacification without specifying which ones he meant.[39] The Huguenots' national assemblies became more insistent; their increasing size and the length of their sessions are one way of measuring this. (See Fig 3.) The one at Saumur in 1595 lasted two months and was attended by under 50 delegates. In the following year, that which commenced its deliberations at Loudun in April lasted six months and included many delegates re-elected from its predecessor. In March 1597, the assembly grew to 70–80 delegates and the assembly which opened in Châtellerault in June 1597 was attended by over 200. By this time, they were in almost constant session and threatening to sit until a new edict was published and also enforced in the provinces. *The Complaints of the Reformed Churches*, the published version of their demands, circulated widely through the kingdom.[40]

The king used some of his most able and moderate catholic diplomats to negotiate with the assemblies – the historian Jacques-Auguste de Thou, Méric de Vic, Gaspard de Schomberg and the protestant Soffrey de Calignon. But they were instructed not to undertake to give further guarantees to the protestant movement at large. Royal insistence that no edict would be undertaken which appeared to be a surrender to weakness or which would be unacceptable to the *parlements* of France was vital at this moment. As Professor Sutherland has shown, this was despite the pressures on the king from the military campaigns against Spain, warfare which Bouillon may have persuaded the king, against his better judgment, to wage in the first place.[41] While Henri IV struggled to recapture Cambrai, La Fère and Amiens, La Trémoille and Bouillon remained in Poitou and the Auvergne in calculated disregard for the king's repeated summons to his presence. At the same time, Huguenot treasurers began to confiscate royal taxes in some areas to pay for their garrisoned troops. The possibilities of their making common cause with catholic malcontents like 'the prodigal son' (as the king called him) comte Charles d'Auvergne, actively fomenting sedition in the same region, were all too menacing.[42]

The different texts of the pacification of Nantes were eventually signed in April and May 1598. The king, having recovered Amiens from the Spanish, sued for peace at Vervins. For a brief moment, the conjuncture of international and domestic pressures provided the conditions for peace and the king grasped the opportunity decisively.

39. Fontanon, IV, 360 (15 Nov. 1594).
40. N.M. Sutherland, 1980, p. 323. Mariéjol, 1904, p. 417.
41. N.M. Sutherland, 1980, pp. 308–20.
42. Ibid., p. 321; also M. Greengrass, 1981, 336–7; Estoile, [1948], p. 504.

He marched his large army towards the Loire, ostensibly to defeat the last remnants of the League in Brittany. In fact, however, the protestant deputies were equally alarmed and it proved to be the ultimate gesture which brought the protestant deputies to accept the royal terms.[43] The pacification was not, in fact, one legal enactment but a series of four. There was a public edict of 92 published articles, undated but almost certainly signed on 13 April 1598. This was, in due course, followed by 57 so-called 'secret articles' to accompany the registration of the edict as a schedule. These expanded on particular clauses in the general edict and dealt with exceptions. They were agreed on 2 May. Finally there were two letters (*brevets*) from the king. The first of these, issued on 13 April, assigned 45,000 *écus* per year of crown revenue to the protestant pastors for their salary. The second *brevet* (of 30 April) allowed the protestants 180,000 *écus* per year for some 50 military garrisons in Huguenot strongholds (*places de sûreté*) spread through western France and across the Huguenot crescent of Languedoc to Dauphiné. In addition, it allowed them about 150 emergency forts (*places de refuge*) and 80 other forts which were to be maintained at their own expense. (See Map 2.)

In the preamble to the general edict, probably drafted by Jacques-Auguste de Thou, there was a delicate path to be trodden between displaying the king's new-found catholicism and his freshly-deserted protestant faith. It spoke of the king's desire to serve God, his recent military successes, his desire to see Christians united. Peace was the ultimate goal; there was no mention of any universal principle of toleration. Although it spoke of the edict as 'perpetual and irrevocable', a phrase which had not been included in any previous edict of pacification, this was not intended, and was never interpreted by its contemporaries as meaning that the edict had become part of the fundamental law of France.[44] Indeed, at one point, the preamble explicitly envisaged an eventual reconciliation of the two churches. The king assured catholics of their security in wealth and their position as the dominant religious faith in the kingdom. The basis of the general edict had already been laid in 1563, 1570 and, above all, in the religious pacification which Henri of Navarre had helped to negotiate and to enforce in 1577. But several of the clauses of that previous edict were tightened up where legal precedents had indicated that the guidelines provided in the edict needed to be more precise.[45]

---

43. d'Aubigné, IX, 281.
44. M. Turchetti, 1993.
45. For example, clause 5 (on protestant fortresses), 18 (on forced baptisms), 28 (the provision of protestant cemeteries), etc.

A major part of the edict was devoted to 'the removal of past disorders'. It attempted to erase the sectarian memories of the past. There was a full amnesty granted for crimes committed in the past in time of war. Ministers and catholic clergy were enjoined not to preach seditious or scandalous sermons. Forced abjurations were forbidden. Exhumations of protestants from catholic cemeteries were prohibited. The edict was robust in tackling a range of sensitive issues between the two religions – the provision of religious buildings, ceremonies, feast-days, funerals and marriages.

The basic 92 articles granted freedom of worship to the protestants on a carefully restricted basis. Huguenot worship was allowed in three categories: firstly, on the estates of Huguenot gentlemen who wished to allow it (the so-called *culte privé*). Secondly, it was to be permitted at two locations in every *bailliage*, the places to be decided by royal commissioners sent to every province of the kingdom (this was called the *culte de permission*). Finally, rights to worship were to be allowed everywhere the Huguenots could prove that it had been openly practised in 1596 and 1597 (up to August). This was called the *culte de concession*. These three categories had been established in the edict of pacification of 1570 and amplified in 1577. They allowed for the edict to adjust to the local conditions of the protestant movement, whether amongst the gentry-based rural religion of Normandy, the dispersed and vulnerable protestant communities of the north-east, or the dense, more urban protestant fabric of the Midi.

The important clause 27 of the edict removed the religious qualification from the right to acquire or inherit any office in the kingdom. This, too, had been enunciated in the edict of pacification in 1577 and included in the letters patent of Mantes in 1591. But it had been ignored by the reluctant *parlements*. So this clause was the least that the king could offer which would satisfy the delegates at the political assemblies who were lawyers with expectation of royal service, or who might reasonably hope for remunerative service in the state's financial administration. Even so, the protestants would require the continued good favour of the king and his council, despite the edict, to combat the prejudices against them from among the royal tribunals who alone registered the letters patent for the nomination of office-holders.

The edict also established bi-partisan chambers of the *parlements* to judge cases involving protestants. The clauses relating to the appointment of these magistrates, their spheres of legal responsibility, the methods of appeal of cases to these courts, and the payment of their judges were, on the whole, more comprehensive than those which had appeared in the previous edict of pacification of 1577 (clauses 40–44, 49–52, 62). The Chamber of the Edict (*chambre de l'édit*) for the province of Languedoc was already in session following the decree from Mantes and half of its judges were protestants. Other provinces had to wait until the pacification at Nantes and, even then, the success of these legal bodies was dependent on continuous pressure from the council of state for the enforcement of the edict. Not all the tribunals enjoyed an equal number of protestant and catholic magistrates. The *parlements* were adept at frustrating their decisions. Nevertheless, a degree of case law and range of precedents did gradually develop in dealing with those sectarian issues at the individual and communal level which came before the court. The lawyers and judges associated with the chambers on the protestant side were those who became most committed to the success of the edict of Nantes and its enforcement. Soffrey de Calignon in Languedoc and Charles du Cros in Dauphiné, for example, were powerful voices for moderation within the protestant movement in the decade after the edict of Nantes and their position as magistrates in these tribunals enabled them to speak out with additional authority.[46]

The so-called 'secret' articles were not a sinister invention and they were never intended to be kept a secret. They were an attached schedule of exemptions and additional clauses which attempted to harmonise the general articles of the edict of Nantes with specific promises made to individual League towns such as Paris or Toulouse when they had capitulated to the king that they would never be required to accept heretic services taking place within their walls and suburbs. Some of the clauses in the secret articles also treated the establishment of protestant universities in France and the training of ministers, clauses which would not, in fact, have been inappropriate in the general articles – for the division between the two was not always clear. But the *brevets* were, in some ways, the most significant concessions of the pacification. In them, Henri IV granted the protestants a very limited measure of independent military and political status. The payment of ministers was assumed to be the king's responsibility (although this had already been accepted in principle in 1589).[47] The payment of the garrisons – the so-called 'guarantee clauses' – was granted for a limited period of eight years from the date

---

46. The point is made in F. Garrisson, 1950, for both the commissioners of the edict and the magistrates in the bi-partisan chambers. It is reinforced by the speeches edited and reproduced in E. Rabut, 1987.

47. Henri III had accepted it in April 1589 as part of his rapprochement with the protestants.

of publication of the edict in the *parlement* of Paris, although the troops were to be deployed in their various strengths according to royal instructions and their captains were to be appointed by the king. However the wording of the letter conceded that these appointments would take protestant wishes into account. The *brevets* were juridically distinct from the rest of the pacification, issued as private letters from the king under his privy seal rather than under the great seal of the chancery – the king's personal promises to the protestants rather than acts of state. They would be confirmed in 1611 but withdrawn by Louis XIII in 1629 at the peace of Alais and, from that date, the Huguenots lost one of the main advantages which the pacification at Nantes had afforded them.

On the basis of these *brevets*, it has been claimed that the edict of Nantes created a 'state within a state'.[48] The claim is difficult to substantiate, given their juridical status. By paying for their churches and garrisons, the king bought protestant loyalties (as with the League) and bound them more closely to the monarchy rather than separating them from it. The main articles of the edict (clause 82) specifically prohibited the protestant political assemblies at either national or regional level so that the 'united provinces of the Midi' were officially disbanded. Article 43 of the secret articles, however, permitted colloquies and provincial synods, but only for a religious purpose and meetings had to be held before a royal judge. It is true that the protestants were allowed separate chambers of the *parlement* for their cases, but it was royal law which was enforced there (even in cases of matrimonial law, where protestant rules of consanguinity were less strict than catholic ones). Royal catholic judges were always present. Protestants were required to pay tithes and respect the festivals of the catholic calendar, the only dispensation being that they were relieved of any requirement to decorate their house frontages for the purposes of a festival (municipalities would undertake this for them). The protestant movement was still not allowed as a corporate entity to possess any school, hospital, church or consistory property. Protestant property was recognised only as the property of an individual. In fact the whole tenor of the edict is not the extreme degree of independence that it granted to the Huguenots to live under their own law, but the degree of dependence which, in practice, it demanded of them, on the pleasure of the king.[49] We might say that it attempted to create, not a 'state within a state', but rather (as is

---

48. Mariéjol, 1904, p. 423.
49. Points all made by C. Benoist, 1900, and reviewed in D. Ligou, 1968, pp. 20–2.

promised for contemporary Hong Kong when it reverts to Chinese sovereignty) 'one state, two systems'. In comparison with the modest freedoms granted to the protestants in the religious sphere, the extensive cash payments, indemnities and exemptions from taxation granted to the League towns, not to mention their rights to practise the catholic religion to the exclusion of any other, put *them* into the category of a 'state within a state' rather than the protestants. At most, the edict made the Huguenots an 'estate' of the realm in a kingdom already generously endowed with 'estates', that is to say, groups protected by certain privileges. In some respects, the support accorded the protestants' educational institutions in the pacification was the most significant longer-term key to the survival of this 'estate'. But, in comparison with the other estates of France – the nobility, the *noblesse de robe*, or the clergy – the Huguenots remained an estate on the margins or confines of traditional French society and liable, in a different climate from that prevailing in the regime of Henri IV, to become more vulnerable.

HUGUENOTS UNDER THE LAW

Pronouncing the edict was the work of a month; enforcing it was that of a decade. Only the main body of it was to be registered in the law-courts and it took ten fraught months to negotiate its passage through the *parlement* of Paris. For the first five months, Henri IV's government stood back, surveying the violent campaign orchestrated against it from the pulpits and in the Parisian press. The king waited for the departure of the papal legate and the registration of the peace of Vervins. Then, in a succession of lectures, private conferences and scarcely veiled threats (which reveal the king's political style) it was finally registered on 25 February 1599. He called the judges before him to the Louvre on 7 February 1599 and subjected them to a harangue of great force and finesse. He stressed that he was not an absolute monarch, demanding obedience without question or debate: 'You see me in my study and I am speaking to you not in royal attire with cape and sword (like a prince addressing foreign ambassadors) but dressed like the father of a family, in his doublet, speaking frankly to his children.'[50] The contrast with the political style of his immediate predecessor could scarcely have been greater. He then stressed that

50. Estoile, [1948], pp. 555–6. See also 'Les paroles que le roy a tenues à Messieurs de la court de Parlement' in *Henri IV*, V, 89–94.

pacification of his kingdom was his objective and that, as judges, their obedience was vital. Stability was in their interests as well as his.

I have made peace abroad, and I now wish to see it established within. You must obey me if only because I am king and all my subjects owe me obedience, but especially those of my *parlement*. I have restored the banished to their property; others have returned to the catholic faith. If obedience was due to my predecessors, it is all the more due to me because I have established the state which was mine naturally by inheritance and conquest. The magistrates . . . would not be in their courts without me.

He then tactfully, but firmly, reminded them of their past disloyalties and their unfortunate consequences:

I know that there are plots in the *parlements* and that seditious preachers are encouraged . . . This is the road that led to the Barricades and the assassination of the late king. I am not going that way. I will strike at the roots of all factions and all seditious preaching, and those that support them will be hurt as well.

Then, warming to his theme, he rounded on the judges, telling them that he knew of all their machinations and reminding them that he was an elder son of the catholic church now:

Those who refuse me this edict want war . . . you in your long robes are like the Capuchins who hide muskets under their cloaks . . . You will be sorry for creating this trouble for me . . . my council finds this edict good and essential for my State – the Constable [*Montmorency-Damville*], the Chancellor [*Cheverny*], Bellièvre, Sancy and Sillery [*the royal secretaries*] – I have acted with their advice and that of the dukes and peers. Not one of them would not call himself a protector of the catholic religion and yet they have advised me to accept this edict.

Finally, he displayed some bare knuckles before dismissing the judges to go away and consider what he had told them and do as he asked:

There is a rumour in Paris that I am about to levy some Swiss or other troops to coerce you. If I did so, it would be justified, and with results, and would be of a piece with my previous actions. I was victorious at Amiens, thanks to the finance which you would not have granted me if I had not come to the *parlement* to demand it of you.[51] Necessity drives me to this edict. In times past, necessity has turned me into a soldier. . . I am a king now and I speak as a king and wish to be obeyed!

51. A reference to the *lit de justice* held in 1597 to secure emergency financial edicts to fund the Amiens campaign. See A. Chamberland, 1904 and below, ch. iv.

In this plain and direct speech lay the stuff of the struggle for stability. On one side stood the king and his regime, anxious to establish themselves as the guardians of stability, yet unwilling to obtain it by a demand for absolute obedience without coupling it with an appeal to the reality of things and a reference to past failures and misfortunes. On the other side stood the representatives of a powerful and independent corporation, collectively aware that past disorders had greatly damaged it, yet unwilling to compromise on matters of principle despite the manifest reality of things. Principles and compromise, past history and present reality, law and its capacity to change things, personalities and their ability to persuade others that loyalty was part of obedience and brought rewards – all these were part of the equation. Even as they registered the edict, however, the *parlement* of Paris modified it. Article 2 was altered to exclude the second *place de concession* from being cited in any episcopal town. Since most main towns in France were episcopal towns, this effectively excluded the Huguenots from having churches sited anywhere in urban France with the exception of their stronghold towns. The majority of the other *parlements* followed Paris a year later, albeit with an ill-grace, often requiring stern letters from the king. One *parlement*, that of Rouen, resisted a full registration until 1609.

Even when legally binding, the edict still had to take root on the ground. Commissioners were sent round the provinces, generally in pairs – one catholic and the other protestant. They were well-chosen royalists with diplomatic experience and local authority. Some were former protestant officers and others were catholic masters of requests and magistrates. The difficulties encountered by these commissioners have, until recently, only been known through the very scattered record of their activities. Now, however, thanks to the discovery and publication of the *procès-verbal* recording the visitations of the commissioners of Dauphiné, we can more accurately assess the problems they encountered.[52] The commissioners were nominated a month before the *parlement* of Grenoble registered the edict in September 1599, the first to do so in the provinces after Paris. They began receiving suits in October and commenced a series of visitations throughout the province in the following month. The bulk of the visitations were completed either by them or their representatives before the end of the year, but contentious matters were still being decided by some of the commissioners even as late as 1601. The commissioners themselves were no strangers either to the province or

52. E. Rabut, 1987.

the problems the civil wars had created. Ennemond Rabot, seigneur d'Illins was the first president of the *parlement* at Grenoble, a catholic royalist of proven prudence and sound judgement. The commissioner for the protestants was their former regional military commander, François de Bonne, seigneur de Lesdiguières. Responsible for a good deal of the destruction caused in the civil wars, he was now given the task of undoing the damage and putting his considerable political abilities to work. The third Dauphiné commissioner was an outsider, Méric de Vic, who had already displayed his abilities to sort out difficult problems when he had been despatched in 1597 to deal with the debts of the city of Lyon.

The hearings of the Dauphiné commissioners reveal, firstly, the sheer intractability of some of the local problems they confronted. Villages where there was a catholic population or a local seigneur of a mind to resist the edict could frustrate the commissioners for years. There were contested accounts of numbers belonging to the rival confessions; differing memories of the supposed ancestry of the Huguenot churches in the neighbourhood; refusals to let refugees back to their property; dreadful testimonies of people frightened by what had happened to them in the past. In the valley of the Oulx, it was only finally in 1614 that the commissioners succeeded in establishing the protestant rights to worship allowed under the edict.

Many of the difficult problems they faced are readily understandable. One curious feature of French protestantism was that the majority of its services up to 1598 were not held in purpose-built churches but in abandoned or seized catholic buildings. Given that the edict of Nantes required these to be returned to the old faith (articles 9, 10, and 11), it was necessary to build afresh. The commissioners were called on to decide the precise location of the new churches (generally off the main thoroughfare and not close to a catholic place of worship), and the money had to be raised to build them (usually by means of subscriptions from the faithful with occasional gifts from localities and prominent local patrons).

These, however, were issues which the commissioners could try to resolve on a practical basis. Others risked placing the commissioners in conflict with powerful local interests. They were asked, for example, to resolve questions relating to the confessional balance of town councils. These were delicate matters, likely to inflame the petty squabbles between local notables afresh. When necessary, the commissioners intervened by means of regulation, thus contributing to the greater interventionism in municipal life which was a feature of the Henrician regime. When it came to matters of ecclesiastical benefices, however, the commissioners stepped into an even more confused world of alienated and disputed rights. In practice they had to lay down some general rules and hope that an episcopal visitation would sort out the remaining problems.

By far the most fascinating part of these records, however, is what they reveal of the mentality of both the supplicants and the commissioners. Through these records, we encounter the reality of the confessional divide, an inherited fact, comprehended in a relatively undogmatic fashion. 'I am a Christian by the grace of God, but not a theologian' said one of their protestant suitors. 'I believe assuredly that I am in the true church, containing the infallible mark of pure doctrine.' As another said, religious unity was 'more to be desired than hoped for'. On some matters, the leading figures from both confessions found, somewhat to their surprise, that they were at one – over, for example, the abolition of abbeys of misrule, masques and charivari which encouraged immorality. For their part, the commissioners encouraged local communities to assemble together and swear solemnly to one another to live in good neighbourliness under the king's authority. Sometimes they persuaded squabbling local notables to give the lead by embracing each other in public and swearing to 'put aside all their adversities'. In this way, stability was nurtured gradually and from below, from the roots of local sociability which the civil wars had only temporarily trampled on.

The experience of the commissioners in Dauphiné could doubtless be replicated in the other localities. There were other provinces besides Burgundy where they encountered opposition from orthodox, crypto-League catholics in provincial estates or town councils.[53] In the provinces of the north and east, with their scattered protestant communities and League loyalties, the siting of the *places de concession*, provoked particular contestation. In the whole of Picardy, only two sites for worship were initially established under the terms of the edict although, even in 1650, there were nearly 10,000 protestants in the province. Henri IV eventually gave personal permission for other sites in Calais and Abbeville to be added to these in order to modify the rigours of the edict. In neighbouring Champagne, the commissioners settled disputes between Huguenot communities, each of which wanted to be chosen as the *place de concession*. There were repeated difficulties with the siting of churches in the suburbs of main towns. In Paris, the village of Ablon was eventually chosen and the protestant church was built in a street called (providentially, according to the

---

53. J. Proudhon, 1959, 225–49. D. Ligou, 1968, pp. 23–5.

protestants) the *chemin des Bannis*.[54] Later, in 1606, the journey from Paris to Ablon was so frustrating to the protestants that the government, under Sully's insistence, allowed the church to move to Charenton, and thus to disregard the strict terms of the edict. In this, as in numerous other instances, the edict of Nantes was rendered a success because it was not enforced too rigidly on either side.

In some respects, therefore, the Huguenots were not so much under the edict as under the king's good favour. Henri IV tried to ensure that his own personal religious persuasions remained out of the public gaze, 'one of the great mysteries of Europe' as he declared. In its public response to the series of religious issues following the edict, Henri IV's regime acted like a gently rolling boulder which, as it went, knocked out for itself a broader path. Each decision which favoured one side was paralleled by a similar gesture towards the other. If the government supported the Jesuits' college at La Flèche, then he granted the protestants their college at Die. If he accepted the Jesuits back into Paris, then he agreed to move the protestant church to Charenton. If he appointed the Jesuit Father, Pierre Coton, as his confessor, then he promoted the protestant theologian and controversialist, Pierre Du Moulin, as his almoner. Only occasionally did a more personal agenda for attempting to unite the two faiths, perhaps under a national council or colloquy, rise to the surface. When it did so (as in 1607–8) it was promptly rejected by both sides as apostasy.[55] The notable royal tact was deployed too. Henri IV remembered past loyalties and forgot past wrongs. He ensured that protestants – even the zealot Agrippa d'Aubigné – were welcomed at his newly-established court. Protestants who abjured (following the example set by the king) were not given such special preference by the king as to give offence to their former co-religionists. In the management of the Huguenot grandees, he displayed the combination of tact and firmness which characterised all his relations with the nobility. (See below, ch. 6.) It was partly as a result of this achievement that the protestant aristocrats – Lesdiguières in Dauphiné and La Trémoille in Poitou – did not associate themselves directly with Huguenot zealots in the decade after Henri IV's death. He also neutralised, albeit with more brusqueness, the influence of aristocratic Huguenot ladies who proselytised for the faith without always considering the consequences. Madame de Condé remained

54. J. Pannier, 1911, pp. 101 etc.
55. W.B. Patterson, 1975, 223–44. Estoile, [1948], pp. 271–2. François Hotman's son, Jean Hotman de Villiers, a diplomat, was much involved in the proposals of 1606–7.

permanently incarcerated and the king's sister, Catherine de Bourbon, was put under enormous pressure to follow the king's apostasy. She did not give way. But her marriage in January 1599 to the catholic Henri de Lorraine, marquis du Pont, was part of the king's linking the marriages of his higher nobility to his broader strategies.[56]

In a larger context, the government used protestant talents at court and in administration. Sully's Arsenal employed Huguenot artillery experts like Gillot and treasurers like Claude Arnauld. His financial ministry enjoyed the support of protestant bankers like the Tallemand family and the Héroard.[57] The court physicians – the most famous of whom was Théodore Turquet de Mayerne, later a physician to James I, who appreciated his irenicism – were mainly protestants.[58] Henri's châteaux were reconstructed by individuals from the dynasties of protestant architects at work in France, such as Salomon de Brosse (1562–1624) and J. Androuet du Cerceau.[59] Inside, côteries of Huguenot decorators and artists provided their décor. Protestant engravers provided the drawings for emblematic coins at the royal mint. They were never, however, a dominant influence amongst Henri IV's image-makers.[60] Although purveyors and decorators at court, these protestants still retained a distinctive mental view as a result of their religion and background. Their presence provided a distinctive flavour to the first Bourbon's court. They curtailed the elaborate baroque tendencies of Henri III. They supported French culture as against Italianate influences. They helped to develop French classicism as the expression of beauty through ordered, yet simple, classical proportions. In their propaganda, they stressed that the court played a positive part in achieving peace through royal beneficence and obedience to the law.

In some respects, the edict of Nantes completed the process of shaping protestantism into a marginal religion in France. By placing their churches on the margins of French cities it indicated their position in French society at large. In some cities, they gained new adherents; in Rouen, for example, the protestants finally settled down (before the edict, they had behaved like their emblem, the ark, and their meeting place had floated from one location to another in the city during the civil wars), even gaining the adhesion of the prominent

56. R. Ritter, 1985, II, chs xvii and xviii.
57. J. Pannier, 1911, pp. 180–87; B. Barbiche, 1978, p. 191.
58. R. Mousnier, 1970, pp. 57–60.
59. E.g. R. Coope, 1972.
60. F. Bardon, 1974, pp. 177–89.

merchant family, the Legendre.[61] In Paris, a number of resolute protestants took advantage of the brisk trade in offices and invested there. Some, like Gilles de Maupeou, an intendant of finances and the grandfather to Louis XIV's ill-fated financier, Nicolas Fouquet, turned to protestantism to secure Sully's patronage.[62] Sully certainly advanced some protestants in the provincial administration of roads, bridges and artillery, for which he was responsible. Even Mère Angélique – a kind of spiritual St Theresa to many Parisian magistrates – briefly found refuge in La Rochelle in 1607–8. In the Midi, despite some abjurations in traditionally strong protestant cities like Montpellier, protestantism remained alive and vigorous under the edict of Nantes. Indeed, in 1621, the financial administration and many of the town councils of at least three dioceses of the Midi deserted to the Huguenot rebel cause. Historical estimates tend to suggest that, under Henri IV, French protestantism held its own, but not much more. (See Fig. 3.) It was the decade of the 1620s which would prove the test of fire for French protestantism.

But an edict could not change people's minds. The old venomous sectarianism remained in people's language and memories. A police officer, reliving the collective memories of 1572 perhaps, was astonished to find himself in one of his own cells in 1598 for calling someone a Huguenot dog. In 1605, there was an outbreak of sectarian disorders in Paris caused by some student handbills.[63] The duke of La Force warned his wife of another St Bartholomew's Day massacre. After the construction of the protestant church at Charenton in the suburbs of Paris, the consistory court was obliged to cover the classical marble frontage of the new building with plaster in order to remove the offensive slogans which had been painted there.[64] This church was, in fact, destroyed by arson in a street riot in 1622, but it is easy to imagine that such destruction might have occurred a decade earlier in the weeks of tension leading to Henri IV's assassination.[65]

There is a sense in which it was important that religious debate and controversy continued, for this meant that neither side had gained a decisive victory. So long as this was the case, there was also hope on

---

61. P. Benedict, 1981, pp. 230–2; cf. the example of Caen, explored in M.S. Lamet, 1979, pp. 439–40.

62. G. de Maupeou, 1959, pp. 120–37; see also, n. 53, above.

63. Estoile, [1948], p. 170. The incident coincided with the season of St Bartholomew and the time when the protestants were due to surrender some of their *places de sûreté*.

64. J. Pannier, 1911, pp. 454–61.

65. Ibid., pp. 544–61.

both sides. Henri IV never destroyed these hopes. In practice, although he made no secret of his dislike for Huguenot assemblies, he was reluctantly persuaded to let them meet from time to time. (See Fig. 3.) The assembly of Saumur in 1601 prevailed upon him to accept the nomination of two protestant deputies to reside permanently at court to bring to his attention their particular problems. He agreed to allow the assembly of 1605 at Châtellerault so long as the assembly did not prepare any general *cahier* of grievances but merely nominated two further protestant deputies. At the assembly of 1608, the king's letters ordered the delegates merely to elect their deputies and dismiss without further discussion; however, the letters were diplomatically 'held up in the post' for five days so that some debate of issues in common was able to take place.

Some attempts to find another 'protector' may have taken place from time to time; but James I of England (on whom such hopes were centred) refused to give them any encouragement. The assemblies therefore became something of a sounding board where protestant zealots could let off steam. All this, of course, would change once a government in Paris appeared to threaten protestant rights. At the first political assembly following Henri IV's assassination, the old warrior-poet d'Aubigné was elected to represent Poitou. Once arrived at Saumur, he argued that the queen mother, Marie de Médicis, was not a legitimate ruler since she had not been elected by the estates general. Although his views apparently scandalised some of his audience, he was nonetheless elected to represent the assembly at court and to present its grievances. When it came to his audience with the queen mother, he refused to kneel, boldly explaining that 'reverence, not bowing the knee, was all that they owed the king'.[66] But the political theory which d'Aubigné was evoking in this gesture had largely been eclipsed by this date. His fellow delegate to the court from the assembly at Saumur, André Rivet, was so shocked by d'Aubigné's audacity that he was scarcely able to maintain his own composure. His own speech stressed the personal and unreserved loyalty owed by everyone in the land, including protestants.[67] He referred proudly to the articles of the protestant discipline and confession of 1559, affirming the divine origins of all forms of political sovereignty and enjoining believers to obedience to their monarchy. In this speech, Rivet reflected the monarchical cult which had developed amongst the professors at the protestant academy in Saumur.[68] It was

66. d'Aubigné, [1877], XI, 83–4.
67. Bib. Prot. MS 708 ff. 100–1.
68. H. Kretzer, 1977, 54–75.

left to a Scot there to continue to argue the case for a 'mutual obligation' between prince and people.[69] In any case, Henri IV's regime did not deny the reality of a mutual obligation. At every turn, royal spokesmen emphasised that the king took his responsibilities to his people more seriously than anything else. Bouillon, among many others, had found it difficult to argue against the royal spokeman, sent to him in 1594–95, who openly said that nothing was more pernicious than princes who believed that they could legitimately use an absolute authority over their subjects as though kings were gods.[70] A belief in 'sovereign power' was clearly nonsense, the representative had continued, because no one could, given man's corruption, render up everything to his sovereign. But because a prince and his people were mortals, this was no reason not to continue 'loving, serving and revering' them. Princes had to inspire a 'true sense of godly affection'. And here was where there was a continuing division between those protestants like d'Aubigné who continued to believe that an elective assembly constituted the only mechanism by which that 'mutual obligation' could be secured, and the rest who were persuaded that a more informal, personal and 'affective' form of politics, such as Henri IV had done so much to foster, would provide an equally satisfactory guarantee.

So the 'universal quarrel', as James I called the polemics across the confessional divide, went on. The fact that the protestants were only a small minority in France was not apparent from the quantity of their publications: almost half the hundred editions noted for 1600 in a recent inventory, were by protestants.[71] Towns like Nîmes, Orange, Die and Montélimar arranged their own municipal disputations to acquire a little brief glory in it. The provincial printing centres still echoed to the debates and pamphlets of the sectarian past – Lyon answering those produced in Geneva, Bordeaux replying to those from Saumur.[72] The king only intervened occasionally to censor particularly obnoxious examples – those which touched on Antichrist, a particularly sensitive doctrine, or those plays which had a contemporary political message underneath their religious theme.[73] His

69. Boyd was professor at Saumur from 1604–14. His *Commentary on the Epistle to the Ephesians* was later published by André Rivet in 1652.

70. Sully, [1970–88], I, 508–19.

71. *Henri IV et la reconstruction du royaume*, 1989, p. 148.

72. Pierre Du Moulin, the chief protestant controversialist, is treated in L. Rimbault, 1966, esp. pp. 26–61. For provincial disputations, see M.S. Lamet, 1979, pp. 433–6 (Caen); P. Koch, 1940, 9–21 (Nîmes); P. Joutard, 1976, pp. 26–31 (Lyon); L. Desgraves, 1960, pp. xvi–xxxii and bibliographical descriptions (La Rochelle).

73. A. Soman, 1973, pp. 273–88.

promises – given in equal measure to both sides and equally tardily put into practice – encouraged hopes. Promises to allow Jesuits back into the realm in 1601 (not performed until September 1603); to accept the decrees of the Council of Trent (never enacted); promises to support the salaries of pastors (always in arrears) – all acted as useful tensions in France's delicately cantilevered state. With some justice, Henri IV could say – as he did to the English ambassador, Sir George Carew – that 'in according the factions of religion, or at least in containing of them in peace the one with the other . . . il pouvoit faire leçon à tous les autres Roys, *viz* He might read lecture to all other princes'.[74]

74. G. Carew, [1749], p. 441.

CHAPTER FIVE
Financial Recovery

THE SECRET OF FINANCE

French royal finances were a complex arcanum in the *ancien régime*. Besides the king, only the two (from around 1600) intendants of finance who advised the council of finance (*conseil des finances*), the *contrôleur* of finance and (when there was one) the *surintendant* of finance were privy to its secrets. Each year, the intendants drew up a draft budget (*état du roi*) by December. When the king had approved it, three copies of the budget were retained, one for the king, one for the royal treasurer and a third for the archives of the council. On the basis of this budget, the main tax, the *taille*, was repartitioned among the financial regions with the assistance of regional treasurers, beginning each August. In 16 regions (*généralités*) they supervised local officials called *élus* dispersed through 140 *élections* which, in turn, saw to the appointment of the tax among the 23,200 or so parishes in the *pays d'élection*.[1] There were, in addition, the 'small generalities' in the provinces of Burgundy, Provence, Languedoc and Dauphiné – 'small' because the amounts of revenue they collected for the central treasury were much smaller than the others in relation to their geographical size. In some provinces (Brittany, Dauphiné and Normandy), *élus* or

---

1. This account is based on the widely known *Treatise of Finance* which was drawn up under Sully's instruction and which took the budget of 1607 as its exemplar. It was perhaps the first budget to receive widespread circulation. It was used by deputies to the estates general of 1614 as the basis for their own deliberations on French finances (BN MS Fr 4020 f. 355 *et seq.*). Cf. D.J. Buisseret, 1968, pp. 57–8. This chapter has been revised particularly in the light of the fundamental new work by Françoise Bayard, (1984), and (in a regional perspective) that of J.B. Collins, (1988).

other royal officials oversaw the apportionment and collection of the *taille*. In others (Languedoc, Provence, Guyenne and Burgundy), officials appointed by local representative assemblies did the job. These assemblies retained a degree of authority over how much tax was collected and these were the true *pays d'états*. Periodically money was transported from the provincial treasuries to the central treasury, but, wherever practicable, local expenditures were 'assigned' on local receipts to avoid the enormous costs (*charges*) and risks of transporting large sums of money by pack-horse around this huge kingdom. All the details of repartition, collection and transhipment were supposed to be kept secret and, one month after the end of the financial year, the provincial treasurers were required to submit their accounts to the chief treasurer who accumulated them into a final account (*état au vrai*) which was eventually verified by the intendants and the council of finance. All accounts eventually fell under the scrutiny of the *chambre des comptes*, a sovereign court with awesome powers over all royal treasurers.[2]

Most other sources of revenues – indirect taxes, *gabelles* (the tax on the sale of salt in various regions of France) and internal customs (most of which was known as the *cinq grosses fermes*) – were the subject of individual contracts with tax farmers. Bids for tax-farms went to the highest bidder at an auction (*aux enchères*) which gave a certain transparency to this part of the taxation system. However, the individual presenting the bid was often a front-man (*prêt-nom*) for a syndicate of officers and financiers. In the bid, vetted by the intendants and submitted to the council of finance, the bidder had to give detailed information about his backers (*cautions*) before a contract was finally issued. It was in the nature of the exercise that the precise details of tax-farm syndicates rarely became public knowledge although the process itself was both widely known and vociferously criticised. Sales of royal offices were undertaken in a similar way with revenues from the sales being handled by a special treasurer.

The debts of the French monarchy cannot be readily separated out from the tax-farming mechanisms. This was because advances on tax-receipts were often negotiated as part of the contract with tax-farmers, or bankers were assigned tax-farm revenues as security for their loans to the king. The majority of loans from individual bankers were assigned in some fashion upon receipts or guaranteed upon a public body, although this was not the case in respect of loans from

---

2. Ibid., chs iii and iv. Cf. the *règlements* on the subject of the budget in BN MS Fr.16626 (Feb. 1571, May 1582, Apr. 1600).

foreign princes and governments. Before and during the civil wars, the French monarchy relied extensively, though never exclusively, on loans negotiated with Italian banking syndicates, headed by the Bonvisi, Rucellai, Zametti and Capponi clans. The civil wars had, however, made loans to the French monarchy a particularly risky enterprise for those who were not *régnicoles*, i.e. those whose origins lay outside the kingdom. In any case, some of the remaining Italian-based syndicates backed the League. In all such loans, secrecy was regarded as particularly important to sustaining the king's creditworthiness with his bankers.

In sum, the French fiscal system was an extraordinary edifice. It was decentralised, cumbersome, informal and secretive, yet capable of raising prodigious revenue and undoubtedly the centrepiece of the monarchy. But every fiscal system breathes through its evasions and these were equally awesome. Estimating the likely yield of taxes, not to mention future expenditures, was a highly speculative affair. Even Sully, who invested a good deal of time in the process, was often adrift in his estimates by over a third. Ensuring a regular receipt of revenue in the central treasury was an intractable problem and, in wartime, a severe constraint. By the accession of Henri IV, most of the royal treasurers were office-holders who had purchased their offices. The accounting procedures were slow and legalistic; thus Vincent Bouhier, the chief treasurer in 1605, did not present his accounts to the *chambre des comptes* until 1617.[3] So the possibilities for peculation and corruption were endless, the hallmark of the *ancien régime*. Yet demands for reform from the estates general were treated with suspicion, like their desire to be told of the king's true financial position; all statistics which were released were massaged to suit the occasion. Any reform of royal finance therefore had to come from within. The suspicion of corrupt practices remained deeply ingrained among those who were not a party to its secrets. The author of the book entitled *The Secret of the Finances* (1581) supported the demands of the provincial estates for greater public accountability. It complained that no account was taken of the people's ability to pay, and that there were 60,000 surplus officers in royal service; it threatened, too, to reveal the names of 214 families who had grown rich from the profits of royal financial administration and tax-farming.[4]

This system did not completely collapse during the civil wars but it

3. F. Bayard, 1984, p. 115.
4. N. Froumenteau (probably a pseudonym for the protestant publicist N. Barnaud), *Le secret des thrésors* (2nd edn *finances*), (n.p. 1581).

proved hopelessly inadequate.[5] The civil wars cut the king's income from the *taille* and at the same time increased his military expenditure. The king had to borrow money, sometimes from the financial officers themselves. Once peace came, however, he was obliged to attempt to liquidate these debts at a time when it was politically imprudent to increase taxation. By 1588, when the king was forced to present a budgetary statement to the estates general, he chose to declare a capital debt of 138 million *livres* and a deficit of 12 million *livres* on that year's income.[6] Like all such figures, however, these should not be taken at face value. Contemporaries generally included the mortgaged royal domains and forests amongst the capital debt, much of which had already been alienated by 1560. It also embraced the *rentes* as well as other secured and unsecured loans to Italian financiers and other foreign powers. The French king owed money to, amongst others, Elizabeth I, many German princes, the grand duke of Tuscany and the Swiss cantons. There was also an outstanding debt of about 1.8 million *livres* on Lyon, some of it originating before the civil wars began. Even the crown jewels were mortgaged to Orazio Rucellai, to whom the king owed in 1589 over a quarter of a million *livres*.[7]

So, by Henri IV's accession, there was a surreal quality to French finances which it is as difficult for historians to interpret as it was for contemporaries to accept. It was undoubtedly the case that the levels of extraordinary taxation had risen substantially in the reign of Henri III, but so had the debts. Contemporaries tended to ignore the effects of inflation and to regard the discrepancy as the results of corruption. They also did not include the creation of offices, their sale and resale, as part of royal borrowing, although it was a process intimately connected with the national debt. It offered an immediate, additional source of revenue; yet, in the longer term, the payment of salaries to newly created officers constituted another kind of interest charged to the revenue, even though the king regularly defaulted on their payment. Contemporaries were only too keenly aware of the money raised and despatched from local treasuries to the exchequer. Yet the king regularly claimed to be without ready money, and unable to satisfy the realm's most immediate and pressing needs. The truth of the matter was that, especially in a time of war, these resources were all too easily ransacked and diverted by provincial warlords and their treasurers, sometimes with perfectly valid assignations granted by the

---

5. Martin Wolfe, 1972, chs vi and vii.
6. R.J. Bonney, 1981, p. 34.
7. B. Barbiche, 1978, pp. 80–2. AN 120 AP 34, ff. 15–51.

council of finance.[8] To contemporaries, however, the problem lay in corruption. The spiralling creation of supernumerary offices to pay for debts gave them good cause to believe that they faced a dropsical administration, limp with malversation and apparently incapable of undertaking its own reform.

The *surintendant* of finance and his colleagues as intendants of finance were the most vulnerable to these charges of corruption. François d'O, seigneur de Frênes and Maillebois (1551–94), was *surintendant* from 1578 until his death and widely held to have presided over a cabal of tax farmers and foreign financiers which had diverted large sums of public money into private pockets.[9] When he died, his house in Paris was ransacked by angry Parisians claiming to be his creditors.[10] Royal treasurers, *trésoriers de l'épargne* and others were also suspected of corruption because there was no public treasury and large supplies of money were thus often stored in their private houses. The office of treasurer was an expensive one and attracted rich individuals to it because there was a handling charge on all cash which passed through the treasurers' hands as well as interest on all short-term loans.[11] A succession of treasurers required special royal immunity from investigation for their alleged financial irregularities.[12] The popular perception as to their corruptibility was strengthened by the discovery of a large coin hoard under the floorboards of the study of Pierre Molan, the current royal treasurer, by the *Sixteen* in March 1589.[13] In 1597, Molan was the first to pay for an exemption from an enquiry into financial malpractice although, according to one senior government official, he was 'the most culpable'.[14]

To members of the *chambre des comptes* in Paris, the chief auditing court of royal finances, corruption lay most evidently in the growth of the *comptants*, directives to the royal or provincial treasurers to disburse

8. See the example cited in J.B. Collins, 'Un problème toujours mal connu: les finances d'Henri IV' in *Avènement d'Henri IV*, (1990), p. 146.

9. BN MS Fr 16626 f. 150 (the opinions of a later commentator); Cf. P. Champion, 1939, pp. 521–6 and R.J. Bonney, 1981, p. 33.

10. Estoile, [1948], pp. 433–4. Sully, [1970–88], I, 530–1. An indication of François d'O's wealth in Paris is to be found in the inventory of his Paris residence (AN (*minutier centrale*) LXXVIII, 156, 29 Oct. 1594).

11. R.J. Bonney, 1981, pp. 10–12. Cf. BN MS Fr 16626, f. 148.

12. BN MS Fr 16627 f. 47 (*règlement* on the *remonstrance* from the *chambre des comptes* in Paris following the discharge granted to François Sabatier in 1577 – which also refers to discharges for Pierre Molan and Jean de Baillon in 1563 and 1565).

13. Estoile, [1943], pp. 618–19, 647.

14. Estoile, [1948], p. 504. A. Chamberland, 1904, pp. 40–2.

money without regard to the budget and for undisclosed purposes.[15] One of its judges went through selected years of the royal accounts to show how the use of *comptants* had grown dramatically in the course of Henri III's reign in order to provide cash benefits to favourites and financiers, thus destroying the validity of the budgets and threatening the sovereignty of the *chambre des comptes*.[16] In reality, however, the budget was bound to be disrupted in wartime and, in 1586, even the fundamental distinction between ordinary and extraordinary revenues was dropped in order to release all available resources for the military effort.[17] In any case, by the accession of Henri IV, military governors, provincial estates and towns were all levying taxes without royal permission. In November 1589 a royal edict − neither the first nor the last of its kind − forbade the governors of towns from levying taxes for their garrisons without royal permission.[18] In April 1590, another prohibited all levies without proper royal authorisation. In January 1593, there was another effort to outlaw the practice and all military commanders were instructed not to seize royal funds which had been collected in local treasuries. In February 1593, taxation without royal permission was condemned in Brittany; in August illegal taxes on vineyards were prohibited.[19] These and many other expedients became part of the wartime financial burdens. The secrets of finance threatened to lie close to the butt of a pistol.

ROYAL DEBTS AND THEIR CONSEQUENCES (1589−96)

In a famous aphorism, Henri IV is supposed to have remarked that he ascended the throne as 'a King without a kingdom, a husband without a wife and a warrior without money.'[20] The search for resources dominated his military strategy as well as his political endeavours in ways which are not always fully appreciated. His dogged campaigning

---

15. For the history of the *comptants* generally, see H. Michaud, 1972, 87–150; F. Bayard, 1974b, 1–27; R.J. Bonney, 1976, 825–36.

16. BN MS Dupuy f. 52 *et seq.* (The figures are tabulated in detail in the first edition of this book).

17. BN MS Fr 16627 f. 49 (Letters patent, Paris, 16 Mar. 1587).

18. Isambert, XV, 10.

19. Ibid., 20. Valois, I, Nos 23, 118, 119, etc. See, generally, Martin Wolfe, 1972, pp. 213–16.

20. S.H. Ehrman, 1936, I, p. xxxix, quoted in R.J. Bonney, 1981.

in Normandy and his deployment of troops in Brittany during the period 1589–92 are, at first sight, incomprehensible; but his purposes are more clearly revealed in resource terms. In peacetime, these two provinces raised over a quarter of the crown's revenues; their mints coined the silver which their export markets in Spain procured. There was every reason for both sides to concentrate on winning the war here.

Henri IV also needed the expertise of the royal financial administrators of his predecessor and he was prepared to tailor his politics to secure it. In August 1589, he negotiated with François d'O for his loyalties and those of his financial circle.[21] A convinced catholic, an able soldier, someone who carried the confidence of the monarchy's creditors as well as enjoying a following in his native Normandy, François d'O was able to extract considerable concessions from the new king and, as we have seen, was amongst those responsible for the king's declaration of August 1589 whose leniency towards catholics in royal office was so offensive to his co-religionists. This was merely the first of a series of consequences to flow from the king's financial plight. In September 1589, he accepted responsibility for the discharge of Henri III's debts although he had no immediate means of satisfying these creditors.[22] This was an essential prerequisite for gaining further foreign credit from them. Some of these debts were, in fact, to the Elector Palatine (old Huguenot war debts underwritten by the king as part of the pacification of 1576) and the Elector was likely to be a significant political ally for the new king among the German protestant princes.[23] Similarly it was vital to hold the Swiss alliance and not to alienate the cantons by reneging on their loans. In a more general sense, it may have been important to try and preserve the myth that the French king would, unlike his Spanish counterpart, honour his international debts.

The king's lack of means came to dominate his military campaigns and short-term objectives. His principal mercenary captain in 1587–89 had been François, Baron de Dompmartin with whom he reached a complex agreement on 14 August 1589 to raise 1,500 cavalry for the royal army.[24] That kept an army in the field for the first few critical

21. A. Poirson, 1862–5, I, 19–31.
22. R.J. Bonney, 1981, pp. 34–5. On 24 August 1589, Henri IV accepted Henri III's debts to the duke of Württemberg and the comte de Montbéliard in return for new loan arrangements (BN MS Fr 4019, f. 36).
23. See BN MS Dupuy 848 f. 270 ('Estat au vray des sommes de deniers deues par le Roy au prince palatin . . . ').
24. L. Anquez, 1887, pp. 52–4, 206–20.

months. In December 1589, however, the king lamented that nothing defeated him more than the lack of money to pay his troops.[25] The victory at Ivry in March 1590 was not exploited because François d'O had to negotiate with the Swiss troops and satisfy their demands for pay before they would advance further. In September 1590, Henri IV was forced to lift the siege of Paris, not only because the duke of Parma had reinforced the capital, but also because part of the royal army had 'broken'. Elizabeth I's envoy reported the disbanding of her own troops from this army as 'so strange unto me as seeing of it I kanne scarce believe ytt'.[26] In July 1591, the siege of Noyon had to be abandoned in order to pay the remaining Swiss off and collect new forces raised by Christian of Anhalt from Germany. A year later, in July 1592, Anhalt also threatened to retire as he was owed over 3 million *livres*. In March 1593, there were further problems with new contingents of Swiss – the debts to Swiss cantons and colonels by this date were between 9 and 12 million *livres*. The English and Palatine governments had effectively refused to advance any further credit.[27] In 1595, the Burgundy campaign was halted because the Swiss refused to cross the Marne until they were paid what they were owed.[28]

Other consequences of royal indebtedness appear in a memorandum to the king in July 1591, prepared in all probability by François d'O at the camp of Epernay. The realm, it said, had suffered a 'great and cruel war' for three and a half years. The means to sustain it were exhausted. The domain was almost completely mortgaged; no further loans could be anticipated from towns, merchants or provincial estates with any reliability or on any scale. Even the *taille* was faltering in Normandy (the most productive province of the kingdom) where 'a great proportion of the villages were either abandoned or half depopulated.' Financial assistance from abroad was the only remaining resource. If the king's protestant allies merely gave him 'sweet talk' ('*belles parolles generalles*') then he must consider conversion to the catholic religion within six months as the only possible way to gain a general truce and open up new sources of revenue both at home and abroad. Huguenots, then and later, advised him to exploit the wealth of the catholic church more energetically, but the political dangers in

25. Henri IV, *Lettres*, III, 107–8.

26. J.B. Black, 1914, p. 27.

27. R.J. Bonney, 1981, pp. 36–7. J.B. Black, 1914, pp. 70 *et seq*. M. Greengrass, 'Henri IV et Elisabeth: les dettes d'une amitié' in *Avènement d'Henri IV*, (1990), pp. 353–70. The Palatinate began charging high rates of interest; its last major loan to the French government was on 10 April 1592.

28. R.J. Bonney, 1981, p. 35.

alienating moderate catholic opinion were far too great and, in any case, ecclesiastical wealth was already badly damaged or leased out in many places.[29] So the king ignored the advice from both sides but, by March 1593, the financial position was desperate and François Dompmartin was trying to scrape together 50,000 *écus* from the Normandy receipts to meet the most pressing and immediate of the mercenary soldiers' demands and keep them in the field.[30] While the more immediate political considerations dominated the royal decision to convert, as we have seen, there is no doubt that financial pressure pushed him in the same direction.

The pacification of the League was not, in the short term, of great financial benefit to the king. The enormous gratifications to League nobles and cities were, on paper, huge financial commitments for the royal treasury – precisely how much in total depends on when the account was drawn up, because the money was not all paid out at once.[31] Sully's account in 1605 was for just over 32 million *livres*. Already in 1594, the scale of the *comptants* reflected the enormous strains that these pensions placed on the financial administration. These pressures were increased by a string of arrears granting release from or postponement of arrears of taxation which were unpaid.[32] In April 1594, these were applied generally so that all unpaid *tailles* and military levies for the years 1589–92 were cancelled in the loyal parts of the kingdom; at the same time a delay was granted for the payment of the *tailles* in 1593.[33] The taxes levied on the French church were also abandoned for the years from 1589 to 1592.[34] The justification for these measures is to be found in the peasant rebellions and popular sedition in the south-west as well as more vocal resentments towards tax-collectors elsewhere. In the Paris region, tax receivers had to be protected by armed guards in January 1594.[35] The search for expedients to meet the royal debts continued. There were new and extensive sales of royal offices (including *alternats* – those supernumerary positions where two men shared the same office and its

29. Cf the memorandum in BN MS Fr 16626 f. 136.
30. BN MS Fr 10839 f. 40.
31. The figure of 32 million *livres* comes from Sully's memoirs (Sully, [1881] XVII, 28–30). A Poirson, 1862–65, I, 660–9 compares this with other accounts. Martin Wolfe, 1972, regards this as an inflated figure.
32. In the year 1594, just over 200 surviving decrees of the council granted tax relief to inhabitants – Valois, I, Nos 342–1873.
33. Valois, I, Nos 693, 701, 726 etc.
34. Ibid., Nos 1044, 1095, 1536 etc.
35. J. Russell Major, 1974, 6.

salary). Titles to nobility were sold in Normandy and elsewhere. The *élus*, theoretically exempt from taxation, found themselves among those who paid revenues to the king. Other officers were pressed for forced loans.[36] Inevitably, there were vigorous protests from the *chambre des comptes* and the *parlement* in Paris as well as among representative assemblies in the provinces.[37] In Dauphiné, the first royal levy to be raised without the consent of the estates began in 1594, while the estates of Normandy were also not summoned.[38] The financial problems of Henri III's reign appeared to be repeating themselves.

Like his predecessor, Henri IV publicly committed himself to reform. Although he assumed Henri III's debts and inherited his *surintendant*, Henri IV tried to distance himself from the court and its supposed corruption. When François d'O died in October 1594, the king placed the direction of finance into commission, appointing tough military commanders like Montmorency-Damville, Schomberg and the duke of Nevers to serve on it.[39] At the same time, the council of finance was to observe strict budgetary propriety, to investigate every pension and assign it properly on the revenue, to ensure that every imposition was correctly authorised by royal commission, and to record every creation of a royal office with the name of the individual who had purchased it, for how much, and the amount of the salary which was to be paid.[40]

The council set to work and, with the assistance of its administrators like Pierre Forget de Fresnes (1544–1610), Nicolas Harlay de Sancy and Pomponne de Bellièvre, it ordered investigations into alienations of the royal domain, the salt farmers and the military levies. It issued a general decree to regulate many aspects of tax collection.[41] Provincial treasurers were asked to enumerate every extraordinary tax levy and investigate the royal officials, their salaries and rights. Efforts were made to ensure that all those who should pay tax, actually did so and that villages whose tax had been reduced

36. Valois, I, Nos 1544, 2499, 1857, 2058, 2694, 2842–6, etc. R. Mousnier, 1971, pp. 132, 135.

37. Valois, I, Nos 883, 2251, 2606, 2713, etc. J. Russell Major, 1974, 7. A. Poirson, 1862–65, I, 105–8, 117–20.

38. L. Scott van Doren, 1975, 36–48. J. Russell Major, 1974, 6.

39. Bn MS Fr 16626 f. 20 (27 Nov. 1594, St Germain-en-Laye). R.J. Bonney, 1981, p. 44.

40. BN MS Fr 16626, ff. 22–3.

41. J. Russell Major, 1974, 9. R. Mousnier, 1971, pp. 151, 157 for the reform of office-holding which it attempted. DBF, XIII, cols 480–1 for Forget de Fresnes, an important royal pamphleteer, negotiator and financial administrator.

because of wartime devastation were, in fact, the ones that had suffered most. Provincial treasurers complained about the vigour of these enquiries and suggested that some of them (notably that on usury) was itself being undertaken for fiscal motives.[42] They were afraid that the council's zeal for rectitude was actually preventing the collection of essential revenue for the war against Spain.

The declaration of war against Spain in 1595 proved to be a disastrous step for the royal finances. The assistance expected from abroad by those who had advised the king to undertake the war was miserly. Catholic powers in Italy, with the exception of the duke of Tuscany, were unprepared to leave their Spanish tutelage without clear signs of the French king's ability to protect them.[43] Protestant powers did not trust him after his conversion. German princes and England offered virtually nothing while the Dutch and Swiss alone provided loans and some troops.[44] Resources had to be located within the kingdom and, as a result, expedient finance quickly overtook attempts at reform. Reductions in the *tailles* for those areas worst hit in the civil wars were authorised but the threats to the lives of tax-collectors increased. In 1596, the inhabitants of one Normandy village were accused of attacking and killing members of the armed guard sent to assist the receiver.[45] An attempt to reduce the interest paid to the *rentiers* in Paris resulted in a hostile reaction in the *parlement* of Paris while the proposal to introduce taxes on walled towns was blocked by the *cour des aides*.[46] Outright sales of the royal domain also ran into stiff resistance from the constituted bodies of the realm, and representative assemblies in provinces like Normandy demonstrated their ability to defend provincial rights as vigorously as they had done in 1579.[47]

Meanwhile, the war against Spain did not go well. The cardinal-archduke of Austria took Calais for the Spanish on 17 April 1596 and threatened the whole of Picardy. The siege of La Fère proved hard and expensive. The correspondence between Henri IV and his council of finance in the spring of 1596 is a long litany of complaints. To the Constable of France, Montmorency-Damville, he wrote in March: 'If my finances were well-regulated and I was able to pay my army and satisfy those who merit it such as the delegates from

---

42. BN MS Fr 3447 f. 60 (*remonstrances* to the council of finance, 26 Mar. 1596).
43. A. Poirson, 1862–5, II, 168. Mariéjol, 1904, pp. 408–9.
44. J.B. Black, 1914, pp. 103–7. R.J. Bonney, 1981, pp. 37–8.
45. Valois, I, No. 34128 (30 Nov, 1596 – village of Touquette near Lisieux).
46. *Revue Henri IV*, 1905–6, I, 152–63. There was also some opposition from the city of Paris (*Registres de Paris*, [1866], XI, 210–4).
47. H. Prentout, 1925, I, 338–9. Valois, I, Nos 3015, 3130.

the [*Swiss*] League, nothing would be beyond me'.[48] To Bellièvre, he demanded that a forced loan be accepted by the judges: 'I desire your reply in writing and that it be a simple "yes" or "no".'[49] Meanwhile he wrote a letter to Sully, parts of which were almost certainly fabricated by its recipient in its surviving version, but whose tone may authentically represent the king's exasperations:

> My shirts are torn, my trousers are worn out, my larder is often bare and, for two days, I have had to dine and eat out with others. My purveyors say that they can no longer feed me because they have received no money for the past six months. By this, you may judge whether I should be thus treated and whether I ought any longer to permit financiers and treasurers to let me die of hunger while they sit at well-laden and stocked tables.[50]

He was eventually driven, like his predecessor, to hold an assembly of notables. It was called, at very short notice, to Rouen for 31 August 1596; letters of invitation to participants and to constituted bodies in the polity were only issued on 25 July 1596. Henri IV was clearly anxious to avoid an estates general, believing that, as one of the members of his council of finance said, 'It was too dangerous to assemble the estates of France when the minds of those who attend are filled . . . with factions, private interests and disobedience.'[51] In all 11 bishops, 26 nobles, 24 members of the sovereign courts and 18 treasurers attended as royal nominees. There were also deputies from 15 towns who were present at the opening session of the assembly which, after many delays, began on 4 November with a speech from the king. In it, he promised that he would follow their advice and put himself in tutelage to them.[52] It was remarked in Paris that Gabrielle d'Estrées, the royal mistress, who was hidden behind a tapestry to hear his speech, later expressed some surprise at his submissiveness. 'Ventre saint gris! It is true!' he is supposed to have replied, 'But I said it with a sword at my side.'[53]

Certainly this was an assembly for which there had been little time to prepare and whose principal task was to provide the king with a

48. Henri IV, *Lettres,* IV, 512 (4 Mar. 1596).

49. J. Russell Major, 1974, 11.

50. Henri IV, *Lettres,* IV, 567.

51. J. Russell Major, 1974, 12 – quoting a remark from the memoirs of the chancellor, Philippe Hurault, comte de Cheverny.

52. Ibid., 10–14. His opening speech is reprinted in *Revue Henri IV,* 1905–6, I, 5–7.

53. Estoile, [1948], pp. 490–1.

justification for raising more taxes. The council of finance came to the
assembly with hastily drafted proposals which involved the reduction
of pensions, diminishing the interest on *rentes* and salaries, with some
additional revenues proposed in order to avoid the further sale of royal
domain. Bellièvre proposed that a specific sum – 16.05 million *livres* –
should be assigned on particular revenues and administered by a special
'Council of Good Order', perhaps nominated by the assembly of
notables, in order to ensure the regular payment of the interest on the
public debt. This would, he estimated, leave about 15 million *livres*
free for the war effort.[54] His calculations were almost certainly too
optimistic and the council of finance was dissuaded from offering this
version of the Great Contract of 1610, famous in English financial
history, to the assembly of notables. Instead, the assembly was
encouraged to investigate the numerous allegations of weaknesses in
the French financial system – the private levies of *daces* or war-time
tolls, the over-assignation of expenditures on provincial receipts and,
above all, the corruption of provincial treasurers (their *bureaux* were
disbanded in September 1596). But, by 16 January 1597, the notables
had still been unable to find the necessary financial savings or accept a
new financial resource. Henri IV was desperate and on 10 January
1597 he had been forced to enter into a major new contract with the
financiers of Italian origin, Zamet and Cenami, who agreed to advance
almost 1.5 million *livres* with which the king could meet his
immediate needs.[55] He therefore recommended that the notables
accept a five per cent sales tax (one *sol pour livre*) on all merchandise
sold in towns. Two weeks later, the proposal was reluctantly accepted
and the assembly had submitted its ponderous advice to the king for
his consideration. Many of their suggestions were laudable and
reflected recommendations made previously in 1576 and 1588. The
key question remained, as the cardinal of Florence, papal representative
in France, said, 'whether they could be put into practice'.[56]

This question was answered, at least in the short term, during the
crisis provoked by the Spanish capture of Amiens on 11 March 1597.
This victory threatened Picardy and even Paris, encouraging others to
take advantage of royal weaknesses. In addition to the protestant
malcontents, there were the dukes of Tuscany, Savoy, Mercoeur and
the comte d'Auvergne. The anticipated receipts from the sales tax
were overestimated with the result that a new series of purely financial

54. J. Russell Major, 1974, 15.
55. BN MS Fr 3447 f. 70 (copy, 10 Jan 1597).
56. R. Ritter, [1955], p. 109. The deliberations at the assembly are discussed at
length in R. Charlier-Méniolle, *l'Assemblée des notables de 1596*, 1911.

measures was quickly required. These included new offices in every lesser jurisdiction in the kingdom, the sale of nobility, the renewed sale of royal domain and forced loans on officials in Paris.[57] There was a predictable response from the constituted bodies of the realm. The *chambre des comptes* in Paris refused to register some of the measures, saying that it had heard all too much about the king's necessity and not enough about the needs of his subjects.[58] The *parlement* of Paris proved even less sympathetic. The judges submitted a lengthy memorandum to the king which echoed many of the public complaints voiced by Froumenteau.[59] They wanted to relieve the people's poverty by reforming the royal finances. The latter needed better management. Court pensions, gifts and salaries should be reduced, surplus offices removed and the practice of assigning expenditures to revenues which were already committed elsewhere should cease. They demanded an investigation into the profits of financiers and suggested the establishment of a standing 'Council of Good Order'. Each *parlement* would nominate six *conseillers* and the king would choose from amongst the nominations 12 collaborators to undertake the task of reform. All this would have to occur before the *parlement* would register any of the proposed new taxes. On 13 April, the king attempted to win their support with important concessions.[60] He offered to establish a *chambre de justice* to investigate financial corruption – the fourth since 1574. He also agreed to set up their special council to administer the interest on the public debt.

Henri IV never forgot this critical month. His sense of weakened authority is expressed in the recorded version of the speech he made when he finally paid a visit to the *parlement* on 21 May 1597 to enjoin the magistrates to register the nine disputed fiscal edicts in a formal *lit de justice* ceremony.[61] Despite the explicit royal command, however, the magistrates refused to cooperate. As Louis XIV's chancellor, the third Pierre Séguier, noted three quarters of a century later, the edicts were not to be found in the *parlement*'s register. For his part, too, Henri IV did not keep his promises. The *chambre de justice* was abolished in July after it had extracted some money from royal financiers. The special council was never given any money to

---

57. R.J. Bonney, 1981, pp. 50–1. *Revue Henri IV*, 1909, II, 113–15.
58. Ibid., and *Registres de Paris*, [1866], XI, 361–72.
59. BN MS Fr 3888 ff. 133 et seq. ('Une remonstrance au roi sur les désordres de l'état et la mauvaise administration des finances').
60. J. Russell Major, 1974, 24–5. A. Chamberland, 1904.
61. Henri IV, *Lettres*, IV, 764; Sarah Hanley, 1983, pp. 223–5.

administer and it fell into disuse very rapidly, if it ever effectively met at all. By July 1597, the king was even abandoning the council of finance itself and approaching individual intendants of finance like Sublet d'Heudicourt, Saldagne d'Incarville and Harlay de Sancy to provide him with revenue and financial management.

The failure of his council of finance, the uselessness of mercenary armies without financial reserves to pay for them, the handling of royal debts in wartime, and the stubborn protectiveness of the constituted bodies were all important political lessons. The problem which remained was this: in what direction, and how, could financial reform be made to assist the exercise of political authority, rather than being its endless, unhappy and destructive burden.

SULLY'S RISE TO POWER

Genuine financial recovery was out of the question so long as the monarchy remained at war. It only began in earnest after 1598 and has always been associated with Henri IV's famous finance minister, Maximilien de Béthune, baron (later, in 1606, duke) of Sully. He was born in December 1559 into a cadet line of the House of Béthune, which had just converted to protestantism. Sully made much of this lineage, claiming descent from the Counts of Flanders as well as affinities with the Houses of Horne and Montigny.[62] In fact, although his memoirs carefully disguised the fact, both his marriages were to well-placed families in royal administration. His first wife, Anne de Courtenay, whom he married in 1583, was descended from a family which had provided several *présidents* to the *chambre des comptes*. His second wife, Rachel de Cochefilet, whom he married almost three years after Anne's death, had been previously married to François Hurault, a *maître des requêtes*. In 1572, Sully had pledged himself to Henri of Navarre and followed him to Gascony at the age of 16. He rose through the Huguenot army and, by his fidelity to Henri IV and the respect in which he was held by catholics (amongst whom he counted both friends and relatives), he acquired positions of trust in royal service towards the end of the wars of the League. His first

---

62. In a dispute with the duke of Nevers, for example, Sully was aggrieved that his adversary treated him as 'un simple gentilhomme' whereas, as he informed the duke of Nevers, the princes of the House of Béthune had been counts of Nevers well before the Gonzaga family had acquired the title (Sully, [1970–88], I, 189). Cf. B. Barbiche, 1978, pp. 23–7; D.J. Buisseret, 1968, ch. ii.

experiences with royal finances involved the fleecing of merchants on barges on the Seine close by his family château at Rosny.[63] Sully prided himself on one capture of 7,000 *écus* which he retained as a recompense for his own losses from his estates whilst in the king's service.[64]

From 1594, he was a reporter to the privy council and the king had him in mind (according to Sully) for the new council of finance, formed after François d'O's death on 25 November 1594.[65] In fact, he was not appointed to it and became, instead, one of the commissioners delegated by the council in 1595 and 1596 to go round the *élections* to conduct broad-ranging investigations of maladministration and corruption. Sully later exaggerated the success of his own mission (two generalities visited became four, four *receveurs* arrested became eight, 300,000 *écus* raised in revenue became 500,000 *écus* . . .), but it is clear that his ruthless zeal earned him the dislike of provincial treasurers and the respect of the hard-pressed king.[66] Sully later pretended in his memoirs that, from this moment, he was the king's most respected councillor. In fact, he was still inexperienced in comparison with Bellièvre, Forget de Fresnes or Harlay de Sancy. He was a protestant and they were catholics. He was also rather younger than they were. He still had some way to go and, in some respects, he remained a distinctive, even unusual, figure, a soldier-financier, a captain of the accounts. At the assembly of notables, the difference between Bellièvre's cautious, compromising and conciliatory approach and Sully's more brutal expedients for taxation was apparent.[67] It should not be drawn too strongly, though, for Sully and Bellièvre were both aware of the enormous difference between income and expenditure and the need to reconcile interest groups to the king when demanding extra taxation from them. They were both similarly ambiguous towards the *sol pour livre* which was the only concrete proposal to emerge from the assembly of notables to solve the short-term deficit. During the recovery of Amiens, Sully's fiscal expedients became imperative, however, and his ruthlessness at that time earned him the king's enduring confidence. In 1598, he was appointed superintendent of finance (*surintendant des finances*) and, thereafter, rapidly increased his authority.[68] He was named successively

63. Sully, [1970–88], I, p. 211.
64. Ibid., pp. 279–80.
65. B. Barbiche, 1978, p. 40.
66. A. Chamberland, 1905–6, in *Revue Henri IV*, 1905–6, I.
67. J. Russell Major, 1966.
68. B. Barbiche and D.J. Buisseret, 1965, 538–43.

grand voyer de France (in charge of roads and bridges) and *grand maître de l'artillerie* (in charge of fortifications) in 1599.[69] After 1600, his authority grew at the expense of the council of finance which gradually merged into another branch of the king's council, the council of state. Within the privy council, Sully became (with Bellièvre and Villeroy) a member of the king's inner cabinet. Villeroy was in charge of foreign affairs and Bellièvre was chancellor. Not until December 1604, however, was Bellièvre relieved of his grip upon internal affairs by the appointment of Sillery as Keeper of the Seals.[70] Even then, the chancellor refused to surrender the seals until October of the following year. Until then, the budgets and important accounts carried the signatures of Bellièvre, Sillery and other members of the council as well as Sully's. After 1605, they appear with Sully's signature alone. According to the specialist on Sully's papers, Bernard Barbiche, it is no coincidence that the royal budgets in Sully's private archive date from 1605. The years from 1605 to 1610 are those of Sully's administrative superintendency *par excellence*.

Sully was the first to sing his own praises. After his resignation from Marie de Médicis' regency government in January 1611, he spent the next five years writing the first draft of his memoirs. He then decided to publish the first half of these in December 1638, spurred on by the success of Scipion Dupleix's work, *Henri IV*, in which his own role had been almost completely ignored, and also by the publication of the memoirs of Villeroy and the favourable reception of the published letters of cardinal d'Ossat.[71] His memoirs appeared under a longer title, now generally abbreviated to the *Oeconomies royales*. They were composed with an artificial conceit as though his secretaries, Balthazar, Maignan Moréli and others, were writing *aides-mémoire* to him ('In your travels you [*Sully*] met . . . ' etc). In fact, it is clear from his extensive annotations to successive drafts in manuscript that the work was carefully written and revised by Sully himself. His oversight of the publication even extended to setting up a printer in his château at Sully-sur-Loire to undertake the work under his own roof. To write his memoirs, Sully relied not just on a carefully organised archive of materials, but also on journals that he had dictated to his secretaries at various moments in his public life and to which he refers at various points in the text. This did not prevent considerable exaggeration, special pleading and even falsification being introduced into the

69. B. Barbiche, 1978, p. 45. Sully, 1881, XVI, 362–3.
70. B. Barbiche, 'De l'Etat de justice à l'Etat de finances (1605)' in *Avènement d'Henri IV*, 1989, p. 97.
71. Sully, [1970–88], I, intro. E.H. Dickerman, 1972.

Oeconomies royales. Some passages were rewritten for later editions. As a result, the work requires careful historical use, but its record of Sully's energy, administrative zeal and grasp of affairs is not false. It is entirely typical of the man that, in a month's enforced seclusion in his château at Rosny because of the plague in 1587, he should devote himself to drafting a complete map of his house, gardens, plants and surrounding lands, making extracts from books on topics which currently interested him, and digging and completely replanting one of his orchards.[72]

Prudent husbandry of state resources ('une bonne mesnage' was one of his favourite phrases) was his great aim. His economic thought was a domesticated version of those to be found in classical sources such as Xenophon. National budgets, like those of any seigneury, had to have an equilibrium. Revenues could not be assigned where there were no assignable funds. These modest nostrums are confirmed in his private papers which were deposited in the National Archives in Paris in 1955.[73] They reveal Sully's jackdaw eye for detail, his understanding of the budgetary mechanism and of accounting procedures as well as his imaginative use of statistics. He made personal copies of his royal budgets and codified and cross-referenced them with a key of over 2,000 symbols.[74] He compiled lists of the royal gifts and pensions as well as the household expenses as though it were his own estates that he was directing.[75] His extensive enquires ranged into legal intricacies and back to the malversation of the previous reign.[76] This is how the *Oeconomies royales* described his activity on the commission (*chevauchée*) around the generalities of Orléans and Tours in the Autumn of 1596:

> The treasurers, *élus*, controllers and their clerks in the revenue offices were found to be so recalcitrant, and some of the receivers of tax so stubborn, that they refused to reply to your enquiries or to show you their tax-rolls, and made off when you set foot in their localities. In the end, given that, if you had suspended them all from their offices you would have had none to work with at all, you chose two treasurers and two *élus* from each tax office to carry out the tasks of them all and remain in office . . . . Thus, to the astonishment of these officers, you presented them with the evidence of all the acounts, both past and present, all the orders, quittances, patents, assignations and ascriptions levied on these revenues as well as the accounts for the preceding three years. You gleaned so much for the king, especially from the assignations raised to pay for old debts,

72. Sully, [1970–88], I, 170.
73. R-H. Bautier and A. Karcher-Vallée, 1959.
74. D.J. Buisseret, 1968, p. 59. Sully, [1881], 17, 298.
75. E.g. AN 120 AP 12.
76. Ibid., 30.

reimbursements for loans, old arrears for wages, *rentes* and pensions to individuals who did not merit them . . . that you put together fully 300,000 *écus*.[77]

It was a similar kind of energy which Sully brought to the management of his own estates where he cannily exploited the possibilities for horse-dealing in the civil wars, for tolls on the Loire and generally made the life of his stewards unpredictable and occasionally thoroughly miserable.

Sully enjoyed the advantages of a long period in office and the support of a king who, as Carew remarked, had an 'economical faculty for looking into matters of profit'. Henri IV sustained Sully 'in all his rough courses which he hath taken for the increasing of the revenues of the crown.' Sully's surviving correspondence, particularly with the provincial treasurers, provides ample evidence for this dictatorial high-handedness. It also displays his firm grip on the financial administration and his acute political acumen.[78] Carew added that the finance minister 'hath found great profit thereby himself.'[79] So most contemporaries believed – and the envy thereby generated returned to plague him following his disgrace in 1611. According to cardinal Richelieu's memoirs, even Henri IV had his doubts: 'The contradictions of the duke of Sully, and the suspicion that he [*Henri IV*] had of him, not as regards the fidelity of his heart but in respect of the cleanliness of his hands, meant that he was in great doubt as to whether he should support him further.'[80] The sieur d'Elbène, a lieutenant in the king's cavalry and an astute observer at court, reckoned that Sully had amassed a personal fortune of at least 2 million *écus* (6 million *livres*) and that, with the king's assassination, he ran a great risk of having his malversations exposed.

It is therefore not surprising that Sully devoted a good deal of the *Oeconomies royales* to quantifying, justifying and demonstrating the legality of the personal fortune he had acquired. The thorough research of Sully's personal fortune by Isabelle Aristide has proved, however, that he legitimately enjoyed substantial salaries, pensions and gifts from the king. (See Fig. 5.) These provided the means whereby he was able to establish a considerable landed fortune, valued at over 2

77. Sully, [1970–88], II, 105–6.
78. L. Romier, [1910], pp. 93–205 and D.J. Buisseret, [1963], edited the surviving correspondence between Sully and the generality at Caen which provides an excellent case-study of the *surintendant* in action.
79. G. Carew, [1749], pp. 480, 485.
80. Cited I. Aristide, 1990, p. 61.

million *livres* in 1610, purchasing three major estates before 1610 as well as renovating his existing estates at Rosny and Sully.[81] But Sully was scrupulous about securing letters of confirmation from the king for all gifts and pensions and having these registered in the courts. In comparison with Richelieu (whose appropriation of royal funds was on a more massive scale), Sully's fortune was modest.[82] In any case, as the *Oeconomies royales* were concerned to prove, his industry in the king's service had earned him his rewards.

THE LIQUIDATION OF THE PAST

Sully later told Sir George Carew that, when he came to the management of the revenues in 1598:

> he found . . . all things out of order, full of robbery of officers, full of confusion, no treasure, no munition, no furniture for the King's houses, and the crown, indebted three hundred millions; that is three millions of pounds sterling. Since that time . . . in February 1608, he had acquitted one hundred and thirty millions of that debt, redeeming the most part of the revenues of the crown that were mortgaged . . . [and] had brought good store of treasure into the Bastille, filled most of the arsenals with munition, [and] furnished most of the King's houses with rich tapestry.[83]

The latter part of this achievement was what most pleased the king. On 20 July 1602, the king decided (in the aftermath of the revolt of the duke of Biron) to create a contingency fund 'to provide for the security, maintenance and conservation of the state' with a treasure stored in a strong room of the Bastille to which Sully kept one of the three keys.[84] Revenue was paid *comptant* to this special treasury and, by 1605, it was becoming a remarkable sight. Four large coffers contained pieces of eight and sixteen (*sols*) in 1,465 sacks, while a further 55 sacks were in another cabinet. Forty-two barrels also contained over 2,000 sacks in them. By this date, the treasure was about 3.4 million *livres*.[85] Despite the fact that over a million was withdrawn in 1606 to raise the army of Sedan, there were over 7

81. Ibid., p. 92.
82. J. Bergin, 1985.
83. G. Carew, [1749], p. 486.
84. BN MS Dupuy 848 f. 191. *Revue Henri IV*, 1912, III, 200–9.
85. BN MS Dupuy 848 f. 192.

million *livres* in store by 1607.[86] When Henri IV died, there were still 5 millions in the store and just over 11 millions of budget surplus 'on hand' in provincial treasuries. A steady replenishment of arsenals had also been undertaken both in Paris and the provinces. Sir George Carew described the king promenading on the palisade between the Bastille and the Arsenal, boasting that 'none other hath such an alley to walk in, having at the one end thereof armour for 40,000 men ready prepared: and at the other end money to pay them, even to the end of a long war.'[87] There was an exaggeration here, since the events of 1610 would demonstrate how quickly a contingency fund would be used up on the preparations for a campaign. But, so long as it lasted, it was an important means of ensuring that the periodic crises of temporary liquidity did not afflict Henri IV's government as they had its predecessors. It was Sully's canny means of reminding the king's bankers and backers that his creditworthiness was sound and that they could not drive too hard a bargain with him. To France's neighbours it demonstrated that the king had the means to mobilise military force very quickly if this were needed.

Underwriting the growth of this treasury was an 'undeclared bankruptcy' which Sully shrewdly and effectively negotiated without endangering France's future credit. As the French historian Mariéjol put it, France's financial recovery rested upon the 'liquidation of the past'.[88] Foreign creditors required the most delicate handling, and none more so than the Swiss cantons who had invested so heavily in the French monarchy. The Swiss (who were owed 35.8 million *livres* in 1598) expressed their resentments by threatening to arrest the French ambassador to the League cantons.[89] Swiss troops were an essential part of the French royal army (the contract for them was renegotiated every five years) and the friendship of the cantons was essential to the maintenance of French influence in the Alps. In the Savoyard war, the French government accepted new terms for the Swiss contingents. In the treaty of Soleure on 20 October 1602, it was agreed to pay 1.2 million *livres* annually until the Swiss debt was entirely repaid.[90] It would have taken thirty years for this to happen but Swiss cantons and Switzer colonels were sometimes unprepared to wait so long and so they settled privately for a token repayment. In 1609, Marc Escher from Glarus, who had 13,050 *livres* of *rente* assigned

86. Ibid., ff. 194–6, 198.
87. BN MS Fr 3447 f. 54. D.J. Buisseret, 1968, ch. viii. G. Carew, [1749] p. 436.
88. Mariéjol, 1904.
89. AN 120, AP 34, ff. 79–256. R.J. Bonney, 1981, p. 55.
90. R.J. Bonney, 1981, p. 55. E. Rott, 1882, pp. 181–98.

to him and who had used every weapon of the creditor to extract the interest and principal of his debt, finally accepted 1,500 *livres* of discharge. He was later angered to learn that the difference between the *rente* and the payment he was given was transferred to the king's coffers in the Arsenal.[91] By 1607, the government in Paris thought that the debt to the Swiss had been reduced to 16.7 million *livres*, or half the amount it had been in 1602. These private deals were sometimes not as unfair as they sounded because some of the original contracts had included payment substantially in excess of the soldiers or service received.[92] Even so, the financial stability of Henri IV's government in this, and other affairs, rested on the impotence of the creditor.

Other debts with England and Tuscany were reduced in different ways. Henri IV once remarked to Elizabeth I that he wanted a speculative marriage with a dowry which would repay his debts. His engagement to Marie de Médicis in 1600 was a purely financial affair. Ferdinand I, grand duke of Tuscany, was owed 3.5 million *livres* by the king who hoped that the dowry would pay it all off. The grand duke was horrified at the size of the proposed dowry – even the Holy Roman Emperor would not have asked for so much. Eventually, by a contract drawn up on 7 March 1600, it was agreed that the grand duke should pay Henri IV 600,000 *écus* (1.8 million *livres*), of which 350,000 *écus* were to be paid *comptant* and the rest accepted as debt repayment. The deal was a favourable one to the French king (who had pressed the grand duke to act quickly by promising to marry his mistress, Henriette de Balzac d'Entragues, marquise de Verneuil, within six months if she became pregnant) and the outstanding debts of Tuscany were quietly ignored afterwards.[93] To the equally parsimonious English queen, the French debts of 4 million *livres* owed to her, with additional debts to London merchants which she had underwritten, became increasingly irksome. 'The king was waiting for her to die' before paying up, Elizabeth told the French ambassador roundly.[94] Henri IV was the 'anti-christ of ingratitude' for failing to satisfy her legitimate requests for repayment. Responding to the growing spirit of naval and commercial aggression in London, she threatened trade restrictions by way of reprisal.[95] Eventually Sully

91. *Revue Henri IV*, 1909, II, 50–60.
92. Ibid.
93. R.J. Bonney, 1981, pp. 56–7.
94. M. Greengrass, 'Henri IV et Elisabeth: les dettes d'une amitié' in *Avènement d'Henri IV*, 1989, p. 365.
95. See below, ch. vi.

negotiated a treaty in 1603 which allowed a third of France's subsidy to the Dutch to count towards France's debt repayments to England. Whether the amounts that France paid to the United Provinces (3.05 million *livres* were expended over the following five years) satisfied the entire English debt was a matter of dispute between the two countries which was not settled until after 1610.[96] It is clear that subsidies to foreign allies, disguised as debt repayments in order to continue the war against Spain while remaining at peace officially, were a useful piece of diplomacy. A past debt had, once more, been turned to a present political advantage.

The German princes were treated to a worse deal. Henri IV wrote to Prince Christian of Anhalt in 1599 that he was sure that the prince would understand the constraints: 'Those who understand the ways of the world, know that it is not only very difficult, but even impossible to re-establish oneself after such a desperate affliction as our poor state has suffered.'[97] The prince of Anhalt was accommodating but, by 1602, his patience was beginning to wear thin. The Dutch, English and the Swiss had all received compensation but the Germans, who had done the king's fighting, had received nothing.[98] It is not surprising that some German princes contemplated support for the duke of Biron's revolt in 1602. In the years from 1602 to 1605, some German princes' debts were partially satisfied but the towns, with the exception of Strasbourg, received hardly anything and the Elector Palatine was kept waiting the longest.[99] This was perhaps condign treatment for the country whose Elector had been rumoured to encourage French protestants to look to him as their protector.

If princes could not secure repayment of their debts, what chance was there for financiers of Italian origin unless there were special circumstances to assist them? Orazio Rucellai held the French crown jewels but did not succeed in reaching a settlement for his debts. It was left to his heirs after 1606 to accept payment of half of the amounts incurred by Henri III, thus releasing the crown jewels for Henri IV. Other Italian financiers – among them the Bonvisi, Sardini and Capponi – died without recompense. The Gondi received payments of 45,000 *livres* on the *cinq grosses fermes* and, in 1609, the king paid them 100,000 *livres* as the remainder on one loan and 26,490

96. R.J. Bonney, 1981, p. 56.
97. L. Anquez, 1887, p. 56.
98. Ibid., p. 58.
99. Ibid., pp. 58–67. Some of the debts were later satisfied, as with the Dutch, in the form of renewed pensions in return for promises of loyalty (BN MS Dupuy 852 f. 308).

livres as that on another.[100] Whether these represented the totality of
their loans and interest is unknown. The influence of these Italian
banking clans faded away, their role being replaced by the tax-farming
syndicates which would play a discreet but more significant role as the
century wore on. Only Sebastien Zamet managed to blend into the
changing environment. This was partly because of his immense wealth
(he claimed to be 'seigneur of 1,700,000 *écus*') and also because of the
huge loans which he made in 1597–98 to sustain the king. It was also
due in part to the fact that his political position at Henri IV's court
was a secure one.[101] He was the king's gambling partner, a personal
friend and also superintendent of the queen's household. His eldest son
and heir would marry the duke of Epernon's niece; the younger son
became the royal almoner and coadjutor to the bishop of Langres in
1607. His huge Parisian residence in the rue de la Ceriseraie was
placed at the king's disposition to lodge visiting ambassadors and royal
mistresses. Gabrielle d'Estrées died there; a pretty dancer, Angélique
Paulet, daughter of another financier, awaited the king's attentions at
Zamet's house on the day of his assassination in 1610.[102] Zamet was
repaid between 1.5 and 1.6 million *livres* during the reign; but his
rewards also came in other than purely financial form.[103]

Internal debts were also complex. Firstly, there were the various
assignations on revenues for past debts incurred by the king. Treasurers
had already been instructed not to accept any assignations from the
past unless they were currently assigned on the revenue.[104] This led to
a scramble for new assignations and pressure from the localities for
quittance from the old ones. There was a market in discounted paper
assignations and, by brusquely reflecting political realities, these
discounted debts were another harsh way of liquidating the past. Sully
spoke of 'wailing, accompanied by all kinds of special pleading' by
provincial governors and military captains.[105] Even the great officers of
state such as the Constable of France, whose own financial position
was somewhat bleak as a result of debts incurred in the wars, lamented
that his 'little assignation' on revenues in his province of Languedoc

100. J.B. Collins, 1988, p. 71.
101. Zamet's loans in Valois, I, Nos 3229, 3428, 3496, 3777–8, 4042, 4254, 4483, 4633, 4990, 5121. See Valois, II, No. 7121 for his position in the queen's service. For Zamet as the king's gaming partner, see Estoile, [1948], pp. 494, 537, 570, etc.
102. Françoise Bayard, 'Les financiers' in *Henri IV et la reconstruction du royaume* (1989), pp. 272–3.
103. J.B. Collins, 1988, p. 71.
104. BN MS Fr 16626 f. 21v.
105. Sully, [1881] XVI, 294.

had been curtailed.[106] Sully promised him that he would receive a replacement assignation and one which would be worth more than its predecessor. The message for the future was a clear one. Assignations would be harder to get and more valuable when acquired. Epernon, governor of Poitou and Saintonge, a man with a different political style from that of the Constable, proposed to appropriate for his own purposes a particular levy in his own government. Sully tore up the suggestion, calling it a 'robbery'. This almost resulted in a fight in council which Henri IV settled in Sully's favour.[107] A similar dispute occurred with the comte de Soissons, who threatened to have Sully assassinated unless his assignations for debts incurred in royal service were met. Thereafter, Sully maintained a bodyguard for his own protection. Other debts and pensions, promised to League aristocrats, were only satisfied tardily. The duke of Guise was still owed 5,000 *livres* in 1610 for a debt, the settlement of which was agreed in 1596.[108] The duke of Mayenne's debts were also not finally satisfied until 1611.[109] One of the first actions of the Regency of Marie de Médicis was to use the *comptants* to remedy these outstanding payments to League nobles.

A more difficult task was the liquidation of the *rentes*, since these creditors formed a sizeable part of the Parisian bourgeoisie which had revealed its political influence during the League. Sully's first aim was to discover the full extent of the king's liabilities and, in March 1599, a five-member commission was appointed to verify the *rentes* since 1560.[110] They identified over 36 million *livres* of *rentes* of which 7 million had been constituted as gifts of the crown and had never provided any revenue to the monarchy. By 1605, some *rentiers* had been paid no interest for seventeen years and the city provost estimated that the arrears on payments were over 60 million *livres*. Once the scale of the problem had been identified, another commission produced its recommendations in 1604 to restructure the debt. These were that certain *rentes* should be automatically discontinued without compensation, especially those of dubious legal title. Interest due in the past should be written off. Current interest

106. M. Greengrass, 1986, 291, 294.

107. G. Carew, [1749], pp. 484–6. L. Mouton, 1924, pp. 55–9. Sully, [1881], XVI, 298.

108. BN MS Dupuy 85 (Estat des deniers receues par M. de Guise . . .). Cf. BN MS Fr 10839.

109. BN MS Fr 10408 (Paiement des debtes contractés par feu Monsieur le duc de Mayenne . . .).

110. B. Barbiche, 1978, pp. 83–4.

should be reduced at varying rates, depending on how long the *rente* had been issued and on what revenues it was assigned. Thus *rentes* on the *taille* were paid at half their face-value and those on the *cinq grosses fermes* at three-quarters their value. A scheme to repurchase the *rentes* with compensation (for those that remained) would be instituted. It was an even-handed approach which attempted to preserve the validity of the legal title to *rentes* whilst reducing their practical burden to the treasury.

There was, however, a storm of protest at the measures proposed. There were genuine fears that Paris would see a repeat of the disorders which had occurred in 1588. The city provost, François Miron, conducted an able campaign against them, arguing that they went against the king's promises in *parlement* in 1597, that they would lead to lawsuits and public disorder and that the only beneficiaries would be the financiers who had failed to provide the assigned revenues for the *rentiers'* interest in the past.[111] Miron seized the treasurer's house and insisted that, since *rentes* were contracts issued, officially, in the name of the provost and the city of Paris, it was *his* credit-worthiness which was being attacked. Some changes were made to the proposals but they did not satisfy Miron. As he ruefully observed: 'Kings cannot be constrained – only in so much as it pleases them – to pay debts to their subjects.'[112] He thus raised the sensitive issue of the *mutua obligatio* which was at the centre of the struggle for political stability. But, as the king said in another context, he wanted Sully 'to increase his revenue and not to deliver justice.'[113]

Two other operations to liquidate debts led Sully into conflict with provincial authorities. One was the attempt to repurchase royal domain. In January 1603, letters of commission were sent to the treasurers, asking them to search out 'all sorts of means to accomplish the repurchase of our domain.'[114] In the following year, Sully proposed to establish a sinking fund, run by tax-farmers, who, in return for the farming of certain revenues, would undertake to repurchase part of the alienated royal domain. The scheme met with systematic objections from the sovereign courts which were not without some justice on their side. Most of these proposed contracts would run for a long time, perhaps fifteen years or more which was 'a

111. B. Schnapper, 1957, ch. 7. A. Miron de l'Espinay, 1885, pp. 206–37. Cf Sully, [1881], XVII, 16. B. Barbiche, 1978, pp. 54–6. AN 120, AP 35, ff. 68–189.

112. A. Miron de l'Espinay, 1885, pp. 230–1.

113. G. Carew, [1749], p. 487.

114. B. Barbiche, 1978, pp. 78–9. AN 120, AP 36. L. Romier, [1910], p. 235 (15 Dec. 1602).

century . . . for peace and stability to last in a state as large as this one.' The tax farmers would be guaranteed against any losses but there was no way of knowing how much domain they had redeemed if the contract was stopped before its termination. There would be endless legal cases. There was an attempt to involve provincial estates in the project, tempting them with the prospect that they could expect to pay less tax in the future if the king had a larger domain. Numerous contracts were issued after 1608 but, in the end, they would not make a great deal of difference to the king's overall financial position.[115]

Next, Sully investigated municipal debts. These are often ignored but the larger cities of France had their own budgets and had generally run up large deficits, either in attempts to protect themselves, or in pursuit of the urban political adventures of the civil wars. Marseille, for example, owed an estimated 1.55 million *livres*, Arles 700,000 *livres*.[116] Dijon's creditors, often local officials, held it to ransom for at least 240,000 *livres* in 1596. At Troyes, the mayor was arrested in 1602 by an angry creditor trying to distrain for payment.[117] Secondary towns like Dinan (debts of at least 60,000 *livres*) or Quimper (166,000 *livres*) may have carried proportionately an even heavier burden.[118] Communal property had often been mortgaged or sold off completely. Urban treasuries were, in reality, independent of royal control but, in order to raise additional funds, they generally had to gain royal permission. This was, therefore, an opportunity for Sully to investigate their debts and to use such investigations as a way of eroding some of the urban notables' adventurism which had rocked the monarchy during the civil wars. In other cases, Sully exploited his subordinate officials of roads and bridges. Progressively, Marseille, Troyes, Bordeaux and many other cities found the same even-handed, but tough-edged approach which Sully had applied to the problem of the *rentes* being applied in respect of their own debts. Commitments of dubious legal title were cancelled. Additional local levies were permitted for interest payments, repayment and even the repurchase of alienated communal property, even though some of the town oligarchies then devoted the proceeds to trying to repurchase some of

---

115. BN MS Dupuy 848 f. 131. Sully claimed in 1610 to have repurchased 80 millions; the reality was much less – perhaps 30–35 millions (Sully, [1881], XVII, 266, 437). For these efforts in Brittany, see R.S. Trullinger, 1972, p. 389 *et seq.*

116. R. Pillorget, 1975, p. 207.

117. Valois, I, Nos 2115, 5993, 7150 (imprisonment of the mayor of Troyes, 7 Sep. 1602). Statement of *rentes* issued by the Troyes municipality in BN MS Fr 10839, f. 63.

118. Figures cited in J.B. Collins, 1988, p. 74.

their franchises from the king rather than amortising their debt.[119]

So the process of liquidating the past went on, stretching out to include the rural communities, who also found themselves indebted, having contracted to pay soldiers, purchase war-supplies or provide fodder for armies. In many instances, although the interest payments were met under Henri IV, the debt remained with them for many years to come. Some Burgundian villages, for example, were still paying interest on debts incurred during the civil wars into the 1660s. Almost a decade after the pacification of Nantes, a sixth of the king's income was still devoted to paying for the civil war. Yet, in the process, tax-farms and *rentes* had re-established their value and this would have profound social consequences for the longer term.

FINANCIAL REFORM

The main contours of Sully's financial achievement appear in Fig. 4. The principal feature was a shift from direct towards indirect taxation. The total levy from the *taille* decreased from 18 million *livres* to an average of 15.85 million *livres* per year for the first decade of the new century. At the same time, Sully increased the returns from indirect taxation. This was supplemented after 1608 by significant returns from the *paulette* to the bureau of casual revenues.

The rise in indirect taxation was not entirely painless. Most of the increase came from more competitive farming of these taxes – in other words from tax farmers rather than the population at large.[120] The auctions of tax-farms were well-attended and it was a sellers' market.[121] There were numerous 'augmentations' of contracts and these were probably assisted by Sully's relentless efforts to secure the best value possible for the crown. But the main indirect tax, the *gabelles* or salt tax, was unequal in its repartition; and the areas of heavy *gabelles* found themselves burdened by increases in the price of salt and the quantities that each inhabitant was required to purchase. As the

119. For verification of debts at Troyes, see Valois, I, Nos 7825, 9637; II, Nos 10141, 10187, 14206. At Marseille, ibid., I, Nos 5058, 7891. At Clermont-Ferrand, ibid., I, 7146, 9154, 9389 etc.

120. G. Carew, [1749], p. 486: 'and where the farms of the whole realm amounted then but to 800,000 pounds sterling, this year, 1609, he had let them out for 1,000,000 pounds and that without exacting any more upon the people than was paid before, but only by reducing that to the king's coffers, which was embezzled by under-officers'.

121. F. Bayard, 1984, p. 306.

English ambassador in France, Sir George Carew, noted, this was
storing up a potential problem for the future.[122]

Not all reforms were successfully implemented. The one major
innovation in indirect taxation in the early seventeenth century, the
introduction of a shilling in the *livre* or 5 per cent sales tax on all
goods for sale at markets in the walled towns in the kingdom, proved
to be a political liability, the 'poll-tax' of its day. Known as the *sol pour
livre* or *pancarte* after the posters advertising the tax to be paid on
different kinds of goods, it had originally been proposed by the
chancellor, Bellièvre, and accepted at the assembly of notables in
1596–97. It had been expected then to raise 2.1 million *livres*. The
opposition from the constituted bodies was, however, energetic and it
was only introduced as an emergency measure for three years.[123]
There were complaints of numerous abuses in its collection, especially
in respect of the traffic in cattle and wine past the customs posts.[124]
Several walled towns sued successfully to be free of the tax in return
for a lump sum to the treasury. In 1601, when its trial three-year
period was coming to a close, the government again tried to use the
case for imperative necessity – this time provided by the war with
Savoy – to extend the tax. But the opposition was more determined
and more vocal and the risk of such opposition becoming exploited by
disgruntled elements in the upper nobility was greater. There were
riots in Poitiers and Angers in May 1601, and a more serious
disturbance in Limoges in April 1602.[125] The latter involved a city
where League bitterness was still close to the surface. Foreign
ambassadors at the French court were well-informed about the
possibilities of a major noble insurrection and expected it to turn into
a revolt against Sully's growing predominance in the government.[126]
There were internal rivalries amongst the ministers which added to the
overall nervousness. The king moved to Blois in early April 1602 and
the possibility of an expedition to Poitiers and then Limoges was
actively canvassed. In the end the sedition was quelled but, in
November 1602, the *pancarte* was dropped. What had seemed like a

122. Carew, [1749], p. 462.

123. For the opposition in Paris, see *Registres de Paris* [1866–], XI, 354–5, 376,
389, 485.

124. Ibid., XI, 514–15; XII, 15, 18, 57–8, 79–80, 94 etc.

125. F. Lebrun, 1965, 120–1. M. Cassan, 1988, 276–8. Annette Finley-Croswhite,
'Absolutism and Municipal Autonomy: Henri IV and the 1602 Pancarte Revolt in
Limoges' in M.P. Holt, 1991, pp. 81–3. A. Thomas, 1882, p. 2. P. Ducourtieux, 1925,
pp. 114–15. AN 90 AP 32, dossier 1.

126. A. Desjardins [1859–86], V, 487–95.

shrewd way of raising revenues from the tax-privileged towns had, instead, become a way by which those towns could become the focus for opposition from both town and country.

On the whole, Sully's budgets probably bore more relation to what was being actually levied. Unrealistic arrears of tax were written off in January 1598 and, in the following August, commissioners were despatched to the *pays d'élections* to conduct a sustained campaign against corruption in the financial administration of the *tailles* and to reapportion the burden around villages where this was necessary.[127] This *régalement* (or *re-également*) was no novelty – the process had been undertaken in 1567, 1578 and 1593; but it had never been so thorough, so well-supported from the centre, or so determined to remove local opposition to investigation. Later, the privy council issued an authoritative edict in March 1600 which itemised and outlawed abuses in the *tailles*.[128] This was to be the most comprehensive statement of the proper procedures to be observed in the levy of *tailles* to appear in the *ancien régime*. Commissioners also interpreted the royal will to the *pays d'états*. In Brittany, for example, Sully remained in Nantes after the province finally submitted to Henri IV in May 1598. He dismissed the provincial treasurers and appointed two men more favourably disposed to the king. When Sully went, he left behind his client, Gilles de Maupeou, as a 'commissioner, deputed . . . for the direction of finance' with responsibility for Brittany.[129] Maupeou's achievement was considerable. He settled the arrears owed by former receivers of the province. He negotiated revenues from the provincial estates and limited their financial independence. In 1599 and 1600, he codified the tax farms in the province and began to investigate the municipal debts of Nantes.

Throughout his period in office, Sully inspired the provincial treasurers to a prompt despatch of their responsibilities. In December 1598, he suppressed the colleges (*bureaux*) and presidents of the provincial treasurers and, in November 1601, he carefully delineated their functions by royal edict.[130] To enforce his will, he sometimes threatened to suspend a whole generality of treasurers for failing to comply with royal requests. At other times, he hinted that wages would be curtailed or that they would be plagued with special enquiries. He demanded swift responses and this was how he addressed

127. B. Barbiche, 1960, 58–96.
128. Isambert, XV, 226–38.
129. Sully, [1881], XVI, 275, 280–3. R.S. Trullinger, 1972, p. 130 *et seq.* J.B. Collins, 1988, p. 87.
130. B. Barbiche, 1978, p. 61. D.J. Buisseret, 1968, pp. 61–8.

the treasurers in Caen in 1610 about the failure of a receiver to present his account to the council of finance:

> He [*the receiver*] should have presented them several months ago because it
> is sixteen months since he was in office. I do not know if you have
> checked his final accounts yet, but I can assure you that he has not
> presented them to the council. In this, I blame him for his negligence and
> would prefer to have some evidence of your diligence in order to
> stimulate some in him . . . [*Addition in Sully's handwriting*]: Messieurs,
> Your negligence is a great disgrace to us; if you do not mend your ways,
> I shall inform the king and he will take the necessary action which
> assuredly will not be to your advantage. Give me a prompt reply. M. de
> Béthune, duke of Sully.[131]

The result was that the regional treasurers ceased to spend significant amounts of revenue outside the budget on their own authority.

At the same time, Sully tackled tax-farmers ('the great destroyers of the kingdom's revenues' as he described them) and financiers ('great rich robbers') by holding specially constituted judicial inquiries (*chambres de justice*). They were held so often that they even appeared to become part of the normal institutions of the kingdom.[132] The first was established, as has been noted, on 8 May 1597, but it was suppressed a month later when the king, aware that he needed finance from any quarter to recover Amiens, accepted a gift of 3.6 million *livres* from the financiers in return for a promise of a limited pardon. A similar judicial investigation began in August 1601 and lasted until September 1604, when Henri IV accepted the offer from two financiers of a 'loan' of 600,000 *livres* in return for an amnesty. Some royal officials refused to subscribe to the loan and they were investigated by a third enquiry from January 1605 to 1607. In March 1607, a fourth *chambre* was instituted which went vigorously to work, inculpating several of Sully's clients (particularly the treasurer, Etienne Puget, and the war treasurer, Jean de Murat). Sully harangued the royal prosecutor of the tribunal and threatened to incarcerate him in the Bastille. Two months later, Henri IV closed the investigation, requiring guilty officials to repay the funds they had embezzled. Over 1 million *livres* was involved but only a fraction of the money was ever recovered. Clearly, *chambres de justice* were used for a political, rather than a reforming, purpose. They were quite expensive, did not distinguish between the important and the insignificant cases of fraud

131. D. Buisseret, [1963], 298–9.
132. J.F. Bosher, 1973, 19–40. F. Bayard, 1974a, 121–40.

and were reliant on the quality of information that came before them. But they were useful in persuading members of the sovereign courts that financiers were not spared Sully's rough courses.

Lastly, Sully exercised a tight control on expenditure. As superintendent of buildings, artillery, roads and bridges, he was in charge of the major spending departments of state. In addition, he managed the king's privy purse. Expenditure on the court was not lavish. The queen was allowed to establish her own entourage between 1601 and 1605 and thereafter Henri IV refused to pander to her expensive tastes.[133] Military matters remained the main item, but were only a fraction of the costs of wartime expenditure. The *deniers comptants* were not abolished but used to pay pensions to the Dutch and the Huguenots, rather than gifts towards the king's favourites.[134] If the *Oeconomies royales* are to be believed, Sully did not spare the king upright, puritan lectures on expenditure:

> I beg His Majesty most humbly, since I recognise his commitment to advance his honour, glory, triumphs and renown to their sovereign degree of merit, to have in mind what I have always advised him, namely, that (in order to achieve these with success) it is vital to avoid all expenses on luxuries, not to waste money destined to advance his glory, and to divert all expenditures on pleasures and distractions, of whatever sort, to purely military expenditures.

Sully had in mind the king's prodigality with regard to his preferred vices of mistresses and gambling. Neither, however, were as politically damaging or costly as Henri III's *mignons* and neither threatened the budgetary surplus. Although deflationary in impact, the Bastille war-chest quickly restored the king's credit. Sully's accounts reckoned that the king was worth over 32.5 million *livres* in 1608; in bullion terms this was worth about 355 tons of silver. By comparison, the annual imports of silver from the New World Spain were about 350 tons a year during the decade. This perhaps explains why Sully could contemplate a trial of strength with Spain in 1610. Henri IV was more cautious, aware that the financial position was contingent on political stability. Sully's difficulties in balancing the budget in 1611, given Marie de Médicis' higher expenditure, suggest that he was right to be prudent.[135] The next decade would demonstrate how vulnerable financial solvency could be to renewed political instability.

133. B. Barbiche, 1978, pp. 99–101. D.J. Buisseret, 1968, table 4.
134. Bayard, 1974a, 45–80. Cf. BN MS Dupuy 848, f. 52.
135. J.M. Hayden, 1974, p. 21.

SULLY AND THE CONSTITUTION

Sully's vigorous political style created resentments within the official bodies of France, and these have led historians to argue that Sully was responsible for constitutional changes which made his period in office the prototype for ministerial absolutism in France as it was later practised under Cardinals Richelieu and Mazarin. In particular, it has been asserted that Sully used special commissioners like intendants in the government of distant provinces. He wanted to eliminate representative institutions in France. He trespassed in a permanently damaging way on the jurisdiction of the sovereign courts and he established a ministerial style of government.[136] For Bernard Barbiche, the change occurred around the turning-point of 1605 with the establishment of Sully's supremacy within Henri IV's administration and he defined it as a moment of transformation for the French monarchy. It ceased to be a 'justice state' and became a 'finance state'.[137]

It is worth observing that Sully was not a fundamental political theorist. His style was more military and abrupt. When, for instance, the duke of Bouillon discussed Huguenot political aspirations with him, these were dismissed as incomprehensible.[138] Sully differed from his colleagues in the king's council in his political style, but not in his fundamental attitudes. Disagreements over the way to enforce royal authority came at the level of tactics, rather than strategy. The chancellor, Pomponne de Bellièvre, was more cautious, 'an excellent negotiator' as Carew said, 'the treasurer of promises' as he was known.[139] He believed that it was better to enjoy the new-found peace, rather than embark on any vigorous reconstruction of the administration in outlying provinces or among powerful institutions lest it awake old or slumbering sectarian hatreds. As chancellor of France, he had an exalted view of his responsibilities to defend the multiple powers attached to the great seal of the chancellory of which he was the guardian.[140] All royal nominations to offices, letters obliging the sovereign courts to register edicts (*lettres de jussion*) and judicial instruments relevant to the head of the judicial hierarchy were

136. J. Russell Major, 1966, 363–83; 1974, 3–34.

137. B. Barbiche, 'De l'Etat de justice à l'Etat de finances (1605)' in *Avènement d'Henri IV*, 1989, pp. 95–109.

138. Sully, [1970–88], I, 502–8.

139. G. Carew, [1749], pp. 481–3. R. Mousnier, 1941, 68–86.

140. H. Michaud, 1967, ch. i.

issued through his office. It gave him, as it had his predecessors, a particular perspective on the French state and its exalted judicial traditions. Sully, on the other hand, thought that, in order to prevent the recurrence of abuses, changes in government should be made while the memory of past disorders was fresh and could be exploited to advantage. At the time of his accession to power, he inherited no established office of state and no secretariat. The issue in debate was not the king's absolute authority in his state or the constitution which, since it was unwritten, would bend and sway before issues and personalities as it had done in the past. Sully and Bellièvre differed over language, style, different official positions in the government and divergent historical perceptions of the French state. The issue was how best to avoid future civil troubles; stability, not absolutism was the immediate question.

Sully certainly used commissioners to regulate provincial problems, but this was not a novelty. From the beginning of the civil wars monarchs had resorted to commissioners to establish edicts of pacification, administer a royal army or investigate abuses in administration. The word 'intendant' was sometimes applied to these commissioners, as it was commonly adopted to describe overseers of great noble estates and fortunes. But these intendants were not the equivalent of the regular, permanent intendants established by Richelieu under the pressures of the Thirty Years' War. They were never systematically sent out through the *pays d'élection*. Their use was haphazard in the *pays d'états*.[141] Sully's attitude, as that of Richelieu after him, was ambiguous. He was worried lest too many commissioners should damage the ability of the treasurers to extract revenue. He wrote to the municipality of Rouen in 1603 to say that he had tried to revoke certain commissioners but that he had been overruled in council. In October 1607, he encouraged the treasurers of Burgundy to oppose an officious commissioner who had been despatched to their province.[142]

Both Henri IV and Sully mistrusted representative assemblies. The king's memories of the protestant political assemblies were unhappily recent. His experience of governing a state where parliaments had a constitutional role, a state 'of estates', had been similarly frustrating. It is often forgotten that Henri IV's determination to uphold the absolute monarchy in France emerged from his having experienced the politics of its counterpart at close quarters in Béarn. This was how he addressed the estates of Burgundy in 1608:

141. D.J. Buisseret, 1966, 27–8. R.J. Bonney, 1978.
142. D.J. Buisseret, 1966, 27–8.

I know how business is conducted in these Estates. Before this crown descended to me, the country which I possessed governed itself by means of Estates. I summoned them annually. In their deliberations, the one who talked the longest and the best, the one who cited the pretexts of institutions or emperors – whilst all those who understood nothing about it whatsoever, said 'He has spoken well' – he was the one they made syndic. And this is the first one to lead a League.

He was determined to sustain the absolute monarchy in France and quite prepared to support Sully's more martial approach to the constitution in the process.

Sully's attitude is most graphically expressed in numerous passages from the *Oeconomies royales*. Nobles, soldiers, and men of finance deal with realities, substantial matters of state, practical effects and consequences. Parliamentarians, scribes and lawyers argue, dispute, waste time and strike attitudes. The provincial estates were talking shops which artificially protected some areas of the kingdom from taxation at the expense of the rest. Opposition in the previous reign had taken root in the provincial estates. Social resentments in the popular risings during the League had focused on the provincial assemblies. Politically, financially and socially, they threatened future stability and gave a platform to aspiring politicians who would meddle in the state's affairs.

There was an alternative case to be made, of course. Aristocratic governors of provinces protected their representative assemblies. They argued that to remove them was to endanger provincial privileges (occasionally enshrined in old charters) and to invite renewed rebellion. The provincial estates themselves claimed that they defended distant provinces and administered themselves cheaply. To attack them was to threaten municipal privileges and to generate lasting rancours which would lead to political instability.

For much of Henri IV's reign, the council of state was divided on the issue, aware of the strength of provincial feeling but suspicious of provincial privileges. Sully presented the case for introducing *élus* (officers to raise royal taxes) in those *pays d'états* without them, but this frequently became the basis for negotiating better revenue contributions to the exchequer. In Brittany, the only change occurred on the border when, in 1606, thirteen parishes on the marches between Poitou and Brittany were finally declared an *élection*.[143] In Languedoc, the province was protected by the Constable, Henri de Montmorency-Damville. Damville arranged for a written guarantee of

143. R.S. Trullinger, 1972, p. 372.

its privileges in return for a large gift to the king in 1600 and again in 1604. After Damville retired from active politics in 1608, the province became more vulnerable and lost some of its considerable financial independence but retained its immunity from *élus*.[144] In Dauphiné, the levy of taxes without the consent of the estates had already begun before Sully came to power and the process was continued in a province where there was a bitter and long-running battle over the system of tax assessment between nobles and commoners.[145] To preserve the province in harmony, it was clearly important for the king to make a decision and enforce it in the province, while not alienating any social group in the process. This was almost impossible, and the decision was delayed until 2 March 1602 when the king ordered his council to devote a fortnight to deciding the merits of the case. They eventually declared in favour of the nobles and royal office-holders and against the delegates of the towns of Dauphiné. The provincial governor, Lesdiguières, was satisfied because this followed his advice. But the council proceeded cautiously in implementing its decision in order not to upset the third estate in a province uncomfortably close to the troubled Alpine region.

The issues were clearest in Guyenne and in the newly acquired small territories of Bugey, Bresse and Gex, adjacent to the province of Burgundy.[146] In Guyenne, Sully sent two commissioners to the province in 1602 to investigate 'the abuse and corruption of the province's finances since 1585' with a proposal to introduce *élections* in mind. The lieutenant of the province, Alphonse d'Ornano, was alarmed at the disruptive effects of such 'novelties' and he sent his intendant, Raymond de Viçose, to the king and the chancellor, Bellièvre, to warn them of the possible unrest in the province. When the affair came before the privy council, Sully was absent and it was shelved while the commissioners were revoked. In 1604, Sully's position in council was stronger and the province's was weaker. Bouillon's conspiracy had not produced widespread revolt in the south-west. The divisions between the towns and surrounding countryside (the *plats pays*), evident during the League, were still present in the locality. Sully exploited them and reintroduced his proposal for *élections*. A meeting of dubious legality of the estates of Guyenne was hastily convoked in the province and a deputy urgently

144. P. Gachon, 1887, chs i–iii. J. Russell Major, 1980, pp. 306–18.

145. L. Scott Van Doren, 1975, 35–53. E. Le Roy Ladurie, 1979, chs ii and xiv. The pamphlets produced by the controversy are important and very revealing. The whole debate is carefully reviewed in D. Hickey, 1986, chs iv–v.

146. J. Russell Major, 1966; 1980, ch. ix. R. Tait, 1977.

despatched to Paris. Despite importunate letters from d'Ornano, and the diplomacy of Viçose, the council accepted the case for *élections* in Guyenne and the edict was passed. Yet the change was only introduced cautiously. The issue was suspended in 1605 for fear of popular sedition. *Elus* only began to collect taxes after the lieutenant d'Ornano had died in 1609. Personalities, the politics of a province, the facts of the case, all played a part in determining the survival of local representative institutions.

The same conclusions hold good for the treatment of town councils. League cities were readily accorded their privileges and autonomies by Henri IV in return for their loyalty. As he told the *échevins* (municipal councillors) of Amiens: 'The past is pardoned and I intend to conserve the privileges, freedoms and liberties of the inhabitants and even to augment them if I can.' France's urban notables were greeted like prodigal sons as they made their peace. 'With open arms we are, and shall for ever be, ready to receive and embrace with paternal good-will and clemency the most errant and deviant of our subjects' he assured the notables of Troyes.[147] Yet there were ways of reminding the urban elites to have regard for the royal interest. In 1596, municipal elections at Amiens were suspended by the king, fearing the city would be divided by dissension. In 1599, a year after the submission of the city of Nantes, Henri IV chose as the city's mayor a magistrate of known royalist sympathies and ignored the list of three candidates submitted to him. In a minority of cities, the electoral arrangements were rewritten to limit the scope for disorder or reform corruption. In Lyon, for example, the large elective town council was replaced by a municipal government composed of five municipal *échevins*. The latter were still elected officers but the elections were more readily overseen by royal magistrates. In Poitiers, Dijon and Marseille, substantial changes were made to prevent electoral gerrymandering but always with the effect of increasing royal surveillance.[148] Following the *pancarte* sedition in Limoges in 1602, a senior judge was despatched to the town who stripped the town councillors of their robes of office because of their alleged complicity in the uprising. The king chose six new consuls, half the old number, to govern in their place. The electorate was reduced in size to only a hundred bourgeois to be elected from the various *quartiers* of the city for the task. The results were striking; in a town where factionalism

147. Cited by Annette Finley-Croswhite, 'Henri IV et les villes' in *Avènement d'Henri IV*, 1989, p. 197.
148. R. Pillorget, 1972, 705–30.

(*partialités*) had been endemic, a tight oligarchy of *bons bourgeois* was put in control of the town. Thus it would remain in Limoges until the French Revolution.[149] The desire to strengthen the grip of the *bons bourgeois* upon the urban fabric of France was the clear overall drift of the Henrician regime. If this resulted in the restriction of urban autonomies, this was a by-product, but one which was by no means always a necessity. For many towns (including even Paris) Henri IV respected the traditional electoral arrangements without direct interference because loyal *bons bourgeois* were already firmly in the saddle.[150]

Sully had some of the attributes of a minister of the Richelieu and Mazarin period. He tried to make the provincial treasurers responsible to him in the same way as royal officers traditionally had been to the chancellor. The sovereign courts of France fought a rearguard action to frustrate his powers as minister in charge of roads and bridges (*grand voyer*). This was because they rightly perceived Sully's intention to create a network of administrative officials exercising quasi-judicial functions. Sully came into conflict especially with the *chambre des comptes*. He regarded their procedures as cumbersome and corrupt. A memorandum of 1601 listed the various abuses which he had discovered:[151]

> In Provence . . . the *chambre des comptes* orders expenditure on
> delegations, reimbursements, gifts and other expenses outside the royal
> budget. In Languedoc, the *parlement* sanctions the full payment of the
> *rentes*, notwithstanding the fifty per cent reduction made by the budget
> . . . the *cour des aides* releases tax officials imprisoned by the treasurers
> who had suspended them from office for failing to pay their deposits. At
> Limoges, the *chambre des comptes* ordered in one year and on one account,
> expenditure of 10,000 *écus* not included in the royal budget on its own
> authority. In Normandy . . . the *cour des aides* at Rouen has given an
> order against the commissioners for the reorganisation of the *taille* and
> instructed officials to pay no attention to them now or in the future'.

Sully demanded documents from the *chambre des comptes* in Paris which had never previously left the chamber. He also created his own clientèle in the financial administration and used it to restrict the privileged courts. However his loss of favour in 1611 removed his

149. Annette Finley-Croswhite in M.P. Holt, 1991, pp. 84–92.
150. R. Descimon, 1988, 113–50.
151. AN 120 AP 37, ff. 120–1 (*c.* 1601). Occasionally, the *chambre des comptes* assisted in these investigations – e.g. BN MS Dupuy 854, f. 102 (memorandum on abuses in the *chambre des comptes* of Montpellier).

clients, dismantled much of the administrative officialdom which he had created and allowed the sovereign courts to reinforce their position once more. The French administrative monarchy was a result, rather than a cause, of political stability. When the conditions were right later in the seventeenth century, it would be re-established and, eventually, on a permanent basis.

The most significant constitutional change was not directly the result of Sully's activity (although his own position reflected the change) and this was the growth in the importance of the privy council. A memorandum by Jérôme Luillier in 1606 for the keeper of the seals explained why it had happened.[152] The privy council (the *conseil privé* or, as it was known before the reign of Henri III, the *conseil des parties*) had grown in significance during the civil wars. The various edicts of pacification (which allowed appeals to the privy council) and the inevitable bitterness of conflicts in a civil wars had expanded its jurisdiction. So, too, did the 'factions and partialities' of the *parlements*, the treaties of pacification with the League (which also gave a right of appeal to the privy council), and the insistence by tax farmers that their treaties should contain an automatic right of appeal to the privy council in cases of legal dispute concerning their tax-farm. This growth was mirrored in the number of masters of requests (*maîtres des requêtes*) who prepared its briefs and carried out its decisions.[153] In time, they would provide the intendants in French provinces. By 1606, there were fifty-six or fourteen per quarter, of these well-rewarded officials in service. Their offices sold for exalted sums, reflecting the power and status their posts enjoyed. In his memorandum, Luillier looked forward to the day when the reasons for the growth of privy-council affairs would no longer apply and when the harmony of French society would no longer require the incessant intervention of the privy council. But the whole trend of French government and society was against that. The privy council was essential to the struggle for stability and, coordinated by ministers like Sully, it had a permanent place in the constitution of the Bourbon monarchy.

152. BN MS Dupuy 851 f. 4 *et seq.*

153. For their growing significance during the civil wars, see M. Etchechoury, 1991.

CHAPTER SIX

Economic Reconstruction

THE TERRIBLE YEARS

In 1582, the Venetian ambassador, Priuli, remarked that it was a tribute to the wealth of the country that warfare had not generated the funereal consequences which would have naturally occurred elsewhere.[1] Regions had, of course, been temporarily ravaged by passing armies. Priuli's predecessor, for instance, was shocked at the consequences of the campaigns of 1577 for the villages on the poor soils of Champagne: 'Everywhere is in ruins; the oxen have, for the most part, been destroyed so that, generally, the land remains fallow. Many inhabitants have abandoned their homes'.[2] But most areas seem to have recovered quickly. From such figures as exist for population, yield from tithes, production of cloth in Amiens and other textile centres in northern France, it is reasonably clear that massacres, troops on the march, currency instability, increasing royal taxation and poor trading conditions had been patchy and temporary in their effects before 1580.[3] In some northern regions, there was a continuation of

1. BM MS It 1732, ff. 261–2.
2. G. Fagniez, 1897, p. 7.
3. A. Croix, 1974, chs iv and v, esp. pp. 116–26. P. Benedict, 1975, pp. 232–3. J. Jacquart, 1974, pt II, ch. v, esp. pp. 171–89. P. Goubert, 1976, pp. 171–94. F. Lebrun, 1965, pp. 49–50. P. Deyon, 1963, pp. 948–9. R. Gascon, 1971, II, pt ii. G. Cabourdin, 1977, esp. I, pt II and pt IV, chs 2 and 4. J. Goy and E. Le Roy Ladurie, 1972, pp. 21, 44–57 (Paris region); pp. 146–7 (Burgundy); pp. 176–7 (Lyonnais); pp. 198–9 (Auvergne); pp. 236–9 (Toulousain). E. Le Roy Ladurie, 1966, I, pts II and III. P. Leclercq, 1979. No attempt has been made to analyse in detail the economic data included in these works which, for the period of the wars of religion, must be regarded as providing only tentative conclusions. The detailed and illuminating regional studies on the seventeenth century in France have not yet been matched by research of comparable quality for the period before 1598.

the demographic and economic expansion of the earlier half of the century. In the Midi, where the effects of the wars were more prolonged and intense, however, some places did not always manage to recover so easily.[4] Yet it cannot be emphasised too strongly that the statistical evidence on which this impression is based is sketchy in the extreme.[5]

The wars of the League from 1585 to 1596 were of a different quality and took place in a different economic environment. Their impact was much more prolonged. The distress was more widely expressed. From 1589 to 1596, warfare took place in the north of France on a scale which had not been witnessed before. The mortality figures in cities like Rouen and regions like the Nantais and the indices of prices for Paris, Toul, Beauvais, Lyon and Toulouse present a grim statistical reality which historians have to translate into human consequences as best they can.[6] The historian of the rural world of the Ile de France, Jean Jacquart, spoke of this period as 'the terrible years'.[7] Burgundy's historian, Henri Drouot, said that the province had not suffered so greatly since the high middle ages.[8] Economic historians tend to look beyond the civil wars for explanations for France's problems which include the movements of silver bullion, the patterns of international trade, world meteorological conditions and the incidence of plague to explain demographic crisis, bad harvests or depression. As various studies have proved, there was no automatic correlation between the years of demographic crisis and those of civil war.[9] Contemporaries, however, remained more naively convinced that economic miseries and civil wars were intimately and inseparably associated, and that both were signs of the imminent judgment of God.

4. For a comparison between the experiences of northern France and the Midi see the contributions of Philip Benedict and Mark Greengrass to P. Clark, 1985, chs v and vi.

5. See the proper scepticism towards both price and demographic data expressed by M. Morineau in R. Sauzet, 1992, pp. 294–6.

6. M. Baulant and J. Meuvret, 1960 (Paris). P. Goubert, 1960, p. 77 (*graphiques*) (Beauvais). P. Benedict, 1975, pp. 232–3 (Rouen). A. Croix, 1974, pp. 80–4, 126–38 (Nantes). A. Latreille, *Histoire de Lyon*, (Privat, Toulouse), 1975, p. 167. G. and G. Frêche, 1967, (Toulouse). R. Baehrel, 1961, pp. 534–5, 554 and *graphiques* (Grenoble, Arles and Aix). E. Le Roy Ladurie, 1966, II (*Annexes*) (Montpellier, Béziers and Narbonne).

7. J. Jacquart, 1974, pt ii, ch. v. Cf. F. Braudel's remarks about 'cette étonnante montée de misère du XVIe siècle finissante' quoted in P. Leclercq, 1979, p. 33.

8. H. Drouot, 1911, 361.

9. A. Croix, 1974, esp. graphs 57 and 58.

It is clear that France's economic problems began before the wars of the League but were made much worse by them. The progressive weakening of the economic fabric began to show more clearly in holes and tatters. The two most important arteries for France's international commerce lay through the Atlantic and the Mediterranean. Both were interrupted in the civil wars and completely constricted during the League. Catholic towns on the Atlantic coast were periodically blockaded by Huguenot privateers, and merchants like the Ruiz family had almost ceased to trade by 1589.[10] Only well-fortified protestant ports like La Rochelle prospered.[11] In the Mediterranean, Spain dominated the trade routes across the Gulf of Lions so that the shipping through Marseille and Narbonne was reduced, partly because both ports were isolated from their hinterland by enemy troops. Royal taxation damaged Marseille's position as a trading port by charging duties on foreign ships and their cargoes which entered the port.[12] The Hermite brothers, important factors in the Marseille trade to the Levant, gave up business for politics during the League.[13] Between the economies of the Atlantic and the Mediterranean lay the city of Lyon, the pre-eminent trading, banking and printing city of France in the sixteenth century. Lyon's greatness was already threatened in the 1570s when the Huguenots broke the delicate tissue of its merchant commerce and conditions turned unfavourable for the city.[14] The Bonvisi, the greatest merchant bankers in Lyon, managed to survive that onslaught, but the number of letters of exchange that they handled began to decline from 1583 and so did their value from 1585.[15] In the wars of the League, their fortunes and the city's difficulties veered towards a débâcle. Lyon's commercial fortunes seemed beyond repair by 1594.

The traditional staples of much of French commerce were also threatened. The export of canvas and textiles from Brittany and Normandy was, as a Rouen city father said, 'The true gold and silver mines of this kingdom'.[16] Normandy canvas equipped the English navy, Vitry cloth was used as packing in Amsterdam and for doublets throughout western Europe. Buckrams from Brittany provided shirts, pillowcases and lining materials in England and elsewhere. In the wars

---

10. H. Lapeyre, 1955, pp. 251–3.
11. E. Trocmé and M. Delafosse, 1952, ch. vi, esp. p. 145.
12. J. Billioud, 1951, pp. 186–202.
13. M. Baulant, 1953 pp. xxv–xxvii.
14. R. Gascon, 1971, II, pt ii.
15. F. Bayard, 1971, 1234–60.
16. *Rouen, Inventaire sommaire des délibérations* (Series B – 10 May 1601).

of the League, French exports collapsed. Production at Amiens began to decline from 1586 and imports to London in 1587–88 were at half the level they had been in 1568.[17] Instead, imports of English woven and finished cloths increased into France, with the dyeing and finishing of the cloths undertaken with French skills and techniques acquired from refugees.[18] The Dutch also broke into the French markets. From 1587, Dutch ships appeared regularly in the ports of Rouen, Bayonne and St Malo, bringing with them grain, salt, fish and cloth. When they left, they swept the bullion from the towns, leaving them with a shortage of good coin.[19] One mint in the Netherlands was kept at work during the wars purely by minting silver from the trade with France. The English traders gained bourgeois status in towns like Caen and exemption from port dues in Rouen.

Meanwhile, the production of cloth in the Midi for the Levant market also declined as some of the centres for the industry – Nîmes, Alès and Uzès – went protestant. At the estates general in 1576, there was a complaint at 'the great number of His Majesty's subjects in Poitou, Languedoc and Dauphiné who, seeing their manufactures cease, have taken up arms'.[20] The estates of Languedoc lamented the decline of their native textile industry and there were increasing calls for protection of French industries, even from traditionally free-trade centres like Lyon. 'Foreigners', it was said, 'had gained little by little over the French.'[21] The other international trade to suffer was that in wine through Bordeaux. The wars of the Midi and a harvest failure in 1572–74 left wine in short and irregular supply. Parts of Gascony suffered as parts of Germany would suffer during the Thirty Years' War. Montaigne's description of the civil wars is an accurate representation of the damage that had been done, as it was seen by a judge from Bordeaux.[22] *Daces* or river tolls made it expensive to ship wines from 'the high country' while the convoy charges and taxes at

---

17. P. Deyon, 1963, pp. 948–9. H.A. Nicholle, 1976, p. 89, appendices 7–9.

18. Ibid., pp. 154–69.

19. F.C. Spooner, 1958, pp. 203–5, 218–19. R. Boutruche, 1966, p. 124 (for their appearance in Bordeaux). E. Trocmé and M. Delafosse, 1952, p. 104 (La Rochelle).

20. R. Gascon, 1971, II, 614.

21. AN H 748[17] f. 46. The trend towards protectionism in the traditionally free-trade city of Lyon is documented in R. Gascon, 1971, II, 675–731. The distinction between duties on imported primary products and manufactured products appeared in an edict on tariffs in 1570.

22. T. Malvezin, 1883, II, 224–6. R. Boutruche, 1966, pp. 91–138. C. Higounet, 1971, p. 277. As Montaigne said, the wine trade was 'un moyen des guerres religieuses'. The complaints of London merchants appear in BL Harleian MS 288.

Royan and Blaye were bitterly resented by English merchants. Wine shortage worried the English privy council for the amounts shipped through Bordeaux at the end of the civil wars were less than a third of the tonnages of thirty years previously.

The vulnerability of French capitalism during the wars of the League is strikingly demonstrated by the monetary instability. France possessed during this period both a money of account (the *livre tournois*) and a circulating coinage in silver (*testons* and, in the 1570s, *francs*), gold (*écus*) and small change (*pinatelles, vaches de Béarn, sols au fer forgé*, etc, some in copper after 1578).[23] France began to feel the effects of the imported silver from the New World in the appreciation of the price of gold and the depreciation in the price of silver (all relative to the money of account). The crises tended to occur at the same time as grain or raw material shortages so that, in the periods of bad harvest in 1572–74, the official rate for an *écu* rose from 52 *sols* to 58 *sols* and eventually to 65 *sols*.[24] The unofficial rate went, on some occasions, two or three times higher than that. Smaller denominations of coins became so scarce that barter had to take over for minor transactions. In the face of monetary inflation and a risk of currency collapse, Henri III attempted to produce stability in the coinage by a modest devaluation in the money of account and by harnessing the money of account to the inherently more stable gold currency.[25] After September 1577, all transactions in France over a certain minimum amount were to be expressed in *écus*. The measure was a palliative which worked rather by luck than by good management. The rates of exchange were stabilised until the wars of the League when, once more, gold began to appreciate rapidly in its value whilst silver depreciated in its value in terms of the money of account. Spanish subsidies to the League and their payments of troops on French soil flooded the French market with silver specie, causing monetary inflation.[26] In Provence, for example, the *écu*, its official value fixed in 1577 at 60 *sols*, or 3 *livres tournois*, appreciated on the money market at Aix to 66 *sols* in January 1590, 92 *sols* in 1592 and reached a maximun of 240 *sols* for a brief period in March 1593.[27] Monetary inflation

23. F.C. Spooner, 1972. A. Blanchet, 1930, pp. 235–7.

24. R. Gascon, 1971, II, 549–72. *Coligny (Actes du colloque, 1972)*, 1974, pp. 672–701. F.C. Spooner, 1972, pp. 157–97.

25. R. Gascon, 1971, II, 576–7. F.C. Spooner, 1972, p. 163. LN, No. 921. The edict was only enforced with difficulty in the Midi.

26. F.C. Spooner, 1972, pp. 164–7, 212–47. Money minted at Paris from Spanish sources enumerated in BN MS Fr 4019, f. 206v.

27. F.C. Spooner, 1972, pp. 582–93.

excited price rises in basic commodities which were already high because of war. The national grain market fractured into a series of very local, volatile markets in which barter, hoarding and speculation were inevitable.

Currency problems were made more chaotic by the creation of mints. Both sides exploited the minting of sub-standard coins as a way of paying for their armies. By 1590, the number of mints had risen to over twenty and many produced small denomination silver coins with a silver content as much as three-quarters below that of their face value.[28] Many mint masters themselves made great profits from the speculative enterprise which depreciated the value and inflated the amount of coinage in circulation. Eustache Piémond, a diarist from a small catholic *bastide* town in Dauphiné, reported that, in March 1593, the *pinatelles* of Valence were worth only 1s. 6d. (instead of 2s. 6d.), those of Nyons, 9d., some from Grenoble only 4d.[29] He recorded the appreciation in prices too, especially from September 1592 to January 1593, when foodstuffs increased by 50 per cent and manufactured products like cloth and silk by 60 and 300 per cent respectively.[30] In eastern provinces, copper coins, imported from Germany, made their way into France and began to supplant the French coinage. But they were vulnerable to fraudulent clipping and quickly became a discredited coinage too. Attempts to stabilise the smaller denominations of coins were as painful as the inflation they had caused. Languedoc merchants anticipated such moves and unloaded their poor quality coins in Dauphiné (where they were still accepted) in exchange for goods. Some coins ceased to be legal tender and this resulted in months where coin disappeared from some villages, leaving them, as Piémond said, 'in desolation, without cash, and yet pestered for the payment of *tailles*'. The imminent collapse of the coinage was a presage of the scale of economic damage inflicted by the wars of the League.

Towns felt the impact most severely. They were faced with a multitude of difficulties but the fears of famine, plague and the effects of war overshadowed other problems. 'These are terrible afflictions', wrote Eustache Piémond and added, 'God have mercy on those poor people suffering from them.'[31] His diary chronicles their impact on his region from 1577. Plague assumed a new virulence in French towns

28. Ibid., pp. 105–15.
29. J. Brun-Durand, [1885], p. 310. Cf. the works of J. Bailhache on the various small mints in French provinces during the League in *Revue numismatique* (1928–32).
30. J. Brun-Durand, [1885], p. 311.
31. Ibid., p.77.

during the civil wars and was frequently preceded or accompanied by dearth. In Rouen, Beauvais, Amiens and Paris, outbreaks of plague occurred during the first civil war in 1562–63. Biraben, the historian of bubonic plague in France, attempted to chart its incidence; his results suggest a new breadth and intensity to its manifestation after 1577.[32] There were other infectious diseases too, especially malaria, smallpox, and something called the *grande coqueluche* which afflicted many major towns in 1580 and claimed numerous victims. In some cities, the plague of 1586–87 was to be the most serious attack during the century. Some of the popular psychology of the League may be ascribed to the return of the plague – processions and confraternities were traditional responses to the scourge of infectious diseases. The mortality figures of the region around Nantes and Rouen and the amounts spent on plague relief in Toulouse reveal the seriousness of the attacks.[33] According to Piémond's own estimates (and they may have been exaggerated to gain tax relief for the locality), St Antoine lost half its population in the course of the year 1586–87 – but if its victims had all survived they would never have been fed by the meagre harvest of 1586.[34]

Dearth in towns was the result of falling levels of agricultural production but the grain shortages were exacerbated by the political problems of the wars. Catholic cities like Aix, Toulouse, Paris, Chartres, Rouen and Marseille were, at various times, besieged by armies and cut off from their food supplies. In Rouen, the city fathers bought large amounts of Baltic grain to feed the poor, only to have the ships taken by pirates and the grain sold at Southampton. At the height of the dearth in the early summer of 1586, 14,000 people were in receipt of relief in the city and plague was carrying away a great number each day: 'They dye in evrie streete and at evrie gate, morning and eveninge, by viii or xii in a place, so that the like hath not byne heard of. And the poore doth not onely die so in the streete, but the riche also in their bedde, by 10 or 12 in a daye.'[35]

In the rural world, there was also starvation. In the Lyonnais, the dearth was so great that some communities sold their church bells to raise money to nourish their poor.[36] One diarist reported people dying

32. J-N. Biraben, 1975, I, 377–88.
33. A. Croix, 1974, pp. 126–39 (Nantes region). P. Benedict, 1975, pp. 214–22. M. Greengrass, 1979, 263. F. Rolle, 1865 (deliberations of the town of Lyon – analysis of registers BB104–117).
34. J. Brun-Durand, [1885], p. 199.
35. P. Benedict, 1981, p. 173.
36. A. Latreille, *op. cit.*, p. 167 (cited in note 6 above).

'of necessity' in the fields. Lyon itself, a town with an enlightened poor-relief tradition, found itself besieged by the migrant poor and did its best to limit the number begging on its streets and entering its workhouse.[37] Overall, it would appear to be a reasonable hypothesis that, in some places, the cumulative effects of famine and infectious diseases temporarily wiped away the population increase during the century. Population decrease on the scale of that which occurred in neighbouring Castile in the 1590s also threatened France.[38]

In the countryside, falling agricultural production can be measured in the returns of tithes to churches and in the leases of lands. In the Parisian region, the product of the tithes began to fall away from its high point on the eve of the civil wars after 1570 and particularly after 1585. In the Normandy Vexin, it declined by about 25 per cent during the wars of the League. In Burgundy there was a similar decline.[39] This was partly the result of bad harvests and poor weather conditions. Piémond was an amateur meteorologist and he noted the late frost of the 1580s and 1590s and the accompanying cyclonic conditions which frequently lasted well into July and accompanied the pre-harvest frosts. Piémond speaks of seven sterile years from 1584 to 1591 and only records one harvest from 1580 to 1590 as 'reasonably fertile'. The decade 1590–1600 was only a little better with good years in 1593, 1595 and 1599. With the evidence of advancing glaciers around Chamonix destroying villages, late harvests of grapes and other meteorological data, some historians have spoken of a 'mini ice-age' during the latter half of the sixteenth century.[40]

There was also the direct impact of military campaigns. Contemporaries talked of two sorts of war. There was the *grande guerre*, the movement of royal armies, the great set sieges. There was every sign of the effect of this on the countryside. The German troops invaded in 1587, pillaging and stealing, cutting a swathe through Lorraine, Burgundy and the Beauce that was observable in tithe accounts ten years later.[41] After 1589, the *grande guerre* moved to the valley of the Seine, out towards Picardy and south towards the Loire at Tours and Orléans. The impact can be seen in the Paris *mercuriale*

37. J-P. Gutton, 1970, esp. pp. 298–300. For the effects on Marseille, see J. Billioud, 1951, p. 183.

38. B. Bennassar, 1969.

39. J. Goy and E. Le Roy Ladurie, 1972, pp. 50–7, 140–1, 146–7, 151–2.

40. E. Le Roy Ladurie, 1971, ch. iv.

41. P. de Saint-Jacob, 1961, pp. 34–49. A. Tuetey, 1883. The methods of fighting the *grande guerre* are amply referred to in the memoirs of François de la Noue, Jean de Saulx-Tavannes and Blaise de Monluc.

(the register of grain prices) and many contemporary accounts. Antoine Richart describes the effects of the siege of Laon on the survivors in a dispassionate way.[42] Bread was bought with people's possessions in the town. Peasants either sold up or left their property and fled. Bodies lay in the fields, unburied. Wolves were a menace because, having fed on human corpses, they became more ready to attack children and unprotected humans. For Piémond, the royal armies were no different from any other soldiery. Their strategy was 'just a mockery', their battles 'a tennis match' which would 'ruin the people'.

Beyond this, there was the *petite guerre*, the war of châteaux, the *guerre guerroyable*, fought by provincial armies, garrisoned soldiers, brigands who had never fought in any army at all, a confusing picture of cattle-rustling, skirmish, pillage and raid. Piémond describes the effects on his own small walled town in Dauphiné. *Commissaires des vivres*, army provisioners, arrived without warning and herded up cattle, sheep and farm produce to fulfil their commissions. By March 1590, sowing and tilling had become impossible, since there was no seed corn to sow and commissioners were besieging the town like an enemy army. Billeted troops pillaged, imprisoned local peasantry, ran protection rackets and seized food supplies without authorisation. It was pointless to appeal to their commanders, for they were frequently responsible for it. Bribery of a regimental sergeant or a captain could be effective, but it could also advertise a town's willingness to be blackmailed.

Compensation for these burdens was theoretically given by 'assigning' the costs on the provincial *tailles*, but this handed taxation over to the militia with its inevitable consequences. In any case, more 'assignations' were issued than there was tax to pay for them and, by 1594, there was a distinct possibility that the king would issue an amnesty for all wartime debts. So nobles who still had outstanding 'assignations' began to imprison town deputies, billet companies of soldiers on villages and charge extortionate expenses and rates of interest to constrain them to a quick settlement. As Piémond said, with a private sarcasm, the military captains had 'the mercy of Nero'.[43] The conditions created by the *petite guerre* are revealed in tithe investigations and reports on the *tailles*. One from Autun in Burgundy

---

42. J. Jacquart, 1974, pp. 179–88. A. Richart, [1869], pp. 480–90. Cf. the remissions for *tailles* and *décimes* in Valois, Nos 1790, 1873, 1914, etc. Henri IV fought in the Beauce, Paris' main source of provisions and permanently changed the pattern of Paris' provisioning. See P. Goubert, 1961, 797–801.

43. J. Brun-Durand, [1885], p. 187.

in 1596 presents a tragic picture which could be repeated for many other localities.[44] The reduction in numbers being taxed was over 50 per cent in many villages. Beasts of burden had been seized and could not be replaced. Village communities, having borrowed money to pay for protection against soldiery and ransom, were selling their commons to relieve their debts. Individual peasants with overwhelming debts turned to share-cropping (*métayage*) as the only way of finding working capital for the land; others sold up to local bourgeois, seigneurs, or more prosperous peasants.[45] Here, as in the uplands of the Cévennes in Languedoc and the inland Breton peninsula, packs of wolves proved a menace for sheep and travellers.[46] The registers of marriages of the age cohort whose youth was spent during the wars of the League reveal a degree of illiteracy among the rural population which eliminated the increased rates of literacy which had apparently been achieved in the course of the sixteenth century.[47]

It seems clear that the cumulative effects of plague, dearth and war on rural communities reinforced the pressures for structural change which were already present from a high population and a serious shortage of resources in cultivatable land and new techniques. The indebtedness of villages meant they were less able to resist seigneurial demands in the law-courts and had to sell communal land on which many members of the village community relied for marginal resources which kept them alive. The resources of individual peasant proprietors could only be recovered by entering into mortgage or rental agreements for their land or their livestock which, ultimately, involved a new dependence on someone else. The civil wars enforced the polarities of rural society between an élite of *laboureurs* and *fermiers* and a mass of cottagers, share-croppers and wage labourers which typical of the French *ancien régime* in the countryside. One historian has used the legal contracts for debts and property transfer registered by notaries to illustrate this process.[48] He found that the number of contracts in which villagers either mortgaged land or borrowed grain

44. P. de Saint-Jacob, 1961, 34–49. There is other similar evidence from commissioners investigating the non-payment of *décimes* around Toulouse (AD Haute-Garonne 1G 187). Cf. records of tithes around Rouen in P. Benedict, 1981, pp. 224–5.

45. L. Merle, 1958, pp. 179–80. J. Jacquart, 1974, pp. 200–53. E. Le Roy Ladurie, 1966, I, 33–53.

46. H. Wacquet, [1960], p. 275 – this evocation of the deprivations of Breton peasants at the time of the League ends by saying that, if he attempted to describe them all, his diary would be accounted a fairy story.

47. E. Le Roy Ladurie, 1966, I, 333–56 and accompanying tables.

48. G. Cabourdin, 1977, pp. 377–424. A similar process is revealed in P. Leclercq, 1979, pp. 58–67.

to tide themselves over to the next harvest increased in line with grain prices after a bad harvest. The loans for grain, usually for six or seven months, were taken out in April or May and these were followed by a second series of land sales in December or January, as those peasants unable to pay off their loans had to surrender some of their land. The total volume of transactions was particularly high during the years from 1586 to the end of the century. Those who profited from the sales included prosperous peasants (they bought 17.5 per cent of the land sold), nobles and newly ennobled families (35 per cent) and urban merchants, lawyers and artisans acquiring their first parts of the rural world (29 per cent), leaving a small proportion for the clergy (13 per cent) who also had cash to spare to invest in the rural world. This investigation was carried out on the borders of France in the Toulois, where the great engraver, Jacques Callot was brought up. His famous series of engravings, the *Miseries of War*, was produced at the time of the Thirty Years' War, whose tragedies it is rightly taken to illustrate.[49] But Callot might also have been reflecting the bitter collective memories of the wars of religion, conveyed to him in his youth.

Rural distress could be ignored by neither side. There was a widespread use of 'truces for cultivation' (*trèves de labourage*). These were agreed at provincial or local level – initially for the period covering the sowing and the harvesting of grain – at least partly so that the armies could live to fight another year. They began in areas of marginal cultivation like the uplands of the Vivarais and then spread to include the plains of the Ile de France and Picardy. Clauses included freedom of commerce, movement of refugees, medical personnel and clergy returning to their churches, arrangements for garrisoning châteaux, and patrols by both sides.[50] By the end of the League, some of these truces had extended into properly maintained truces lasting a full calendar year, a genuine sign that physical exhaustion played its part in bringing the wars of the League to a close.

Warfare certainly amplified social hatreds in the *plat pays*. Agrippa d'Aubigné's epic poem, *Les Tragiques*, first circulated in manuscript in 1593.[51] It included a long passage on the plight of a wounded and starving peasant from the Périgord who had witnessed the slaughter of

---

49. DBF, VII, cols 707–9.

50. G. Fagniez, 1897, pp. 14–15. Examples from the Midi to be found in L. Ménard, 1750–68, IV, 187, 239, 146. For the north of France, examples in BN MS Fr 3646, f. 82, 3982, f. 137; (Ile de France, 1 Sept. 1592); 3983, f. 4 (Orléanais, 10 Jan. 1593).

51. A. d'Aubigné, *Les Tragiques*, ed. J. Bailbé, (Garnier-Flammarion, 1968), p. 17.

his wife and children by marauding soldiery.[52] The third estate of the estates general of Blois in 1588 demanded the right of hot pursuit against plundering troops.[53] The Venetian ambassador said that it was the lesser noble captains of the army that were the worst offenders.[54] The *Dialogue between the Noble and the Townsman* said it had become a war against the inhabitants by the nobility and soldiers.[55] In the *Pleasant Satyre* the Baron de Rieux was the representative of the lesser nobility. His oration to the estates general began:

> Let warre live; there is nothing but to have it, of what part soever it befall . . . Touching myselfe, I mean nothing of all this, provided that I levie taxes daily, and that they pay my appointments, I care not what betide the Pope, or the pretie wench his wife. I am after my intelligences to take Noyon; if I can bring it about and to effect, I shall be Bishop of the towne and of the fields too . . . In the meane while I chase the cowe and the inhabitant also, as much as I can, and there shall not be a peasant, husbandman or merchant round about me, and within tenne miles compasse, that shall not pass by my hands, and that shall not pay me custome and ransome.[56]

The smaller market towns of the *plat pays* shared the resentments of the surrounding countryside. Some of them had suffered most from the *grande guerre*. La Ferté-Milon was besieged and sacked three times during the wars; Dreux was sacked twice. Châteaudun was besieged and then sacked. Noyon was sacked and two-thirds of its houses burned. Sully described the treatment of Mantes (where his brother was governor) which was sacked and yielded 1,000 *écus* in booty for each of the six captains responsible.[57] According to Piémond, the nobility were deeply hated for treating the inhabitants like swine. He reserved his particular venom for the new nobles, the Kentucky colonels of the civil wars, who had become *riches et opulents* through war contracts or captaincies.[58] In the peasant insurrections towards the

52. Ibid., pp. 68–9.
53. G. Picot, 1888, II, 214.
54. G. Fagniez, 1897, p. 7 (Priuli, 1582).
55. Morin, [1977], p. 75. Cf. the comments in G. Fagniez, 1897, p. 9 on the *casaniers*, gentlemen who remained neutral during the wars and protected their estates. The same problem would occur during the English Civil War.
56. *A Pleasant Satyre or Poesie; wherein is discovered the Catholicon of the League* (London, 1595).
57. G. Fagniez, 1897, p. 79. Sully, [1970–88], p. 87.
58. Piémond's hostility towards the nobility was typical of the small town officials of the *plat pays*. It would also be present in the leadership of the *Croquant* rebellion. J. Brun-Durand, [1885], pp. 235–6, 252, 295, etc. Cf. D. Hickey, 1978, 25–49 for an interesting analysis of the newer nobility which claimed exemption from taxation in Dauphiné.

end of the wars of the League there was a striking unanimity of purpose between the smaller towns and the *plat pays* countryside which gave those revolts a degree of confidence and sense of purpose which rendered them particularly dangerous to established authority.

PEASANT INSURRECTION AND THE END OF THE WARS OF THE LEAGUE

Organised popular unrest against royal taxation and noble brigandage first became a feature of the civil wars in the wake of the edict of pacification in 1577.[59] There were movements in Provence in 1578 (the *Razats*), in the Rhône valley in 1579 (the *Ligue des Villains*) and in Normandy (the *Gaultiers* around Caen). Peasants of either religion became involved in them. They were led by the smaller towns of the *plat pays* such as Montélimar and Romans. Their aims included the reduction of royal taxation on the countryside and a proper representation in provincial assemblies so that taxes could be more fairly distributed between principal towns and the rest of the province, as well as an end to unjust exemptions for newly ennobled individuals and military captains. They also demanded the right to act against noble brigands. Each movement included manifest expressions of hostility to the local nobility and demands for liberty which were not just rituals in popular revolts and which seriously alarmed contemporaries.

Widespread popular risings also accompanied the end of the wars of the League a decade later. The *Gaultiers* reappeared in 1589, attacking the troops of the duke of Epernon (already renowned for their disobedience) and those of the duke of Montpensier who was besieging Falaise for Henri III.[60] The peasant army was repulsed with great violence by Montpensier, but peasant insurrections remained just below the surface in Normandy. Two years later, the *Francs-Museaux* and the *Châteauverts* directed peasant hostilities against plundering League nobles in the province.[61] Their example was followed in other regions. In nearby Brittany, Jean Moreau, priest at Quimper, described the sufferings of the *paysantaille* and their determination to exterminate

---

59. E. Le Roy Ladurie, 1979. J.H.M. Salmon, 1979, 25–40.
60. J.H.M. Salmon, 1975, pp. 278–9 and refs. The papers of La Popelinière (BN MS Fr 20782, ff. 573–6) give an account of the beginnings of the *Gaultiers*.
61. R. d'Estaintot, 1862, pp. 95–8, 109–13, 124–7 describes the problems around Falaise through the surviving letters of a tax collector.

the brigand nobles.[62] Their targets included the one-armed pirate of the island of Noirmoutiers (Anne de Sanzay, comte de la Magnanne) and a dangerous brigand called Guy Eder de la Fontanelle who withstood an attack from a large peasant force by retreating to an island and eluded capture until 1602.[63] Further south appeared the *Campanelle* of Comminges who expressed their purpose as 'to rally and declare war on the nobility and take possession of the fortified towns of the countryside'.[64] As in Normandy, their enemies were League nobles who were conducting a campaign of terror in the locality. The most serious peasant uprisings occurred at the end of the wars of the League in Burgundy (the *Bonnets Rouges*, 1594, 1597), in the Velay (1595) and, above all, in the south-west (the *Croquants*, 1593–95). The *Croquants* began in the autumn of 1593 in the viscounty of Turenne. By the time that the royal lieutenant in the Limousin had defeated the peasant army in his province in July 1594, the rising had spread throughout Guyenne, creating a movement as serious as the more renowned *Croquant* rising in 1636–37.

In a comprehensive recent study of popular revolts in south-west France, Y-M. Bercé concluded that the *Croquants* of 1593–95 were principally 'a party of the countryside', that they were opposed to the towns and that they did not consciously break the 'vertical solidarity' – the 'fidelity towards their seigneur'.[65] There was, he said, no 'structural social antagonism'. Was this, in fact, the case? Initially, the peasants called themselves the *Chasse-Voleurs* because their chief purpose (in an area heavily dependent on pastoral agriculture) was to prevent theft of livestock by noble captains. Later, they called themselves the *Tard-Avisés*, the late-comers.[66] They saw favours and privileges being heaped on League nobles and cities and feared that, being the last in the queue for concessions, they would pay for the favours assigned to others. In a sense, they were correct in their fears.

---

62. H. Wacquet, [1960], pp. 80–3.

63. J. Baudry, 1920, unravels the mythology connected with Fontanelle. He was executed in Paris in September 1602 with some popular satisfaction (Estoile, [1958], 80).

64. This revolt was partially encouraged by the League lieutenant for the region (J. Lestrade, *Les Huguenots de Comminges*, 2 vols, (1900–1901), II, 239). Cf. H. Drouot, 1937a, II, 272–93 for the *Bonnets Rouges*.

65. Y-M. Bercé, 1974, I, 291–2.

66. Y-M. Bercé, 1974, I, 258 presents the explanation for their name rather differently. His bibliography of sources is the fullest, but the account of J.H.M. Salmon, 1975, 282–91 is also interesting. J. Nouaillac, 1912, should be added to the accounts mentioned in Y-M. Bercé, 1974, pp. 258–9. I have drawn on some documents mentioned in R.G. Tait, 1977, ch. vii. His analysis of the *Croquants* modifies that of Bercé in important respects.

In 1594, Henri IV was hoping to raise about 21 million livres through the taille and a further 8 millions by indirect taxes. Bercé is therefore correct to see the *Croquants* within a tradition of anti-fiscal agitation in Gascony and it is true that the revolt took place in areas which had refused taxation in the past and would continue to do so in the seventeenth century. But the demands to relieve the weight of taxation and the oppressions of the nobility were intertwined one with another. It was impossible for local communities to distinguish between the military *tailles*, imposed on them by League nobles as assignations on their revenue, and other royal taxation. Brigandage was not just a local difficulty with a few captains, for the nobles that the *Croquants* complained about were prominent local figures.[67] Some villages which joined the *Croquant* movement specifically complained of their own seigneur.[68] Initially, it is true, the *Croquants* assembled in April and May 1594 at Abzac wood, Limeul and Montpazier to call on their social superiors to lead and direct their large forces. Their manifesto in June hoped that they would be assisted by 'all seigneurs and gentlemen without reproach'.[69] Such cooperation was not unthinkable, for peasant armies had been raised in Gascony by seigneurs in the course of the League. But even in their initial meetings, enough was said to alarm some nobles and capital cities. One assembly called on peasants 'to take arms and raze to the ground many noble *châteaux* belonging to those who only stole the cattle and beefstock of their neighbours'.[70] At another, they complained about the town of Périgueux, whose inhabitants closed their doors on poor peasants from the countryside in need of shelter, and cooperated in illegal taxation.[71] Among the individuals they mentioned were two

67. Already in the *cahier* of the third estate of Périgord to the estates of Blois in 1588, there were complaints that the nobility had appropriated royal taxes and forced an 'infinite' number of *corvées* from peasants, interfering with their rights to commons and demanding huge rents from peasants in places where their rent rolls had been destroyed in the civil wars. The Périgord *Croquants* complained that their nobility had taken over royal taxes and imprisoned more than 200 peasants 'for their *tailles*'. The community of La Linde, which played a prominent part in the Périgord rising, complained in 1594 that their own seigneur oppressed them and sold them to the enemy side, leaving them to pay their ransoms. There were similar complaints from the villages surrounding the fortified site of Penne in the Agenais.

68. BN MS Dupuy 744, f. 147. Cf. Y-M. Bercé, 1974, I, 272–7.

69. Cayet, XII, 574–5.

70. BN MS Fr 23914, f. 373v.

71. Deputies sent from the peasant assembly at Abzac wood in April 1594 to the king asked for royal permission to deal with 'the king's enemies' at Périgueux, Bergerac and Sarlat. They also demanded the right to appoint a syndic to represent the *plat pays* at the local estates. This demand had been previously expressed in 1583, at the time of the provincial commissioners for reform, despatched by Henri III.

receivers of the Périgord and Ogier de Gourgues, a merchant of Bordeaux, who had made immense profits from war contracts and tax farming and who died one of the wealthiest men of the province.[72] They also demanded the right to elect their own syndic of the countryside to the local estates. A similar demand had been presented by the smaller towns of the Périgord in 1583 and its reappearance in 1594 suggests that the organisation of the *Croquants* was influenced by the smaller towns and *bastides*.

Bercé writes of 'an imagined subversion' among those in authority in the province. At the time, they thought that the threats were real enough. From Sarlat, the cathedral canon, Jean Tarde, wrote of the anti-noble aspirations of the revolt.[73] The secretary to the town council in Périgueux reported: 'They openly speak of destroying the nobility and being free of everything. The share-croppers (*métayers*) turn against their masters . . . The brutish people have several times tried to stop grain and other provisions coming to town.'[74] A Limousin observer recalled that: 'They menaced the nobility, held them to ridicule, and did the same to the towns . . . In fact, they terrorised and frightened many and it seemed as though the world had turned upside down.'[75] Social antagonisms became more marked still when anti-peasant noble bands (mainly around Sarlat) were formed from League captains and Huguenot nobles who buried their differences to fight against those who 'want to establish a democracy like the Swiss'.[76]

The *Croquants* placed Henri IV in a delicate position. Concession would easily be misinterpreted as weakness, yet military force would damage his credibility and was not easily spared in the last stages of the wars of the League. The king was personally disposed to leniency. According to Estoile and Agrippa d'Aubigné, he remarked that, if he had not inherited the throne, he would have become a *Croquant* himself. [77] He accepted their demands, presented to the council on 23 May 1594, and sent a commissioner to the Limousin to disperse their armies by persuasion and to spread the news of his 'clemency,

---

72. For Ogier de Gourgues, see Y-M. Bercé, 1974, I, 274–5, 281–2.

73. Jean Dupont, sieur de Tarde, canon at Sarlat cathedral. His diary was edited in 1885. This passage appears in C. Higounet, 1971, pp. 212–15.

74. Y-M. Bercé, 1974, I, 285. There were other alarmed reports from the *parlement* of Bordeaux and the seneschals of Périgord and the Agenais (Bourdeille and Monluc) in BN MS Fr 23194.

75. Y-M. Bercé, 1974, I, 286.

76. Ibid., pp. 287–8.

77. Estoile, [1948], p. 420 (June 1594). d'Aubigné, IX, 121. Cf. *Henri IV*, 1843–60, IV, 112–13, 154–6.

goodness and natural justice'.[78] For a time it looked doubtful whether the king's authority was strong enough to impose the ways of moderation on the provincial nobles, but by harvest 1594, all was quiet again. However, the harvest was a poor one across France. In the spring of 1595, the poor of the Périgord were dying from starvation and the *Croquants* reassembled. The king once more offered concessions on royal taxation but, this time, a force of gentlemen under the seneschal in the Périgord was allowed to attack and disperse the remnants of the peasant army.[79] Their brutality suggests something of the vengeance to be expected from the provincial nobles.

This was the last major popular rebellion under Henri IV. Through its history can be glimpsed the real social hostilities of the wars. It provided a test of fire for Henri IV's government, the memory of which was never forgotten. It advertised the fact that direct taxation had a clear limit beyond which it became unendurable given the limits of production in the peasant economy. It indicated how important genuine peace and recovery were to preserve traditional French society.

REVIVAL AND RECONSTRUCTION

Economic recovery was broadly based after the peace and felt across the whole of France. François de La Noue exaggerated when he said that 'France is so populous and fertile that what war damaged in a year is restored in two' but it is clear that recovery could happen remarkably fast.[80] Economic dislocation always meant tragedy for some, but opportunity for others. One man's famine was another's moment to benefit from high grain prices. One peasant's reluctant sale of part of his land-holding meant investment by another in the property. When Thomas Coryat, an English traveller, went through the country in 1608 he only found one village 'exceedingly ransacked and ruinated by means of the civil wars' still showing the visible signs of its former suffering.[81] Some parts of the countryside reached,

---

78. J. Nouaillac, 1912, 321–50.
79. Y-M. Bercé, 1974, I, 281. R.G. Tait, 1977, ch. vii. The king eventually granted amnesties to the *Croquants* in 1596 on the insistence of the syndic of Périgord to prevent a group of nobles ruining villages in legal suits for damages to their property.
80. F. de La Noue, [1967], p. 190.
81. T. Coryat, *Coryat's Crudities*, Glasgow, 1905, I, 167.

although few exceeded, the population densities of 1580.[82] Tithe returns indicate that recuperation had also taken place.[83] The consumption of salt – partly encouraged by forced sales – increased dramatically from 8,000 *muids* in 1599 to 11,400 *muids* in 1611 in the major salt farms of France.[84] (1 *muid* = a waggon-load of roughly 25 hectolitres). Prices for grain decreased with the coming of peace, helped by a succession of fortunate harvests from 1604 to 1609. There was no dearth and little shortage in the first decade of the seventeenth century. When (as in 1604) the harvest appeared to be mediocre in some regions, royal administration prohibited exports before the crops had been harvested.[85] Low grain prices encouraged a diversification to new cash crops – maize, vegetables, vines and oils – especially around the main towns. These were often the regions where the indebted peasantry had sold up to the new proprietors from the towns who had the cash and incentive to experiment. After 1600, the concurrence of falling grain prices, interest rates and *tailles* was unique in the *ancien régime*. It meant that for the peasant proprietor of 15–20 acres or less, Henri IV's reign brought a welcome respite and was, in reality as well as myth, a golden age.[86] For some of the rural gentry and farmers, however, it meant an end to the exploitative, albeit risky, profit environment which some of them had enjoyed during the civil wars.

The atmosphere of rural recuperation and revival is best discovered in the pages of the *Theatre of Agriculture*, written by France's most famous agriculturalist, Olivier de Serres (1539–1619), in 1600 and dedicated to the king. He was one of those socially unclassifiable people from the Midi: a seigneur who was not really a nobleman, from a merchant family but without mercantile leanings, a farmer only in retirement from his considerable activity in the protestant movement.[87] His family came from near Orange. His elder brother, Jean de Serres, became a pastor and Henri IV's official historian, while Olivier de Serres stayed on the family estates. The *Theatre of Agriculture* was not the only work of its kind to be produced during or immediately after the civil wars. But its subtle blend of observed detail,

---

82. The evidence is summarised in E. Le Roy Ladurie and M. Morineau, 1977, pp. 727–9.

83. J. Goy and E. Le Roy Ladurie, 1972, pp. 22, 145–7, 210.

84. E. Le Roy Ladurie and M. Morineau, 1977, pp. 750–1.

85. D. Buisseret, 1968, p. 172.

86. E. Le Roy Ladurie and M. Morineau, 1977, p. 762.

87. G. Fagniez, 1897, pp. 36–8. E. Le Roy Ladurie, 1966, I, 64–7, 353–5. F. Lequenne, 1942. A. Jouanna, 1976, pp. 1050–54. O. de Serres, *Le théâtre de l'agriculture et mesnage des champs* (Paris, 1600).

theoretical wisdom and practical advice, and its emendations in successive editions, ensured that it became the textbook for the substantial French farmer in the *ancien régime*. De Serres gives invaluable advice on how to rebuild a seigneurie, on the choice of land, the administration of a farm, the cultivation of an orchard, a vineyard or a meadow. New crops – beetroot, rice, melons and artichokes – did not escape his attention. He commented on new techniques too. From the book's pages appears a grand baroque landscape of staged and ordered nature. The work went through five editions in Henri IV's reign and the king had it read to him in half-hour instalments after dinner.

The towns experienced revival too, but it was far more patchy. Some never recovered their former prosperity. Toulouse, for instance, having lost its woad industry in the civil wars, did not recapture it in the face of competition from indigo.[88] Other towns found some measure of recovery on new foundations. Lyon did not regain its banking and trading pre-eminence but it acquired a new strength as a manufacturing centre for the silk industry.[89] Marseille recovered part of its former position in the Levant trade through the import of raw silk from the near East.[90] Henri IV assisted this with the construction of a Mediterranean fleet to combat pirates and the negotiation of a preferential trade treaty with the sultan in May 1604.[91] In the Atlantic, the centres of new prosperity lay in the smaller ports of St Malo, Brest and La Rochelle. Prospering from privateering and blockade, these ports then exploited valuable trade with Spain. This became a principal currency earner for France.[92] The export of grain and cloth to Spain was worth (on one contemporary estimate) 9 million *livres* a year.[93] From these ports were mounted colonial enterprises to the East Indies in 1601 and to Canada from 1598.[94] The government did what it

88. Suggestive pages in P. Chaunu and R. Gascon, 1977, pp. 326–33. For Toulouse, P. Wolff, *Histoire de Toulouse* (Privat, Toulouse, 1974), pp. 309–14. *AD Haute-Garonne* C 2285, f. 36 (The catholic estates of Languedoc estimated in October 1587 that the amount of woad exported from Toulouse had declined from 100,000 bales to 6,000 per year 'since foreigners invented a way to increase their production and export it to France without paying any duty'. Toulouse, like Lyon, demanded the protection of native manufacture.)

89. G. Fagniez, 1897, pp. 126–30. But Lyon was not the only city to develop a silk-weaving industry and there were problems with internal competition. (Ibid., pp. 121–6).

90. G. Fagniez, 1897, pp. 317–22. M. Baulant, 1953, pp. xxvii–xxix.

91. G. Fagniez, 1897, pp. 260–5. D. J. Buisseret, 1964a, 297–306.

92. G. Fagniez, 1897, pp. 26–65. A. Girard, 1932, pp. 50–1, 54–7.

93. G. Fagniez, 1897, pp. 260. G. Carew, [1749], pp. 430–1.

94. G. Fagniez, 1897, pp. 278–88. M. Trudel, 1973, pp. 62–106.

could to assist this commercial sector. A proposed 30 per cent import duty on French goods by Spain in 1604 was removed by retaliatory economic sanctions by France. Privateering was reduced in north-west European waters by a treaty with James I in February 1606. Following the pattern set by the Dutch, the king established trading companies for the East Indies in 1604 and one for 'New France' in 1605. The particular problems of English and Dutch penetration of the French market with their cloth were overshadowed by the growth of the home market in which all, for the moment, could share. In fact, following the seizure of defective English cloth at Rouen in April 1598, the French council prohibited the import of fully finished English textiles.[95] This became part of the disputes over the payments of English debts by the French government. The retaliation by the English government, which prohibited the import of French canvas and linen, temporarily harmed those French industries until, in 1604, an English trade delegation and the English ambassador in Paris succeeded in removing the French prohibition. In fact, the *parlements* of Bordeaux, Rouen and Rennes did not register its removal, so that there was still some import control imposed and English merchants were careful not to export to the French market the kinds of cloth which would bring them into direct competition with the home product.[96]

Sully's most positive contribution to economic revival lay in the creation of a more favourable commercial background. With Sully's assistance, bridges and waterways were improved and the currency stabilised. Commercial rates of interest were reduced in the wake of the reduction in rates of interest on government bonds. He changed the commercial laws of France on bankruptcy, tried to encourage nobles into trade, clarified the jurisprudence of French commercial courts and fostered merchant guilds and corporations.[97] He supported protection of native industries and attempted to acquire foreign techniques by attracting Dutch drainage engineers like Humphrey Bradley (who began to drain the Poitevin marshes) and Italian

---

95. H. A. Nicholle, 1976, pp. 178–80. English merchants said that the actions of the French 'showeth evidentlie that the Edict was procured by them of Roan for their privat good ther to restraine draperie or to gain the cullouringe of our English draperie to themselves'. Henri IV was more concerned at the loss of the English alliance than the loss of English trade as his letters to his English envoy make clear. For Benedict Webb, see J. Thirsk and J.P. Cooper, 1972, pp. 206–8.

96. H.A. Nicholle, 1976, pp. 182–3.

97. G. Fagniez, 1897, pp. 170–285. There is a discussion of Sully's attitude towards trade protection in D.J. Buisseret, 1968, ch. ix.

architects like the Piedmontese Bartholomeo Ricardo.[98]

The creation of the post of *grand voyer* for Sully in 1599 was not without opposition from the sovereign courts. It eventually led, however, to an impressive programme of capital investment in roads, bridges and canals. Sully insisted on the strict estimation of costs and supervision of contracts in his regulations of June 1604 and January 1605. The declaration of 1604 gave him powers to create lieutenancies in each generality – an extension of Sully's patronage. He chose pliant treasurers, technocrats and former clients to form an inspectorate of all roads and bridges. These officials met opposition from provincial estates which Sully was able to overcome in Brittany and Burgundy, but which defeated him in Languedoc. The bulk of his work, therefore, came in the *pays d'élections*. In 1608, eight per cent of the ordinary revenues was spent on carefully conceived bridge and canal schemes, with as much finance again probably coming from provincial or municipal sources.[99] At no stage before the eighteenth century was so high a proportion of the national product invested in the 'primary sector' of the economy. By 1610 there were new bridges on the Somme at Ham, Péronne, Corbie, Amiens and Abbeville. The Pont-Neuf in Paris and a new bridge at Châtellerault were completed and many others were begun.[100] At the same time, Henri IV's agents in the *voyerie* investigated river tolls and road charges, cancelling some and reducing others. River improvements and canals were effective in linking land-locked parts of France to the Atlantic economy. By Henri IV's death, Châlons, Reims, Troyes and Dijon were connected to the sea by canal. Ambitious schemes to link the Atlantic with the Mediterranean via the Garonne and also from the Seine (through the Loire, Saône and Rhône) were proposed.[101] In fact, the first stage of the latter project, a scheme to join the Seine and the Loire, was begun in 1604 in the canal at Briare, which, with Sully's protection, was nearly completed in 1610, although the regency stopped further work on it and it was not opened until 1642. These improvements had appreciable regional effects, especially in Sully's governorship in Poitou.[102] They also represented additional employment opportunities

---

98. G. Fagniez, 1897, pp. 84–6, 102, 269. J. Nouaillac, [1908], p. 133. D.J. Buisseret, 1964b, on the *ingénieurs du roi*, some of whom were foreigners employed in royal service too.

99. D.J. Buisseret, 1968, ch. vi. B. Barbiche, 1978, ch. vi.

100. G. Fagniez, 1897, pp. 174–87.

101. Ibid., pp. 188–208. D.J. Buisseret, 1968, pp. 107–8, 117–18, 117–19. G. Carew, [1749], pp. 431–2, 470–1.

102. D.J. Buisseret, 1965, 43–53.

and investment in technically advanced areas.[103] Sully's period in office witnessed the establishment of dynasties of technocrats – civil engineers, cartographers, drainage specialists and surveyors – who would serve the French crown through the century.

Some of the currency problems disappeared with the end of the wars; the circulation of defective silver and of debased copper coins was stopped by reform in the mints and the enforcement of an edict in 1596.[104] But the underlying problems of the coinage were still present. A scarcity of gold in 1601 began another round of speculation against the coinage and a marked appreciation in the price of the *écu*, measured against silver. Inevitably, the old parity crumbled and, in an important edict of September 1602, Sully restored the *livre tournois* as the basic accounting unit in France and devalued it against both gold and (slightly less) against silver.[105] The edict met determined opposition from both the sovereign courts and the mint (*cour des monnaies*). The *parlement* of Paris opposed a devaluation as (like the reduction of the rate of interest on the *rentes*) illegal and an attack on individual property rights. The mint in Paris disliked a change in the gold/silver ratio because it marked an interference in their own arcane science. In fact, the devaluation probably did not go far enough to restore the competitive edge to French exports in a period of expansion. Other moneys of account had devalued further than the *livre tournois*, and Sully's measure of 1602, while in the right direction, did not prevent currency speculation reappearing at the end of the reign.[106]

The currency problems of 1601 formed a background to the most ambitious programme of industrial stimulation undertaken in France before the ministry of Colbert. Sully argued that only the restoration of French industrial fortunes would solve France's monetary difficulties. He persuaded Henri IV to appoint a controller of mines and one of commerce in 1601–2 and to initiate regular meetings of a council of commerce to investigate and recommend new industrial ventures.[107] The first controller of commerce was Barthélemy de Laffemas (*c.*1545–1611). Like de Serres, he came from uncertain social origins in Dauphiné. The civil wars ruined his business but released his

103. G. Carew, [1749], pp. 461–2.
104. F.C. Spooner, 1972, pp. 167, 170.
105. Ibid., pp. 168–9. Fontanon, II, 227.
106. B. Barbiche, 1963, 3–17. F.C. Spooner, 1972, pp. 172–5.
107. G. Fagniez, 1897, pp. 31–4, 100, 353–5. Sully, [1881], XVII, 404 for the search for precious metals behind the interest in mining.

considerable talents as a publicist.[108] He used his position at court (he was appointed master of the wardrobe) to advance his schemes. In his substantial literary output, de Laffemas argued the case before the assembly of notables in 1596 for a grand, nationally conceived, manufacturing effort.[109] Laffemas was France's equivalent to the *arbitristas* in Spain or the mercantilists in England. The council of commerce was the French equivalent to the junta on reform in Spain and the parliamentary committees on the decay in trade established in England. It was more successful than the English or Spanish counterparts. It held 150 meetings and investigated many industrial ventures, submitting detailed reports on them to the council of state. In one sector, its recommendations produced genuine and striking success. Louis XI and François I had already tried to establish a native silk industry in France. Their methods were employed on a larger scale under Henri IV. With Laffemas' backing and against Sully's scepticism, silk production developed in Lyon, continued at Tours and spread round Montpellier and Nîmes.[110] A Lyonnais craftsman, Dangon, put the finishing touches in 1605 to a new technique for weaving silk which permitted the construction of the complex and multicoloured fabrics which laid the foundation for Lyon's silk-industry's long-term success. Henri IV granted Dangon a patent and had mulberry trees (on whose leaves the silkworms were cultivated) planted in his gardens. The Place Royale in Paris was conceived originally as the site for a royal factory whose ouput would rival the luxury cloths produced and imported into France from Milan. By 1646, imported silk had declined to one-sixth of its value on the eve of the civil wars.

Other textile ventures also took root – fine fabrics in Rouen, Flemish tapestry in the *maison* Gobelins in Paris, gold and silver point in the galleries of the Louvre and muslin in Reims.[111] The idea of offering lodging to highly-skilled craftsmen in the Louvre was probably also encouraged by the queen; her father had introduced the

---

108.   G. Fagniez, 1897, pp. 88–91. Estoile was suitably sceptical of de Laffemas' position and influence [1958], pp. 61, 221.

109.   G. Fagniez, 1897, pp. 109–12. *Règlement général pour dresser les manufactures en ce royaume* (Paris, 1597). Cf. H. Champollion-Figeac [1841–74], IV, pt. 2. Arch. cur. de l'hist. de France, XIV, 221–45 (*Recueil présenté au Roy de ce qui se passe en l'assemblée du commerce au palais à Paris*, 1604).

110.   Sully, [1881], XVI, 514–16. More generally, Sully and de Laffemas were both flexibly protectionist and Sully supported de Laffemas' schemes (D.J. Buisseret, 1968, pp. 174–5).

111.   G. Fagniez, 1897, pp. 83–4, 147, 151, 160, 237–8. Also pp. 101–2. Cf. P. Benedict, 1981, pp. 229–30.

same idea at the *Casino di San Marco* many years before.[112] There is an implicit Anglo-Saxon refusal to take such state encouragement to skill-intensive crafts seriously. Yet the evidence for its significance is strong. It is not too much of an exaggeration to suggest that, if the corpus of Flemish tapestry-makers had not been attracted to Paris and Amiens by Henri IV, there would have been no Gobelins tapestry manufactury under Louis XIV; the same is true of carpet-manufacture, cabinet-making, glassware, ceramics and clock-making. Metallurgy, however, remained the weakest sector of the French economy. The ironmaster, Antoine de Montchrétien, remarked that, if a French peasant wanted to buy a decent spade, he had to buy an imported one.[113]

De Laffemas was only one of the numerous 'projectors' active in France under Henri IV. The atmosphere was alive with economic proposals from Parisian bourgeois, protestant gentlemen, tax-farmers, financiers and court aristocrats. Such schemes included mining (Henri IV ordered an enquiry into mineral wealth in 1600 with the prospect of leasing out concessions for exploration through a controller of mines in 1601); drainage (his council created a master of dykes in 1599, and parts of Poitou, Guyenne and Picardy were drained); and the establishment of a national bank (1608).[114] The council of finance received a stream of propositions from projectors and tax-farmers. Some proposed to eradicate corruption in particular areas of royal service. Others held out tempting prospects of exploiting national wealth more efficiently – generally in return for the grant of a monopoly to a particular individual.[115] The king's personal interest in projects of all kinds was evident. He was excited by the prospect of a *canal des deux mers*, planned a museum of machinery in the Louvre, and established a variety of artisans there.[116] But it would be wrong to suggest that everything went through royal channels. Far more was planned and achieved through individual initiatives than through state intervention. Henri IV's achievement was to give some schemes a sense of direction and to link them to the success of his administration.

Nowhere was this better illustrated than in the reconstruction of Paris. Among the public buildings that were transformed in the reign were the Hôtel-Dieu, the Hôpital de la Charité, the Arsenal, the

---

112. *Henri IV et la reconstruction du royaume*, 1989, p. 319.

113. A. Lublinskaya, 1968, pp. 112–13.

114. G. Fagniez, 1897, p. 234. The dramatic increase in the number of patents issued by the king is noted in J.U. Nef, 1957, *Industry and Government in France and England* (Ithaca), p. 84.

115. F. Bayard, 1984, pp. 199–211.

116. Ibid., pp. 102–3.

Louvre and the Pont-Neuf. As the newspaper, the *Mercure François* reported in 1610: 'No sooner was he [*Henri IV*] master of Paris, than the masons were at work.'[117] Parts of the city were paved and the sanitation improved. Even the pyramid, erected against the Jesuit, Barrière, for his attack against the king in 1594, was taken down in 1605 and replaced with a fountain and a Latin inscription which ended: 'To prevent the passions [*of civil war*] from breaking out and destroying everything, fresh water here will flow for ever.'[118] Aristocrats also returned to the capital and reconstructed their town houses.[119] Henri IV and Sully took part in the speculation. They planned three major squares. Two of them were built at the Place Vendôme and the Place Royale (now the Place des Vosges), while some streets of the third, the Place de France, were begun.[120] All three projects were designed as an advertisement for the reign, with street names and statues indicating the fact. They involved a new sense of stylistic unity and a degree of cooperation from the office holders and the Parisian magistrature. The Place des Vosges still survives, an ambitious Italian piazza, designed by Androuet du Cerceau and Claude Chastillon, with a central market square cut off from through traffic, surrounded by thirty-six pavilions leased to merchants of the new French enterprises. Above the galleries ran smart town houses which were rented to the office holders and courtiers, especially to Sully's clients. Meanwhile, Sully was involved in the construction of a completely new town in the principality of Boisbelle in the Nivernais, which he had acquired from Charles de Gonzague, duke of Nevers.[121]

117. J-P. Babelon, 1965, p. 13. Cf. Henri IV, 1843–60, VII, 219–20 (Henri IV to the cardinal of Joyeuse, Fontainebleau, 3 May 1607) – 'at Paris, you will see my large gallery which runs to the Tuileries, now finished . . . the Place Royale near the Porte Saint-Antoine and its factories is three quarters completed and will be finished next year; at the end of the Pont-Neuf a beautiful new street runs to the Porte de Bussy and the houses along both sides of it will be up by the end of next year; more than two or three thousand workshops are employed here and there for the embellishment of the city so it is impossible that you will not notice a change'.

118. A. Miron de l'Espinay, 1885, p. 106.

119. R.R. Harding, 1978, pp. 172–3. Cf. H. Sauval, 1724, II, 67–8, 120, 122, 123, 127, etc. for the speculative development of town houses by aristocrats in Paris. Henri IV joked that the rebuilding of the *hôtel* de Nevers would take so long that no one alive would ever see its completion.

120. J-P. Babelon, 1965, pp. 16–25.

121. B. Barbiche, 1978, pp. 121–5. Charles de Gonzague, duke of Nevers, also constructed a new town (Charleville), beginning in 1606 with the architect, Clément Métezeau (who had designed royal buildings in Paris). The duke of Montmorency planned a grand new port on the Languedoc coast (Montmorencette – now Sète), while Henri IV was enthusiastic for a new planned addition to the city of Rouen (P. Benedict, 1981, p. 230).

In December 1608, the charter for the new town of 'Henrichemont' was unveiled. Its subscribers included Sully's financiers and colleagues in the Arsenal. The purpose was to create a show-case fortress-city. It was part of Sully's complex campaign of self-advertisement which was designed to persuade the king of his indispensability when it came to advancing the military strength of the regime.[122] When Sully fell from power, however, the clients backed away from the project, leaving Sully with a half-finished enterprise. The Place des Vosges was more fortunate and was completed in April 1612, a good example of the union of privilege, wealth and productive enterprise which was at the heart of France's new-found and delicate equipoise.

122. E.H. Dickerman and Anita M. Walker, 1992.

CHAPTER SEVEN

The Long Robe

THE PROFESSIONS

There was a traditionally close association between the professions of the law and the catholic church. Judges and clerics shared a common educational background, a similar official dress (the professional classes were recognised by their long black or red robes) and a series of shared assumptions about professional conduct. As the Chancellor Bellièvre remarked, justice was a 'Holy thing'.[1] To François le Breton, the lawyer and League martyr: 'Religion and Justice are bound up so closely with each other that they are inseparable; the same zeal guides and inspires us and strengthens our courage'.[2] In courtrooms, large missals or paintings of the Crucifixion were used as objects of veneration on which witnesses swore to tell the truth.[3] Some clerics were members of the *parlements* and some magistrates were canons of cathedral chapters. Some lawyers trained to become clerics (or to *faire la profession*, as the taking of Holy Orders was commonly called) before turning to the study of civil law. Many of the qualities commonly regarded as most edifying in a cleric were, with the exception of chastity, also taken to be most becoming in a judge. Modesty in dress, gravity of gesture, propriety in conduct and association were qualities regularly alluded to in the speeches made to the assembled barristers at the beginning of each new legal session by the royal attorney. Eulogies and biographies turned judges like Achille de Harlay (the first president of the *parlement* of Paris) into something approaching counter-reformed

---

1. *Revue Henri IV*, 1905–6, I, 187.
2. F. le Breton, *Remonstrances aux Trois Etats de la France* (n.p., 1586), p. 72.
3. M. Rousselet, 1957. J. Dewald, 1980, p. 21.

saints.[4] La Roche Flavin, the lawyer from Toulouse, wrote an extensive account of the sovereign law-courts of France in which he devoted a chapter to the question of judicial proprieties and included a number of malicious stories of judges who had failed to live up to their calling. This resulted in an effort to have the book suppressed.[5]

Professions have conservative tendencies, and the legal and clerical world of sixteenth-century France rested heavily on history and precedent to prove the importance of tradition as the basis for legitimacy and consent to the law and the catholic church.[6] Lawyers used 'the old authors' and studied ancient chronicles in order to cite them in courtrooms in the same way as theologians and clerics consulted the biblical canon and church fathers. To contemporaries, the conservatism of the Latin language used by clerics and the fossilised legal jargon of the courtrooms were very striking. The professions shared a number of common interests and concerns where their conservative instincts were noticeable. The judges, for instance, punished offences against the moral order most severely. These included homicide, perjury, blasphemy, brigandage, infanticide (which Jean Bodin thought was a crime resulting from a pact with the devil) and parricide.[7] The law and the church were inevitably drawn close together in certain other public affairs. Cases of sorcery and witchcraft were judged by royal courts but frequently required clerical testimony. To judge from the number of cases being presented on appeal to the *parlement* of Paris and from the contemporary alarm, fear of witchcraft had grown considerably during the civil wars. Both clerics and lawyers were perturbed that 'the practices of sorcerers are in such profusion that a majority of people and families are in continual peril and apprehension, both on their own account and also on the account of the fruits of the earth and their cattle'.[8] Jean Bodin, among others, urged judges to relax their standards of evidence and testimony in order to close the legal loopholes through which, he claimed, many sorcerers escaped conviction.[9] Administration of poor relief and the operation of hospitals as well as the problems of education were also matters of mutual concern. The church had responsibilities towards the poor and the sick and the judges wanted to prevent civil disobedience. In the civil wars, charitable institutions and hospitals did little to

4. C. Kaiser, 1982.
5. B. de La Roche Flavin, [1617]. Biography in P. Boyer, 1921.
6. J. Dewald, 1980, pp. 31–41.
7. J. Dewald, 1976.
8. A. Soman, 1978.
9. J. Bodin, *De la démonomanie des sorciers* (2nd edn, Paris, 1581).

alleviate poverty and private charity was often uncoordinated. Royal legislation demanded that both *parlements* and clerical administrators cooperated in the management of what resources there were.[10] The universities were in a somewhat analogous position to hospitals in respect of their relationship to the professions, both of the robe and the cloth.[11]

There were also common differences of opinion within the professions. One debate concerned the position of the Jesuit colleges in France, which had been set up especially in the first decade of the civil wars.[12] On the one hand, these were opposed because they appeared to challenge the rights of established universities to issue degrees and they were felt to expropriate the education of youth – frequently to foreign-born teachers. On the other hand, some prelates were anxious to encourage the Company of Jesus in their diocese and some judges wanted a cheaper education for their sons. The Jesuit issue was but one part of a wider debate about the Gallican rights of the French church. These rights had been articulated from the early fifteenth century when the schism in the papacy permitted the French church to express certain aspirations to independence both from the papacy and from French kings. The Pragmatic Sanction of 1438 represented clerical aspirations at their fullest but this was revoked by François I in all but its purely internal disciplinary decrees by a Concordat reached with the papacy in 1516. The Concordat removed the French church's claims to elect its senior clergy, denied it the right to hold councils of the church without royal permission and restored papal taxation. The Concordat was bitterly disliked by the judges of the *parlement* of Paris and by the theologians of the Sorbonne.[13] In 1560, there was an attempt to re-establish the Pragmatic Sanction through the estates general and in 1579 the clergy asked for internal elections of senior clergy to be instituted, but all without success. In 1586, an assembly of the French church vigorously resisted a further alienation of church wealth which had been proposed by the king and supported by the papacy, and appealed to the Gallican rights of the French church. Although judges were naturally prudent in their treatment of the Gallican question, barristers, scholars and

10.   R. Doucet, 1948, II, 802-12. The edict of 1561 was confirmed in 1566 and 1579, giving the laity a major power over hospital and Poor Law management. For charity in Paris, see C. Paultre, 1906, p. ii. Cf. J. Dewald, 1980, p. 98.

11.   R. Doucet, 1948, II, 791–802. For the *parlement* of Paris and the university of the capital, see E. Maugis, 1914, II, app. ii.

12.   R. Chartier, *L'éducation en France* (SEDES, 1976), p. 187.

13.   A. Thomas, 1910, III.

constitutional lawyers were more straightforward in their support for the clergy's rights to a freedom from interference from royal or papal power.[14] Jacques Faye d'Espesse expressed them trenchantly at the estates general of Blois in 1588. The primacy of the papacy within the universal church was not an absolute authority but limited by the canons and councils of the church and local customs. In addition, the papacy had no rights to intervene in the temporal jurisdiction of the French crown. These freedoms were as essential a professional requirement for the *ecclesia* as for the *parlementum*.

THE SALE OF OFFICES

Contemporaries frequently remarked on the corruption within the French church and alluded to the widespread non-residence, nepotism, pluralism and simony among the senior clergy as one of the principal causes of the French reformation.[15] However, in the case of simony, or the sale of offices, royal service was far more afflicted than the church. This 'vile commerce' (as Estoile described it) was widely regarded as an evil in the state for the same reasons as it was in the church, namely, that it promoted unsuitable individuals to a sacred task and involved the possibility that they would attempt to profit from the procedures of punishing sins and enforcing justice.[16] In theory, the money paid into the bureau of casual revenues (the *bureau des parties casuelles*) for the right to hold a royal office was a loan to the king and reimbursable.[17] Royal office-holders had to swear an oath on taking up their posts that they had paid nothing for the privilege of exercising royal authority, an oath which survived until 1598, by which time theory and practice were too far apart to be sustained.[18] The market in royal offices was already widely known in the reign of Henri II and the prices for various posts were openly discussed. The numbers of offices for sale began to increase as the king attempted to finance his

14. J. Powis, 1983.

15. For example, Guy Coquille: 'Que les maux de la France pendant la Ligue venoient faute de réformation principalement de l'estat ecclésiastique'. (*Oeuvres*, 2 vols (Paris, 1666), I, 310–11).

16. Estoile, [1958], p. 234 (Mar. 1611). The dislike of venality is widely expressed towards the end of the sixteenth century. R.E. Mousnier, 1971, p. 76 (for the views of Montaigne). F. Hotman, [1972], pp. 519–21.

17. M. Rousselet, 1957, I, 97. J. Dewald, 1980, p. 136. C. Stocker, 1978, 25.

18. *Revue Henri IV*, 1905–6, I, 265.

wars on resources beyond the revenues of the *tailles*. The *parlement* of Bordeaux doubled its size in the first half of the sixteenth century; its twin at Toulouse tripled.[19] The formation of the lesser legal tribunals known as *présidiaux* in 1555 created 550 new offices at once. In Paris, the practice of having more than one officer to a post (and a rotation between them) began in the 1550s.

The civil wars turned a stream of new offices into a flood. In 1573, there were about 146 senior magistrates and 741 lesser office holders in 502 posts in the city of Rouen. By 1604, there were 162 senior magistrates, with 1,932 lesser officials in 922 posts.[20] In the generality of Montpellier, it has been estimated that the overall number of royal officers quadrupled during the sixteenth century. As the lawyer, Charles Loyseau, commented: 'in every town, the *honnêtes hommes* have offices'.

With the increase in royal offices went an increase in lawyers, clerks and notaries to service the professions. The numbers of solicitors in the *parlement* of Dijon increased fivefold between 1550 and 1580, and La Roche Flavin commented on the 'many regiments, even a small army' of attorneys in Toulouse by the beginning of the seventeenth century.[21] The sale of new offices went on at all levels of royal administration and the prices of offices also began to rise rapidly, particularly after the revenue of the *parties casuelles* was put out to farm in 1575.[22] The tax farmers sold offices more aggressively to the highest bidder and dropped the pretence of the purchase price being a loan. In Rouen, the price of a councillorship in the *parlement* doubled between 1575 and 1588.[23] It was probable that royal office-holding may have become more attractive as an alternative to mercantile or even landed investments in the unstable conditions of the civil wars. There was certainly no shortage of lawyers wanting to move into a royal office.

It was also relatively easy to obtain the reversion, or inheritance, of an office for a son, heir, or relative. The pattern was rather similar to the *resignatio in favorem* procedure which the church allowed for cathedral prebendaries and other clerical posts.[24] Individuals could

---

19. R.E. Mousnier, 1971, pp. 41–3.

20. J. Dewald, 1980, p. 69.

21. B. de La Roche Flavin, [1617], p. 238. The number of solicitors at the *parlement* of Rennes increased from 60 to 80 in the period from 1555 to 1572 and there were 110 in 1600. For the number of attorneys in Paris, see M. Yardeni, 1966, 483–6.

22. Estoile, [1943], 115 (Mar. 1575).

23. J. Dewald, 1980, pp. 138–40.

24. G. de Maynard, *Notables et Singuliers Questions du droit écrit*, (Toulouse, 1751), p. 43. R. Doucet, 1948, I, ch. xviii.

purchase the right to hand on their post for what was called the third or fourth penny (a third or fourth of the value of their office) paid to the king in return for letters of resignation. As in the church, these letters had to be granted at least thirty-nine days before the death of the incumbent in the office in order to prevent fraudulent resignations. Estoile recorded the competition for offices and resignations in Paris in the civil wars:

> As soon as His Majesty has thought of creating an office, no matter how small, there are disputes about who shall have it, and he [*the king*] is importuned about the reversion of it; for there is no officer so poor that he does not wish to secure his estates and cannot find the ready money to buy the rights of reversion, and yet who does not criticise the king and blame him for the multiplication and sale of offices of which he is the first and prime mover.[25]

The right of reversion to an office was, literally, a fatal issue. Sudden death could come to the most eminent office-holder in the realm, through an attack of the plague, a riding accident or the hangman's rope: the descendants of Pierre Hennequin, Christophe de Thou and Barnabé Brisson (to take examples from amongst the most eminent judges of France) had good cause to regret the precipitate deaths of their ancestor and the loss to the family of the large investment which each had made in their office of president in the *parlement* of Paris.

Others recorded how the increase in the number of judges also encouraged a recourse to the law so that, as one contemporary put it, 'never was a kingdom, province, country, estate or manor, so occupied in litigation as France'. The chancellor remarked on this 'great deluge' of lawsuits which he blamed on 'the multiplication of offices in all the nooks and crannies of the kingdom'.[26] Sully, too, noted the lamentable consequences for the council of state where the 'crowd of masters of requests and other legal bigwigs [*bonnets cornus*] created chaos in council and would willingly confute by chicanery all the affairs of state and finance'.[27] By the end of the wars of religion, therefore, office-holding represented a significant social fact in France. Some commentators like La Roche Flavin spoke of the office-holders as a kind of 'people of the middling sort'. He regarded them as

25. Estoile, [1943], p. 115 (Mar. 1575).
26. P. Bugnyon, *Traité des loix abrégées et inusitées*, (Paris, 1605), p. 12. According to the chancellor de l'Hôpital: 'the great deluge of lawsuits began under the reign of Henri II with the establishment of the *présidiaux* and the multiplication of offices in all the nooks and crannies of the kingdom'.
27. N. Valois, [1886], I, cvii.

Aristotle had done, as 'the steadiest element, the least eager for change' in society.[28] In doing so, La Roche Flavin chose to ignore the widening gap between senior officers and those in posts of little value and to overlook the distinction between judicial and other posts in royal service, both of which made it difficult to regard the office-holders as a coherent group in society. When it came to the holding of the estates general in 1576, the second estate rejected any notion of a 'fourth estate' of office holders and reminded the deputies of the third estate (the majority of whom were royal officials) that they belonged to the bourgeoisie.

The lesser nobility were particularly alarmed at the rapid spread of venality and its effects on the price of offices. They recited the commonplace that those who bought offices of justice 'sold retail what they bought wholesale'.[29] At the estates general, they said that members of old noble families were being squeezed from royal office by the rise in prices. There is considerable evidence to suggest that this was, in fact, the case. In the early sixteenth century, there had been a significant number of old nobles serving among the magistrature.[30] In the civil wars, this ceased to happen. This was partly because of the military demands of the civil wars which emphasised the demeaning character of professional duties. Monluc, for instance, could not understand why 'so many of our fine youth live uselessly' among the lawcourts when they could be discovering honour and valour on the battlefield.[31] Even judges like Michel de Montaigne or lawyers like Etienne Pasquier admitted that nobility in France was, in practice, to be associated with the military.[32] It was also because the costs of entering the magistrature increased beyond the pockets of many lesser nobles, however. Legal education almost certainly became more expensive in the sixteenth century, as the cost of books and travel and the length of time required to acquire a qualification rivalled the costs of purchasing military livery and becoming a lackey in a military

---

28. B. de La Roche Flavin, [1617], p. 350. Quoted in J. Dewald, 1980, p. 70. This lack of 'people of the middling sort' was much lamented by the *arbitristas* in Castile during this period (J.H. Elliott, *Imperial Spain* (Arnold, 1963), p. 305).

29. F. de La Noue, [1967], pp. 126–7. Bugnyon, *op. cit.*, p.15 (cited above in note 26).

30. J. Dewald, 1980, pp. 70–80. Cf. J. Powis, 1973, 27–36.

31. B. de Monluc, [1964], p. 345.

32. M. de Montaigne: 'La forme propre et la seule et essentielle de noblesse en France, c'est la vocation militaire' ([1962], II, 165). Etienne Pasquier: 'tant est demeurée recommandée entre nous cette vieille impression des armes sur laquelle nos premiers Français establirent le fondement de leur noblesse' (*Recherches* (1621 edn) p. 128). See A. Jouanna, 1976, pp. 241–452.

company. The rising prices of offices made it more difficult to raise the necessary money without resorting to borrowing or to selling the patrimony. At the same time, observers like La Noue expressed the resentments of lesser nobles, who felt that judges were becoming more wealthy and more established as a provincial nobility in certain regions around the cities where the sovereign courts resided.[33]

In fact, the return on an investment in a royal office probably changed its character in the wars of religion. The salaries (*gages*) of royal officials failed to keep in line, either with inflation or with the price of offices, and especially so after the 1570s. For instance, a senior judge in the *parlement* at Rouen around 1570 could expect about a 10 per cent *per annum* return on the capital value of the office, but this figure halved by the end of the century.[34] The costs of the growing bill for wages to the new officers explained why the monarchy could not contemplate raising its servants' salaries. As it was, expenditure on official salaries rose (at least according to the estimates produced for public discussion) from 2.3 million *livres* in 1576 to 5 million *livres* in 1585.[35]

Alongside salaries, however, there were the notorious 'emoluments' (*épices*) paid to magistrates by suitors and at a rate agreed by the judge of the case, having regard to the casework it had required. Such emoluments were substantial, at least if you were a senior judge. They ensured that senior royal office remained a very attractive proposition, offering annual returns on investment which were generally better than those from landed rents or government bonds and more secure than any prospective investment in a commercial venture, especially during the fraught trading conditions of the civil wars. For ordinary judges or lesser judicial officials in courts of first instance where salaries were only a few hundred *livres*, however, it was a rather different matter.[36] They were less able to make up for loss of salary by legal fees, commissions and emoluments. They were unlikely to be offered the royal pensions available to presidents of *parlements* and other senior officials who were regarded as particularly important for monarchical authority. As one councillor in the *parlement* of Rouen said in 1570: 'The president wants to rule the councillors by tyranny and fear; he gets the honours and the large salary, while the councillor receives

---

33. F. de La Noue, [1967] pp. 126–7. Cf. R.E. Mousnier, 1971, pp. 74–7, 462–9. Also J. Dewald, 1980, ch. iii. G. Snyders, 1965, pp. 36–7.
34. R.E. Mousnier, 1971, pp. 74–5. J. Dewald, 1980, pp. 148–50.
35. R.E. Mousnier, 1971, p. 74.
36. *Ibid.*, p. 148.

nothing and is ill-treated.'[37] Whether it was the case, as La Roche Flavin complained, that an ordinary case judge only achieved a return of, at best, 2 per cent on his investment in public office, remains an open question.[38]

In any case, the office-holding robe had even greater attractions in terms of status and social pretensions. Charles Loyseau, a distinguished lawyer at the Paris bar, defined an office as a 'dignity with a public function'. By 'dignity', he meant the corpus of privileges attached to the office and its tribunal.[39] Among the individual privileges for judges in sovereign courts were an exemption from the billeting of troops on their town houses and, for all office holders, an exemption from payment of *tailles*. First presidents of the courts were treated as the equivalent of princes of the blood in that it was regarded as a treasonable act to plot against their lives.[40] Many magistrates purchased letters of nobility and others married into the high magistrature to create a series of cohesive groups of families in each tribunal.[41] In some *parlements*, there were efforts by some judges to prevent those who were not from good families gaining offices.[42] One protestant pamphleteer sneered at these pretensions and called the *parlement* of Toulouse a 'consistory of princes'.[43]

The corporate privileges of the tribunals of judges were also to become more important. The most notable of these was the right to refuse to register royal edicts in the sovereign courts. This was, in essence, a right to review all royal legislation. In order to overcome it, the legislation had either to be modified, or the king had to present it himself before the sovereign court in person and demand its registration in a *lit de justice*. According to one recent evaluation, this

---

37. Examples of the pensions to *présidents* are to be found in the lists of royal pensions in BN MS Dupuy 852 (1576, 1578, 1603, 1605 etc). The average pension was about 2, 800 *livres* in Henri IV's reign. Remark from the councillor in Rouen quoted in J. Dewald, 1980, p. 149.

38. B. de La Roche Flavin, [1617], p. 350.

39. C. Loyseau, [1611], p. 7.

40. Isambert, XIV, 245 (Jan. 1572).

41. The *parlement* of Rennes granted itself noble status in 1544, 1545, 1562. The *parlement* of Grenoble confirmed its noble status in 1573. In 1546, the *parlement* of Paris was the first to authorise the nobility of its judges and this edict was the subject for Tiraqueau's notable treatise *De Nobilitate* in 1549 and the debate about nobility which began with it. The king attempted to limit the claims to exemption from taxation by all office holders in royal edicts (Isambert, XIV, 540–8, Mar. 1583). The growth of endogamy in the senior tribunals can be measured at Rouen (J. Dewald, 1980, p.76) and Toulouse (M. Greengrass, 1979, 72).

42. J. Dewald, 1980, pp. 100–1.

43. N. Froumenteau (pseud. N. Barnaud?), *Le secret des finances* (n.p. 1581).

ceremony had only been used twice in the period from 1515 to 1559, but was used at least five times between 1550 and 1598. Constitutional lawyers of the period of the civil wars invested the ceremony with a great mystique, emphasising the necessity for a monarch to act according to the law, and making it a moment of accountability for French kings.[44] Some judges spoke as if they saw themselves as Roman senators, self-appointed guardians of the *res publica*. La Roche Flavin said that they 'mediate ['*metoyenne*'] between the king and people'. Others wrote extensively on the origins, the privileges and importance of the French sovereign courts.[45] It is not surprising that some lawyers disputed the pre-eminence of military virtues as the prerequisite for noble status and suggested that the dignity of a judge was, in some ways, more secure than that of a military nobleman. Jacques de La Guesle, the *procureur général* to the *parlement* of Paris, told the assembled judges in 1594 that the nobility of the law was above the caprices of princes: 'It enlarges itself ceaselessly and, with the king's authority, it extends to all Frenchmen, embracing their lives, wealth and honour.'[46] La Roche Flavin said that 'their [*the judges'*] authority is so exalted that there was no seigneur, no prince even, no subject so over-mighty, that did not hold in respect and fear their censure, judgments and decisions'. Their growing eminence in French society was beyond dispute.

Personal and corporate ambitions became so enmeshed that history can only be written at this stage by resorting to example. Thanks to the intimate diary of his son (a record, as he said, of 'the means to success'), the apparently irresistible rise of a senior office holder at the end of the sixteenth century can be documented.[47] Born in November 1525, Olivier Lefèvre d'Ormesson was the son of a legal clerk, and his mother was the daughter of a solicitor. His son candidly admitted that his family was 'mediocre in extraction and property'. After attending the college of Navarre in Paris, he was apprenticed to an attorney to learn 'to write and earn a living'. Good fortune attended him, and Olivier was attached to the service of André Blondel, sieur de

---

44. S.H. Madden, 1982. The *parlements* also increased their jurisdiction in the church and, in 1560, the *parlement* of Paris registered the recommendations of the estates general.

45. There was a flood of literature on individual styles and judgments of the various courts of France as well as discussions of judicial authority.

46. J. de La Guesle, *Les Remonstrances*, (Paris, 1611), p. 281. Cf. A. Jouanna, 1976, pp. 945–51.

47. A. Chéruel, [1860], pp. ii–viii. The diary was used by G. Huppert, 1977, pp. 50–7, whose account is closely followed here.

Roquancour, treasurer to the future Henri II. Attached to the coat-tails of this up-and-coming man, Olivier bettered himself. He became first clerk to Roquancour and helped his brother to the post of treasurer of special war expenditures (*trésorier de l'extraordinaire des guerres*). The investment was repaid in the first year of office, and when his brother died, Olivier became heir to an estate worth over 25,000 *écus* and an office which he was able to transfer to his own name. Henri II was a good patron and Olivier subsequently never spoke of 'the king who loved him well' without emotion.

Wealth, once achieved, needed to be protected. Olivier bought the respectable seigneurie of Ormesson, near Nemours and, henceforth, always called himself 'M. d'Ormesson . . . for the name of Lefèvre was too common'. This proved inadequate to screen him from the charge of embezzling public funds and he was forced to surrender his office (although he was compensated for his losses). Thereafter, 'realising how difficult it was to survive for any length of time . . . without support and assistance, he resolved to marry and thus to ally himself with some well-chosen family'. He chose Anne de Morvilliers, a great niece of the bishop of Orléans. It was a shrewd choice and the bishop protected him during the civil wars. Olivier became a treasurer in Picardy and then an *intendant des finances* and a *conseiller d'état* in 1573. When the bishop died in 1577, he hastily retreated from public life. He sold his offices and retired to Ormesson to live the life of a country gentleman. But the life bored him, not being (his son tell us) a 'cultivated man'. Although over fifty years old, he deployed every vestige of his influence to obtain a respectable, secure judicial office. Eventually, he persuaded the chamber of accounts in Paris to overlook his embezzlements and, with 40,000 *écus*, bought the office of president there. His dress, manner of life and investments, all became more conservative to match his new-found dignity. At last, the *nouveau-riche* financier could feel secure in the knowledge that, at least for his children, his family was among the great notables of France. He sent his three surviving sons to the best schools, bestowed seigneuries on them, married them into the best legal families in Paris. But, even then, Ormesson was vigilant, aware that security was never complete and that ambition bred resentments. In his last years, he shored up the family's defences by offering lavish entertainments to Henri IV at his smart town house in the Rue Beaubourg. Even the king warmed to his hospitality and remarked that, 'without the *président* d'Ormesson, there would be no fun in Paris. He is the father of youth'. But on 29 May 1600, riding back from Ormesson to Paris, he fell from his horse and died. To those in the council of state who tried to prevent the inheritance of the office passing to Olivier's eldest son, Henri IV is supposed to have replied, 'I was fond of the *bonhomme*' and the reversion was granted. Olivier's prudence had not been in vain. He had risen to nobility in one generation and his family had 'arrived'.

Other families – the Séguier, Harlay, Camus, Bellièvre or Hennequin – might have been chosen to illustrate the aspirations of what one contemporary described as 'the demi-Gods of our age'.[48] There is no doubt that their success caused resentment among those judges who were either not so lucky or not so enterprising. Among the lawyers without offices, there was a pronounced feeling of being excluded from any chance of fame and fortune. The scabrous French humanist Joseph Scaliger spoke for the disappointed scholar of every age: 'All the Harlay [*clan*] are peculiar and avaricious, and the lord president is chief amongst them'. Referring to the first president of the *parlement* of Paris who had been hanged by the radical League, he wrote: 'Brisson was rich. He had made a fortune by unjust means. He was a wicked man'.[49] In the placards on the Pont Neuf in Paris as well as the pages of the diary kept by the respectable Pierre de l'Estoile, the senior judges of its *parlement* are not treated with the dignity which they believed their status and profession accorded them. Had they not bought and sold offices, played politics, enjoyed powerful political protectors, and made it to the top by corrupt or underhand means? There were rumours aplenty, some lies or half-truths – yet believed because individuals wanted them to be true.

So the failure to reform the realm, and in particular, its office-holding structure, turned out to have serious consequences for French society. The structure created hopes of reward and possible social advancement which were unrealisable. This led to great resentment. Individual and collective disillusionment displayed itself both in the exaltation of the professional ideal of the office-holder and the excoriation of the debased and corrupt specimens who represented the reality. The dislike for the '*politiques*' in Paris and other provincial cities at the time of the League was, in various ways, a resentment directed by lawyers and lesser office-holders against those who had been more successful than themselves. The extraordinary and bizarre events in the kangaroo court which hanged the first president of the *parlement* of Paris, Barnabé Brisson, on 15 November 1591 are best

---

48. Pierre de Saint–Julien de Balleure, *Meslanges Historiques* (Lyon, 1588), p. 600. The author was a canon at Châlons-sur-Marne and his biography is in L. Raffin, 1926. Cf. A. Jouanna, 1976, pp. 658–63. Cf. D. Richet, 1991, pt 2.

49. Cited in E. Barnavi and R. Descimon, 1985, pp. 134–5; for the remainder of this paragraph, see Robert Descimon's subtle analysis in *ibid.*, ch. vi.

explained, as Robert Descimon has put it, in the context of 'the crisis of the judicial system, a reflection of the total crisis felt by a society which had failed to reform itself.'[50] Some historians have spoken of a 'blocked society' (*société bloquée*) where increased heredity in offices caused promotion blockages in the legal professions.[51] In reality, the accumulation of resentments was much broader. There was a distaste for venality, a dislike for the spiralling costs of office and a jealousy of those notables who had successfully manipulated the system. It was never a simple division between 'ins' (those in senior office) and 'outs' (those without an office or without hope of promotion). The League preachers best expressed the sense of frustration felt, not just by office-holders but by all social groups. As one of the League orators said:

> You, Lords of justice, with palms lined with gold, purses full of coins and houses full of money, whence comes your luxury, your shining success? How did you come by your tunics, red as the blood of Christ? By stealing from the poor! I tell you that the blood of Christ cries out for mercy on behalf of those so unjustly and unfairly treated and your robes call for vengeance against you because they represent the blood of so many poor people.[52]

PRELATES AND PREACHERS

It will be a long time before we are as well informed about the state of the catholic church in France during the civil wars as we are about royal officialdom. The church was a vast and diverse institutional conglomeration. There were 117 dioceses in France (not counting the three suffragans of Avignon) in 1600 but they varied enormously in size and prestige.[53] Some, like Paris, Reims, Rouen, Bourges or Chartres, were geographically large and traditionally prestigious sees. Others, especially in the Midi, were tiny, though none was smaller than Toulon with its two-score parishes. Although, however, these southern sees were not necessarily unremunerative, at least as far as the bishop was concerned. They were, however, the dioceses which experienced most severely the deleterious effects of the civil wars.

---

50. *Ibid.*, p. 173.
51. J. Dewald, 1980, p. 97 and P. Benedict, 1981, pp. 182–3.
52. B. d'Estang, *Les Parlements de France* (Paris, 1857), p. 173.
53. The only recent, comprehensive study is the remarkable work of M. Venard, 1993.

The senior clergy of France, especially its archbishops and bishops (and, to a degree, its senior regular clergy, the abbots, priors and prioresses) were theoretically appointed on royal nomination.[54] In reality, however, all sorts of pressures were brought to bear on the outcome of episcopal nominations, generally with the aim of securing a patrimonial influence in a particular see, furthering an ecclesiastical career or bolstering the revenues of a grandee's family. Episcopal sees could be resigned in favour of a particular, named individual (*resignatio in favorem*). Although simony was prohibited both by royal and ecclesiastical decree, it was perfectly possible to arrange a resignation so that the departing incumbent retained a pension on the diocese in return for his resignation. Such agreements, although frowned on in the Tridentine hierarchy, were common in civil-war France, leading to the nomination of 'straw-bishops' (*custodi nos* or *confidentiaires*) whose role was to be the nominal incumbent to the see whilst someone else enjoyed its revenues. As a result, an ambitious and energetic ecclesiastical careerist like the cardinal Joyeuse could accumulate the revenues of several bishoprics whilst laymen (like his father, the vicomte de Joyeuse in the case of the bishopric of Nîmes) could also enjoy the fruits of ecclesiastical office without any ensuing responsibilities.[55] The rather similar practice of laymen holding monasteries 'in trust' (*in commendam*) was more openly practised – and even encouraged – by the Holy See. The result, however, was a French ecclesiastical hierarchy of extraordinary geographical, social and intellectual diversity.

A similar diversity was also the case at the parish level. Until we have more studies such as that undertaken for the ecclesiastical province of Avignon, however, the overall picture will remain far from clear. The most striking and significant minority were those who rose to prominence as preachers during the civil wars. Some of these were established parish priests in their locality, endowed with a prebend, salaried by the town council or residents of neighbouring monasteries. Others, however, were outsiders, brought in to the parishes of the larger cities at the traditional preaching seasons of Lent and Advent. Many were mendicants, particularly Franciscans and Dominicans. Many of those most active during the League shared a common background in the Sorbonne during the tumultuous early years of civil war, where they had doubtless listened to the oratory of Simon Vigor and imbibed the prophetic eschatology of that period.[56]

54. For the episcopacy, see F. Baumgartner, 1986, ch. ii.
55. For an example, see M. Greengrass, 1987a.
56. See D. Crouzet, 1990, chs 4–6. B. Diefendorf, 1987.

The target of the preachers in the 1560s had been the Huguenots. By the late 1580s, they offered a more general denunciation of public corruption. In their sermons they portrayed the judicial system as corrupt, the aristocracy as degenerate and the church as subverted from above by a monarchy which alienated its wealth. In the surviving sermons and printed works of the Parisian clergy – Julian Pelletier (parish priest (*curé*) of St-Jacques-de-la-Boucherie), Jean Guincestre (installed in the parish of St Gervais by the radical League in 1588) or Jacques de Cueilly (parish priest of St-Germain-l'Auxerrois) – there is a sustained prophetic denunciation of the oppression of the poor people of France and a finger pointed directly at the monarchy as the cause of all corruption and malaise. From the League preachers in provincial cities – Jacques Le Bossu, for example, in Nantes – there came the equally familiar call to renew fidelity through public oath-swearing.[57] Le Bossu painted a picture of those who had suffered exclusion from office, property or exile during the civil wars in devotion to the 'holy cause'. Their moral purity was contrasted with the alleged selfishness and corruption of catholic royalists who had made their peace with Navarre in order to enjoy an ill-gotten advancement.

THE ALIENATION OF ECCLESIASTICAL WEALTH

The forced sale of ecclesiastical wealth, demanded of the catholic church by the last Valois kings as a way of financing royal debts, had as disruptive an effect on the church as the sale of offices had on the legal profession. It was widely condemned among catholics, indeed, and Papire Masson, who wrote a defence of the massacres of Saint Bartholomew, could not decide who had damaged the church more, Charles IX or the Huguenots. The *parlement* of Paris repeatedly condemned the alienations of church rights and property as the sale of the Lord's domain, an infringement of the church's independence as well as an illegal attack on property rights. The senior clergy reluctantly accepted papal bulls and royal authorisations to alienate wealth in order to assist the king at critical moments, and to protect the kingdom from heresy. They risked (as in 1586) being criticised in the assemblies of clergy unless there was papal authorisation for the alienation. This sale of church wealth was in addition to the *décimes*, a regular contribution from

57. R.R. Harding, (1981).

all the benefices of the realm, organised on the basis of a contract drawn up at Poissy in 1561, and renewed and renegotiated (always to royal advantage) roughly every five years by the assemblies of clergy.[58] The amounts that were alienated were considerable, although not as large as the sale of royal domain which also took place in the wars of religion.[59] The operation was a complicated one, partly because of the need to equalise the quota for alienation between wealthy and poor dioceses. In the first alienation, Charles IX used royal officials to undertake the task, but the results were unsatisfactory to all parties. Greedy royal officers in protestant areas sold more church property than was necessary to meet the diocesan quota and were reluctant to organise its repurchase in 1564, when the king agreed that churches could recover their wealth and rights if they could reimburse the new owners to whom it had been sold.

Aware of ecclesiastical sensibilities on the issue of church freedom, Charles IX and Henri III left all other alienations in the hands of the church itself. As a result, some alienations were imposed as subventions and involved no sale of property or rights. When something was sold, minor rights and outlying properties were surrendered first, especially those which had proved difficult to collect during the civil wars.[60] In some dioceses, bishops and prominent lay catholics bought the alienated property to prevent it falling into protestant hands. Some of the large northern dioceses avoided having to sell much before the alienation of 1574–75.[61] The dioceses of the Paris basin and central France were obliged to sell something to meet their quotas from 1563 onwards.[62] In a band of southern dioceses, the regions were in protestant hands and no sales of ecclesiastical wealth could be undertaken in wartime. The tithes were already expropriated to Huguenots' coffers and the properties leased to protestant farmers.[63]

58. R. Doucet, 1948, II, 831–45. J. Viguier, 1906. L. Serbat, 1906.

59. I. Cloulas, 1958, 6–19. In Languedoc, for example, provincial institutions resisted the alienations vigorously (AD Haute-Garonne B56, ff. 395–6; AD Hérault G 316, etc). The diocese of Nîmes alienated more than it needed to and exceeded its quota by over 300 per cent, while the diocese of Montpellier exceeded its quota by 400 per cent. In Béziers, one of the royal commissioners sold himself some of the best church properties (J. Hilaire, 1952, 146–58).

60. This appears from case studies of individual dioceses – L. Welter, 1946; N. Becquart, 1974; I. Cloulas, 1964.

61. I. Cloulas, 1958, 17, 47-8.

62. *Ibid.*, 18.

63. The process of farming ecclesiatical properties was governed by regulations laid down by protestant political assemblies. For the operation and accounts of Languedoc's protestants during the civil wars, see M. Dainville, *Inventaire sommaire des archives départementales de l'Hérault* – Series B(VI) (Montpellier, 1951), cols 381–462.

Farms and properties were inevitably despoiled in the process and the revenues from bequests and church courts declined. In some dioceses, there were intermittent tithe strikes by both catholic and protestant inhabitants.[64] Where the farmers of ecclesiastical properties were protestants, the cathedral chapters or episcopal officials were forced to negotiate in order to obtain a proportion of the revenues. Some tithes and rents remained completely unpaid for twenty-five or thirty years. The extent of the problem by the middle of the civil war period appears in the remissions granted by the king on the alienation of church wealth in 1576. A decade later, in the alienation of 1586, fifteen dioceses defaulted on at least half their quota and a further seven still owed at least a quarter of the amount in the years 1599–1600.[65]

The condition in the worst affected dioceses can be substantiated by visitation records and investigations for the non-payment of tithes. In the diocese of Toulouse, for instance, the damage done to churches alone was enormous: 138 churches, or 41 per cent of the total in the diocese were damaged, of which 45 had been set on fire, 37 destroyed and 23 badly affected. A further 19 had no roof and 14 had been pillaged. A much larger proportion lacked essential fabric to celebrate catholic rituals – fonts, altars, holy ointment and sacramental vessels.[66] At the same time, the visitations conducted in the nearby diocese of Agen by the bishop, Nicolas de Villars, revealed a still more sombre picture.[67] Only 24 churches in the main towns of the diocese were in an acceptable state. The majority of the 427 parishes had churches with no roof, no glass in the windows, cemeteries appropriated by local landowners and ruined presbyteries.

Alienations and *décimes* generated an enormous amount of paperwork and many disputes. Some of the latter occurred between the assemblies of clergy and the general receiver for clerical revenues. There were also acrimonious exchanges and altercations between the provost of the city of Paris and the receiver, for these revenues went to pay the *rentes* on the *hôtel de ville* in Paris. Philippe de Castille, the receiver for much of the later period of the civil wars, was imprisoned

64. E. Le Roy Ladurie, 1966, I, 375–89. Cf. AD Haute-Garonne B57 (21 Jan. 1564). In 1569, a deputy of the clergy of Béziers claimed that 40 benefices were occupied and in 69 others there was a tithe strike (J. Bellaud-Dessalles, 1902, pp. 106–7). There were regular complaints over tithe impropriation by gentlemen of both religious persuasions.

65. I. Cloulas, 1958, 52–3.

66. G. Baccrabère, 1956.

67. L. Bourrachot, 1963, 129–43.

once and threatened with imprisonment several times over. The alienations and taxes on the church inevitably reinforced the clerical support at various levels in the church for the catholic League.

Those who profited from the alienations can be analysed from the registers of sale preserved by the general receivers. They included notable protestant leaders like the prince of Condé who purchased a substantial amount of wealth in 1563.[68] But catholics like the royal secretary, Jules Gassot, also invested in the spoils of their church.[69] Merchants prudently took up some of the wealth, and peasant proprietors who had the means, bought out the obligations they owed to the church or extended their patrimony. As the civil wars progressed, the proportions of nobles and military captains participating in the purchases increased – a way to invest the profits of war. According to the third estate in Dauphiné, some captains gained nobility on the basis of the seigneuries they bought.[70] Taken with the alienation of the royal domain in the civil wars, this considerable speculative opportunity offered a significant shift in landed fortunes in the French *ancien régime*.

THE DIVIDED LOYALTIES OF THE LEAGUE

For the senior clergy and magistrates, the League presented invidious choices. There is a tendency to suggest that the prelates were *predominantly* supporters of the League while the senior magistrates assisted Henri IV by their *fundamental* royalism. In fact, their reactions were both more complex and alike in their response to the difficult decisions which faced them after the assassinations at Blois in 1588. At the estates of Blois, it is true that a majority of prelates were supporters of the League. The most prominent among them was the archbishop of Lyon, Pierre d'Epinac, the so-called 'courier of the League' in 1588.[71] Others present included Arnaud Sorbin of Nevers and Aymar Hennequin of Rennes, both of whom had defended the massacre of St Bartholomew and whose ardent catholicism drove them to the League.[72] But there were also some royalist bishops who were

68. I. Cloulas, 1958, 14.
69. I. Cloulas, 1964, 95–6.
70. D. Hickey, 1978.
71. P. Richard, 1901, pp. 272, etc. For the political affiliation of the episcopacy during the wars of the League, see now F.J. Baumgartner, 1986.
72. C. Labitte, 1849, pp. 7–8, 28.

articulate and influential supporters of the king. These included Claude d'Angennes, Bishop of Le Mans, Renaud de Beaune, Archbishop of Bourges and (although he was in Rome at the time of the estates) the cardinal Joyeuse, archbishop of Toulouse.[73] After the assassinations, some royalist prelates, such as Joyeuse, joined the League under the influence of the decrees of the Sorbonne. Nevertheless, despite the excommunication of Henri of Navarre by the Pope, about 36 bishops became royalist, with 51 declaring for the League and a further 12 remaining neutral, abandoning their dioceses, retiring to monasteries or returning to Italy.[74] Some of the League bishops declared their support under duress, and Nicolas Fumée of Beauvais was taken prisoner by League forces and then ransomed in 1590 for 900 *écus*. The royalists retaliated with the capture of the League incumbents of Embrun, Riez and Evreux. Claude de Sainctes, bishop of Evreux, was even put on trial for his treasonable pamphlet praising the assassination of Henri III. While the support of the League bishops to the catholic cause as diplomatic and military agents was occasionally significant, it was not as important as the royalist bishops would become to Henri IV's propaganda. By the end of 1589, Henri IV could depend on the loyalty of two archbishops and only one cardinal (Lenoncourt).

For these new royalist bishops, Gallican aspirations suddenly acquired a new significance. In September 1591, at Chartres, nine royalist prelates issued a declaration against the papal bull threatening the clerical supporters of Henri of Navarre with excommunication.[75] Their statement declared that the papal bull was against the privileges of the Fench church and would create a schism. One royalist prelate, Renaud de Beaune, archbishop of Bourges, campaigned to become patriarch of France in order to set up an independent French church discipline in the spirit of the Pragmatic Sanction. The importance of de Beaune to the royalists became clearer in 1593. He was the only royalist prelate among the royal negotiators at Suresnes for the conference with the League.[76] He played a conspicuous part in the discussions with the archbishop of Lyon there. Scripture, canon law, French customs were cited by the two prelates in defence of their positions, but de Beaune was able to secure from d'Epinac a declaration that the League's only objection to Henri of Navarre's kingship was his religion. The scene was set for de Beaune's announcement in May that Henri IV intended to convert. Two

73. F.J. Baumgartner, 1978, 102–4. F.J. Baumgartner, 1979.
74. F.J. Baumgartner, 1986, ch. ix.
75. Ibid.; pp. 289–90.
76. Ibid. Cf. the classic account in A. Poirson, 1862–65, I, 396–408.

months later, the archbishop of Bourges lifted the excommunication of the king in the name of the French church. Once Henri had attended his first Mass, numerous League prelates rallied to his cause, leaving only a minority of catholic diehards. Some of these did not accept him as king, despite the papal absolution in 1595. The bishop of Vannes in Brittany continued to use the clause 'until there is a catholic king in France' in episcopal documents until the pope, Clement VIII, reminded him in September 1596 that this was an offensive anachronism.[77]

The senior magistrates proclaimed their royalism more frequently than the prelates but it was, in some respects, less evident during the League. After the Day of Barricades in May 1588, the first president in Paris firmly reminded the duke of Guise that 'My bench [*of judges*] is founded on the *fleur de lys* and, since it has been established by the king, it can only function in his service. We would all rather sacrifice our lives than consent to act differently.'[78] A year later, all but about 10 judges of the *parlement* were in revolt against the king and 41 had been led to the Bastille by the *Sixteen*.[79] On 26 January 1589, 108 *conseillers*, 2 presidents and a royal attorney had sworn allegiance to the League. In May 1589, 11 judges were among 44 principal felons condemned by Henri III for rebellion against the king.[80] Of the 8 *parlements* of the realm, 6 went over to the League and only one *parlement*, that of Bordeaux,remained royalist and continued to support Henri III and Henri IV. Many judges later claimed that they were terrified into supporting the League and there was some veracity to their claims. Estoile recalls the famous incident when the first president was placed in a difficult position by a League preacher in Paris. He was asked to demonstrate his support for the *Sixteen* or risk being declared a heretic from the pulpit as well as being publicly humiliated: 'Raise your hand, *Monsieur le Président*, raise it high, still higher', cried the preacher, 'so that the people can see it.'[81] Other judges said that they stayed in their posts to protect their property or to spy for the king. But by November 1589, only 21 magistrates from the *parlement* of Paris had assembled at Tours and there were only 9 judges in the royalist *parlement* at Caen.[82] A majority of magistrates in Paris

77. F.J. Baumgartner, 1979, 292.
78. E. Maugis, 1914, II, 53, questions whether the speech was ever made in the form that has now been preserved.
79. F.J. Baumgartner, 1979, 36.
80. E. Maugis, 1914, II, 127.
81. Estoile, [1943], p. 604.
82. F.J. Baumgartner, 1979, 37. A. Desjardins, 1879, p. 482. E. Maugis, 1914, III, 282–5.

supported the claim to the throne of the cardinal de Bourbon. By implication, they lent support to the fundamental law that only a catholic could inherit the throne and they also denied the legality of the case for the Gallican liberties of the French church, partly by putting a cardinal on the throne, and partly by legalising the excommunication of Henri III and Henri IV. Letters patent from the *parlement* of Paris in March 1591 even began their preamble: 'Our Holy Father, in accordance with the jurisdiction which should be his in matters relating to the preservation of the crown of France . . .'[83] This submission to the papacy increasingly worried many fundamentally Gallican councillors and was responsible, with the fears of the *Sixteen* in the capital, for causing a drift of magistrates towards the royalist *parlements* and away from the League *parlements*. By 1592, there were 76 League judges in Paris, as compared to 89 royalist judges at Tours and Châlons.

The failure of the estates general of the League in 1593 to agree on a candidate to elect as king was accompanied by an edict from the League *parlement* on 28 June 1593. One of the spokesman in the debate was, as we saw in chapter three, Guillaume du Vair (1556–1621).[84] He had attacked the League before, but in a speech of great fervour, he reminded magistrates of their obligation to defend the rights of the crown and the laws of the kingdom (including Gallican rights): 'Therefore arouse yourselves, sirs, and display today the authority of the laws which are entrusted to you. For, if their faults admit of any remedy, you alone can provide it.' The court resolved by a majority on a decree outlawing any *elected* king as against the Salic (and fundamental) law. This step has been called a courageous act of political conviction by fundamentally royalist magistrates.[85] It certainly brought the recognition of Henri IV one stage nearer and annoyed the duke of Mayenne who demanded its revocation. But it was as much an act of realism as of courage, a response to de Beaune's declaration that Henri IV was preparing to convert to catholicism. There was an air of desperation in their relieved discovery of the Salic law.

In the course of these years, the senior magistrates found themselves required to take political decisions and to show political leadership. They did so unwillingly, their procrastination displaying the scruples of their consciences as well as their aversion to becoming too closely

---

83. Ibid., II, 76.
84. DBF, V, cols 905–1.
85. For example, J.H. Shennan, *The Parlement of Paris,* 1968, pp. 230–1.

connected with the world of politics. The prelates, on the other hand, were not so reticent, for many of them had been appointed because of their political usefulness or as a result of their political skills. The magistrates acted from their most conservative instincts. They were aware that their property, wealth, privileges and laws were vulnerable to the pressures of war, the fates of military commanders, the wiles of popular movements outside their control, and their own divisions. The prospect of a state of federated communes run by an independent, zealot clergy had been a frightening one, even for those like Brisson who were supposedly in a position to influence it. No judge could fail to be aware of how fragile the rule of law had proved to be. Equally, the ruined episcopal palaces, badly damaged or ruined parish churches, alienated fabric, and numerous contested claims to episcopal sees were amongst the tangible consequences of the civil wars which no bishop could ignore. As a result, there emerged, on the one hand, a magistrature somewhat humbled and chastened, and willing to pay some price for the existence of a strong monarchy; on the other hand, the numerous contested claimants and vacancies to French sees meant that Henri IV had a rare opportunity to create a French episcopacy of his own devising, one which would tame the parish preachers and contemplate church renewal.

THE PAULETTE

Like most contemporaries, Henri IV believed that many superfluous offices would be discontinued once hostilities had ended. As early as 1593, a familiar proposal was resurrected to prune the excess number of royal posts. From 1594, Henri IV granted few reversions of office and enforced the forty-day rule with rigidity.[86] More proposals were laid before the assembly of notables in 1596, involving a reduction in the number of offices to cut the costs of salaries from 2.5 million *livres* per year to 1.5 million.[87] But these well–rehearsed schemes evaporated during the expensive campaign to recapture Amiens in 1597 and then again during the Savoyard War (1600–1). There were also deeper reasons why reform was stillborn. The fundamental pressures towards venality and inheritance were too great to be resisted. Lesser tribunals fought tooth and claw to maintain themselves against extinction

---

86. R.E. Mousnier, 1971, pp. 134–5.
87. Ibid., p. 136. *Revue Henri IV*, 1905–6, I, 18.

through any reduction in the number of offices.[88] The *partisans* – tax-farmers and projectors for office creation and sale – also exercised influence on the council of state. Sully recorded the example in his *Oeconomies Royales* (for which there is independent corroboration) of one financier who offered diamonds worth 2,000 *écus* to two mistresses of councillors (besides other payments to Sully's wife) if, between them, they secured approval for a set of newly proposed offices.[89] In the face of this corruption, Henri IV's reliance on Sully's vigilance to check each creation as it was proposed was insufficient.

The pressures on magistrates to secure the inheritance of their posts, were great and grew ever greater. This was, at least in part, because an individual's freedom to dispose of his (landed) property other than to his immediate descendants was circumscribed by French customary law. Offices, however, did not count as 'property' but as 'movables' and therefore, so long as one could secure the reversion of an office, it became an attractive way of gaining flexibility in determining the succession of a family fortune.[90] Among lesser office-holders, the edict on the *tailles* in March 1600 ruled that, for the purposes of tax, an office which had passed from father to son in three generations granted the third-generation official and his successors the right to hereditary nobility.[91] Three generations – or 100 years – also became the recognised period over which old nobles had to prove their family nobility to commissioners for tax purposes.[92] This edict created many problems in French jurisprudence, as Loyseau admitted in 1610, but it also increased the pressures for a formal system of reversion of offices.[93] By enforcing the forty-day rule strictly, Henri IV encountered fraud at a local level. An unsavoury case came to light in 1600 in the *parlement* of Toulouse of a president paying for a *survivance* to an office twelve days *after* the death of the incumbent, and arranging with a doctor to keep the body of his predecessor on his death-bed for forty-five days, as though alive, in order to circumvent the forty-day clause.[94] One enterprising jobber offered – for a fee – to create an office to investigate such scandals. Other tribunals, it was also

---

88. For example, the provincial treasurers, whose *bureaux* were abolished in 1589, following the advice of the assembly of notables, but were re-established in 1608, on payment of 600,000 *livres* (R.E. Mousnier, 1971, pp. 139–40).
89. Sully, [1881], XVI, 250.
90. R.E. Giesey, 1977.
91. Isambert, XV, 234.
92. J-M. Constant, 1977.
93. Ibid., p. 83.
94. R.E. Mousnier, 1971, pp. 226–32.

discovered, ignored the king completely, and did not bother to secure proper inheritances to their offices at all.

There was also the problem of the king's revenue. Fewer offices created, fewer reversions sold, meant a decrease in the revenues of the *bureau des parties casuelles*. The civil wars had left a legacy of royal debts and, if offices were a curious form of royal debt, it could not be denied that they were more solidly funded and on a longer-term basis than other parts of the royal debt. It was more important to clear the short-term debts rather than try to tackle a fundamental reform which would require time, patience and political strength. This is the background against which the criticism of Henri IV's failure to tackle the fundamental problems of office-holding must be seen. Reform is notoriously difficult from within, and it is clear that he did attempt some changes. It is also clear that his failure was because a change of any dimension would require a shift in attitudes and mentalities among a group whose support was very important for both political and financial stability. His task was to provide a basic stability for the magistrature as a necessary precondition for the administration of law and for consent to the monarchy. He did not wish to undertake a reform whose implications would shake the pillars of his scarcely secure state. Venality and heredity were not abandoned for any length of time in the later history of the *ancien régime* and this is perhaps a sign that the task of reform had gone beyond the reach of anyone working within the regime itself.

This is a necessary prelude to a discussion of Henri IV's most notorious measure, the institution of the *paulette* in 1604. In essence, the *paulette* was a tax on heredity. The proposal arose – at least superficially – from among the speculators in the royal administration, the *partisans*. It was presented to the council of state with the approval of Sully in 1602 by a consortium of financiers and administrators headed by Charles Paulet, sieur de Corbéron, a Languedocian from a family of financiers and a secretary of the king's chamber.[95] The idea was to invite a cash payment (called the *droit annuel*) each year of one-sixtieth of the assessed price of each office from every magistrate in return for a grant to them of the inheritance of their office and a waiving of the forty-day clause. The strength of the *paulette* proposal lay in its equal appeal to all parties. To the office holders it made financial and social sense. The annual rate was a reasonable insurance proposition; universally available in return was the guarantee of heredity and the continued enjoyment of their investment by their

95. Ibid., pp. 234, 242–3.

heirs. To the king, it was administratively easy and politically sound. Collecting the money each year was farmed out to the company of the financiers (initially to Paulet). It ensured a steady annual revenue to the *bureau des parties casuelles* at a time when the revocation of the *pancarte* tax had created a shortfall in the royal budget.[96] It also controlled the political pressures on the council and discouraged fraud. Richelieu later recorded in his *Testament Politique* that he 'learnt from the late duke of Sully that this consideration was the most pressing on the late king [*Henri IV*] for the institution of the *droit annuel*; he was less concerned about the revenue it would raise than about the political embarrassments it would avoid in the future'.[97] Henceforth, every office holder who paid the *droit annuel* would be reminded each year that he owed his loyalty to the king, rather than to any intermediary through whose favour he might (otherwise) have gained the office or its reversion.[98]

When the *droit annuel* was first proposed in council, Sully supported it but was opposed by the chancellor, Pomponne de Bellièvre. The objections were long, detailed and shrewd ones.[99] The measure would provide ammunition to the king's critics who would claim that 'peace is harsher than war'. It abandoned 'holy and necessary promises' undertaken by monarchs before numerous estates general to reduce office-holding. It was offensive to the professional dignity of magistrates and 'all the discipline of the *parlements* will be dissipated'. Since it was proposed that tax-farmers would take over all vacant offices and all those offices without a reversion to them, kings would no longer control their servants and 'dangerous monopolies' would occur. When offices became private property the king would no longer be able to reward his faithful servants. The price of offices would be bound to increase still further as 'the boldest and most corrupt speculators' acquired royal posts. The magistrature would be despised by the rest of society and industry would be starved of investment capital which would be siphoned off into royal administration.

Bellièvre only succeeded in postponing the measure for two years and the contract with Paulet was passed on 6 December 1604, part of

---

96. B. Barbiche, 1978, p. 98. R.E. Mousnier, 1971, p. 234. R.J. Bonney, 1981, pp. 61–2. *Revue Henri IV*, 1905–6, I, 184.

97. R.E. Mousnier, 1941, pp. 68–86.

98. G. Carew, [1749], p. 474 – 'so many tenures which draw necessary dependence on the king'.

99. *Revue Henri IV*, 1905–6, I, 182–96.

it being published a week later.[100] It has been plausibly suggested that it was timed (at least in part) to appease the Paris magistrates who had invested heavily in *rentes* and who were outraged at the proposed reductions in their interest payments. A large register of assessed prices of the major offices of the kingdom was drawn up for use by the tax-farmers.[101] Paulet did not remain the farmer of the tax for long, but his name became the term for the popular new 'insurance' of heredity offered to royal servants. Some of Bellièvre's financial predictions proved correct. His prophecy of a continued rise in the price of offices was an accurate one for senior legal positions. (See Fig. 6.) Loyseau claimed that, on average, prices had doubled in the period from 1594 to 1609. In his book on the jurisprudence of office-holding, he described how, during the frosts of January 1608, he went to spend an evening with the tax-farmer of the *paulette*, only to find his office besieged by anxious customers:

> I found him still busy with a host of them pushing and jostling one another to be the first to pay their money. Some of them still had their boots on, not having bothered to take them off when coming in. I noticed that, after they were dealt with, they went straight to a notary to register their letter of resignation, and it seemed to me that they walked as though to avoid any patches of ice for fear of losing their footing and dying in the street. Then, when it was quite dark, the tax-farmer closed his register and I heard a great clamour from those who were still in the queue demanding that their cash be taken from them because (they said) they knew not whether they would still be alive the following day. Thinking this over, I began to reflect to myself: Lord, if only we were as concerned to save our souls as we are to save our offices! . . . Both are imperilled by dying but what a difference lies between them. For, once dead, what is the use of an office, and (on the other hand) how important it is to save our souls for eternity.[102]

Estoile, less philosophically, despised:

> the miserable conception of the century, the vain and scandalous ambition of men of the age, which makes the prices of offices rise so high and so fast that you can see them go up, not year by year, nor month by month, but day by day and week by week, a despicable and infamous prostitution . . . Councillors of the court go for 46,000 francs; masters of requests at 70,000 francs . . . that is 46,000 follies and 70,000 stupidities.[103]

100. Fontanon, II, 576–8.
101. BN MS Fr 3435 ('Estat de la Valleur et estimation faicte au Conseil du Roy de tous les offices de judicature').
102. C. Loyseau, [1611], p. 143.
103. Estoile, [1958], 498–9 (Aug. 1609).

In other respects, Bellièvre was proven wrong. The *paulette* may not always have automatically increased the trends to heredity and endogamy beyond the pressures which were already there. In Paris, for example, it has been proved that more new officers entered the *parlement* of Paris in the twenty years after 1604 than in the twenty years before that date.[104] Turnover in offices was brisk, encouraged by rising prices, and this attracted new families – generally from lesser offices – to broaden their investment. The *paulette* did not immediately create a caste of office holders in the French administration at the expense of ability or loyal service. It is also unlikely that the *paulette* diverted wealth from trade to royal posts. The revenue that it created was useful and, if it had not been generated from the office holders, it would have come from other sources – perhaps from indirect taxes – which would have affected commerce more seriously.

Bellièvre's arguments were repeated in a continuing debate about the merits of the *paulette* which lasted beyond 1610.[105] For brief periods the *paulette* was even suspended (as in 1617 and 1648) but political crisis ensued. Although many judges were convinced that behind the *paulette* lay a monstrous engine for corporate corruption, yet they loved it dearly. By 1604, a major reform which challenged the existence and privileges of the robe was impossible. What was possible, and what the *paulette* did, was to strike a bargain between the monarchy and its officials in which corruption was open, institutionalised and to the monarch's advantage.

PERCEPTIONS OF REFORM IN THE CATHOLIC CHURCH

In a carefully prepared speech before the assembly of clergy in 1605, Henri IV flattered his audience and congratulated himself: 'As to elections [*of prelates*] you see how I go about it. I am proud to find I have installed prelates that are different from those of the past.'[106] The assembly in fact contained examples of both a reforming and a complacent prelacy. Among the latter were bishops who had never been ordained, a cavalry captain who only visited his diocese once a year for its festival, and the blind bishop of Clermont who showed an

---

104. M. C. Cummings, 1974, pp. 139, etc.
105. Ibid. Cf. D. Bitton, 1969b.
106. Quoted in F.T. Perrens, 1872, I, 249–50.

immodest eagerness to identify his female visitors using his hands.[107] Among the former were bishops who attempted to reform their dioceses by holding synods, developing clerical education and persuading the religious orders to undertake their own reform.[108] The path to reform was clear, although the practical obstacles from the large and intricate Gallican church establishment were considerable. Some of the most distinguished prelates of the period, such as cardinal Du Perron, appear, in retrospect, bland and lacking in zeal. Even the energetic François de Sales (1567–1622) was almost overwhelmed by the problems in his diocese at Annecy.[109]

Most reforming bishops were appointed by Henri III, a result of his misunderstood catholic concern. Nicolas Villars, a *conseiller* at the *parlement* of Paris, was appointed to the diocese of Agen in 1587 and proved to be a vigorous reformer.[110] Even his predecessor, Janus Frégoso, the last Italian bishop in the see, attended a regional council at Bordeaux to introduce Tridentine decrees into the archdiocese.[111] In Provence, the Italian bishops in the diocese of Aix and Arles were responsible for the first steps towards Tridentine reforms.[112] During the wars of the League, Henri IV had been less concerned about the quality of his bishops and more interested in their loyalty and the revenues of their sees. He used the dioceses as a source of patronage and posts were sold for money.[113] By 1594, about six archdioceses and thirty dioceses were vacant, either because no appointment had been made, or because the bishops had not been confirmed at Rome.[114] By 1596, the number of vacancies had risen to about forty.[115] It took many years for the political pressures surrounding League and royalist candidates to vacant sees to be resolved. Some royal nominees were ill-regarded at Rome and had to wait for their confirmations. Arnaud de Beaune was kept waiting for eight years until he was transferred from Bourges to the see of Sens as, metropolitan to Paris – one of the most prestigious posts in the French church. At Grasse, the League nominee was eventually accepted in place of the royalist, whose marriage and four children embarrassed his candidature. At Nîmes, the

107. Examples in J.M. Hayden, 1977, pp. 28–9.
108. Ibid., pp. 30–1.
109. R. Kleinman, 1962. For a less than flattering portrait of Du Perron, see F-T Perrens, 1872, I, 237–8.
110. L. Bourrachot, 1963, 129.
111. Ibid., 136. R. Boutruche, 1966, pp. 369–83.
112. J-R. Palanque, 1975, ch. v.
113. F.J. Baumgartner, 1979, 293–4.
114. Ibid., 292.
115. R. Ritter, [1955], p. 69.

209

bishopric became the object of rival aristocrats' clients in 1597. On the one hand, there was the Dominican Louis de Vervins (later, archbishop of Narbonne), a client of the cardinal Joyeuse. On the other, there was Jean Valernod, brother of the secretary to the constable, Henri de Montmorency-Damville. Valernod was eventually victorious, thanks to the support of his patron both at the royal court and in Rome.[116] The results, politically speaking, of the disposal of many bishoprics to royalists was a compliant prelacy which put up little resistance to the edict of Nantes in 1598. If it was also a reforming prelacy, this was perhaps more by luck than good management. It is nevertheless an interesting reflection of the close identity between the long robe and the clergy that the most determined and successful reformers were originally members of the magistrature, particularly from the *parlement* of Paris.[117]

Some clerical requests for reform in the French church were satisfied by royal edict. Henri IV restored the catholic church to its property in an edict of May 1596, repeated in the edict of Nantes in 1598.[118] In 1606, he gave the church rights to reacquire any alienated property for which it could provide compensation for the original purchase price.[119] Also in 1606, another edict confirmed the ordinances of Blois in 1579 and agreements reached at Melun in 1580 to exclude laymen from abbeys and priories and forbid gentlemen from farming tithes and other ecclesiastical revenues without special clerical consent.[120] More often, the king invited the church to reform itself and amalgamate benefices to attract well-trained, literate clergy to its ranks. What could be achieved by a vigorous bishop in an unpromising diocese can be demonstrated by the achievement of Nicolas Villars at Agen.[121] When he arrived in his diocese, his initial visitations revealed that he was satisfied only with 18 of the 307 *curés* and 146 *vicaires* in his see. He deposed 7 *curés* and 36 *vicaires* immediately for irregularities and ignorance. One was a collector of *tailles* who had suborned the parish chest; several others were

---

116. R. Sauzet, 1979, pp. 54–6.

117. J.M. Hayden, 1977, p. 38. Examples can be found among the families of the Potier, Miron, Hennequin, Hurault and Zamet.

118. Clause three of the edict of Nantes, Isambert, XV, 173.

119. *Ibid.*, 313 (Dec. 1606).

120. *Ibid.*, 303–13. Poirson, 1862–67, I, 743–9 overestimates the importance of the edict.

121. L. Bourrachot, 1963, 142–3. R. Doucet, 1948, II, 799–801 is unenthusiatic about the achievements of the seminaries. But see L. Lestrade, *Revue des Pyrénées*, VIII (1906), 551–69 for pioneering efforts in Toulouse. Cathedral accounts reveal more being spent on preaching and fabric in the period 1598–1610.

renowned vagabonds and pickpockets according to village testimony (although village testimony should not be taken too uncritically, for it was often an amalgam of spite and petty quarrels). Forty-eight priests were disciplined and many vicars did not know the name of the rector of the parish. By 1608, the efforts of the seminary established at Agen were beginning to have an effect on clerical standards in the diocese, although more in urban than in rural parishes. The evolution towards a Tridentine catholic church in France was bound to be a long and uneven process. Henri IV did not encourage it to the extent of accepting the decrees of the Council of Trent in their entirety in his realm and by royal edict. As the papal nuncio wrote in 1608: 'This is a lost cause, at least for the present.'[122] Henri IV also refused categorically to have anything to do with a revived Inquisition in France, aware that Gallican sentiments would be aroused against such a proposal from all quarters.[123] He did accept that the clergy should set aside some funds to persuade heretic ministers to return to the Roman faith; however, the assembly of clergy in 1605 was unwilling to accept an additional burden of 10–15,000 *écus* on the *décimes*.[124]

The spirit of evangelical catholicism was more alive among the regular religious orders and, by 1610, the Capuchins, Feuillants and Récollets, as well as reformed houses of cloistered monks, had active groups in Paris. The corrosive oratory of the Paris parish clergy and some of the regulars was not suddenly switched off, but it found politically less sensitive channels of expression in the back-eddies of the emerging *dévot* movement. More surprisingly, the Jesuits were allowed back to France after long and complicated negotiations in 1603.[125] They had been expelled in 1594 by the *parlement* of Paris, anxious to demonstrate its royalism and eager to exercise its new unity against what senior and effective lawyers like Pasquier argued was an ultramontane, papal and Spanish fifth column in France. Henri IV allowed them back under strict conditions which made them more responsive to royal influence than any other religious order in the kingdom. In the debate over the registration of the edict for their reinstatement, the king let it be known that he wanted the Jesuits to return because of their skills as teachers. More privately, he may have

122. F-T. Perrens, 1872, I, 299 (19 Aug. 1608).

123. Ibid.

124. Ibid., 301.

125. *Revue Henri IV*, 1909, II, 94–110 for the negotiations leading to the edict of 1603. For the Jesuits in France, the fundamental work is H. Fouqueray, *Histoire de la Compagnie de Jésus en France*, 5 vols (1910–25), esp. II. For anti–Jesuit pamphlets in this period, see C. Sutto, 1977.

wanted to prevent the Jesuit order becoming too dependent on Spanish Habsburg influence. Once they were reinstated, the king patronised the Jesuits with zeal. Through the influence of his favourite, Guillaume Fouquet, and some royal pensions, they established a new college at La Flèche in the jurisdiction of the *parlement* of Paris.[126] Later, the king's heart would be buried at La Flèche. He gave another pension to the Jesuits to found a house in Canada and introduced the order to Béarn. In 1608, he took the able and seductive preacher, Pierre Coton, as his confessor and sponsored the 'commemoration' of Loyola and Xavier at Rome as the first step towards their canonisation by the Vatican. In October 1609, the Jesuits obtained the necessary royal permission to teach theology at their college in Paris, and thus directly challenged the Sorbonne, the theological faculty of the university of Paris. Gallican theologians and lawyers attempted to discredit the Jesuits by refuting at length the theoretical arguments advanced by some members of the order for the superiority of papal over royal jurisdiction. Edmund Richer, the austere principal of the *collège* Cardinal Le Moine and one of the reformers of the university of Paris in 1600, edited the works of Jean Gerson in 1606. Gerson was the leading Gallican theorist of the early fifteenth century, and the papal nuncio in Paris immediately asked the royal professor at the Sorbonne, André Du Val, to answer the edition when it appeared in Venice.[127] Henri IV largely stood aside from the debate, not wishing either to alienate the papacy or to outrage the Gallicans. But the Roman Inquisition banned several Gallican works in 1609, including the royal edict against Jean Chastel for his attempted assassination of the king in 1594. Also banned were the published volumes of Jacques-Auguste de Thou's history of the civil wars, which had reached the year 1584. Henri IV then diplomatically asked the papacy to remove the Inquisition's ban on the royal edict against regicide but did not press for the ban to be lifted on de Thou's history. When the first volume had appeared in 1603, it had been warmly received by the king who ordered the laudatory preface to him to be translated and reproduced as a separate work (it went into six editions by 1617). But the first volume had treated the period to 1560 and, as the history proceeded to more uncomfortably recent times, the king was less keen to encourage its publication.[128] He preferred his subjects to forget

126. *Revue Henri IV*, 1905–6, I, 8–14, 97–9.

127. The debates surrounding Richer are usefully summarised in F-T. Perrens, 1872, I, ch. v. The fundamental (but prejudiced) work on Richer is E. Pujol, 1876. Cf. E. Préclin, 1930, pp. 241–69.

128. F-T. Perrens, 1872, I, 341–5. Cf. S. Kinser, 1966, ch. ii.

more recent events and remember that regicide was never justified under any circumstances.

THE NEW ORDER

Politically chastened by the events of the League, the professions of the long robe lost none of their privileges or social position. Peace enabled them to consolidate their corporate strength within society. Economically, too, it provided the climate for a good return on their investments. With the coming of peace, house prices in Paris rose dramatically and the senior magistrates who had prudently invested in real estate there found it paying handsome dividends. Those who had not done so, hastened to construct elegant town houses in the reclaimed marshlands in an area to the north-east of the city known as the Marais.[129] They made it as exclusive a residential suburb for Bourbon Paris as Harley St, Wimpole St or Portland Place would be to Hanoverian London. Henri IV participated in the speculation himself by organising the construction of his new squares. In the countryside, the seigneurial investments of the *robe* benefited from the favourable economic climate at the end of hostilities. Rentals began to rise and some prudent *robins* were encouraged to farm their estates directly. Those who wanted to consolidate their estates did so by acquiring (at low prices) parcels of land from ruined peasants or desperate villages selling their commons to pay off debts. Henri IV ensured that the interest on investments in government securities (*rentes*) was paid, albeit at a lower rate than during the civil wars. Wages were also paid on time. The numbers of cases before tribunals increased as the litigation resulting from the civil wars passed through the courts, so that there were large fees still to be gained.

In provincial cities, the same trends were at work. In Montpellier, for example, they had considerable effects on the city's social structure. There was a redistribution of wealth among Montpellier's urban élites, a flight from commerce into office, accelerated by the effect of the parlous state of the civil wars on the profitability of bourgeois mercantile activities. It was the office-holders who increasingly made shrewd landed investments in the farms situated towards the Mediterranean coast close to the city; the dowries of their daughters

---

129. B. Veyrassat-Herrem and E. Le Roy Ladurie, 1968, pp. 541–55. Also E. Le Roy Ladurie and P. Couperie, 1970, pp. 1014–15.

also reflected the growing wealth of the office-holding robe group.

The social tensions which had scandalised the *robins* were also reduced with the coming of peace. Peasant rebellions and popular risings were much less likely to occur after 1600. The army was garrisoned or disbanded so that the possibility of undisciplined soldiers roaming the roads and countryside receded. Judges in the *parlements* were employed to survey town constitutions, limiting town franchises where possible to prevent 'factions and monopolies' in municipal government. A commission from the *parlement* of Paris reformed the university of Paris in 1600.[130] The judges were used to censor libellous and blasphemous publications and to oversee cases of demonic possession. The sovereign courts were entrusted with the enforcement of order in the provinces. They were given general powers to deal with seditious preaching and treasonable plots to assassinate the king. They took their duties seriously and investigated rumours of plots with considerable vigour. They also enforced the laws against duelling, and themselves passed new edicts against the crenellation of castles, the carrying of firearms and the manufacture of offensive weaponry. Since the provincial governors became largely absentee during the reign, the *parlements* became the policemen of the provinces.

Within the judicial profession, too, the old self-regulating mechanisms of a code of ethics and accepted patterns of behaviour became more believable in the more stable context. Estoile recorded a case in February 1608 of a councillor in the *Grand Chambre* in Paris who was 'about to commit a signal and new infraction of justice in judging a second time a case which had already been adjudged and lost' when the president upbraided him with the words: 'Monsieur P., remember Poile [*a notorious case of injustice, committed by a magistrate of this name in the 1580s, much advertised during the League*] – he almost found himself on the gallows; you will sacrifice your honour'.[131] In the court-rooms and outside on the *parquets* of the court-houses, the older ideals of the Christian magistrate began to prevail, reinforced by an ascetic, puritan reformed catholic piety adopted by many of the Henrician senior magistrates and an elevated sense of their own dignity. When the advocates in Paris went on strike in 1602 it was apparently because the president of the *parlement*, Antoine Séguier, had suggested to the council of state that their emoluments should be taxed. Reform would begin at home.

Between the magistrates and Henri IV there developed a consensus,

130.   C. Jourdain, 1867, I, 18 *et seq.*
131.   Cited in E. Barnavi and R. Descimon, 1985, p. 172.

based on a shared view of society, which was more important than the differences of opinion which occurred between the king and his magistrates over individual issues. This can be glimpsed through the extensive writings of one of the lawyers of the period, Charles Loyseau. Loyseau began his career as a *lieutenant particulier* (a minor royal officer) in Sens and ended it as a barrister, having retired to a prudent seclusion in the period of the League.[132] He was a direct heir to the flourishing tradition of legal philosophy in sixteenth-century France and his family was related to that of Guy Joly as well as to François Hotman. He was well read and in all his works he successfully orchestrated legal theory and jurisprudence, never becoming too abstruse or overburdened with citations, or losing sight of his (considerable) legal and classical knowledge. He wrote in French, which ensured him a large audience, and almost everything that he published was of direct, practical and immediate importance. His treatises on mortgages, bankruptcies and seigneuries explained in clear language the detailed complexities of the law on debt, real estate and liability, concentrating on the common problems which were occurring at the end of a long period of civil wars.

One of his most popular works was his treatise on offices (*Des Offices*, 1608). It would not be an overstatement to say that, singlehanded, Loyseau codified the practices and precedents behind the venality and heredity of royal and seigneurial offices. He put to one side most of the moralising criticism of office-holding, and systematically analysed it as a new branch of the law with its own rules, precedents, actions and damages. It is impossible to imagine the work being written a decade earlier, given the confusions that prevailed in the law on office-holding, and the opposition felt towards the magistrature. Its appearance in 1609 is a witness to the importance of the officers as a legal and social fact in seventeenth-century France.

Loyseau's most ambitious work was undoubtedly his last, the treatise on orders (*Traité des Ordres et simples dignitéz*, 1610). In it, French society was stratified and arranged into a neat hierarchy. An order, he explained, was a 'rank with a particular fitness for public authority . . . and, in France, it has the special name of "estate". . .'[133] Each of the main estates, however, was then subdivided into ranks. The ecclesiastical order, Loyseau described as a hierarchy running from the cardinals, primates and patriarchs down to those who had 'just taken the tonsure', since that was, 'what makes a man a cleric and

132. J. Lelong, 1909.
133. R.E. Mousnier, 1979, I, 4–16.

distinguishes [*him*] from the people'. Likewise, the order of nobility was divided into princes of the blood, princes, the chivalric orders of the higher nobility, down to the ordinary gentlemen who enjoyed the profession of arms. The third estate was the most intricate in its gradations. At the top of the order came the 'men of letters' – doctors, licentiates and bachelors of arts. Then came the barristers. Lower down the scale were the financiers, next the 'practitioners of men of affairs'. Below the merchants in their various 'honest professions' (all of which were graded) appeared those 'who depend more on manual labour than on trade or on the sharpness of their wits and whose occupations are therefore the most base'. These too were graded from the top (the *laboureur*) to the very bottom (vagabonds and tramps) who lived 'in idleness and without care and at the expense of others'. Loyseau explained at length how the various orders of society were maintained in their position. Each order had 'its special mark or outward ornament' – robes, hats, gloves, rings etc, for public appearances. Each possessed its own titles and forms of address; '*Sire*' for kings, '*Monseigneur*' for princes, '*Monsieur*' for knights and ordinary nobles and '*Maistre*' for men of letters. He outlined the principles behind common rules for precedence, such as who should give way to whom in the street, in the pews of a church or at a municipal ceremonial. Each different rank, he noted, had its own corporation or fraternity which dedicated itself towards maintaining its status. This was a picture of a stable, hierarchical society. But it was not entirely static. Individuals could acquire new ranks in society through good fortune, wealth, education or the king's favour. They could also lose them through failing to live up to their rank (*dérogéance*), through treason or criminal activity. Nevertheless, the ranks of society themselves remained clearly delineated and did not change.

Loyseau's picture was based on Aristotelian principles.[134] It was immensely popular and his complete works went into six editions in the seventeenth century. His theoretical exposition of a hierarchical society was not new, but it had never been presented so coherently or with such observant attention to the detail of day-to-day social customs. Its date too – coming at the end of a reign dedicated to the re-creation of a stable society – is immensely significant. The legal and financial professions had, in their corporate ambitions in the sixteenth century, disproved the existence of the static hierarchical society by becoming a new *couche sociale* (the term is more appropriate than the formal 'order' or the anachronistic 'class'). Having glimpsed the

---

134. H. Lloyd, 1981, pp. 53–82.

consequences of such mobility at the end of the sixteenth century, they espoused the most traditional view of French society and worked hard to see it enforced in laws, ordinances and their own social customs. In the process of assimilating them to the world of traditional French society, Henri IV's regime played a significant role.

The king was the guarantor of the stable, organic society of Loyseau, for every organ required a governing principle, a *pars principans*. The king could govern only when there was a commonly accepted harmony between himself and the polity. This harmony came from the divine basis of the social and political bonds of the community. Loyseau's catholicism was essential to his conception of a hierarchical society in harmony with itself. Other lawyers and theologians of the period drew on the writings of Neoplatonists – Christian, Gnostic and Jewish – to explain this harmony. They strongly influenced Jean Bodin when he came to write the *Six Books of a Commonweal* in 1576. Replying to the *Francogallia* of François Hotman and the Aristotelian political thought of Louis Le Roy, Bodin explained his theory of monarchical sovereignity in terms of mystical oneness. Society itself required geometric (or harmonic) proportions, as in music, to keep the various orders in tune with each other and in harmony with their sovereign king.[135] Bodin's theories of sovereignty would become important among seventeenth-century French judges, but this was partly because they were reinforced by other theological contributions. The divine right theories of the absolute monarch (as preached, for instance, on the death of Henri IV) and the theory of celestial hierarchies expounded by Pierre de Bérulle from the writings of the Neoplatonist Denis the Areopagite reinforced the picture or ideal of the society of orders which became so prominent in the aftermath of the civil wars.

135. D. Parker, 1981, 277–82.

CHAPTER EIGHT

The Old Nobility

THE TITLED NOBILITY AND ITS CLIENTS

Among the buildings which house the National Archives in Paris are the remains of the *hôtel* Clisson, the Paris residence of the dukes of Guise. To its rear, the severe, military aspect of the edifice reflects something of its sixteenth-century past when, in the civil wars, it had served as a citadel in the capital. The building had seen more glorious moments, especially in 1559–60 when the Guise family was at the height of its prestige. The wealth and interests of its owners were best depicted in the fine chapel, built in the 1550s. The décor included a painting by Primaticcio of the *Adoration of the Magi* in which François, duke of Guise, appears as one of the three kings, proudly standing (rather than kneeling!) before the Almighty.[1] A few hundred yards away stood the most elaborate of the four houses in Paris owned by the duke of Montmorency. Although now destroyed, its magnificence can be reconstructed from contemporary inventories which described the forty splendidly furnished apartments, the sumptuous library and the marvellous collections of linen and glass, a testimony to the wealth and interests of the Montmorency family.[2]

These two powerful families characterised the closely knit French titled nobility of the sixteenth century. Both were recently created dukedoms, dating from the first half of the sixteenth century when a significant number of laymen, both foreigners (the Guise came from the House of Lorraine) and natives (the Montmorency stressed their ancestry as 'first barons of France'), were raised to the peerage.[3] Both

1. J-P. Babelon, 1958 and 1983.
2. L. Mirot, 1918–19.
3. J-P. Labatut, 1972, ch. ii.

possessed substantial landed inheritances spread through many provinces. Properties of the dukes of Guise were to be found mainly in Champagne, while those of the dukes of Montmorency were concentrated in the Ile de France. Marriages increased their wealth and influence. The House of Montmorency was related to foreign nobles (the Horn and Montigny in Flanders), French courtiers (Coligny), and influential provincial nobles (the Montmorency had married the richest and most powerful families of the Midi – the Turenne, the La Trémoille, the Ventadour and the Candalle). The Guise family was closely related to the House of Stuart as well as to the dukes of Montpensier and Nevers.[4] Through this network of kinship, these two 'potent Houses' exercised political influence.

The power of the peerage had traditionally been exercised through membership of the royal council which enabled nobles to obtain favours and privileges for their followers.[5] This was still the case during the reigns of François II and Charles IX and the registers of the royal council record at whose request pensions and other favours had been granted. Then, in 1574, Henri III limited his council to the princes of the blood and trusted *fidèles*, removing from it other princes and titled aristocrats.[6] At the same time he merged this 'privy' council with his council of finance and made it more difficult for Montmorency or Guise to obtain patronage. This explains some of the difficulties the last Valois experienced in obtaining the confidence of his aristocrats.

In any case, during the civil wars, the peerage was also able to exercise its powers through the post of provincial governor.[7] The most important governments lay on the borders of France, in Guyenne, Languedoc, Provence, Dauphiné, Burgundy and Champagne. In theory, these were not permanent posts but temporary commissions granted to 'great and notable persons' to exercise during the King's good pleasure. In practice, there was a strong trend towards heredity, especially during the reign of Charles IX.[8] By that time, the members of the House of Montmorency regarded themselves as hereditary governors of Languedoc, having controlled the province since 1526, and hoped to gain control of the government of the Ile de France

4. H. Forneron, 1893. F. Decrue de Stoutz, 1889, pp. 377–420.

5. R.R. Harding, 1978, pp. 34–5.

6. Villeroy, [1881], XI, 108. I. Cloulas, 1979, pp. 276–7. For a contemporary view of the privy council, Claude Figon, *Discours des Etats et Offices tant du gouvernement que de la justice et des finances de France* (Paris, 1580), fols 2–3.

7. R.R. Harding, 1978, pp. 88–107.

8. Ibid., p. 121.

which had been in the family since 1538. The House of Guise installed itself in the province of Champagne in 1524 and extended its influence over neighbouring Burgundy in 1543 so that, by the wars of religion, the family was ensconced in both localities. An increasing number of cash transactions accompanied the growth of heredity so that governorships threatened to become as venal as judicial posts.[9]

Letters of commission to governors gave them wide and unspecified powers to oversee every aspect of provincial affairs including imports and exports, the summoning of provincial estates, the investigation of royal officials. If they were charged with a part of the royal army during wartime, they were given authority to exercise justice and levy money too.[10] In some provinces, like Dauphiné and the Nivernais, governors had certain prerogative powers as a matter of custom.[11] But their principal function involved the military disposition of the province, its security, and the payment and upkeep of its garrisons. During the civil wars, therefore, it was natural that the governors would become both more numerous and more important in French politics. In some provinces, they appeared to act like viceroys; cities anxious to acquire their protection offered them lavish entry ceremonies with royal canopies. The mayor at Dijon during the League told the duke of Mayenne, its governor, that he was 'the image of God'.[12] Pasquier said that fidelity to a provincial governor could be used to hide treason in the civil wars.[13] Loyseau recorded: 'Of all the dangers that menace France, there is not one greater than the tyranny of the governors . . . who, by means of their governments in provinces and towns, have made themselves lords, practically sovereigns, over their localities'.[14] The estates of Blois in 1576 petitioned the king to reduce the powers of military governors, compel them to run well-ordered households and undertake their military duties conscientiously.[15] In practice, the authority the king possessed in provinces where there was a powerful governor was to

---

9. Ibid., pp. 125–6. M. Greengrass, 1979, 22–5.

10. Ibid., ch. i. G. Zeller, 1964, pp. 207–39. R. Doucet, 1948, I, ch. ix.

11. Rights of governors in Dauphiné noted in M. Greengrass, 1979, 16. Cf. Isambert, XIV, 484 for the edict of 4 July 1580 against these prerogatives. It seemed that they might have survived until the time of Richelieu (R.R. Harding, 1978, p. 29). For the Nivernais, see L. Despois, *Histoire de l'authorité royale dans le comté de Nivernais* (1912), p. 482.

12. 'The image of God and one of his ministers on earth' quoted in R.R. Harding, 1978, p. 13.

13. E. Pasquier, [1723], II, cols 447–8.

14. C. Loyseau, [1611], p. 348.

15. R.R. Harding, 1978, p. 70.

appoint a loyal lieutenant. Lieutenants were generally not peers but chosen from well-established noble families and sometimes kinsmen of the governor himself.[16]

Governors possessed substantial, armed, noble retinues. In 1556, for instance, the governor of the Ile de France, François de Montmorency, arrived in Paris accompanied by 200 noblemen.[17] In 1561, his father, the constable, entered Fontainebleau with 800 noblemen in his train. Companies of cavalry (*gens d'armes*) formed the most important part of these retinues. The gendarmerie was a unique force in western Europe – a paid, standing army reserved exclusively for the nobility. The *gens d'armes* were organised into companies under captains who controlled their recruitment and promotion.[18] They wore the captain's livery on their cassocks (*hocquetons*) and it was illegal to remove the livery or enlist in another company without his consent. The captain's name, reputation and colours were the focus of their pride and morale. Theoretically, each company consisted of 100 men-at-arms with a further 150 archers to assist them. Many were relatives of the captain and all were theoretically required to be nobles. By 1560, there were about 6,500 serving in the gendarmerie and on it came to rest much of the theory and practice of 'clientage' among the French nobility.[19] The Italian wars glamorised the 'pastime' and 'game' of war among the nobility. Writing in the civil wars, Blaise de Monluc, a catholic gendarme captain, lieutenant of Gascony and, eventually, marshal of France, described the great battles of the Italian wars and also revealed the ethos of the relationship between noble and captain, between lieutenant and governor, and between captain and gendarme, that of honour, service and protection.[20] Jean de Saulx-Tavannes (*c.*1533 – *c.*1629), the lieutenant in Burgundy for much of the later part of the sixteenth century, looked back in his memoirs to his father's great exploits in those wars and stressed his family's 'fidelity' – that powerfully diffused sense of honour, duty and service, developed from military origins to form a code of behaviour which permeated the French nobility.[21] André de Bourdeille, sieur de Brantôme, wrote in his retirement in the last stages of the League, his memoirs of *Famous Men and Great French Captains*, a kind of Valhalla

16. *Ibid.*, pp. 9–10, 132–4.
17. R.R. Harding, 1978, p. 21.
18. *Ibid.*, pp. 22–6. R. Doucet, 1948, II, ch. vi. Fontanon, III, 62, etc. contains numerous edicts on the *gens d'ordonnance* or *gendarmerie*.
19. R.R. Harding, 1978, p. 23.
20. A. Jouanna, 1976, pp. 638–50. cf. P. Courteault, 1909.
21. G. Saulx-Tavannes, [1881], VIII, 3–21, 68 etc.

in which various sixteenth-century nobles were immortalised for their chivalry, fidelity, catholicism and military prowess.[22] He reserved his highest praise for 'Monsieur de Guise le Grand' (François de Guise, 1519–63) and Anne de Montmorency (whose shield, he remarked, carried the legend '*sans fraude et très-fidèle*').[23] These were all works by authors who were, in some measure, discontented by the civil wars. Monluc and Saulx-Tavannes felt their prowess was not rewarded by their king; for his part, Brantôme looked back to a golden age of French military valour. For a number of reasons, the bonds of fidelity had become strained during the wars of religion.

For several historians, these strains had their roots in a structural crisis for the French nobility which had contributed materially to the causes of the civil wars in the first place. Some have tried to argue that there was a 'failure of clientage' during the civil wars.[24] The case for a structural crisis leading to the civil wars, however, remains unproven and the argument that there was a 'failure of clientage' has also attracted criticism.[25] Nevertheless, there were evident strains and these were a function of the civil wars themselves. Unlike the Italian campaigns of the first half of the sixteenth century, the civil wars divided the aristocratic families in France both within and among each other. Attempts to appeal to family loyalty fell on deaf ears. Nobles found it difficult to exploit the loyalties of religious parties in order to extend their own support because Huguenot political assemblies or League councils were responsive to religious faith as well as to aristocratic fidelities.[26] The patterns of civil war cut across the familiar filigrees of noble clientage and the habitual ways by which the noble honour code was exemplified in warfare, and devalued the language of fidelity.[27] Secondly, the aristocracy was affected by a progressive decline in the number and value of aristocratic royal pensions. The swiftest contraction of patronage occurred during 1559–61, but the whole period of the civil wars remained one of austerity. Payments of pensions, gifts and wages were periodically postponed, curtailed or diverted. In the reign of Henri III, the problems were exacerbated by the *mignons* so that, as Villeroy (one of the royal secretaries) remarked: 'It was no longer possible for princes and seigneurs of quality to

---

22. Brantôme, [1864–82], III and IV. Cf. A. Jouanna, 1976, pp. 696–703.
23. Brantôme, [1864–82], III, 294–350; IV, 187–279.
24. R.R. Harding, 1978, pp. 68–87.
25. See M. Greengrass, 1986; also, with different nuances, S. Kettering, 1989 and K.B. Neuschel, 1989.
26. R.R. Harding, 1978, chs iii–iv.
27. K.B. Neuschel, 1989.

intercede with the king on behalf of others, as they did in the past, which greatly angers them'.[28]

Among the problems of the higher nobility generally, the greatest during this period was their indebtedness on the king's behalf. Provincial governors and lieutenants raised armies and provided loans to the king but they were not repaid. Other members of the aristocracy became heavily indebted by their revolts against royal authority. In 1586, the Savoyard ambassador recorded that the poverty of the duke of Guise was well known and was forcing him to sell some of his best estates.[29] In November, the duke begged the royal secretary, Brûlart, to ask Henri III for assistance: 'You know my funds and my credit and I do what I can. All that I can mortgage has been mortgaged. I beg you to solicit the king for me as there is nothing else to be found.[30] It is not surprising that several friends counselled him to be cautious in 1588 to save the family fortunes. In 1594–96, 300,000 *écus* of debts were accepted by Henri IV on behalf of Charles de Guise and his father, and 600,000 *écus* on behalf of the duke of Mayenne.[31] Other examples of indebtedness are more astonishing. Louis, duke of Nevers, died in 1595 leaving a debt of over 1 million *livres*, having spent the civil wars trying to keep his estates intact.[32] The debts of the prince de Condé were disavowed after his death in 1588 because they were so substantial.[33] Henri de Montmorency-Damville's family wealth was already mortgaged when, in 1586, his estates were confiscated by the king. In 1597, the income from his devastated lands was so low that his banker, Sebastien Zamet, threatened to withdraw further credit.[34] In the same year, Montmorency-Damville was informed by the son of the lieutenant of Guyenne, Charles de Matignon, that his father (who had gained a reputation for rapacity in office) had died 'with a world of debts on his shoulders'.[35] His colleague, the lieutenant in Lyon, François de Mandelot, had died in 1588 in similar circumstances.[36] The growth in size of aristocratic dowries did not help aristocratic fortunes, but the opportunities for

28. Villeroy, [1881], XI, 108.

29. R. de Lucinge, [1954–5], pp. 118–9; [1966], p. 106 (14 Mar. 1586); p. 160 (1 May 1586). Cf. J. Russell Major, 1981.

30. de Croze, 1866, II, No. 40 (Guise to Brûlart, 24 Nov. 1586).

31. BN MS Fr 3646, f. 77 (Charles de Guise); 4019, f. 360 (Mayenne).

32. R.R. Harding, 1978, pp. 143–9, amplified and corrected in D. Crouzet, 1984.

33. Carew, [1749], p. 447.

34. M. Greengrass, 1986, 291–2.

35. BN MS Fr 3549, f. 20 (Charles de Matignon to Henri de Montmorency, 24 Aug. 1597).

36. R.R. Harding, 1978, p. 127.

making a wealthy marriage were still present for individual hard-pressed aristocrats. Some nobles were more able to press their 'assignations' on royal revenues and obtain cash from provincial treasuries or grants of profitable alienated royal domain. François de Bonne, seigneur de Lesdiguières (1543-1626) was widely believed to have profited from the wars in Dauphiné both before and after he became lieutenant in the province in 1597.[37] Nevertheless, it is not difficult to understand why some aristocrats – Guise, Montmorency-Damville, Mercoeur, Joyeuse and Epernon – should seek pensions from Spain or Savoy to maintain their political influence and protect them from bankruptcy.

Decline in royal favours, the growth of aristocratic indebtedness, the rival attractions of new religious beliefs and the bitterness of civil war eroded the fabric of fidelity elsewhere in society, especially among the gendarmes. As a result, the standards of discipline declined. One captain reported from Brittany that his troops, their wages unpaid, had deserted him to pillage the surrounding region: 'There is so much due to the men of my company . . . that I am neither feared nor obeyed. I was never a happier man than when it pleased His Majesty . . . to give me an ordnance company but it seems now that I have only a company of 100 horses.'[38] He was luckier than Captain Jarnac who, in the same year, reported that his company, unpaid for a year, had eaten its horses and retired home. In the course of the civil war, at least ten edicts of considerable ferocity attempted to assert royal authority over the gendarmes.[39] Their reputation grew more tarnished as complaints of their pillage spread. One edict in February 1574 bluntly said: 'The gendarmerie, which ought to contain gentlemen respecting their honour, has committed (to our grave regret) as much pillage of our subjects as foreigners and vagabonds.'[40] The offences of stealing, pillaging, and the various abuses in their muster and payment were to be heavily punished, some by martial hanging and strangling. But, a decade later, Henri III lamented in another edict that the civil wars had 'corrupted the police and discipline' of the gendarmerie, and proposed to assign a priest to each company to restrain its lawless elements.[41]

37. C. Dufayard, 1892, ch. xiii. Cf. the example of Blaise de Monluc in R.R. Harding, 1978, pp. 149–54. See also the optimistic assessment of J. Russell Major, 1981.

38. Morice, 1742–6, III, cols 1295–7.

39. R.R. Harding, 1978, pp. 74–6.

40. Fontanon, III, 111 (1 Feb. 1574).

41. Ibid., 129 (9 Feb. 1584).

The most evident sign of indiscipline was the growth of duelling and feuding.[42] The cavalry returned from the Italian wars carrying the contagion of the private duel to the French provinces. The protestant captain, François de La Noue, recorded in his *Discourses* (1586) that more noblemen died in France from 'private discords' than from the civil wars.[43] Jean de Saulx-Tavannes estimated that 6,000 noblemen of his generation had died in duels.[44] Both authors thought that duels led to feuds and vendettas which encouraged civil wars. In the army, duels were controlled by the marshals; both the catholic Church and the protestant synods outlawed the practice. In the provinces, however, it went on largely unchecked and even involved provincial lieutenants.

In another respect, the gendarmerie was but a tattered remnant of its former noble glories. Although officially still reserved for nobles, increasing numbers of non-nobles appeared in its ranks. Foreign-born gendarmes had always been exempt from proving their noble status. To those native-born cavalrymen who were not noble, the king resorted to the distribution of nobility and knighthood instead of payment of salary. The abuse was at its worst during the reign of Charles IX, and the royal edict of February 1574 which lamented the 'disdained, despised and devalued' quality of noble service was both true and somewhat hypocritical.[45] The changing nature of warfare also gave rise to uncertainty. Infantry and artillery were becoming more important, especially in sieges. As Montaigne said; 'Valour has become popular in our civil wars'.[46] The third estate in Dauphiné claimed in 1596 that the 'common people' had done as much fighting as the nobility and should thus share some tax exemption.[47] The unease among the nobility remained widespread and emerged in complaints from the second estate at the estates of Blois in 1576 and 1588.[48]

For the fact was that the civil wars represented a challenge to the inherited ideal of nobility. This ideal was an amalgam of traditional medieval social theorising and some Renaissance popular philosophising.[49] In essence, the basis of nobility lay in virtue. As one (thoroughly typical) treatise on noble virtue explained in 1567:

42. F. Billacois, 1990, chs 3–4.
43. F. de La Noue, [1967], p. 281.
44. G. de Saulx-Tavannes, [1881], VIII, 154.
45. R.R. Harding, 1978, pp. 80–84 and refs. Cf. D. Bitton, 1969a, ch. ii.
46. *Ibid.*, p. 76. Changes summarised in R.R. Harding, 1978, p. 75. M. de Montaigne, [1962], II, 661.
47. Cf. memorandum quoted in A. Jouanna, 1976, pp. 656–8.
48. D. Bitton, 1969a, pp. 18–26.
49. See E. Schalk, 1986, pt. 2.

> To fight to maintain the honour of God and a peaceful kingdom, to
> spread more widely the king's authority against his enemies, and, on such
> occasions, not to be afraid of cold or heat, but to offer one's life
> courageously; these are the proper qualities of virtue. And that is how
> Nobility originated and why it is worthy of its privileges.[50]

But wherein lay the 'honour of God' in a religious war, and how did
'gent-pille-hommes' maintain the king's authority? Some noble
commentators were compelled to condemn noble violence, ignorance
and inability to prevent usurpation by commoners, especially during
the League. The greater the gap between the ideal and the reality of
nobility, the more they relied on a more stark justification for nobility
in terms of birth, blood and lineage.

HENRI IV AND THE TITLED NOBILITY

Henri IV attempted to rebuild the bonds of fidelity with his aristocracy
by generous pensions, careful management of the provincial
governorships and sensitive creations of new peers, and by a
(sometimes contrived) cultivation of the old-fashioned virtues of
'loyalty to a prince'. He was most successful in winning over the
League nobles and most ruthless to those who had a claim to his
throne and their supporters.

The treaties with League nobles recognised the importance of
fidelity and did not try to obtain loyalty on any other terms. The
treaty with Charles de Guise, for example, involved Guise giving the
king a solemn oath in writing of his fidelity and that of his followers
'such as good and faithful servants and subjects ought, and are by
nature obliged, to render to their legitimate and natural king'.[51] In
return, Henri IV accepted 'these good subjects into his obedience and
especially because he holds them dear to him'. Even the corpulent
Mayenne bent the knee in formal submission before the king, while
the avaricious marquis de Villars in Rouen expressed his new loyalty
to Henri IV in the rich, emotive imagery of fidelity which had so
often been denied to Henri III.[52] They were given lavish pensions,
matching in some cases those of the princes of the blood, and they

---

50. P. d'Origny, *Le Hérault de la noblesse de France* (Reims, 1578), p. 31. Cf. E.
Schalk, 1976, pp. 20–21.

51. BN MS Fr 3646, f. 77 etc. Sully, [1970–88], I, 455–6. Sully, [1881], XVI, 226.

52. R.E. Mousnier emphasises the importance of fidelity in 1979, pp. 99–111.

raised no further problems during the reign. Mayenne retired to Soissons, an ill man, dying in seclusion in 1611. Mercoeur went on crusade to Hungary, and died in Nuremberg in 1602. Henri de Bouchage-Joyeuse, the last of the Joyeuse brothers, retreated in 1599 from his lieutenancy in the province of Languedoc to the world of mental purgation and severe seclusion in a monastery in Paris which he had left in 1592 to take on his family duties and head the Toulouse League. Henri IV was delighted and remarked that 'peace will be here to stay for a long time since our captains are turning into Capuchins'.[53] At *frère* Ange's (Joyeuse) funeral in 1609, a procession of monks and gendarmes formed a cortège through the streets of Paris both incongruous and pathetic after a decade of peace.[54]

Towards others in revolt, Henri IV was less disposed to be generous. The duke of Epernon, for instance, had supported the king in the early years of his reign but he then joined the League in Provence. In his final treaty with the king, he failed to acquire any satisfaction to his demands for the government of Provence and only a portion of his war debts was underwritten. His compensation lay in the less significant government of Angoumois, Aunis and Saintonge, which lured him away from his landed influence in Guyenne. The king encouraged him to spend his time (and considerable fortune) in building a vast palace for himself on the Garonne at Cadillac.[55] He retained the important frontier government of Metz, but a royalist lieutenant reduced his influence there.[56] Epernon continued to cause periodic tension both at court and at Guyenne, being suspected of formenting revolt in 1602, but Henri IV's delicate combination of firmness and tact reduced his power for mischief.[57]

Some royalist aristocrats felt that Henri IV had rewarded League nobles at their expense, and that they were alienated from the new regime. Their continued exclusion from the king's council was particularly disliked. The constable's brother, at the time of the revolt

---

53. Estoile, [1948], p. 565. P. de la Guesle, *Lettres et ambassades de Messire Philippe de Canaye* (1635), p. 532.

54. Estoile, [1954], pp. 463–4. A certain religious austerity overcame several of Henri IV's aristocrats. The constable seems to have been influenced by it and was eventually buried in the habit of a Capuchin at Notre Dame de Grau, in Agde (P. Appollinaire, 1892, p. 192). His son-in-law, the duke of Ventadour, became very pious through the influence of his wife. Charles, duke of Nevers became involved in an elaborate project for a Crusade against the Infidel and went to fight the Turk at Buda in 1603 (E. Baudson, 1947, pp. 44–84).

55. J. d'Welles, 1960.

56. C. Derblay, 1927, pp. 135–50. L. Mouton, 1924, pp. 72–4.

57. Ibid., ch. v.

of Biron, expressed the resentments of many royalist aristocrats when he told Villeroy:

> Why are these factions in the state? Does the king think he can govern this huge kingdom through Rosny [*Sully*] and Villeroy, that God has given these two prudence enough to manage it on their own? The remedy lies in establishing a good council [*bon conseil*] with governors in their dignity, for, otherwise these upheavals will never end. Who would put up with it? We are deprived of all our dignity and only the title is left for us.[58]

The complaint was comprehensible but the remedy was unacceptable to the king. He could not restore power to royalist governors and loyal aristocrats without also giving it to League princes. However, loyal aristocrats were also rewarded by the increasing value of royal pensions to governors, so the reign was not without some dividends for them. Montmorency-Damville was made constable and the king became the protector of his infant son and heir.[59] Hunting expeditions, in which the king took great pleasure (unlike his predecessor), gave the aristocracy an illusion of being involved with royal affairs, even if they no longer had an open access to obtain the favours and privileges that they had enjoyed in the past. The king ensured that provincial governors no longer exercised powers of justice or finance. He did his best to see that provincial government rested in the hands of those he could trust. Governors were encouraged to reside at court, rather than in the provinces.[60] In their place, the king utilised loyal provincial lieutenants, where venality and heredity was not yet a major problem, and chose them from the secondary nobility in the provinces rather than from the peerage. These lieutenants – Alphonse d'Ornano in Guyenne after 1597, Anne de Lévis-Ventadour in Languedoc from 1594, François de Bonne-Lesdiguières in Dauphiné from 1597 – were significant figures in limiting the extent and seriousness of those provincial noble revolts which did occur in the realm.

Towards those who had a claim to his throne, Henri IV was more ruthless than tactful. Although he had legitimacy on his side, he was still weak in his fundamental dynastic right. If he could gain the throne, then it was open to almost any prince of the blood to claim

---

58. J. Nouaillac, [1908], p. 147 (reported in 19 Apr. 1602). cf. A. Desjardins, [1859], V, 496.

59. R.R. Harding, 1978, p. 139. M. Greengrass, 1979, pp. 283–7.

60. R.R. Harding, 1978, ch. xii.

the succession too in the event of the lack of direct heirs. In addition, the validity of the king's divorce from Marguerite of Valois and, therefore, of the claims to the throne of Marie de Médicis' children, were still questioned in some quarters. Hence, in December 1602, it was reliably reported that the king's avarice and ingratitude had ensured that, if he died, many aristocrats would proclaim the prince of Condé, rather than the dauphin, as king; shades of the Old Adam, returning 'vel canis ad vomitum', commented the Dutch envoy, d'Aerssen, on similar rumours in 1601.[61] As a result, the king treated the young prince of Condé with scant respect, casting doubts on his legitimacy, providing his household with inadequate pensions, encouraging his disordered education and ensuring that he was brought up a catholic, as opposed to his family's protestantism.

Condé's nephew, the count of Soissons, also possessed a claim to the throne and was financially well-endowed, not having ruined his fortune in the civil wars. Henri IV deliberately excluded him from his councils, favoured Sully at his expense, and, as with Condé, interfered with the upbringing of his son.[62] Charles d'Auvergne, the illegitimate son of Charles IX, who had been encouraged by Henri III to think that he had a claim to the throne, plotted against the king in 1597 and again in 1602 and spent a period of time in prison before being released on good behaviour. The pleas of the royal mistress, the marquise de Verneuil, saved him from the scaffold, but the extent of his betrayal of other noble conspirators to the king meant he was never trusted again in noble conspiracies against Henri IV.[63] The king's rigour ensured there was no uprising from the princes of the blood for most of the reign, but it was short-sighted and his success was short-lived. In 1609, the prince of Condé, suspecting the king of wishing to make his fiancée, and then, bride – Charlotte de Montmorency – a royal mistress, fled with her across the border to Brussels. Attempts to repatriate them caused a major diplomatic incident which was worsened by Condé's journey from the Low Countries to the Spanish fortress at Milan.[64] There, Condé learned of the death of Henri IV and quickly made peace with Marie de Médicis,

---

61. J. Nouaillac, [1908], p. 112 (15 June 1601).
62. G. Carew, [1749], pp. 447–50.
63. B. Zeller, 1879, pp. 146–50, 158. J. Nouaillac, [1908], pp. 159, 182. Cf. M. Greengrass, 1981, pp. 336–7 for d'Auvergne's part in 1597.
64. P. Henrard, 1870, presents the best case for the obsession of the king with the princess of Condé and the distress it caused royal ministers (pp. 96 and 115–16). The affair was clearly a potential danger to Franco-Spanish relations at the delicate period of the Jülich-Clèves dispute (*infra*, pp. 246–8).

lest he become accused of having plotted to assassinate the king.[65] Whether, had the king lived, the exile of Condé would have been a serious threat to the regime is difficult to assess. It is clear that, in the conditions of a minority, princes of the blood had a different constitutional position, so little can be inferred from Condé's later rebellions. The history of seventeenth-century France suggests that, although there was no permanent solution to the ability of princes of the blood to break any political consensus, there were limitations on their success in raising rebellion and putting anything constructive in the place of royal government.

'Discontented persons of greatness and reputation' (to use Francis Bacon's phrase) still raised revolts. The two most serious ones centred round nobles from the province of Gascony. The first concerned Charles, duke of Biron (1562–1602), whose château in the Périgord is a massive feudal bastion from which (on a clear day) one can see the Pyrenees. The other involved the duke of Bouillon from the neighbouring viscounty of Turenne, who had extensive patrimonies in the Périgord and the Limousin. Both were close personal friends or protégés of Henri IV and had benefited from royal favour. Biron had been made an admiral in 1592, a marshal in 1594, and a provincial governor in Burgundy in 1596.[66] His disillusionment with the king arose after the siege of Amiens and was fostered by agents from Brussels and Turin.[67] It intensified and, during the war with Savoy, he negotiated with the enemy and planned to assassinate the king.[68] In January 1601, Biron confessed some of these plots to the king, who pardoned him, hoping to draw a line under this pattern from the past. However, the peace with Savoy discontented Biron still further and he continued to negotiate with Savoy and Spain and may even have reached some kind of treaty of association with them. By February 1602, the English ambassador was receiving reports of meetings of disaffected nobles in the Auvergne and Gascony who were planning to capture major strongholds in France.[69] As always, there were rumours of potential support from amongst the senior French aristocracy, including officers of the crown. Henri IV acted quickly, dispatching

65. Ibid., pp. 148–9.

66. B. Zeller, 1879, p. 132.

67. Ibid., pp. 133–5. cf LN, No. 2313.

68. B. Zeller, 1879, p. 136. Also A. Dufour, 1965, pp. 434–5, which assesses Savoyard policy in the light of Biron's proposed coup; the case for Biron's treachery is reinforced.

69. B. Zeller, 1879, p. 143. J. Nouaillac, [1908], p.141. References to meetings in G. Lacoste, 1883, I, 285. D. Buisseret, 1984, pp. 111–14.

troops to all the affected areas and summoning Biron to court. On 13 June, both Biron and Charles d'Auvergne were arrested at court. Gascony remained calm while Biron was found guilty of treason in a show trial, stage-managed by Sully. Sully may have manufactured some of the damaging testimony against him, but much of the important evidence came from Biron's duplicitous secretary, Jacques de La Fin, who had revealed the conspiracies and provided incriminating documentation. Biron's supporters and relatives met the king on their knees, 'bearing the supplications of more than a hundred thousand men', begging him to commute the sentence to life imprisonment. Biron was executed for treason a fortnight later on 31 July, but the king did not confiscate the family estates, resting (he said) 'content that he has been punished as he merited'.[70] The king's tactics worked and, although there was a 'large assembly' of nobles at the funeral service of the duke in the ample chapel of the château Biron in the Périgord, there was 'more rumour than malevolence' towards the king among those who attended it.[71] In Paris, catholics thronged to the lying in state of the body at St Paul's Church (the king had arranged for the execution to take place at the Arsenal to avoid a public riot) but, as the Dutch envoy noted, 'the more intelligent' realised that the king had acted justly.[72]

The execution of Biron was rightly regarded as 'one of the great coups of the century', and the implications of the revolt were far-reaching.[73] Charles d'Auvergne implicated many other aristocrats in the rebellion. The constable, his father-in-law, feared that he would be disgraced.[74] The duke of Montpensier had to go down on his knees and beg for forgiveness.[75] La Trémoille was told he had been suspected and he also sued for a royal pardon. The duke of Bouillon, also d'Auvergne's relative, was clearly involved too.[76] He held hastily arranged conferences with his advisors and then left the court, first going to the protestant Midi where he hoped to find friends and where he intended to present his case before one of the courts of the edict (*chambres de l'édit*).[77] The case was dismissed by the chamber at

70. R. G. Tait, 1977, ch. viii. M. Dumoulin, 1895, pp. 170–286.
71. Henri IV, 1843–60, V, 648. Also BN MS Fr 23197, f. 54 (Ornano to Henri IV, 26 Aug. 1602).
72. J. Nouaillac, [1908], p. 172 (6 Aug. 1602).
73. Ibid., p. 184.
74. Ibid., p. 182 (4 Oct. 1602). cf. A. Desjardins, [1859], VI, 499–501.
75. B. Zeller, 1879, p. 142. J. Nouaillac, [1908], p. 184.
76. Ibid., pp. 186, 198.
77. BN MS Fr 15598, f. 235; 23197, f. 562; 3589, ff. 104 and v.

Castres and, a pathetic figure, Bouillon fled the country to Geneva and his sovereign territory at Sedan. Two years later, rumours of renewed conspiracy in Guyenne became strong and, by October, it was clear that Bouillon was behind a renewed series of noble assemblies in Quercy and Périgord.[78] These involved former League nobles as well as protestants. Premature discovery by the king ruined the revolt and Henri IV was quickly inundated by confessions.[79] One noble went to court to confess and submit on behalf of 120 gentlemen who had plotted to take the town of Villefranche-en-Rouergue.[80] By the time Henri IV reached Limoges on his way to Gascony with an army, almost all Bouillon's strongholds had surrendered. Over 1,000 nobles came from the province to visit the king there to demonstrate their loyalty, and, although the king established a special tribunal to sentence the ring-leaders to death, only a handful were finally executed in December 1604.[81] Bouillon, in exile in Sedan, held out for a few more months with a few hundred troops hoping for reinforcements from German princes. However, in April 1606, he also submitted before a powerful siege train in return for a pardon and a confirmation of all his offices.[82] Henri IV was exultant about his victory, vaunting that, like Caesar, he could say 'I came, I saw, I conquered.'[83] The Bouillon revolt was the most ambitious aristocratic revolt against Henri IV. Its failure was partly a measure of the inherent weakness of a purely factional aristocratic conspiracy, but it was also a demonstration of stability from a province which had been among the most disaffected in France during the civil war.

THE LESSER NOBILITY

The end of the wars of the League saw a determined effort to reduce the numbers of gendarmes in the standing army. Many companies had been, or were, transformed into units of *chevau-légers* which were cheaper and which had fewer, or no mounted archers to accompany the cavalry officer.[84] Those cavalry companies which remained were

78. Henri IV, 1843–60, VI, 234 (Henri IV to La Force, 23 April 1604). Ibid., 306–6, 330.
79. G. de Gérard, [1887], p. 403.
80. For example, AD Dordogne 2E, 599/15 pièce 15. *Henri IV, Lettres*, VI, 526.
81. Ibid., pp. 514, 552–3.
82. D.J. Buisseret, 1968, pp. 158–9.
83. *Henri IV, Lettres*, VI, 601–2 (5 Apr. 1606).
84. R.R. Harding, 1978, p. 74.

retrenched to thirty *lances* by the Constable, who also attempted to reduce the number of garrisoned and fortified strongholds in the country.[85] He met with considerable opposition from those with substantial arrears of pay or with expectations of captaincies and, in the short term, retrenchment probably contributed to the support of some nobles for the revolts of Biron and Bouillon. In the long term, Henri IV mitigated its effects by increasing the number of pensions in church and state for the lesser nobility, on which the English ambassador remarked:

> Touching the inferior nobility in general, consisting of Gentlemen of private families, or of great families who have but small means; he hath them much more obsequious to him than to any of his predecessors; and thereof his Majesty has to myself both vaunted often, and shewed me the effects and tokens of it. The course, which he taketh therein is this; that those who are anywise eminent for military or civil ableness, he bindeth them to this obsequiousness, by giving them pensions, (of which there are a great number, and well paid), so long as they continue in their dutifulness. But upon the least disobedience, they are sure to have their pensions stopt; which maketh them very careful, not to do anything against his will, neither in great matters or in small.[86]

Old mentalities died hard, however, and noble feuds reached unprecedented heights of violence in this period. When the new president of the *parlement* of Toulouse arrived in the province from Paris in 1600, he was horrified to find up to forty nobles at a time settling their quarrels by force 'with an excess, licence and brutality which made them seem more like wild beasts than men'.[87] As the commissioners establishing the edict of Nantes perambulated the provinces, they too were confronted with the sectarian aspects of duels. Henri IV had already been compelled to prevent noblemen from carrying offensive weapons and, in April 1602, following reports of several duels involving his provincial lieutenants, he published a controversial edict against duelling.[88] Henri IV had originally taken the view (like Jean Bodin) that duelling was a kind of safety valve, purging

---

85. J. Russell Major, 1974, p. 20. There was considerable opposition from the constable's own province. M. Greengrass, 1979, pp. 296–7.

86. G. Carew, [1749], pp. 459–60.

87. BN MS Fr 15598, f. 102.

88. Fontanon, I, pp. 665–6. L. Mouton, 1924, pp. 62–4. J. Nouaillac, [1908], p. 117 on the case of Louis de Cambonasier, sieur du Térail (who had been implicated in the 1597 Auvergne rising). He fled the court for the service of the archdukes in 1601 after having killed a gentleman at the royal court.

the nobility of its evil humours and reducing the likelihood of civil wars.[89] Others, with direct experience of government, viewed duelling as an encouragement to noble disputes and insurrection. The Act of 1602 made it treasonable, punishable by death, to conduct a duel, and encouraged nobles to seek the mediation of the lieutenant of their province or the marshals and Constable of France.[90] The edict was enforced, where possible, by the *parlements*. The first president of Toulouse reported that, in the first six months of its operation in Languedoc, he had ordered the edict to be printed and distributed as widely as possible and he had settled over 200 quarrels, saving over 300 gentlemen's lives.[91] The constable Montmorency was also kept very busy mediating between nobles who were engaged in feuding. But it was impossible to impose a change of attitude overnight. The edict had only a temporary effect and required reissuing in 1609. In some parts of France, notably in Brittany and the Auvergne, noble violence remained endemic (it is significant that Ravaillac, Henri IV's assassin, came from the Auvergne) and only began to wane after 1660.[92]

It was also widely believed that the best way to tame the lesser nobility and to render them useful was to establish academies to educate them to the ways of civil society. The theoretical concern in the treatises on the nobility about the lack of education among the old nobles (especially noticeable in those treatises written by those whose nobility was recently acquired) gave way to practical schemes to form gentlemen's academies.[93] The treatise by Pierre de La Primaudaye called *The French Academy*, written in 1577 by a protestant gentleman in Anjou's service (whose father had served in the royal mint in Paris), was a particularly popular and influential moralising tract.[94] The most famous academy was established in Paris by Antoine de Pluvinel to provide a noble-orientated education which included formal dressage, fencing, deportment, mathematics and modern languages. Other academies emulated Pluvinel's in the provinces, and the example spread to England.[95] Some of them were run by mountebanks and they did not affect a large proportion of the lesser nobilty, but they

89. J. Bodin, *Six Bookes of a Commonweale* (ed. A.D. McRae) 1962, pp. 527–9.
90. Fontanon, I, 666. F. Billacois, 1990, p. 97.
91. BN MS Fr 15598, f. 490 (13 Oct. 1603).
92. A. Lebigre, *Les Grands Jours d'Auvergne, désordres et répression au XVIIe siècle* (1976).
93. E. Schalk, 1986, ch. viii.
94. P. de La Primaudaye, *Académie Françoise*, (1577).
95. F. Yates, 1947, pp. 276–84.

did represent a more settled view of the status of nobility in society.[96] The most popular treatises on nobility in Henri IV's reign (among which were Salomon de la Broue's *French Cavalier* (1610) and Jean Pelletier's *Nourishment of Nobility* (1604)) were less confused about the origins and nature of nobility. Nobility rested on birth; this explained both its pre-eminence and its continued existence. Further speculation was irrelevant. The writers of treatises on nobility reflect, as did Charles Loyseau's writings, a renewed realism about, and confidence in, the stratified society.

96. Sully, [1970–88], I, 64–5 describes his disappointing experiences at a fencing academy.

CHAPTER NINE
Pax Gallicana

The unchallenged assumption of French foreign policy in the sixteenth century was the threat to France from Habsburg power, possessions and influence. Habsburg interests were global and encircled France. The Spanish Habsburgs possessed the territories of Franche-Comté, the Netherlands, and Naples and Milan in Italy as well as numerous claims to territory extending from England to various pockets in the Pyrenean region. The Austrian Habsburgs enjoyed extensive hereditary possessions in Austria, Bohemia and Hungary. The head of the Austrian branch was invariably elected Holy Roman Emperor, which meant that he could claim direct power from the Almighty and some influence over the German empire's princes and territories. The sense of encirclement increased after the revolt of the Dutch in 1566. The Spanish gained the consent of a string of states in Italy, the Alps and Germany to dispatch and reinforce troops through their lands. There were several alternative routes to this 'Spanish Road' (*le chemin des Espagnols*) as the French christened it.[1] Having crossed the gulf of Lions, the route passed from Genoa through the Spanish fortress city of Milan. From this point, the shortest way to the Netherlands lay through the Little Saint Bernard pass, Savoy, Franche-Comté, the duchy of Lorraine and Luxembourg. A longer route ran from Milan to the Tyrol via the shores of Lake Como and through the Engadine or Valtellina passes to southern Germany and then down to the Rhine, avoiding the hostile Rhine Palatinate and three bishoprics of Metz, Toul and Verdun, which had been ceded to the protection of France in 1559.

Henri IV took Habsburg imperialism seriously. Parts of his hereditary sovereign territory of Navarre were in Habsburg hands.

1. G. Parker, 1972, pp. 50–82.

Philip II had supported the catholic League since 1585 through subsidies to the duke of Guise. In 1590, he had sent a contingent of troops to fight at Ivry and a Spanish army under the duke of Parma had raised Henri IV's sieges on Paris and Rouen in 1590 and 1592 respectively.[2] Spain assisted Marseille to remain out of royalist hands until 1596.[3] The Spanish ambassador in Paris had advanced Spanish interests there while Spanish agents offered provincial governors like Mercoeur in Brittany and Joyeuse in Languedoc some subsidies and troops.[4] Spanish allies also advanced their own interests at France's expense. On 30 November 1588, Charles Emmanuel, duke of Savoy, invaded the marquisate of Saluzzo in the Alps, a French territory since 1548, and took the important fortress which overlooked Savoy at Carmagnola.[5] Although this was achieved apparently without Spain's prior knowledge, the invasions of Provence and Dauphiné in 1589 and 1593 and the establishment of Charles Emmanuel's son as governor in Lyon (Charles de Nemours), were doubtless undertaken with Spanish consent.[6] Charles III, duke of Lorraine, also overran the bishopric of Toul in August 1589, again with Spanish encouragement.[7] Philip II's intentions were therefore clearly displayed, even though he was not officially at war with Henri IV before 1595.

THE DEFENCE OF THE FRONTIERS

As the League crumbled, Henri IV felt more acutely the threat posed by Spain to France's security. By the end of 1594, Spain maintained an army of 60,000 men in Flanders, Charles Emmanuel was still on a war footing at the main approaches to Lyon, and the duke of Lorraine was still the 'protector' of Toul. Spanish forces were still sustaining the League in Languedoc and Brittany. Henri IV did not need much persuading to fan popular anti-Spanish sentiment in France and declare war on Philip II on 17 January 1595.[8] His declaration was supported

2. D. Lamar Jensen, 1964, pp. 197, 208–9, 216.

3. F. Braudel, 1973, II, 1209–16.

4. There is no effective study of Spanish intervention in France during the wars of the League beyond that of J. de Croze, 1866.

5. I. Raulich, 1896–1902, I, 314–45. The background to the loss of Saluzzo in given in A. Pascal, 1960.

6. J-H. Mariéjol, 1947, chs iii–iv. J. Saignieux, 1974.

7. G. Cabourdin, 1977, p. 53.

8. LN, No. 1984. M. Yardeni, 1971, pp. 297–330.

from many quarters, including England and Holland. Turenne saw it as an important moment to put together a grand pan-European protestant alliance against Spain and was influential in persuading Henri IV of the merits of such a war. Other protestant leaders like Sully believed (as Coligny had in a previous generation) that 'the true means of setting the realm at rest is by keeping up a foreign war, towards which one can direct, like water in a gutter, all the turbulent humours of the kingdom.'[9] Du Plessis Mornay also advised the king that the Spanish Road was vulnerable to an attack from France in several places. The protestant leader in Dauphiné, Lesdiguières, proved him correct when, in 1597, he occupied the Mauriennne and Tarantaise valleys in Savoy, two crucial arteries which connected Genoa with Habsburg Franche-Comté.[10] Spain countered in March 1597 by occupying the city fortress of Amiens in Picardy. This was a vital point of defence on the Somme for the whole of Picardy. Its recovery became a focus of tremendous military effort. As the cardinal of Florence wrote to the pope in March 1597:

> I recognise that the loss of Amiens is a great blow which gives heart to [*Henri IV's*] adversaries and that there may be worse to follow. However, I do not despair because the Spanish are so hated in this kingdom that if any individual appeals to them in dire necessity, the broad mass will not let the appeal succeed. Already, all the grandees can be seen flocking to the king . . . and there is no distinction of party (League or otherwise) between them because all are for the king who is a great and courageous soldier.[11]

In fact, Amiens was only recaptured in September 1597 after a protracted siege, orchestrated by Henri IV and his military engineer, Jean Errard. The earth-works to protect the royal forces and enforce the siege were so extensive that they are still readily visible on aerial photographs of the city. In July 1597 the army consumed 29,000 loaves a day and supplies came by boat up the Somme to a pontoon bridge over the river, constructed to block access to the city by water. Forty-five cannon were used to overawe the city and there was even a military hospital, established to cope with casualties from amongst the king's forces. The *parlement* of Paris opposed the financial sacrifices which the siege entailed, while the protestants used it as a lever to gain greater concessions. But, having demonstrated to France's new rulers

---

9. D.J. Buisseret, 1968, p. 177.
10. C. Dufayard, 1892, ch. x.
11. R. Ritter, [1955], pp. 127–8.

how vulnerable her frontiers were to attack, an exhausted Spain withdrew to concentrate her forces on a military victory over the northern Netherlands. Hostilities with France were eventually concluded by the Treaty of Vervins, agreed with papal mediation on 2 May 1598.[12] France's allies in the Netherlands, whose envoys to Henri IV at Nantes, Justin of Nassau and the pensionary of the states of Holland, Oldenbarnevelt, had pleaded with him not to sign it, felt betrayed. The Treaty returned Calais, Toul, Metz, Verdun and Amiens to France, thus maintaining France's north-eastern frontier. In return, France agreed to papal arbitration over all France's claims to Saluzzo.

Pope Clement VIII's envoys found negotiations over Saluzzo particularly intractable. Spanish and imperial pressures prevented their making any headway and the pope acknowledged his defeat eighteen months later. The duke of Savoy then came to Paris in December 1599 and Henri IV modified French demands, offering to accept the duchy of Bresse instead of Saluzzo as an attempt to gain a lasting solution to this important frontier question. It was during this meeting that Henri tried to convince Charles Emmanuel of France's resolve to defend its frontiers, as well as demonstrating his own popularity. Hardouin de Péréfixe's later description of the occasion may have been a product of his own imagination, but it was to provide the king with the most enduring of his legendary *bons mots*:

> When the duke of Savoy came to France, the king invited him to play tennis at the *faubourg* Saint Germain (in Paris). After the game, the duke looked out of a window towards a street and, seeing a large crowd, told the king that he could never sufficiently wonder at the beauty and wealth of France and asked him what the royal revenues were worth. This generous prince, deft at handling such questions, replied, 'It is worth what I want.' The duke, finding this reply too vague, asked him to be more specific. The king replied, 'Yes, what I want, for I have the confidence of my people and I can take what I like for, if God grants me life, I will ensure that there is not a peasant in the kingdom without a chicken in the stewpot' and added 'yet I will not neglect to maintain enough soldiers to bring to reason those who challenge my authority.'[13]

A draft treaty was agreed and Savoy was given three months to make its final decisions. But Charles Emmanuel was encouraged to

---

12. On Spanish and papal motives, see F. Braudel, 1973, pp. 1219–22. Bellièvre believed 'it was the most advantageous peace France had secured for five hundred years'.

13. H. de Péréfixe, *Histoire du roi Henry le Grand*, 1749, pp. 558–9.

prevaricate by Spain because it did not wish to see Bresse in French hands and lose the ability to send troops through the Val de Chézery. Eventually, in August 1600, Henri IV was persuaded to declare war on Savoy by Lesdiguières and Sully. It was, as the Dutch envoy, d'Aerssen remarked, a 'timid' declaration so as not to alarm other Italian princes.[14] But the military invasion by a small force of 50,000 French troops turned out to be decisive and, by the end of 1600, France held all Savoyard territory west of the Alps. Spain provided over 2 million ducats to assist its Savoyard ally and, as Spanish military forces congregated at Milan, Henri IV accepted a papal offer of mediation in January 1601. By the treaty of 17 January 1601 signed at Lyon, France ceded the marquisate of Saluzzo in return for the territories of Bresse, Bugey, Gex and Valromey and 800,000 *écus* in compensation for the war effort. By a further clause, the duke of Savoy was permitted to retain the use of the Val de Chézery and the Grésin bridge over the Rhône connecting Savoy and Franche-Comté in return for 100,000 *écus*.[15]

Lesdiguières was disappointed at the terms of the peace of Lyon. He remarked that Henri IV had bargained like a trader and Charles Emmanuel had negotiated like a prince. The shrewd Savoyard ambassador, René de Lucinge, also thought that the treaty was more favourable to Savoy's interests than could possibly have been expected.[16] Other contemporary diplomats like d'Aerssen and Sir Ralph Winwood regarded it as shameful, while the distinguished French diplomatic historian, Edouard Rott, called the peace 'one of the great errors' of diplomacy.[17] Not only was Saluzzo more profitable a principality than Bugey, Bresse and Gex, but it had also presented France's Italian allies with a guarantee of French protection in the region. The peace was even more favourable to the Spanish for, although Henri IV could cut the *chemin des Espagnols* at the Pont du Grésin (and was to do so at the time of the Biron rising), the route would remain open in time of peace. During a war, it would probably have been unusable, even if France had not possessed its new territories in Bresse. France's diplomats would probably have replied to these criticisms that Saluzzo did not dominate the *only* pass from France to the Italian peninsula. If French troops were needed to assist any Italian ally, they could still use the Col de Tende, the Mont Cénis

14.   J. Nouaillac, [1908], p. 87 (15 September 1600).
15.   E. Rott, 1882, pp. 95–7. On the negotiations, see Cayet, XIII, 133–8.
16.   A. Dufour, 1965, 249–31.
17.   E. Rott, 1882, p. 97. J. Nouaillac, [1908], pp. 97–8.

route, the Val d'Aoste or, if the Valais allowed, the Simplon pass. They would also have pointed out that the existence of 10,000 troops in Lombardy rendered the small French garrison at Carmagnola in Saluzzo strategically less valuable. But, that having been said, the peace of Lyon made the task of France's diplomats harder when it came to sustaining French allies menaced by the power of Milan, particularly in the central Alps.

For the rest of the reign, Henri IV, impressed by the barrier fortresses which Maurice of Nassau was constructing to protect the frontiers of the Netherlands, invested in a similar defensive network. Jean Errard, his military engineer, was commissioned to produce new citadels in Amiens and Calais.[18] Defensive works were improved in Champagne by new bastion walls at Metz and Rocroi and reconstruction at Langres and Châlons in Burgundy. French frontier provinces were surveyed and mapped; arsenals and granaries were kept to a full complement.[19] In Dauphiné, Fort Barraux became a good example of the latest military architecture, while the new bastions around Grenoble turned the regional capital into one of the strongest defensive positions in France.[20] Meanwhile, in Paris, the Arsenal became a great centre of instruction for artillery officers who were 'catechised' in the arts of gunnery. At the same time, Sully's artillery corps worked to standardise French artillery and make it more mobile. The Arsenal in Paris also became a testing-ground for a variety of military hardware and technology with military applications. Similar developments took place in the various provincial arsenals, modelled on that in Paris, and established under Sully's lieutenants.[21]

PAX GALLICANA

From 1601–10, there was a delicate peace on France's borders, but it was a wary, cautious affair, unsustained by common interests of a long-term nature. Savoy, having been militarily defeated, encouraged discontented nobles to rise in revolt against the French monarchy; only in 1609 was there a real *rapprochement* with the mercurial

18. D.J. Buisseret, 1964b; 1968, pp. 122–8.
19. Ibid.
20. V. Chomel, 1976, pp. 122–4.
21. D. Buisseret, 'Henri IV et l'art militaire' in *Avènement d'Henri IV*, (1989), pp. 340–9.

Savoyard leadership.[22] In Brussels, the Infanta (Clara Isabella Eugenia) and her husband (Archduke Albert), governors in the Spanish Netherlands, despatched refugee leaders of the League to contact disaffected elements in France until the truce of Antwerp in April 1609 made it imprudent to disturb French internal security. In Madrid, the French ambassador was imprisoned and encouragement was given to the League leaders exiled from Marseille to recapture the city. Various exiles met in Algiers and Naples to plot the assassination of the king, and there was always a ready welcome for those who sought refuge from the French regime at Milan, which was governed by the Spanish general, Dom Pedro Henriques de Azevedo, Count of Fuentes, from 1600–1610.[23] However, after the collapse of the duke of Bouillon's rebellion in 1604, the momentum behind these attempts to destabilise France began to be dissipated.

France's responsibility for maintaining peace in Europe appears in the range of its diplomatic initiatives, for the wars of religion had not reduced royal diplomatic activity, although they had limited its success. An ambassador was dispatched to Constantinople and the old alliance between the king of France and the Sultan was revived.[24] Capitulations were signed with Constantinople in 1597 and again in 1604; in the latter, the trading privileges accorded to the English in the Levant were revoked and those granted to France were reinforced.[25] A similar embassy was dispatched to Sweden to engage a Scandinavian ally to the Bourbon cause in Europe.[26] The king even received overtures from the Spanish Moriscos in 1602 and sent an envoy to them, signing a secret agreement in 1603.[27]

France's most substantial efforts were reserved for the smaller states of northern Italy, Switzerland and Germany, many of them traditional allies of the French crown during the sixteenth century. This was where Henri IV's government deployed its most able and experienced diplomats. Some of these were former Huguenot diplomats like Jacques Bongars (1554–1612), the king's German envoy, or Sully's younger brother, Philippe de Béthune (?–1649), who served in Venice from 1595 to 1601 and then in Rome until 1605.[28] Others were in

22. E. Rott, 1882, pp. 438 *et seq.*
23. R.E. Mousnier, 1973, pp. 44–6.
24. D. Lamar Jensen, 1974, pp. 22–46. Saint Priest, 1877, pp. 64–8, 398–438.
25. C. Desplat, 'Henri IV et les Ottomans' in *Avènement d'Henri IV*, (1989), pp. 396–7.
26. *Revue Henri IV*, 1909, II, 25–33.
27. J. de Caumont, duc de La Force, *Mémoires*, 4 vols, (1824), I, 217–20, 389–445.
28. L. Anquez, 1887, pp. xiii–lxix. E. Rott, 1882, pp. 104–5, R. Couzard, 1900.

the pattern of Méric de Vic (?–1621), Henri IV's ambassador to the Swiss Confederation, a catholic servant of the monarchy of proven loyalty and experience.[29] Some of the king's advisors – especially among the protestants and former servants of the king in his protestant days – were more aggressive in proposing alliances abroad to exploit every Habsburg weakness, demanding a direct benefit from every subsidy or pension granted to a sovereign power. Others – particularly the king's foreign minister, Nicolas de Neufville, seigneur de Villeroy (1543–1617) – were more cautious. They did not wish to encourage France's allies to entertain greater hopes from her support than were realistic. They were anxious to reach a more lasting *détente* with Spain and to avoid committing the king to actions which might eventually leave him isolated and vulnerable against Habsburg power in Europe. They were prodigal with French subsidies abroad, regarding them as an investment in France's ability to influence future events without binding commitments.

The situation in northern Italy indicates how finely matched and intricately interrelated France's alliances became. France's diplomats found it difficult to make any headway against Spanish influence in northern Italy after the peace of Lyon. The French ambassador remarked in 1602: 'Italy is bound from head to foot to Madrid. Once upon a time, the House of Ferrara, the duke of Urbino, the prince of La Miranda and many smaller princes were either French in their affections or neutral . . . Now all that has been lost to Spain.'[30] France's diplomats gradually cultivated new friends – none more assiduously than Philippe de Béthune in Rome, to whom Pope Clement VIII once remarked that he wanted to see more French prelates in the Holy City to balance those from Spain.[31] As gestures to the Holy See, the Jesuits were accepted back throughout France in 1603 and the French government offered to mediate between James I, the new king in England, and Philip III in Spain. The French cardinals and French pensions in Rome made their influence felt in the elections for a new Pope in 1605.[32] Relationships also improved in Venice, mainly as a result of the logic of events. The Venetian Republic's vulnerability to Adriatic pirates (encouraged by Naples) and its need for diplomatic assistance to maintain its sphere of influence in the central Alps made it turn, rather reluctantly, towards a French alliance. When, in May 1606, Pope Paul V placed Venice under an

29. E. Rott, 1882, p. 181.
30. Quoted in Ibid., p. 115.
31. Ibid., p. 122.
32. *Revue Henri IV*, 1905–6, I, 133–41. Cf. R. Couzard, 1900.

interdict for having extended state control over the ecclesiastical and moral life of its inhabitants beyond an acceptable degree, France supported the Venetian council and the interdict was removed in April 1607.[33] It was a small sign of France's new ability to play a difficult diplomatic hand well and protect an important ally in delicate circumstances.

Venice was important to France because, through it, lay a means of influencing the central Alps. Thanks to the diplomatic finesse of Méric de Vic, France's ambassador to the Swiss Confederation, the traditional alliance between most of the thirteen protestant cantons and France was successfully renewed at Soleure in October 1601 (and confirmed in Paris the following year).[34] The Austrian and Spanish Habsburgs had an alliance with the six catholic cantons of the Swiss Confederation. The object of French policy in the region was to try to close the Spanish routes through the Swiss passes to their Austrian relatives or to the Rhine, while opening those passes which led through the protestant Swiss Confederation towards Venice. Apart from the Simplon pass, a long and difficult route through the Valais to the canton of Fribourg, the most important passes lay through the Engadine valley and the Valtelline, both in the territory of the confederation of the *Grisons*, or the Grey Leagues. These were an association of three cantons of local landowners who were predominantly protestant.[35] The *Grisons* were bounded by Milan, Venice, the Tyrol and the Swiss Confederation. The Valtelline was administered by the *Grisons* but it was inhabited by villagers who were largely catholic. The valley was leased out by treaty to the highest bidder for its exclusive military use. Given the vital strategic importance of the valley, no effort was spared by either Habsburg or Bourbon in order to secure exclusive rights to the use of the Valtelline. France was successful in December 1601. Then, in 1603, the Venetians also managed to cajole the *Grisons* into granting them a right of passage through the valley. The Spanish governor of Lombardy, Count Fuentes, was so irritated by this strategic victory that he redoubled his efforts to win over the *Grisons* and sent catholic agents to arouse religious antipathies in the Valtelline. In October 1603, he also began the construction of a formidable fort (the Fort Fuentes) at the entrance to the valley so that he could demonstrate Spain's military might and intimidate the *Grisons*. These moves had

33. W. Bouwsma, 1968, chs vii and viii.
34. E. Rott, 1882, pp. 194–8.
35. Ibid., ch. i and pp. 170–94.

their effect when, in 1607, the Venetians attempted to move some troops through the Valtelline and provoked an uprising among its inhabitants. Eventually the protestant landowners regained control, restored order and executed some of the ringleaders in the Valtelline so that French and Venetian influence was once more reinforced in the valley and the Spanish were, for the moment, excluded. Once again, French diplomacy had proved successful in sustaining its alliances in a sensitive region, but a price had been exacted in terms of the destabilising of the central Alps and these instabilities would re-emerge at the beginning of the Thirty Years' War a decade later.

The most important alliance in northern Europe became the French treaty obligations, arrived at in 1603, to give the Dutch (in conjunction with England) financial assistance disguised as France's repayment of its war debts.[36] The Dutch had initially been suspicious of French passivity after the peace of 1598. Their envoy in Paris, d'Aerssen, was afraid that the French were merely concerned to maintain the war in the Netherlands so that, 'inwardly calm, there would be just enough [*warlike*] exercise to remove the transitory distempers [*from France*] and keep the Spanish occupied.'[37] France's annual subsidies to the Dutch became considerable – over 2 million *livres* in some years – but France did not intervene militarily to assist the Dutch. The siege of Ostend, begun in July 1601, ended in Dutch defeat in 1604. Henri IV put himself at the head of his army in Calais, hoping to intimidate the Spanish into ending the siege, but did not commit his forces to the field. Spanish efforts against Prince Maurice of Nassau succeeded to the extent of bringing at least some elements in the new Dutch Republic to consider a cessation of hostilities. Led by Oldenbarnevelt and the states of Holland, they were favoured by the English king, James I. Henri IV, by contrast, through his ambassadors at The Hague from April 1607, Buzenval, Jeannin and Russy, invited the Republic to continue the war. Their dispatches tell us of the tempting offers which were made to the Dutch to do so: 1,500,000 *écus*, a renewed defensive and offensive alliance with the French, and a personal pension for Maurice of Nassau. By November 1607, however, the emollient Villeroy was adjusting France's diplomacy to the evolving practical necessity of accepting some kind of peace between the United Provinces and Spain. France would countenance a purely defensive alliance with the Republic, such as was signed in January 1608. By October 1608, the king's negotiators were

36. M. Lee, 1970, 21–7. J. Dumont, [1728], V, ii and 30–1.
37. J. Nouaillac, [1908], p. 148.

pushing for a long-term truce and, on 9 April 1609, the twelve-year cessation of arms was concluded at Antwerp under French mediation. This was, in many ways, the most humiliating of all the pacifications accepted by Spain after 1598. It enabled Henri IV to pose as the pacifier of Europe, the arbiter of its local conflicts. It was a fitting climax to the period of peace after 1601 which France had, to a great extent, managed to mould to its own advantage.

The remaining area in which French diplomacy was particularly active lay among the German princes of the Holy Roman Empire. Henri IV had relied on many of them for loans during the wars of the League. The Calvinist principalities of the Holy Roman Empire particularly looked upon France as a potential protector; princes like Christian of Anhalt, governor of the Upper Palatinate, and some of their advisors (like Ludwig Camerarius of the Palatinate) were, by culture and experience, francophile. Their conviction was that the hegemony of the Habsburgs had to be crushed if a thorough reformation was ever to be accomplished; they looked to an international coalition and a great struggle to achieve this. Henri IV was entirely unpersuaded of such objectives and sceptical about the means. The only international coalition which would be achievable would be one under his patronage and towards more benign objectives. He remained unimpressed by the overall ability of the German protestant princes to coordinate themselves into an effective alliance, let alone play a part within a wider pan-European coalition. They had failed to act together in 1591, 1594, 1596 and 1599, and Henri IV remarked sceptically on their 'long-winded Diets [*the estates of the Empire*] which never achieve anything'.[38] Their internal conflicts and divisions made them of little use in any larger diplomatic setting. As a result, Henri IV concentrated on winning the support of neighbouring princes and cities in the Rhine, showing particular regard for Strasbourg, Hesse, the Rhine Palatinate and the duchy of Lorraine.[39]

Of course, France could not ignore what went on in the lower Rhineland. The least stable state was the small, composite territory on the eastern border of the Netherlands, the dukedom of John William the Simple, duke (since 1592) of Clèves, Berg and Jülich, count of Ravensburg and Mark. The lands were in the quadrant of the Rhine, Ruhr and Meuse, of great strategic importance for supplies to Spanish Flanders or for any potential invasion of the Netherlands. John

---

38. L. Anquez, 1887, p. 76.
39. Ibid., pp. 88–95.

William, already senile and childless, proved incapable of resisting an invasion of his territories in September 1598 by a contingent of the Flanders army under Francisco de Mendoza.[40] The Dutch mobilised forces and, along with some German princes of the Westphalian defensive League, rallied to remove these Spanish troops in April 1599. Henri IV did not immediately react to the invasion, despite the strategic importance of the area:

> For I do not wish to draw on myself the fire which consumes them for this is probably what they would like to happen. I have too often put on my knapsack only to find that I have received no support from them or from anyone else. I am above all concerned to establish my authority and restore my realm. This is my sole objective for the immediate future.[41]

Once the Spanish had withdrawn, Henri IV offered to guarantee the security of the principality with a contingent of troops provided to the Elector Palatine. By this date (June 1599), the king was confident that his move would not be misinterpreted in Madrid, that he could call on Clause 24 of the pacification of Vervins (which guaranteed the territorial integrity of the German princes), and that he could maintain the stability of the region against further invasions by either side.[42]

The problem of Jülich–Clèves reappeared, however, when Duke John William died in March 1609. Legally, the position of his inheritance was very complicated since there were at least eight claimants (two of whom were members of the French aristocracy) and no agreement among them as to how to proceed to settle their dispute. In the event, the Emperor Rudolph II proclaimed his right to mediate between the contending parties and appointed an interim administrator to the duchy. The two main claimants, the dukes of Brandenburg and Neuburg, forestalled him and agreed among themselves on a joint administration of the duchy. This openly ignored imperial authority and, in June 1609, the emperor proclaimed the sequestration of the duchy. A month later, Spanish troops moved to invade the citadel of Jülich in support of imperial authority. The French government's initial reactions were cautious. The truce of Antwerp was only signed on 9 April 1609 and France was anxious not to see its ratification postponed or disturbed. Secondly, Henri IV was not convinced that he enjoyed the material support of the German protestant powers. Although his agent, Jacques Bongars, had worked

40. Ibid., pp. 70–4.
41. Ibid., p. 74
42. J. Dumont, [1728], V, 563–4.

tirelessly to secure their loyalty, some of the princes had supported Bouillon against the king in 1606.[43] When the protestant princes eventually signed their famous 'Evangelical Union' at Anhausen in 1608, they explicitly rejected France's direct association with it.[44]

When France hoped to secure the support of a number of German protestant princes, its position became clearer. In October 1609, Henri IV issued an ultimatum to the emperor to remove his administrator and the Spanish troops from the duchy and, in January 1610, the princes of the 'Evangelical Union' began to mobilise. Henri IV also called his troops to muster in Champagne, ready to conduct an invasion of the lower Rhineland. By May 1610, an army of 50,000 – roughly the same size as had been used in the successful Savoyard campaign in 1600 – was prepared to invade the duchy, and the Dutch and the English had agreed to contribute some troops. In addition, France concluded an offensive and defensive alliance with Savoy in which the duke of Savoy was to attack the duchy of Milan with French assistance at some later date in 1610.[45] At this moment of great international tension, Henri IV was assassinated on 14 May 1610, as he prepared to leave Paris to join his army. We shall never know whether, had he lived, the sequence of events would have produced a climax to the *Pax Gallicana*, a further demonstration of France's new-found rôle as Europe's arbiter and a stronger assertion of French influence in Germany, or whether it would merely have been the prelude to a major European armed confrontation.

THE GRAND DESIGN

The events of 1609–10 have led historians to question the motives and purpose of French foreign policy from 1598 until 1610. Some historians have suggested that its purpose was unequivocally to remove all Spanish authority from Europe outside the Spanish peninsula by any means possible. The suggestion is based on a passage from Sully's *Oeconomies Royales* in which he spoke of a 'Grand Design'.[46] But the passage cannot be accepted even as authentic evidence for Sully's point of view during the king's own lifetime. It appeared in the published

43. L. Anquez, 1887, pp. 95–115.
44. Ibid., p. 128.
45. E. Rott, 1882, p. 435.
46. Sully, [1881], XVII, 421 *et seq.*

version of the memoirs in 1662 and was neither in the various manuscripts nor in the printed edition of 1638. It seems as though Sully added it at a late stage in order to prove that he had foreseen France's diplomatic position in 1659. It was undoubtedly the case that some royal advisors pressed the king to be more adventurous in his foreign policy commitments. Sully was widely believed to have advocated on several occasions a French offensive against the Spanish in Flanders.[47] But there is no sign that such advice formed the basis of French foreign policy. Nineteenth-century historians suggested that the 'Grand Design' lay in diplomatic initiatives to formulate strategic alliances of nations rightly struggling to be free – a united Italy, a confederated Switzerland, a concerted Germany – through which France would eventually defeat the Habsburgs.[48] All the evidence suggests that French diplomats and advisors were sceptical of the likely success of overall confederations and as aware of the underlying religious and political issues which divided their allies as of the common causes which might, at any one moment, temporarily unite them.

If there was no 'Grand Design', it is clear that France's foreign policy was operating in a coordinated and effective fashion which suggests a coherent attitude sustaining it. Recent historians have stressed as the important theme France's desire to maintain European peace while articulating France's strength within it. They have shown how prudent and cautious French foreign policy was in the months before the king's assassination.[49] Henri IV kept contacts with Madrid, and the ambassador, Don Inigo de Cardeñas, remained in Paris throughout the period of mobilisation. Henri IV had not offered the Moors any assistance when they were expelled from Spain in 1609. As late as the beginning of May 1610, the Tuscan ambassador in Paris was encouraged to act as marriage broker in a proposed alliance between the Dauphin Louis and an Infanta. Evidence from the first gentleman of the chamber and from Cardinal Richelieu suggests that the king was anxious to restrict his dispute to the Austrian branch of the Habsburgs. There was already some evidence that Rudolph's resolve was weakening, especially as the imperial administrator fled from Jülich in the face of the impending military invasion. Was not Henri IV concerned to maintain the status quo in Germany, demonstrate France's authority to the German princes and come to a lasting *détente* with Spain?

47. J. Nouaillac, [1908], pp. 95, 105.
48. This appears in the works of L. Anquez, E. Rott and others.
49. Principally J.M. Hayden, 1973.

If this *was* the case, it is clear that the maintenance of peace in 1610 would have depended on an international diplomacy of great skill and some brinkmanship. It is impossible to judge whether Henri IV had calculated correctly or not the diplomatic and military strength required to achieve his objective. Villeroy certainly believed he had, and wrote on 3 June 1610: 'If our good master were not dead, he would not have had to bother to cross the Seine. The keys of Jülich would have been brought to him.'[50] Whether this assessment would have proved to be a correct one would also have depended on whether the king could raise a sufficient show of force from his Dutch allies and whether France could restrain more unstable allies like Savoy. The king would eventually have had to dissipate the war fever which he had aroused in France, a country where martial glory and nobility were intimately related and where there were powerful social pressures for external aggression. It is possible to imagine that the show of force which Henri IV clearly intended to mount in May 1610 would have made France's position internationally clear, and that this clarity would have prevented major hostilities breaking out.[51] The uncertainty over France's position in 1620 was an important factor in persuading the Habsburgs in Vienna and Madrid to adopt a robust attitude towards the Palatinate and the expiring Dutch truce and thus became a material cause for the outbreak of the Thirty Years' War.

50. Cited in Ibid., p. 11.
51. N.M. Sutherland, 1992 provides the broad perspective in which this judgement has to be made.

Conclusion

THE ASSASSINATION

Henri IV was assassinated in his coach while it was stuck in congestion in the rue de la Ferronerie in Paris on 14 May 1610. His assassin, a strong, red-haired man called Ravaillac, stabbed him three times with a short knife before being arrested by the king's travelling companion, the duke of Epernon.[1] Ravaillac was interrogated by the *parlement* of Paris but, despite being tortured, he protested that he had acted as a completely free agent and that neither Jesuit nor aristocrat, Spanish pension nor former League fanatic had encouraged him to undertake the regicide. On the scaffold, he was scalded with burning sulphur, red-hot pincers, molten lead, boiling oil and resin before his arms and legs were attached to horses which then pulled in different directions. After an hour and a half, Ravaillac died. The crowd tried to prevent his receiving the usual last prayers and urged the horses to pull harder. After his death 'the entire populace, no matter what their rank, hurled themselves on the body with their swords, knives, sticks or anything else to hand and began beating, hacking and tearing at it. They snatched the limbs from the executioner, savagely chopping them up and dragging the pieces through the streets.' According to Nicholas Pasquier, one woman ate some of the flesh.

The assassination was the work of one individual who found it impossible to forget the recent past. For no king had survived more attempts on his life by 1610 than Henri IV. There at least

---

1. These, and the following details on the assassination, are taken from R.E. Mousnier, 1973. A more recent analysis, strong on the career of Ravaillac and the details of his trial, is P, Chevallier, 1989, pt II, chs iv and v.

another twenty-three known plots to eliminate him, clustering mainly about the times of greatest uncertainty in the reign – 1593–94, 1597–98, 1602 and 1604.[2] The most serious of these occurred on 27 December 1594 when a young law student from a family of Parisian drapers, Jean Chastel (or Châtel), who had studied classics and philosophy at a Jesuit college was apparently inspired to kill the king after reading a devotional treatise. His dagger narrowly missed the king's throat and hit his cheek, breaking one of his teeth. Châtel was tortured, hanged, drawn and quartered, his family's house razed to the ground and a sombre pillar erected in its place bearing as an inscription the edict against such regicide. The Jesuits were implicated and expelled by the *parlement* of Paris. Châtel's failure did not deter others, but plots grew less common after the turn of the century. One of the last serious pieces of evidence for any concerted attempt on the king's life before 1610 comes from the testimony of a former gendarme of the duke of Guise and the duke of Biron. He related the story of a gathering of malcontents in Naples in the wake of the unsuccessful revolt of the duke of Biron. The participants included a former secretary to Biron, a renegade League leader from Marseille, a Jesuit and a captain called Roux from Provence, whose disaffection was known to the French authorities as early as 1597. Ravaillac may also have been present. The plot never materialised; the successful assassination by Ravaillac was, in some respects, a cruel *momento mori* to these earlier efforts.

Few contemporaries believed Ravaillac's insistence that 'I alone did it'. The possibility of the assassination having been instituted by a wider conspiracy was openly discussed, as it has been ever since. The Parisian chronicler Estoile reported the arrest of a soldier, formerly a priest in holy orders, on 16 May, who claimed to have important information on those behind the plot. But, he continued, the 'feeble investigations which have been instituted into this important affair (where it seems as though they are frightened by what they might find) will prevent them from following the matter up to a fruitful conclusion.'[3] Estoile returned to the same point when he discussed the arrest of another informator, who claimed to have information implicating the House of Entragues and the marquise de Verneuil in the affair, and who was found strangled in prison before a proper investigation had been conducted.

The strongest evidence for some kind of wider plot around

---

2. Ibid., pt II, ch. ii.
3. Ibid., p. 239.

Ravaillac comes, however, from a wet-nurse who had been in the service of the House of Entragues and who shared the intimacies of the duke of Epernon's mistress, Charlotte du Tillet. Jacqueline Le Voyer, demoiselle d'Escoman (or 'la Coman'), came forward with her story in January 1611. Epernon and a secretary of state, secreted behind an arras, listened as she explained to Marguerite de Valois how Ravaillac often visited Mlle du Tillet before the assassination. The king's former mistress, the marquise de Verneuil (Madame d'Entragues) had a great part in the affair too. She hoped, apparently, for a popular uprising after the king's assassination in which her son by Henri IV, the illegitimate marquis de Verneuil, would be proclaimed king. She would be married to the duke of Guise and proclaimed regent. The duke of Epernon would become Constable. At this point in her testimony, the duke could bear it no more and broke in upon her testimony, thus bringing the interview to a close. She was duly committed to the *parlement* for further investigation.

During the succeeding months, every effort was made to limit the damage of this affair to prominent figures at the French court. Epernon bent the ear of the senior judge, Pierre Séguier (whose wife happened to be Marie du Tillet, the sister of the duke's mistress). The first president of the *parlement* had an extraordinary interview with the marquise de Verneuil. The royal attorney attempted to charge Mme d'Escoman with sorcery, a charge which (if sustained) would have ensured her death and, with it, the end of any further damaging revelations. The judges remained divided on the affair and eventually chose to sentence her, against much pressure, to life imprisonment. At the same time, they ordered the destruction of all documents relating to the case. At this distance, it is difficult to draw much by way of conclusion. Although parts of her story were unsubstantiated by their enquiries, the judges were apparently impressed by the evidence she adduced for the fact that Ravaillac had consorted with Charlotte du Tillet. They knew, as we know, that the marquise de Verneuil, Madame d'Entragues, claimed to have a signed promise from the king that the son she had borne him would be legitimised and be the next king. The resulting bitterness in the House of Entragues was common knowledge; so was Epernon's ambition to become Constable of France in succession to Montmorency. His own failure to protect the king in the coach on 14 May was not neglected by the magistrates. The bare bones of a plot, emerging from amongst some of the grandees who were not reconciled to the Henrician regime, become discernible amongst evidence which is entirely circumstantial but not wholly insubstantial.

Despite his apparent immunity, popular fear that the king would die a sudden death and that France would be immediately plunged into renewed civil war had remained strong. Astrologers had regularly predicted that he would die a violent death and some had even cited 1610 as the likely year. The first president of the *parlement* of Toulouse received reports of the king's death from various quarters of his province and had to issue denials. Investigations conducted after the king's assassination in 1610 revealed that spontaneous, false rumours of the king's death were current on the days *before* 14 May in places as far apart as Douai, Lille, Antwerp, Maastricht and Cologne. These fears put the Jesuits in a difficult position. They had not been the only catholics to support the notion of tyrannicide during the League, but they fell victim to the disparate guilts raised by such a proposition later in the reign and became the scapegoats for them. The possibility of a Spanish plot to kill the king cannot be entirely dismissed either. The first president of the *parlement* of Provence, Guillaume de Vair, was troubled by a remark made by Fuentes in Milan on the eve of the king's assassination. He apparently said that he had nothing to fear from French preparations for war in Italy, since 'the death of one person would destroy it all'.[4] The timing of the assassination was so precisely orchestrated that it is difficult to dismiss the possibility of a conspiracy, perhaps with foreign compliance, out of hand.

THE LEGEND

The king had sedulously cultivated his image during his reign by careful propaganda which had stressed his indispensability. The manner of his death transfigured the king into an active legend.[5] The preachers who had done so much to popularise the League now rivalled one another in putting their oratorical talents behind the construction of the main elements of this legend in their funeral elegies. They praised his success in war and peace, calling on classical and Christian mythology (as well as French history) to ornament his heroic stature. Justice, pacifism, prudence, frugality, charity: the chorus of praise – based on the perceived benefits of his reign – was unanimous. They

4. Cited D.J. Buisseret, 1984, p. 175.
5. The legend of Henri IV is explored through the funeral sermons in J. Hennequin, 1977, *Henri IV dans ses Oraisons funèbres ou la naissance d'une légende*. A longer perspective of the legend is to be found in the valuable study by M. Reinhard, *La légende de Henri IV* (1936).

stressed his contribution to political stability. He had, like Castor and Pollux (they said) pacified the seas and cleansed the realm of 'polluted waters'. He had made the 'waters of royal finance flow again' and constructed 'reservoirs to store them in'. He 'had extinguished the brazier of discontent in France'. His death was a martyrdom 'for he has died innocently for the purpose of bringing peace to the kingdom'.

Other groups added to the legend. The Jesuits, afraid that they would be blamed for the assassination, hastened to praise the king and acquired his heart to bury in their chapel at La Flèche. The protestants, aware of the prosperity which had come their way in the security of his reign, spoke of him as the best king Providence had granted them. The judges of the *parlements* chose to ignore their dislike of his occasional interference in their jurisdiction, wept at the news of his death and, fearful of renewed sedition, granted full regent powers to his wife. Henri IV proved, in his legend as in his life, a man for all seasons and his stature grew in the generation after 1610. The political changes associated with the government of Richelieu and Mazarin turned Henri IV's reign into something of a golden age. The protestants looked back during the civil wars of the 1620s to the security and protection of the first decade of the century. The judges of the epoch of the Fronde regarded benevolently the tranquil period from 1598 to 1610 in comparison with the political turbulence of the years after 1630. Peasants, faced with unprecedented rises in the *taille* to pay for the Thirty Years' War, declared open revolt in many provinces and were joined by some nobles and towns in support of an old order which Henri IV appeared to cement and which Richelieu and Mazarin seemed intent on destroying. Churchmen and preachers, faced with the task of writing elegies on the deaths of Richelieu and Mazarin, found the contradictions between traditional catholic moral values and the imperative demands of 'reason of state' much more overt than they had been under Henri IV. One of these bishops, Hardouin de Péréfixe, was well placed to express the legend of Henri IV. He was tutor to the young Louis XIV and he wrote a *History of Henry the Great* for use in the king's education. The account is as much moral philosophy as accurate history, with a considerable emphasis on the prudence of the king. The collection of royal aphorisms at the end of the book is a homely French counterpart to the popular maxims associated with the name of Guicciardini. Written in the aftermath of the worst years of the century for the French peasantry (1648-52), it was the first account to mention Henri IV as the king who had wanted to see a chicken in the pot for every French peasant. This aphorism evoked a king who had the welfare of his subjects at heart, but contemporaries would have seen the wider allusion. It was customary to represent anarchy in engravings and prints of the period in terms of reversed images (for instance, the donkey in the cart with a man between the halters). It was also habitual to represent the world as a pot or *marmite*. Therefore, when Henri IV was alleged to have wanted to see a chicken in the pot, the allusion was not just to a king who had put meat into the peasants' diet, but also to one who had set the world to rights and refounded the stability of the old order.

MYTH AND REALITY

Reality could never have matched the legend. Henri IV could not eliminate the forces of instability in France. What he could do was establish a political consensus. Religious fanatics, factious princes, dissident lawyers, Spanish infiltrators, corrupt treasurers, violent provincial nobles, peasants in revolt still existed but the climate was much less kind towards them, and they were much less close to the surface of political life by 1610. The established institutions – universities, law courts, treasury, mints and catholic church – all felt a new confidence in their ability to contain instability. More importantly, the hierarchical society, on which the *ancien régime* depended, had been strengthened. Although based on rank and privilege, the society of Henri IV's France did not prove completely closed to wealth, ideas and change when it was blessed by royal favour. It was, of course, the case that contentious issues which divided social groups in France were avoided – issues such as the relationship between church and state and the extent to which the state should pursue catholic aims at home or abroad. There was an air of relativism about these matters in the first decade of the century. Louis le Caron reminded the king – he scarcely needed to be told – that the 'public good' often 'changes according to circumstances and events'. With this in mind, Henri IV was Gallican or ultramontane as the occasion suited, and pro-catholic or pro-protestant when the circumstances required it. The relativism was justified, not as cynical Machiavellianism, but as the necessary prudence for the existence of public peace and the justification was widely accepted.

It could be argued that it was impossible for France to forget its recent past. Although Henri IV ordered the destruction of all official documents and published memoirs of the troubles, a morbid interest in the events of the wars of religion remained strong in the earlier years of the new century. Stability remained an ideal which was never completely attainable in practice. But it would be wrong to suggest that what was achieved rested on a mere fortunate coincidence of the exhaustion of France after the civil wars and that of Spain from its long struggle against heresy in northern Europe. This would be to fail to recognise that, until 1600, Henri IV's regime was on trial, based on a series of negotiated agreements in which success was not a foregone conclusion. Nor would it acknowledge the extraordinary achievements of Sully in finance, which produced a unique strengthening of the financial position of a major government in western Europe in the early seventeenth century. Finally, it would ignore the important fact that Spain was brought to the negotiating table not by its own exhaustion alone, but by vigorous French military efforts, especially in 1597 and 1598.

When France passed into the hands of an eight-year-old king in 1610, renewed civil war was widely predicted. Contemporaries looked back to the minority of Charles IX in 1560, which had seen the beginning of the civil wars, and were struck by the ominous comparisons. In 1610, as in 1560, France was in the hands of a sickly boy-king. In 1610, as in 1560, the regent came from the Médicis family (and the reputation of the one cast doubts on the prospects for the other). In 1610, as in 1560, there were attempts to envelop the regent in an exclusive catholic wing at court (that after 1560 was called the triumvirate; after 1610 it was the *dévots*). In 1560, a Prince of Condé was ready to lead the oppositon to the regent as the prince of the blood. In 1610, his grandson was in exile in Milan and apparently preparing to do likewise. But the expected explosion did not occur and, in the end, it is the differences, rather than the similarities, which strike the historian. Firstly, Marie de Médicis, while not of the same stature as Catherine, had a series of able and experienced ministers to rely on. She retained nearly all Henri IV's team, save Sully (they became known collectively as the *dotards* because they were all over seventy years of age). Secondly, she never became the prisoner of the *dévot* faction at court in the same way as Catherine became beholden to the triumvirate. The edict of Nantes was reissued in its entirety eight days after Henri IV's assassination and confirmed in 1612, 1614 and twice in 1615. She did not press for the acceptance of the decrees of the Council of Trent at the estates general in 1614–15. Although contemporaries saw the marriage of Louis XIII to the Infanta in October 1615 as similar to the marriage of Charles

IX to a Spanish princess in 1565 at Bayonne, and presumed it would have the same consequences, in fact, Marie de Médicis' government assured France's protestant allies at home and abroad that the marriage indicated no abrupt change in policy. Thirdly, Marie de Médicis was not faced with impending bankruptcy. The reserve treasury established by Sully was not exhausted until 1614 and the revenue from the *tailles* continued to rise until 1616, while the receipts from the *gabelles* remained strong until the economic crisis of 1619–21. It is true that Marie de Médicis spent more and was charged with extravagance at the estates general in 1614. But the spending did not seriously damage the equilibrium of the budget before 1614 and ministers justified the increase in pensions as necessary to consolidate the loyalty of princes during a minority.

Finally, the Prince of Condé faced greater difficulties in raising a revolt in France than his grandfather had done in 1562. Condé left court in January 1614 and initially attracted the support of other princes who felt badly treated by Henri IV. From the fortress of Mézières in Champagne, he attempted to rally troops and secure the loyalties of various provincial governments. But the military forces that were raised were not substantial enough and only the duke of Bouillon had real stomach for a fight. Even he turned into a mediator when faced with a confident royal government which pre-empted the position of the princes by assembling a royal army, negotiating with the princes, calling an estates general and declaring the king's minority at an end. In the months before the opening of the estates general, there was a flood of pamphlets on political affairs, but the princes of the blood gained little popular support for their cause, being accused of breaking the peace. The regent government exploited the popular sentiment and influenced the election of delegates to the estates to ensure that the princes of the blood had few supporters at the assembly. In comparison with the estates general of 1560, those of 1614 were attended by a larger number of royal office-holders among the third estate and this ensured a fundamental royalism. Among the demands of their *cahier* was a request that it be declared to be a fundamental law of France that the king held his crown from God alone. Other demands, it is true, presented a case for reform in the state which included the reduction of taxes, reform of the church, the abolition of venality and the retrenchment of expenditure. Unlike the estates of 1560, the delegates of 1614 found no panacea such as the secularisation of church property behind which they could unite, so that their various demands remained a curious mixture of the realistic and the idealistic. Henri IV's stability had not involved any fundamental reforms and herein lay a substantial hostage to fortune in the period from 1610 to 1630, as would appear in the assembly of notables of 1617 and 1626–27. After the minority of Louis XIII, it is true that there was renewed civil dissension in France. Stability, consciously realised, was also reversible, particularly when government fell into the hands of favourites. But the campaigns against the princes in 1619 and 1620 and with the Huguenots in 1621–22 and 1627–28 were ones which the king did not lose. With the pressures from the Thirty Years' War in the 1630s, they produced the political changes of the government of Cardinal Richelieu and Mazarin which are associated with the first generation of French absolutism.

Bibliography

ABBREVIATIONS

The following abbreviations have been used:

Annales	Annales, Economies, Sociétés, Civilisations
Bib Ec Ch	Bibliothèque de l'Ecole des Chartes
Bib H R	Bibliothèque d'Humanisme et de la Renaissance
BSHPF	Bulletin de la Société d'Histoire du Protestantisme Français
EHR	English Historical Review
FHS	French Historical Studies
PHS	Proceedings of the Huguenot Society
16C J	Sixteenth Century Journal

Works in French are published in Paris, and works in English in London, unless otherwise indicated. Publishers are not indicated for works before 1945.

PRIMARY SOURCES

Barnavi, E. (1976–77) 'Le cahier de doléances de la ville de Paris aux Etats Généraux de 1588', *Annuaire-Bulletin de la société de l'Histoire de France*, 81–154.

Bernard, A. (1842) *Procès-verbaux des états-généraux de 1593*.

Blouyn, M. (1976) *Les troubles à Gaillac*, (ed.) Nègre, E., Editions du collège d'Occitanie, Toulouse.

Bodin, J. (1789) *Recueil de tout ce qui s'est négocié en la chambre du tiers estat 1577*.

Bosquet, G. (1862) *Recueil de pièces historiques*, Toulouse.

Brantôme (1864–82) *Oeuvres complètes*, (ed.) Lalanne, L., 11 vols.

Brun-Durand, J. (1885) *Mémoires d'Eustache Piémond (1572–1608)*, Valence.

Brutus, Etienne Junius (1979) *Vindiciae contra Tyrannos*, Droz, Geneva.

Buisseret, D.J. (1963) 'Lettres inédites de Sully aux trésoriers-généraux de France à Caen (1599–1610), *Annales de Normandie*, 13, 269–304.

Busbecq (1845) 'Les lettres d'Olivier Ghislain de Busbecq', *Archives curieuses de l'Histoire de France*, X.

Carew, Sir George (1749) ' A relation of the state of France . . .' in *An Historical View of the Negotiations Between the Courts of England, France and Brussels*, (ed.) Birch, T., pp. 417–528.

Catherine de Médicis, Lettres, (1880–1909), (eds) La Ferrière, H. de, I–V (1880–96); Puchesse, B. de, VI–XI (1897–1909).

Champollion-Figeac, J. (1841–74) *Documents historiques inédits*, 4 vols.

Chéruel, A. (1860) *Journal d'Olivier Lefèvre d'Ormesson*.

Chevalier, J. (1885) *Mémoires des frères Gay pour servir à l'histoire des guerres de religion*, Montbéliard.

Cheverny (1881) *Mémoires de Philippe Hurault, comte de Cheverny*, (eds) Michaud and Poujoulat, 10, 463–576.

Davila, H. (1647) *The Historie of the Civill Warres of France*.

Desjardins, A. (1859–86) *Négociations diplomatiques de la France avec la Toscane*, 6 vols.

Devic and Vaissète (1872–1904) *Histoire générale de Languedoc*, 16 vols, Toulouse.

Douais, C. (1890) 'Etat du diocèse de St Papoul et sénéchaussée du Lauragais en 1573', *Mémoires de l'Académie des sciences et arts de Toulouse*, 10th series, 473–89.

Dumont, J. (1728) *Corps universel diplomatique du Droit des gens*, 8 vols, Amsterdam.

Du Plessis-Mornay, *Mémoires* (1824–25) *Mémoires et correspondance de Du Plessis Mornay*, (eds) de la Fontenelle de Vaudoré, A.D. and Anguis, P.R., 12 vols.

Estoile (1875–96) *Mémoires-Journaux*, (eds) Brunet, G. *et al.*, 12 vols.

Estoile (1943) *Journal de l'Estoile pour le règne de Henri III*, (ed.) Lefèvre, L-R., Gallimard.

Estoile (1948–58) *Journal de l'Estoile pour le règne de Henri IV*, (ed.) Lefèvre, L-R., 2 vols, Gallimard.

Jean de la Fosse (1866) *Journal d'un curé ligueur de Paris sous les trois derniers Valois*, (ed.) de Barthélemy, E.

Franklin, A. (1876) *Journal du siège de Paris en 1590*.

Gamon, A. (1881) *Mémoires d'Achille Gamon*, (eds) Michaud and Poujoulat, 8.

Gassot, J. (1934) *Sommaire Mémorial (1550–1623)*, (ed.) Champion, P.

Gérard, G. de (1887) *Les Chroniques de Jean Tarde*.

Granvelle (1841–52) *Papiers d'Etat de cardinal du Granvelle*, (ed.) Weiss, C., 9 vols.

Groulart, C. (1881) *Mémoires*, (eds) Michaud and Poujoulat, 11.

Halphen, E. (1872) *Lettres inédites du roi Henri IV au Chancelier de Bellièvre*.

Halphen, E. (1880) *Lettres inédites, Charles Faye et Jacques Faye*.

Haton, C. (1857) *Mémoires contenant le récit des événements accomplis de 1553 à 1582*, (ed.) Bourquelot, F., 2 vols.

Henri III, Lettres, (ed.) François, M., Société de l'Histoire de France, 4 vols in progress.

Henri IV, Lettres (1843–76) *Recueil des lettres missives d'Henri IV* (eds) Xivrey, B. de (vols 1–7, 1843–60) and Guadet, J., (vols 8–9, 1872–76), 9 vols.

Hotman, F. (1972) *Francogallia*, (eds) Giesey, R. and Salmon, J.H.M., Harvard U.P., Cambridge, Mass.

Lalanne, L. (1858) *Mémoires de Marguerite de Valois*.

La Noue, F. de (1967) *Discours politiques et militaires*, (ed.) Sutcliffe, F.E., Droz, Geneva.

La Popelinière [L.de Voisin] (1581) *Histoire de la France*, 2 vols, La Rochelle.

La Roche Flavin, B. de (1617) *Treze livres des parlements de France*, Bordeaux.

Loutchizky, J. (1873–96) 'Collection des procès-verbaux des assemblées politiques des réformés de France', *BSHPF*, 22 (1873) 546–58; 24 (1875) 314–22, 359–67, 402–9; 26 (1877) 351–7, 401–7; 45 (1896) 418–41.

Loutchizky, J. (1875) *Documents inédits pour servir à l'histoire de la Réforme*, Kiev.

Loyseau, C. (1611) *Oeuvres*.

Lucinge, R. de (1954–55) 'Miroir des princes ou grands de France', *Annuaire-bulletin de la société de l'histoire de France*, 95–186.

Lucinge, R. de (1964) *René de Lucinge; lettres sur le débuts de la Ligue*, (ed.) Dufour, A., Droz, Geneva.

Lucinge, R. de (1966) *René de Lucinge; lettres sur la cour d'Henri III*, (ed.) Dufour, A., Droz, Geneva.

Mémoires de Nevers (1665), 2 vols.

Monluc, B. de (1964) *Commentaires*, (ed.) Courteault, J. de, Edition La Pléiade.

Montaigne, M. de (1962) *Essais*, (ed.) Rat, M., 2 vols., Gallimard.

Morin, François, sieur de Cromé (1977) *Dialogue d'entre le maheustre et le manant*, (ed.) Ascoli, P., Droz, Geneva.

Nouaillac, J. (1908) *Un envoyé hollandais à la cour de Henri IV; lettres inédites de François d'Aerssen à Jacques Valcke (1599–1603)*.

Pasquier, E. (1723) *Oeuvres*, 2 vols, Amsterdam.

Pasquier, E. (1966) *Etienne Pasquier; lettres historiques pour les années 1556–94*, (ed.) Thickett, D., Droz, Geneva.

Philippi, J. (1918) *Histoire des troubles de Languedoc (1560–1600)*, (ed.) Guiraud, L., Mémoires de la société archéologique de Montpellier, 6.

Pigafetta, F. (1876) 'Relation du siège de Paris', *Mémoires de la société de l'histoire de Paris*, 2, 1–105.

Pradel, C. (1894) 'Mémoires de Batailler sur les guerres civiles à Castres et dans le Languedoc', *Archives historiques de l'Albigeois*, 3, 1–60.

Quick, J. (1692) *Synodicon in Gallia Reformata*, 2 vols.

Raemond, F. de (1605) *l'Histoire de la naissance, progrez et décadence de l'hérésie de ce siècle*, 2 vols.

Registres de Paris (1866–) *Registres de délibérations de la ville de Paris*, (ed.) Bonnardot, F. *et al.*, 9 vols.

Revue rétrospective (1834) 'Henri III et les prédicateurs de son temps', 2, 267–78.

Ibid., 'Documents historiques sur l'assassinat du duc et cardinal de Guise', 3, 432–55.

Richart, A. (1869) *Mémoires sur la Ligue dans le Laonnais*, Laon.

Ritter, R. (1955) *Lettres du Cardinal de Florence sur Henri IV, 1596–8*, edition B. Grasset.

Romier, L. (1910) *Lettres et chevauchées du bureau des finances de Caen sous Henri IV*.

Saulnier, E. (1913) *Journal de François, bourgeois de Paris, 23 décembre 1588–30 avril 1589*.

Saulx-Tavannes, G. de (1881) *Mémoires de Gaspard de Saulx-Tavannes*, (eds) Michaud and Poujoulat, 8 vols.

Stegmann, A. (1979) *Edits des guerres de religion*, Librairie J. Vrin.

Sully (1881) *Economies Royales*, (eds) Michaud and Poujoulat, 16, 17.

Sully (1970–88) *Les Oeconomies royales de Sully*, (eds) Buisseret, D. and Barbiche, B., 2 vols in progress, Klinsieck.

Taix, G. de (1625) *Mémoires des affaires du clergé de France*.

Tommaseo, N. (1838) *Relations des ambassadeurs vénitiens sur les affaires de France au XVIe siècle*, 2 vols.

Valois, C. (1914) *Histoire de la Ligue, oeuvre inédite d'un contemporain*.

Villeroy (1881) *Mémoires de Villeroy*, (eds) Michaud and Poujoulat, 11.

Wacquet, H. (1960) *Mémoires du chanoine Jean Moreau sur les guerres de la Ligue en Bretagne*, Quimper.

SECONDARY SOURCES

Adams, S.L. (1975) 'The road to La Rochelle: English foreign policy and the Huguenots, 1610–1629', *PHS*, 22, 414–29.

Airo-Farulla, J. (1975) 'Les protestants et l'acquisition des offices à la fin du XVIe siècle', *BSHPF*, 116, 503–12.

Anquez, L. (1859) *Histoire des assemblées politiques des Réformés de France*

Anquez, L. (1887) *Henri IV et l'Allemagne d'après les mémoires et la correspondance de Jacques Bongars.*

Appollinaire, P. (1892) 'Conversion et dernières années du connétable Henri de Montmorency', *Annales du Midi*, 101–9.

Aristide, Isabelle (1990) *La fortune de Sully*, Comité pour l'histoire économique et financière de la France.

Ascoli, P. (1974) 'A radical pamphlet of late 16th century France; *Dialogue d'entre le maheustre et le manant*', *16C J*, 5, 3–22.

Ascoli, P. (1977) 'French provincial cities and the Catholic League', *Occasional Papers of the American Society for Reformation Research*, 1, 15–37.

Aubert, F. (1947) 'A propos de l'affaire de la rue St-Jacques (4–5 septembre 1557)', *BSHPF*, 114, 96–102.

Avènement d'Henri IV (1988–90), *quatrième centenaire*:
 – Colloque I (Coutras) (1988), Association Henri IV, Pau
 – Colloque II (Bayonne) (1989), *ditto*
 – Colloque III (Pau) (1990), *ditto*.

Babelon, J-P. (1958) *Musée de l'histoire de France*, Imprimerie Nationale.

Babelon, J-P. (1965) *Les demeures parisiennes sous Henri IV et Louis XIII*, Le Temps.

Babelon, J-P. (1982) *Henri IV*, Fayard.

Babelon, J-P. (1983) 'L'Hôtel de Guise' in *L'Age d'or du Mécénat (1598–1661)*, CNRS, pp. 69–75.

Baccrabère, G. (1956) *Les Visites pastorales dans les paroisses rurales du diocèse de Toulouse aux XVIe et XVIIe siècles.*

Baehrel, R. (1961) *Une Croissance; la basse Provence rurale*, SEVPEN.

Bailhache, J. (1929) 'Un atelier inconnu, Maringues, 1591–3', *Revue numismatique*, 32, 128–36.

Bailhache, J. (1930) 'L'Atelier temporaire de Melun, 1592–4', *Revue numismatique*, 33, 71–6.

Bailhache, J. (1932) 'La monnaie de Montmorency pendant la ligue à Montpellier, Beaucaire, Béziers et Villeneuve d'Avignon', *Revue numismatique*, 35, 37–91.

Barbiche, B. (1960) 'Les commissaires députés pour le régalement des tailles en 1598–9', *Bib Ec Ch*, 118, 58–96.

Barbiche, B. (1963) 'Une tentative de réforme monétaire à la fin du règne d'Henri IV: l'édit d'août 1609', *Dix-septième siècle*, 61, 3–17.

Barbiche, B. and Buisseret, D.J. (1965) 'Sully et la surintendance des finances', *Bib Ec Ch*, 123, 538–43.

Barbiche, B. (1978) *Sully*, Albin Michel.

Bardon, F. (1974) *Le portait mythologique à la cour de France sous Henri IV et Louis XIII*, A. and J. Picard.

Barnavi, E. (1980) *Le Parti de Dieu* (Publications de la Sorbonne, Series NS Recherches, 34), Nauwelaerts, Louvain.

Barnavi, E. and Descimon, R. (1985) *La sainte ligue. Le juge et la potence*, Hachette.

Batiffol, L. (1930) *Le Louvre sous Henri IV et Louis XIII*.

Baudry, J. (1920) *La Fontenelle – le ligueur et le brigandage en Basse-Bretagne pendant la ligue, 1574–1602*, Nantes.

Baudson, E. (1947) *Charles de Gonzague, Duc de Nevers et de Rethel et de Mantoue*, Edition A. Perrin.

Baulant, M. (1953) *Lettres de négociants marseillais; les frères Hermite, 1570–1612*, A. Colin.

Baulant, M. and Meuvret, J. (1960) *Prix des céréales extraits de la mercuriale de Paris (1520–1698)*, I, SEVPEN.

Baumgartner, F.J. (1973) 'The case for Charles X' *16C J*, 4, 87–98.

Baumgartner, F.J. (1976) *Radical Reactionaries; the political thought of the French catholic league*, Droz, Geneva.

Baumgartner, F.J. (1978) 'Renaud de Beaune, politique prelate', *16 C J*, 9, 99–114.

Baumgartner, F.J. (1979) 'Crisis in the French episcopacy; the bishops and the succession of Henri IV', *Archiv für Reformationsgeschichte*, 20, 276–301.

Baumgartner, F.J. (1986) *Change and Continuity in the French Episcopate. The Bishops and the Wars of Religion, 1547–1610*, Duke U.P., Durham.

Bautier, R.H. and Karcher-Vallée, A. (1959) *Les papiers de Sully aux archives nationales*, Imprimerie Nationale.

Bayard, F. (1971) 'Les Bonvisi, marchands-banquiers à Lyon, 1575–1629', *Annales*, 26, 1234–69.

Bayard, F. (1974a) 'Les chambres de justice de la première moitié du XVIIe siècle', *Cahiers d'histoire*, 19, 121–40.

Bayard, F. (1974b) 'Etude des comptants ès mains du roi sous Henri IV', *Bulletin du centre d'histoire économique et sociale de la région lyonnaise*, 3, 1–27.

Bayard, F. (1984) *Finances et financiers en France dans la première moitié du XVIIe siècle (1598–1653)*, Doctorat d'état, Université de Lyon, II.

Beame, E. (1966) 'The limits of toleration in sixteenth-century France', *Studies in the Renaissance*, 13, 250–65.

Becquart, N. (1974) 'Les aliénations du temporel ecclésiastique au diocèse de Périgueux de 1563–1585' *Annales du Midi*, 86, 325–41.

Bellaud-Dessalles, J. (1902) *Les évêques italiens de l'ancienne diocèse de Béziers (1547–1668)*.

Benedict, P. (1975) 'Catholics and Huguenots in sixteenth-century Rouen; the demographic effects of the religious wars', *FHS*, 9, 209–34.

Benedict, P. (1978) 'The St Bartholomew's massacres in the provinces', *Historical Journal*, 21, 201–25.

Benedict, P. (1981) *Rouen during the Wars of Religion*, Cambridge U.P.

Benedict, P. (ed.) (1989) *Cities and Social Change in Early Modern France*, Unwin Hyman.

Benedict, P. (1991) 'The Huguenot Population of France, 1600–1685: the demographic fate and customs of a religious minority', *Transactions of the American Philosophical Society*, 81, Part 5.

Bennassar, B. (1969) *Recherches sur les grandes épidémies dans le nord de l'Espagne à la fin du XVIe siècle*, SEVPEN.

Benoist, C. (1900) *La condition juridique des Protestants sous le régime de l'édit de Nantes*.

Bercé, Y-M. (1974) *Histoire des Croquants. Etude des soulèvements populaires au XVIIe siècle dans le sud-ouest de la France*, 2 vols, Droz, Geneva.

Bergin, J. (1985) *Cardinal Richelieu. Power and the Pursuit of Wealth*, Yale U.P., New Haven and London.

Billacois, F. (1990) *The Duel. Its Rise and Fall in Early Modern France*, Yale U.P., New Haven and London.

Billioud, J. (1951) *Histoire du commerce de Marseille de 1515–1599*, Plon.

Biraben, J-N. (1975) *Les hommes et la peste en France et dans les pays européens et méditerranéens*, 2 vols, Mouton.

Bitton, D. (1969a) *The French Nobility in Crisis (1560–1640)*, Stanford U.P.

Bitton, D. (1969b) 'History and politics; the controversy over the sale of offices in early seventeenth-century France' in *Action and Conviction in Early Modern Europe*, (eds) Rabb, T.K. *et al*, Princeton U.P., New Jersey, pp. 390–403.

Black, J.B. (1914) *Elizabeth I and Henri IV*.

Blanchet, A. (1930) 'Les pinatelles', *Revue numismatique*, 33, 235–7.

Bloch, M. (1973) *The Royal Touch*, Routledge and Kegan Paul.

Boase, A. (1977) *Vie de Jean de Sponde*, Droz, Geneva.

Boilisle, A.M. de (1873) *Histoire de la maison de Nicolay*, Nogent le Rotrou.

Bonney, R.J. (1976) 'The secret expenses of Richelieu and Mazarin', *EHR*, 91, 825–36.

Bonney, R.J. (1978) *Political Change in France under Richelieu and Mazarin*, Clarendon, Oxford.

Bonney, R.J. (1981) *The King's Debts*, Clarendon, Oxford.

Bontemps, C. et al (1965) *Le Prince dans la France des XVIe et XVIIe siècles*, PUF.

Bosher J.F. (1973) 'Chambres de justice in the French monarchy', in *French Government and Society, 1500–1850*, Athlone Press, pp. 19–40.

Boucher, J. (1986) *La cour de Henri III*, Ouest-France, Rennes.

Bouillé, R. de (1849) *Histoire des ducs de Guise*, 4 vols.

Bourgeon, J-L. (1992) *l'Assassinat de Coligny*, Droz, Geneva.

Bourrachot, L. (1963) 'Le diocèse d'Agen entre 1592 et 1607, vu par son évêque', in *Moissac et sa région. 19e congrès de la fédération des sociétés*, La fédération, pp. 129–43.

Boutier, J., Dewerpe, A. and Nordman, D. (1984) *Un tour de France royal. Le voyage de Charles IX (1564–1566)*, Aubier.

Boutruche, R. (1966) *Bordeaux de 1450 à 1715*, Fédération Historique du Sud-Ouest, Bordeaux.

Bouwsma, W. (1968) *Venice and the Defense of Republican Liberty*, California U.P., Berkeley, Los Angeles and London.

Boyer, P. (1921) *Le barreau toulousain*, Toulouse.

Braudel, F. (1973) *The Mediterranean and the Mediterranean World in the Age of Philip II*, Collins.

Buisseret, D.J. (1964a) 'The French Mediterranean Fleet under Henri IV' *The Mariner's Mirror*, 1, 297–306.

Buisseret, D.J. (1964b) 'Les ingénieurs du roi sous Henri IV', *Bulletin de géographie*, 75, 13–84.

Buisseret, D.J. (1965) 'The communications of France during the reconstruction of Henri IV', *Economic History Review*, Second Series, 18, 43–53.

Buisseret, D.J. (1966) 'A stage in the development of the intendants; the reign of Henri IV', *Historical Journal*, 9, 27–38.

Buisseret, D.J. (1968) *Sully*, Eyre and Spottiswoode.

Buisseret, D.J. (1972) *Huguenots and Papists*, Ginn.

Buisseret, D.J. (1984) *Henry IV*, George Allen and Unwin.

Cabourdin, G. (1977) *Terre et hommes en Lorraine (1550–1635)*, 2 vols, Université de Nancy, II.

Cameron, K. (1974) 'Henri III – the anti-christian king', *Journal of European Studies*, 4, 152–63.

Cameron, K. (1978) *Henri III. A Maligned or Malignant King?*, University of Exeter.

Cameron, K. (ed.) (1989) *From Valois to Bourbon. Dynasty, State and Society in Early Modern France*, Exeter Studies in History, No. 24, Exeter.

Cassan, M. (1988) 'Les lendemains des guerres de religion en Limousin' in *Croyances, pouvoir et société des Limousins aux Français*, Le Louvanel, CNRS.

Chadourne, J. P. (1969) 'Les bouchers parisiens au XVIe siècle . . .' *Positions de l'école des chartes*, pp. 17–24.

Chamberland, A. (1903) 'Recherches sur les réformes financières en Champagne à l'époque de Henri IV et Sully', *Travaux de l'Académie de Reims*, 111, 243–71.

Chamberland, A. (1904) *Le conflit de 1597 entre Henri IV et le parlement de Paris*.

Champion, P. (1939) 'La légende des mignons', *Bib H R*, 6, 494–528.

Charbonnier, F. (1919) *La Poésie française et les guerres de religion*.

Charbonnier, F. (1923) *Pamphlets protestants contre Ronsard (1560–77)*.

Charleville, E. (1901) *Les états généraux de 1576*.

Charlier-Méniolle, R. (1911) *L'Assemblée des notables de 1596*.

Charrière, E. (1848–61) *Négociations de la France dans le Levant*, 4 vols.

Chaunu, P. and Gascon, R. (1977) *Histoire économique et sociale de la France de 1450–1660*, vol. I, i, PUF.

Chénon, E. (1892) *Les marches séparantes d'Anjou, Bretagne et Poitou*.

Chevallier, P. (1985) *Henri III*, Fayard.

Chevallier, P. (1989) *Les Régicides*, Fayard.

Chomel, V. (1976) *Histoire de Grenoble*, Privat, Toulouse.

Clark, P., ed. (1985) *The European Crisis of the 1590s*, Allen and Unwin.

Cloulas, I. (1958) 'Les aliénations du temporel ecclésiastique sous Charles IX et Henri III (1563–1587). Résultats généraux des ventes', *Revue d'Histoire de l'Eglise de France*, 44, 5–56.

Cloulas, I.(1964) 'Les acquéreurs des biens ecclésiastiques vendus dans les diocèses de Limoges et de Bourges sous les règnes de Charles IX et Henri III', *Bulletin de la société archéologique et historique du Limousin*, 91, 87–140.

Cloulas, I. (1979) *Catherine de Médicis*, Fayard.

Coligny (Actes du Colloque, 1972) (1974) *L'Amiral de Coligny et son temps*, Société du Protestantisme français.

Collins, James B. (1988) *Fiscal limits of Absolutism. Direct Taxation in Early Seventeenth-Century France*, California U.P., Berkeley, Los Angeles and London.

Constant, J-M. (1977) 'Quelques problèmes de mobilité sociale et de vie matérielle chez les gentilshommes de Beauce aux XVIe et XVIIe siècles', *Acta Poloniae Historica*, 36, 83–94.

Coope, R. (1972) *Salomon de la Brosse and the development of the classical style*, Zwimmer.

Courteault, P. (1909) *Un cadet de Gascogne, Blaise de Monluc.*

Couzard, R. (1900) *Un ambassadeur à Rome sous Henri IV, d'après des documents inédits.*

Croix, A. (1974) *Nantes et le pays nantais au XVIe siècle. Etude démographique*, SEVPEN.

Crouzet, D. (1984) 'Recherches sur la crise de l'aristocratie en France au XVIe siècle; les dettes de la maison de Nevers', *Histoire économie et société*, I, 5–50.

Crouzet, D. (1990) *Les guerriers de dieu. La violence au temps des troubles de religion (vers 1525 – vers 1610)*, 2 vols, Champ Vallon.

Croze, J. de (1866) *Les Guise, les Valois et Philippe II*, 2 vols.

Crump, L. (1926) *A Huguenot Family in the Sixteenth Century.*

Cummings, M.C. (1974) 'The long robe and the sceptre', Ph.D., Colorado University.

Dareste, R. (1850) *Essai sur François Hotman.*

Davies, J.M. (1979) 'Persecution and Protestantism: Toulouse, 1562–1575', *Historical Journal*, 22, 31–51.

Davies, J. (1991) 'Neither politique nor patriot? Henri, duc de Montmorency and Philip II, 1582–1589', *The Historical Journal*, 34, 539–66.

Davillé, L. (1909) *Les prétensions de Charles III, duc de Lorraine, à la couronne de France.*

Davis, N. Z. (1975) *Society and culture in Early Modern France*, Stanford U.P.

Decrue de Stoutz, F. (1889) *Anne, duc de Montmorency, connétable et pair de France.*

Decrue de Stoutz, F. (1890) *Le parti des politiques.*

Delumeau, J. (1959) *La vie économique et sociale à Rome dans la seconde moitié du XVIe siècle*, Edition de Boccard.

Delumeau, J. (1968) *Naissance et affirmation de la réforme*, PUF.

Derblay, C. (1927) *Roger de Comminges, sieur de Sobole, gouverneur de Metz (1553–1615).*

Descimon, R. (1982) 'La Ligue à Paris (1585–1594); une révision', *Annales*, 37, 72–111.

Descimon, R. (1983) Qui étaient les Seize? Mythes et réalités de la Ligue parisienne (1585–1594), in *Mémoires de la fédération des sociétés historiques et archéologiques de Paris et de l'Ile de France*, 35.

Descimon, R. (1988) 'L'échevinage parisien sous Henri IV (1594–1610). Autonomie urbaine, conflits politiques et exclusions sociales' in *La ville, la bourgeoisie et la genèse de l'Etat Moderne, XIIe-XVIIIe siècles* (Actes du colloque de Bielefeld, 1985; eds Neithard Bulst and J-Ph. Genet), CNRS.

Desgraves, L. (1960) *Les Haultin (1571–1623)*, Droz, Geneva.

Desjardins, A. (1879) 'Les parlements du roi', *Séances et travaux de l'Académie des sciences morales et politiques*, 39, 478–505, 614–33.

Dewald, J. (1976) 'The "perfect magistrate"; *parlementaires* and crime in Sixteenth-Century Rouen', *Archiv für Reformationsgeschichte*, 57, 284–300.

Dewald, J. (1980) *The Formation of a Provincial Nobility; the magistrates of the parlement of Rouen, 1499–1610*, Princeton U.P., Providence, RI.

Deyon, P. (1963) 'Variations de la production textile aux XVIe et XVIIe siècles; sources et premiers résultats', *Annales*, 18, 948–9.

Dickerman, E.H. (1968) *Bellièvre and Villeroy*, Brown U.P.

Dickerman, E.H. (1972) 'The man and the myth; Sully and the *Economies Royales*', *FHS*, 7, 307–31.

Dickerman, E.H. (1976) 'A neglected phase of the Spanish Armada: the catholic League's Picard offensive of 1587', *Proceedings of the Western Society for the Study of French History*, 19–23.

Dickerman, E.H. and Walker, A.M. (1992) 'Monuments of His Own Magnificence: Henrichemont and the Archaeology of Sully's Mind', *French History*, 2, 154–84.

Diefendorf, B.B. (1987) 'Simon Vigor: a radical preacher in sixteenth-century Paris', *16C J*, 18, 399–410.

Diefendorf, B.B. (1991) *Beneath the Cross. Catholics and Huguenots in Sixteenth-Century Paris*, Oxford U.P.

Divers Aspects de la Réforme au XVIe et XVIIe siècles (1975). Société de l'Histoire du Protestantisme Français.

Dolan, C. (1981) *Entre Tours et Clochers; les gens d'église à Aix-en-Provence au XVIe siècle*, Publications du centre d'études de la Renaissance de l'université de Sherbrooke.

Doucet, R. (1948) *Les Institutions de la France au XVIe siècle*, 2 vols, A. and J. Picard.

Drouot, H. (1911) 'Vin, vignes et vignerons de la côte dijonnaise pendant la Ligue', *Revue de Bourgogne*, 1, 343–61.

Drouot, H. (1937a) *Mayenne et la Bourgogne*, 2 vols, Dijon.

Drouot, H. (1937b) 'La première ligue en Bourgogne et les débuts de Mayenne (1574–79)', *Etudes bourguignonnes sur le XVIe siècle*, vol. II.

Drouot, H. (1951) 'Les conseils provinciaux de la Sainte-Union (1589–95)', *Annales du Midi*, 65, 415–33.

Ducourtieux, P. (1925) *Histoire de Limoges*.

Dufayard, C. (1892) *Le Connétable Desdiguières*.

Dufour, A. (1965) 'La paix de Lyon et la conjuration de Biron', *Journal des Savants*, 428–55.

Dumoulin, M. (1895) 'Jacques de la Fin', *Bulletin historique et philologique*, 170–286.

Dussert, A. (1929) 'Le baron des Adretz et les états de Dauphiné, 1562–3', *Bulletin de l'Académie delphinale*, 5th Series, 20, 110–118.

Dussert, A. (1931) 'Catherine de Médicis et les états de Dauphiné, préludes du procès des tailles et arbitrage de la reine mère en 1579', *Bulletin de l'Académie delphinale*, 6th Series, 2, 123–89.

Ehrman, J. (1972) 'Tableaux de massacres au XVIe siècle', *BSHPF*, 118, 445–55.

Ehrman, S.H. (1936) *The Letters and Documents of Armand de Gontaut, Baron de Biron*, 2 vols, New York.

d'Estaintot, R. (1862) *La Ligue en Normandie (1588–1594)*.

Etchechoury, M. (1991) *Les maîtres des requêtes de l'hôtel du roi sous les derniers Valois (1553–1589)*, Geneva, Droz.

Fagniez, G. (1897) *l'Economie sociale de la France sous Henri IV*.

Faurey, J. (1903) *Henri IV et l'édit de Nantes*.

Fayard, E. (1876) *Aperçu historique sur le parlement de Paris*, 3 vols.

Foisil, M. (1976) 'Harangue et rapport d'Antoine Séguier, commissaire pour le roi en Basse-Normandie, 1579–80', *Annales de Normandie*, 26, 25–40.

Forneron, H. (1893) *Les ducs de Guise et leur époque*, 2 vols.

Frêche, G. and G. (1967) *Les prix des grains, des vins et des légumes à Toulouse*, Privat, Toulouse.

Gachon, P. (1887) *Les états de Languedoc et l'édit de Béziers*.

Galpern, A.N. (1976) *The Religions of the People in Sixteenth-Century Champagne*, Harvard U.P., Cambridge, Mass.

Gambier, P. (1957) *Le président Barnabé Brisson, ligueur, (1531–91)*, Librairie Perrin.

Garrisson, F. (1950) *Essai sur les commissions d'application de l'édit de Nantes*, Montpellier.

Garrisson, J. (1984) *Henri IV*, Seuil.

Garrisson, J. (1988) *Les protestants au XVI siècle*, Fayard.

Garrisson-Estèbe, J. (1968) *Tocsin pour un massacre: la saison des Saint-Barthélemy*, Editions Le Centurion.

Garrisson-Estèbe, J. (1980) *Protestants du Midi (1559–1598)*, Privat, Toulouse.

Gascon, R. (1971) *Grand commerce et vie urbaine au XVIe siècle*, 2 vols, SEVPEN.

Giesey, R.E. (1977) 'Rules of Inheritance and Strategies of Mobility in Prerevolutionary France' *American Historical Review*, 82, 271–89.

Gilmont, J-F. (1981) *Jean Crespin: un éditeur réformé du XVIe siècle*, Droz, Geneva.

Girard, A. (1932) *Le commerce français à Seville et Cadiz au temps des Habsbourg.*

Goubert, P. (1960) *Beauvais et le beauvaisis au XVIIe siècle*, CNRS.

Goubert, P. (1961) 'Sur le front de l'histoire des prix au XVIe siècle', *Annales*, 16, 791–803.

Goubert, P. (1976) *Clio parmi les hommes*, Mouton, The Hague.

Goy, J. and Le Roy Ladurie, E. (1972) *Les fluctuations des produits de la dîme; conjoncture décimale et domaniale de la fin du moyen âge au XVIIIe siècle*, Mouton, The Hague.

Graham, V.E. and Johnson, W.M. (1979) *The Royal Tour by Charles IX and Catherine de Medici*, Toronto U.P.

Grant, A.J. (1951) *A History of Europe from 1494 to 1660*, Methuen (orig. edn 1927).

Green, V.H.H. (1969) *Renaissance and Reformation*, E. Arnold (orig. edn 1954).

Greengrass, M. (1979) 'War, politics and religion in Languedoc during the government of Henri de Montmorency-Damville (1574–1610)', D. Phil., University of Oxford.

Greengrass, M. (1981) 'Mathurin Charretier; the career of a *politique* during the wars of religion in France', *PHS*, 23, 330–40.

Greengrass, M. (1983) 'The anatomy of a religious riot in Toulouse in May 1562', *Journal of Ecclesiastical History*, 34, 367–91.

Greengrass, M. (1986) 'Noble Affinities in Early Modern France: The Case of Henri I de Montmorency, Constable of France', *European History Quarterly*, 16, 275–311.

Greengrass, M. (1987a) 'Aristocracy and Episcopacy at the end of the Wars of Religion in France: the Duke of Montmorency and the bishoprics of Languedoc' in *Miscellanea Historiae Ecclesiasticae VIII* (Bibliothèque de la revue d'histoire ecclésiastique, fasc. 72), 356–63.

Greengrass, M. (1987b) *The French Reformation*, Blackwell, Oxford.

Greengrass, M. (1989) 'The assassination of Henry III', *History Today*, 39 (November), 11–17.

Greengrass, M. (1991) 'The psychology of religious violence', *French History*, 5, 467–74.

Guilleminot, G. (1977) 'Religion et politique à la veille des guerres civiles; recherches sur les impressions françaises de l'année 1561', *Position des thèses, école des Chartes*, 77–83.

Gundersheimer, W.L. (1966) *The Life and Works of Louis Le Roy*, Droz, Geneva.

Gutton, J.P. (1970) *La société et les pauvres. L'exemple de la généralité de Lyon*, Société d'édition 'Les belles lettres'.

Hanley, Sarah, (1983) *The Lit de Justice of the Kings of France. Constitutional Ideology in Legend, Ritual, and Discours*, Princeton U.P. New Jersey.

Hanotaux, G.A.A. (1886) *Origine des intendants des provinces*.

Harding, R.R. (1978) *Anatomy of a Power Elite*, Yale U.P., New Haven and London.

Harding, R.R. (1980) 'The mobilisation of the Confraternities against the Reformation in France', *16 C J*, 11, 85–107.

Harding, R.R. (1981) 'Revolution and Reform in the Holy League: Angers, Rennes, Nantes', *Journal of Modern History*, 53, 379–416.

Hauchecorne, F. (1950) 'Le parlement de Bordeaux pendant la première guerre civile', *Annales du Midi*, 62, 329–40.

Hauchecorne, F. (1970) 'Orléans au temps de la Ligue', *Bulletin de la société archéologique et de l'histoire de l'Orléanais*, 5, 267–78.

Hauser, H. (1912–15) *Les sources de l'histoire de France*, 4 vols.

Hauser, H. (1932) *La vie chère au XVIe siècle; 'la response de Jean Bodin à M. de Malestroit, 1568'*.

Hayden, J. M. (1973) 'Continuity in the France of Henri IV and Louis XIII: French foreign policy, 1598–1615', *Journal of Modern History*, 45, 1–23.

Hayden, J.M. (1974) *France and the Estates General of 1614*, Cambridge U.P.

Hayden, J.M. (1977) 'The social origins of the French episcopacy in 1614', *FHS*, 10, 27–40.

Henrard, P. (1870) *Henri IV et la princesse de Condé (1609–10)*, Brussels.

Henri IV et la reconstruction du royaume (1989), Editions de la réunion des musées nationaux, Archives Nationales.

Hickey, D. (1978) 'Procès des tailles et blocage sociale dans la Dauphiné du XVIe siècle', *Cahiers d'Histoire*, 13, 25–49.

Hickey, D. (1986) *The Coming of French Absolutism: The Struggle for Tax Reform in the Province of Dauphiné 1540–1640*, Toronto U.P.

Highfield, J.R.L. and Jeffs, R. (1981) *The Crown and Local Communities in England and France in the Fifteenth Century*, Alan Sutton, Gloucester.

Higounet, C. (1971) *Documents sur l'histoire de Gascogne*, Privat, Toulouse.

Hilaire, J. (1952) 'Une vente de biens ecclésiastiques au diocèse de Béziers en 1563', *Congrès régional, fédération des sociétés savantes du Languedoc*, 146–58.

Holt, M. P. (ed.) (1991) *Society and Institutions in Early Modern France*, University of Georgia Press, Athens and London.

Hours, H. (1952) 'Le conseil d'état à Lyon pendant la Ligue; contribution à l'étude des gouverneurs de province', *Revue historique de droit français et étranger*, 401–20.

Huppert, G. (1977) *Les Bourgeois Gentilshommes*, Chicago U.P.

Hurtubise, P. (1976) 'Mariage mixte au XVIe siècle: les circonstances de la première abjuration d'Henri IV à l'automne de 1572', *Archivum Historicum Pontificae*, 14, 103–34.

Huseman, William H. (1984) 'The Expression of the Idea of Toleration in French during the Sixteenth Century', *16C J*, 15, 293–310.

Jackson, R.A. (1972) 'Elective kingship and 'consensus populi' in sixteenth-century France', *Journal of Modern History*, 44, 155–71.

Jacquart, J. (1974) *La crise rurale en Ile de France (1550–1670)*, SEVPEN.

Jensen, D. Lamar (1964) *Diplomacy and Dogmatism. Bernardino de Mendoza and the French Catholic League*, Harvard U.P., Cambridge, Mass.

Jensen, D. Lamar (1968) 'Franco-Spanish diplomacy and the Armada' in *Essays in Honour of G. Mattingly*, (ed.) Carter, C.H.J., Cape., pp. 205–21.

Jensen, D. Lamar (1974) 'French diplomacy and the wars of religion', *16C J*, 5, 22–46.

Jouanna, A. (1976) *L'idée de race en France au XVIe siècle (1494–1614)*, 3 vols, H. Champion.

Joutard, P. *et al.* (1976) *La Saint-Barthélemy ou les résonances d'un massacre*, Delachaux and Niestlé, Neuchâtel.

Jourdain, C, (1867) *Histoire de l'université de Paris au 17e et 18e siècles*, 2 vols.

Jung, M-R. (1966) *Hercule dans la littérature française du XVIe siècle*, Droz, Geneva.

Kaiser, C. (1982) 'Les cours souveraines au XVIe siècle; morale et contre-réforme', *Annales*, 37, 15–32.

Karcher, A. (1956) 'L'assemblée des notables de St Germain-en-Laye', *Bib Ec Ch*, 94, 115–62.

Kelley, D. (1970) *Foundations of Modern Historical Scholarship*, Columbia U.P., New York.

Kelley, D. (1973) *François Hotman: a revolutionary's ordeal*, Princeton U.P., New Jersey.

Kelley, D. (1981) *The Beginning of Ideology*, Cambridge U.P.

Kettering, S. (1989) 'Clientage During the French Wars of Religion', *16C J*, 20, 221–39.

Kierstead, R.F. (1968) *Pomponne de Bellièvre*, Northwestern U.P., Evanston.

Kingdon, R.M. (1956) *Geneva and the Coming of the Wars of Religion in France (1555–1563)*, Droz, Geneva.

Kingdon, R.M. (1988) *Myths about the St Bartholomew's Day Massacres 1572–1576*, Harvard U.P., Cambridge, Mass.

Kinser, S. (1966) *The Works of Jacques-Auguste de Thou*, M. Nijhoff, The Hague.

Kleinman, R. (1962) *Saint François de Sales and the Protestants*, Droz, Geneva.

Koch, P. (1940) 'Jérémie Ferrier, pasteur de Nîmes (1601–3)', *BSHPF*, 39, 9–21.

Konnert, M. (1989) 'Urban Values Versus Religious Passion: Châlons-sur-Marne during the Wars of Religion', *16C J*, 20, 387–405.

Kretzer, H. (1977) 'Remarques sur le droit de résistance des Calvinistes français au début du XVIIe siècle', *BSHPF*, 123, 54–75.

Labatut, J-P. (1972) *Les ducs et pairs de France au XVIIe siècle*, PUF.

Labitte, C. (1849) *De la démocratie chez les prédicateurs de la ligue.*

Laborde, F. (1886) *François de Châtillon.*

Labouchère, G. (1923) 'Guillaume Ancel, envoyé résident en Allemagne d'après sa correspondance', *Revue d'Histoire Diplomatique*, 37, 160–88.

Lacoste, G. (1883–86) *Histoire générale de la province de Quercy*, 4 vols, Cahors.

Lamet, M.S. (1979) 'Reformation, war and society in lower Normandy, 1558–1610', Ph.D., University of Michigan, Ann Arbor.

Lapeyre, H. (1955) *Une famille de marchands, les Ruiz: contribution à l'étude du commerce entre la France et l'Espagne au temps de Philippe II*, SEVPEN.

Laronze, C. (1890) *Essai sur le régime municipal en Bretagne pendant les guerres de religion.*

Lavisse, E. (1901–1911) (ed.) *Histoire de France*, 9 vols.

Lebègue, R. (1929) *La tragédie religieuse en France: les débuts (1514–1573).*

Lebigre, A. (1980) *La révolution des curés; Paris, 1588–94*, Albin Michel.

Lebrun, F. (1965) 'Registres paroissiaux et la démographie en Anjou au XVIe siècle', *Annales de démographie historique*, 49–50.

Leclercq, P. (1979) *Garéoult: un village de Provence dans la deuxième moitié du XVIe siècle*, CNRS.

Lee, M. (1970) *James I and Henri IV*, University of Illinois Press, Urbana.

Lelong, J. (1909) *Charles Loyseau; une biographie.*

Léonard, R. (1961) *History of Protestantism*, 2 vols, Nelson.

L'Epinois, H. de (1886) *La Ligue et les Papes.*

Lequenne, F. (1942) *La Vie d'Olivier de Serres.*

Le Roux, N. (1994) 'The Catholic Nobility and Political Choice during the League (1585–94): the case of Claude de La Châtre, *French History*, 8, 34–50.

Le Roy Ladurie, E. (1966) *Les Paysans de Languedoc*, 2 vols, SEVPEN.

Le Roy Ladurie, E. (1971) *Times of Feast, Times of Famine*, Allen and Unwin.

Le Roy Ladurie, E. and Couperie, P. (1970) 'Le mouvement des loyers parisiens de la fin du moyen âge au XVIIIe siècle', *Annales*, 25, 1002–23.

Le Roy Ladurie, E. and Morineau, M. (1977) *Histoire économique et sociale de la France de 1450–1660*, vol. I (pt ii), PUF.

Le Roy Ladurie, E. (1979) *Le Carnaval de Romans*, Gallimard.

Les Travaux et les jours dans l'Ancienne France (exposition, catalogue de la Bibliothèque Nationale, 1969), Imprimerie Nationale.

Ligou, D. (1968) *Protestantisme en France de 1598 à 1715*, SEDES.

Lloyd, H. (1981) 'The political thought of Charles Loyseau (1564–1627)', *European Studies Review*, 11, 53–82.

Lods, A. (1889) 'L'édit de Nantes devant le parlement de Paris', *BSHPF*, 36, 124–38.

Love, R.S. (1991) 'Henri IV et Ivry; le monarque, chef de guerre', *Revue historique des armées*, 182, 11–30.

Lozinski, A. (1973) 'L'accroissement de la population de Paris au XVIe siècle', *Srednie Veka*, 37, 146–73.

Lublinskaya, A. (1968) *French Absolutism: the crucial phase*, Cambridge U.P.

Madden, S.H. (1982) 'L'idéologie constitutionnelle en France; le lit de justice', *Annales*, 38, 32–63.

Malvezin, T. (1883) *Histoire du commerce à Bordeaux*, 4 vols, Bordeaux.

Mariéjol, J.H. (1904) *La Réforme et la Ligue*, vol. vi, part 1 of E. Lavisse, *Histoire de France* (1900–11).

Mariéjol, J-H. (1928) *La vie de Marguerite de Valois, 1553-1615.*

Mariéjol, J-H. (1947) *Charles-Emmanuel, Duc de Nemours, Gouverneur du Lyonnais, Beaujolais et Forez (1567–1595)*, Librairie Hachette.

Mattingly, G. (1959) *The Defeat of the Spanish Armada*, J. Cape.

Maugis, E. (1914) *Histoire du parlement de Paris de l'avènement des rois Valois à la mort de Henri IV.*

Maupeou, J. de (1959) *Histoire des Maupeou,* Fontenay-le-Comte.

Ménard, L. (1750–68) *Histoire des antiquités . . . de Nîmes,* 5 vols, Nîmes.

Merle, L. (1958) *La métairie et l'évolution agraire de la Gâtine poitevine de la fin du Moyen Age à la Révolution,* SEVPEN.

Meyer, J.C.P. (1978) 'Reformation in La Rochelle: religious change, social stability and political crisis, 1500–1568', Ph.D. Thesis, University of Iowa.

Michaud, C. (1981) 'Les aliénations du temporel ecclésiastique dans la seconde moitié du XVIe siècle. Quelques problèmes de méthode', *Revue de l'Histoire de l'Eglise de France,* 68, 61–82.

Michaud, H. (1967) *La grande chancellerie et les écritures royales au XVIe siècle,* PUF.

Michaud, H. (1972) 'l'Ordonnancement des dépenses et le budget de la monarchie, 1587–9', *Annuaire-Bulletin de la société de l'Histoire de France,* 87–120.

Miron de l'Espinay, A. (1885) *François Miron et l'administration municipale de Paris sous Henri IV de 1604 à 1606.*

Mirot, L. (1918–19) 'L'hôtel et les collections du connétable de Montmorency', *Bib Ec Ch,* 78, 311–413; 79, 152–229.

Morice, Dom (1742–46) *Mémoires pour servir de preuves à l'histoire de Bretagne,* 3 vols.

Mousnier, R.E. (1941) 'Sully et le conseil d'état et des finances; la lutte entre Bellièvre et Sully', *Revue Historique,* 102, 68–86.

Mousnier, R.E. (1970) *La Plume, la Faucille et le Marteau,* PUF.

Mousnier, R.E. (1971) *La Vénalité des offices sous Henri IV et Louis XIII,* PUF.

Mousnier, R.E. (1973) *The Assassination of Henri IV. The tyrannicide problem and the consolidation of the French absolute monarchy in the early seventeenth century,* Faber.

Mousnier, R.E. (1979–84) *The Institutions of France under the Absolute Monarchy (1598–1789),* 2 vols, University of Chicago Press.

Mouton, L. (1924) *Le duc et le roi.*

Neale, J.E. (1943) *The Age of Catherine de Medici.*

Neuschel, K.B. (1989) *Word of Honor. Interpreting Noble Culture in Sixteenth-Century France,* Cornell U.P., Ithaca and London.

Nicholle, H.A. (1976) 'Anglo-French trade (1540–1640)', Ph.D. Thesis, London School of Economics.

Nicholls, D.J. (1977) 'The origins of Protestantism in Normandy: a social study', Ph.D. Thesis, University of Birmingham.

Nouaillac, J. (1912) 'Henri IV et les Croquants de Limousin. La mission de l'intendant Boissise', *Bulletin historique et philologique*, 312–50.

Orlea, M. (1980) *La noblesse aux Etats généraux de 1576 et de 1588*, PUF.

Palanque, J-R. (1976) *Le Diocèse d'Aix-en-Provence*, Beauchesne.

Pallier, D. (1976) *Recherches sur l'imprimerie à Paris pendant la Ligue*, Droz, Geneva.

Pannier, J. (1911) *L'église réformée de Paris sous Henri IV*.

Papin, Philippe (1991) 'Duplicité et traîtrise: l'image des 'politiques' durant la Ligue' *Revue d'histoire moderne et contemporaine*, 38, 3–21.

Parker, D. (1981) 'Law, society and the state in the thought of Jean Bodin', *History of Political Thought*, 2, 253–84.

Parker, G. (1972) *The Army of Flanders and the Spanish Road, 1567–1659*, Cambridge U.P.

Pascal, A. (1960) *Il marchesato di Saluzzo e la Riforma protestante, durante il periodo della dominatione francese (1548–1588)*, Sansoni, Florence.

Patterson, W.B. (1972) 'The Huguenot appeal for a return to Poissy' in *Schism, Heresy and Religious Protest*, (ed.) Baker, D., Cambridge U.P., 247–57.

Patterson, W.B. (1975) 'Jean de Serres and the politics of religious pacification' in *Church, Society and Politics*, (ed.) Baker, D., Oxford U.P., 223–44.

Paultre, C. (1906) *De la repression de la mendicité et du vagabondage en France sous l'ancien régime*.

Permezel, J. (1935) *La politique financière de Sully dans la généralité de Lyon*, Lyon.

Perrens, F-T. (1872) *L'église et l'état en France sous le règne de Henri IV*, 2 vols.

Picot, E. (1901) *Italiens en France au XVIe siècle*.

Picot, G. (1874) 'Recherches sur les quarteniers cinquanteniers et dizainiers de la ville de Paris', *Mémoires de la société de la ville de Paris*, I, 132–66.

Picot, G. (1888) *Histoire des Etats généraux*, 4 vols.

Pillorget, R. (1972) 'Luttes de factions et intérêts économiques à Marseille de 1598 à 1618', *Annales* 27, 705–30.

Pillorget, R. (1975) *Les Mouvements insurrectionnels en Provence* (ed.) Pedone, A.

Pineaux, J. (1973) *La polémique protestante contre Ronsard*, Didier.

Poirson, A. (1862–65) *Histoire du règne de Henri IV*, 2nd edn, 4 vols.

Powis, J. (1973) 'Officiers et gentilshommes; a *parlementaire* class in sixteenth century Bordeaux?', *Bordeaux et les Iles Brittaniques*,

Université de Bordeaux, pp. 27–36.

Powis, J. (1983) 'Gallican Liberties and the politics of later sixteenth-century France', *The Historical Journal*, 26, 515–30.

Préclin, E. (1930) 'E. Richer, sa vie, son oeuvre, le richérisme', *Revue d'Histoire Moderne*, 5, 241–69.

Prentout, H. (1925) *Les Etats provinciaux de Normandie*, Caen.

Proudhon, J. (1959) 'La réception de l'édit de Nantes en Bourgogne (1599–1600)', *Annales de Bourgogne*, 124, 225–49.

Prouzet, J. (1975) *Les guerres de religion dans le pays d'Aude (1560–96)*, Tulle, Imp. E. Ogier.

Pujol, E. (1876) *E. Richer. Etude historique et critique sur la rénovation du gallicanisme au commencement du XVIIe siècle*, 2 vols.

Rabut, E. (1987) *Le Roi, l'Eglise et le Temple*, Editions de la Pensée Sauvage.

Raffin, L. (1926) *Saint-Julien de Balleure, historien bourguignon*.

Ranum, O. (1980) 'The French ritual of tyrannicide in the late sixteenth century', *16C J*, 11, 63–82.

Raulich, I. (1896–1902) *Storia di Carlo Emanuele, duca di Savoia*, 2 vols, Milan.

Reure, C. (1897–98) 'La presse politique à Lyon pendant la Ligue', *Annales de la Charité*, 26, 161–88; 27, 5–35.

Revue Henri IV (1905–1912) 3 vols, republished Mégariotis, Geneva.

Richard, P. (1901) *Pierre d'Epinac*.

Richet, D. (1991) *De la Réforme à la Révolution. Etudes sur la France moderne*, Aubier.

Rimbault, L. (1966) *Pierre du Moulin (1568–1658)*, J. Vrin.

Ritter, R. (1985) *Catherine de Bourbon, 1569–1604*, 2 vols, Jean Touzot.

Robiquet, P. (1886) *Paris et la Ligue sous le règne de Henri III*.

Roelker, N.L. (1968) *Queen of Navarre – Jeanne d'Albert*, Harvard U.P., Cambridge, Mass.

Rolle, F. (1865) *Collection des Inventaires-sommaires: Lyon*.

Romier, L. (1925) *Catholiques et Huguenots à la cour de Charles IX*.

Romier, L. (1960) *A History of France*, Methuen.

Rosenberg, D.L. (1978) Social experience and religious choice: a case study – the protestant weavers and woolcombers of Amiens in the Sixteenth Century, Ph.D. Thesis, Yale University.

Rott, E. (1882) *Henri IV, les Suisses et la Haute Italie – la lutte pour les Alpes (1598–1610)*.

Rousselet, M. (1957) *Histoire de la Magistrature Française*, 2 vols, Plom.

Russell Major, J. (1966) 'Henri IV and Guyenne; a study concerning the origins of royal absolutism', *FHS*, 4, 363–83.

Russell Major, J. (1974) 'Bellièvre, Sully and the assembly of notables of 1596', *Transactions of the American Philosophical Society*, New Series, 54, 3–34.

Russell Major, J. (1980) *Representative Government in Early Modern France*, Yale U.P., New Haven and London.

Russell Major, J. (1981) 'Noble income and inflation and the wars of religion in France', *American Historical Review*, 86, 21–48.

Saignieux, J. (1974) 'Philippe II et les ligueurs lyonnais', *L'humanisme lyonnais au XVIe siècle*, Presses universitaires de Grenoble, Grenoble.

Saint-Jacob, P. de (1961) 'Mutations économiques et sociales dans les campagnes bourguignonnes à la fin du XVIe siècle', *Etudes rurales*, 1, 34–49.

Saint-Priest, le Comte de (1877) *Mémoires sur l'ambassade de France en Turquie*.

Salmon, J.H.M. (1975) *Society in Crisis: France in the Sixteenth Century*, E. Benn.

Salmon, J.H.M. (1979) 'Peasant Revolt in the Vivarais (1575–80)', *FHS*, 12, 25–40.

Sauval, H. (1724) *Histoire et recherches des antiquités de la ville de Paris*, 3 vols.

Sauzet, R. (1979) *Contre-réforme et réforme Catholique en Bas-Languedoc* (Publications de la Sorbonne, NS Recherches 30), Nauwelaerts, Louvain.

Schalk, E. (1976) 'The appearance and reality of nobility in France during the wars of religion: an example of how collective attitudes can change', *Journal of Modern History*, 48, 19–31.

Schalk, E. (1986) *From Valor to Pedigree. Ideas of nobility in France in the sixteenth and seventeenth centuries*, Princeton U.P., New Jersey.

Schnapper, B. (1957) *Les rentes au XVIe siècle. Histoire d'un instrument de crédit*, SEVPEN.

Schnur, R. (1962) Die Französichen Juristen im konfessionellen Bürgenkrieg des 16 *Jahrhunderts*, Drucker and Humblot, Berlin.

Serbat, L. (1906) *Les assemblées du clergé de France. Origines, organisation, dévéloppement (1561–1625)*.

Skinner, Q. (1978) *The Foundations of Modern Political Thought*, 2 vols, Cambridge U.P.

Snyders, G. (1965) *La pédagogie en France aux XVIe et XVIIe siècles*, PUF.

Soman, A. (1973) 'The theatre, diplomacy and censorship in the age of Henri IV', *Bib H R*, 35, 273–88.

Soman, A. (1974) *The Massacre of St Bartholomew: reappraisals and documents*, M. Nijhoff, The Hague.

Soman, A. (1978) 'The *parlement* of Paris and the great witch hunt (1565–1640)', *16C J*, 9, 30–44.

Sommervögel, C. and Bäcker (1892–1919) *Bibliothèque de la compagnie de Jésus*, 12 vols, Brussels and Paris.

Spooner, F.C. (1958) 'La Normandie à l'époque des guerres civiles; un problème de l'économie internationale', *Annales de Normandie*, 8, 199–213.

Spooner, F.C. (1972) *The International Economy and Monetary Movements in France, 1493–1725*, Harvard U.P., Cambridge, Mass.

Spooner, F.C. (1973) 'Monetary disturbance and inflation, 1590–3; the case of Aix-en-Provence' in *Mélanges en l'honneur de Fernand Braudel; Histoire économique du monde méditerranéan, 1450–1650*, Privat, Toulouse, pp. 582–93.

Stocker, C. (1978) 'Public and private enterprises in the administration of Renaissance monarchy; the first sales of office in the *parlement* of Paris (1512–14)', *16C J*, 9, 4–25.

Sutherland, N.M. (1973) *The Massacre of St Bartholomew and the European Conflict (1559–72)*, Macmillan.

Sutherland, N.M. (1980) *The Huguenot Struggle for Recognition*, Yale U.P., New Haven and London.

Sutherland, N.M. (1992) 'The Origins of the Thirty Years' War and the Structure of European Politics', *English Historical Review* 107, 587–625.

Sutto, C. (1977) 'Le contenu politique des pamphlets anti-Jésuites français à la fin du XVIe siècle' in *XVIIe Colloque International de Tours*, J. Vrin, pp. 233–46.

Sypher, G.W. (1963) 'La Popelinière's *Histoire de France*; a case of historical objectivity and religious censorship', *Journal of the History of Ideas*, 24, 41–54.

Sypher, G.W. (1980) ' "Faisant ce qu'il leur vient à plaisir": the image of Protestantism in French Catholic polemic on the eve of the religious wars', *16C J*, 11, 59–84.

Taillandier, A. (1845–46) 'Election du député de la prévoté de Paris aux Etats-Généraux de 1588', *Bib Ec Ch*, 2nd Series, 2, 422–59.

Tait, R.G. (1977) 'The king's lieutenants in Guyenne, 1581–1610', D.Phil. Thesis, University of Oxford.

Thickett, D. (1979) *Etienne Pasquier (1529–1615)*, Regency Press.

Thirsk, J. and Cooper, J.P. (1972) *Seventeenth Century Economic Documents*, Clarendon Press, Oxford.

Thomas, A. (1882) *Inventaire sommaire des archives communales de Limoges antérieur à 1790*, Limoges.

Thomas, A. (1910) *Le Concordat de 1516, ses origines, son histoire au XVIe siècle*, 3 vols.

Tilley, A. (1899) 'Some pamphlets of the French wars of religion', *EHR*, 14, 451–70.

Trocmé, E. and Delafosse, M. (1952) *Le commerce rochelais de la fin du XVe siècle au début du XVIIe siècle*, SEVPEN.

Trudel, M. (1973) *The Beginnings of New France*, McClelland and Stuart, Toronto.

Trullinger, R.S. (1972) 'The royal administration of Brittany under Henri IV', Ph.D. Thesis, Nashville University.

Tuetey, A. (1882–83) *Les Allemands en France et l'invasion du comté de Montbéliard*.

Turchetti, M. (1993) 'Une question mal posée: la qualification de perpétuel et irrévocable appliquée à l'édit de Nantes', *BSHPF*, 139, 41–78.

Van der Essen, L. (1933) *Alexandre Farnèse, prince de Parme, gouverneur général des pays-bas*, 2 vols, Brussels.

Van Doren, L. Scott (1974) 'Revolt and reaction in the city of Romans, Dauphiné (1579–80)', *16C J*, 5, 71–100.

Van Doren, L. Scott (1975) 'Civil war taxation and the foundation of French absolutism: the royal *taille* in Dauphiné, 1560–1610', *Proceedings of the Western Society for French History*, 3, 35–53.

Venard, M. (1993) *Réforme protestante, Réforme catholique dans la province d'Avignon – XVIe siècle*, Les éditions du Cerf.

Veyrassat-Herrem, B. and Le Roy Ladurie, E. (1968) 'La rente foncière autour de Paris au XVIIe siècle', *Annales*, 23, 541–55.

Viguier, J. (1906) *Les contrats et la consolidation des décimes à la fin du XVIe siècle*.

Villages déserts et histoire économique, XVe–XVIIIe siècles (1965), SEVPEN.

Viñas, A. (1939) 'Felipe II y la Jornada de las Barricadas' in *Hommage à Ernst Martinenche*, pp. 514–33.

Vivanti, C. (1967) 'Henri IV, the Gallic Hercules', *Journal of the Courtauld and Warburg Institute*, 30, 167–97.

Vogler, B. (1965) 'Le rôle des Electeurs palatins dans les guerres de religion (1559–1592)', *Cahiers d'Histoire*, 1, 51–85.

Warren, A. (1967) 'Les pamphlets de 1563 et l'assassinat du duc de Guise', *Bulletin Philologique*, xlii–xliii.

d'Welles, J. (1960) *Cadillac: Le château des ducs d'Epernon*.

Welter, L. (1946) 'Les aliénations du bien ecclésiastique en Auvergne au XVIe siècle', *Bulletin historique et scientifique de l'Auvergne*, 66, 114–51.

Wolfe, Martin (1972) *The Fiscal System of Renaissance France*, Yale U.P., New Haven, Conn.

Wolfe, Michael (1989) 'Piety and Political Allegiance: the Duc de Nevers and the Protestant Henri IV, 1589–1593', *French History*, 2, 1–21.

Wolfe, Michael (1993) *The Conversion of Henri IV. Politics, Power and Religious Belief in Early Modern France*, Harvard U.P., Cambridge, Mass.

Yardeni, M. (1966) 'L'ordre des avocats et la grève du barreau parisien en 1602', *Revue d'Histoire Economique*, 44, 481–507.

Yardeni, M. (1971) *La conscience nationale en France*, Nauwelaerts, Louvain.

Yates, F. (1947) *The French Academies of the Sixteenth Century*, Warburg Institute.

Yates, F. (1954) 'Dramatic religious processions in Paris in the late sixteenth century', *Annales musicologiques*, 2, 215–70.

Zeller, G. (1879) 'La conspiration du maréchal de Biron', *Compte rendu des séances et travaux de l'Académie des sciences morales et politiques*, 111, 130–59.

Zeller, B. (1964) *Aspects de la politique française sous l'ancien régime*, PUF.

Appendix

THE PARIS SIXTEEN: A SOCIAL ANALYSIS

Extensive research on the background and careers of prominent members of the Paris League has been undertaken by Robert Descimon (R. Descimon, 1983). His analysis emphasises how they were, in general, notables of some status. Both lawyers and merchants adhered to it, outweighing those from below and above these groups (*Table I*). It must be emphasised, however, how imprecise social classifications were during the civil wars. We may conclude, though, that the *Sixteen* enjoyed the active support of respectable Parisian bourgeois. This conclusion is reinforced by the fact that nearly two thirds of those whose geographical background is known (143 of 185) were born in Paris of Parisian parents. The age of adherents to the *Sixteen* is estimated by Descimon from the dates of their contracts of marriage (generally undertaken in this period between the ages of 20 and 30). Probably 95 (or 42.2 per cent) were aged between 45 and 55 in 1591 – i.e. were reaching late adolescence when the civil wars began. A further 71 (or 31.5 per cent) were between the ages of 35 and 45 in 1591 and were thus of the generation whose childhood had never known a period without sectarian violence. It is often claimed that the League was an example of a political movement responding to a 'société bloquée' – the radical politics of individuals frustrated in their vocations and alienated. But this is very difficult to prove. Given the difficulties of social classification already mentioned, the precise measurement of social mobility, or its absence, becomes extremely delicate, and the measurement of individuals' realistic aspirations is an impossibility. Descimon's analysis suggests, however, that the adherents of the *Sixteen* enjoyed considerable social stability before 1588 and that only a minority of them achieved modest social advancement during and after the League (*Table II*):

TABLE I: Adherents of the Sixteen; vocational analysis

	%	Adherents
Members of the sovereign courts of Paris	10.22	23
Subordinate tribunals	1.78	4
Financial officials, bankers; handlers of money	8	18
Lawyers; liberal professions; medics; notaries; clerks, etc	40.44	91
Merchants	28.89	65
Artisans	9.78	22
Unknown	0.89	2
TOTAL	**100%**	**225**

TABLE II: Social Mobility among the Sixteen

	Before the Barricades (1588)			After the Barricades		
	S	A	D	S	A	D
Magistrates in sovereign courts	13	10	0	12	2	0
Other Magistrates	2	2	0	2	0	0
Financiers	8	9	1	7	1	2
Lawyers	76	14	1	42	5	2
Merchants	61	4	0	40	4	2
Artisans	20	2	0	10	0	0
Unknown(2)						
TOTALS (2)	**180**	**41**	**2**	**113**	**12**	**6**

S= No mobility   A = Advancement   D = Decline

Figures and Maps

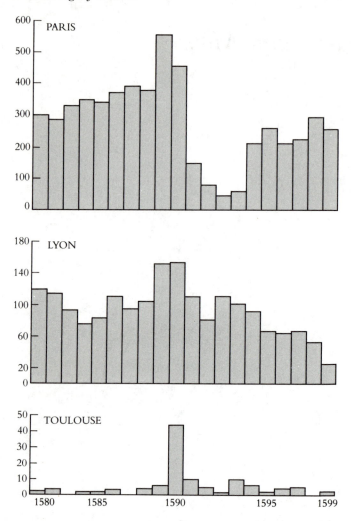

Note

It must be remembered that extant imprints do not accurately reflect the total number of titles printed each year in any centre. Surviving books and pamphlets represent only a small fraction of the total material in print in any year in the sixteenth century. In addition, there are numerous dubious imprints which have been excluded from these calculations.

Sources used: 1. H.L. Baudrier, *Bibliographie lyonnaise,* 13 vols, Lyon, 1895–1921.

      2. J. Mégret and L. Desgraves, *Répertoire bibliographique des livres imprimés en France au seizième siècle,* Bibliotheca Bibliographica Aureliana, lxiii, fasc. 151. Baden-Baden, 1975.

      3. D. Pallier, 1975.

Fig.1   Extant imprints from the presses at Paris, Lyon and Toulouse

The following is a simplified genealogy which illustrates the conflicting claims of strict primogeniture and consanguinity.

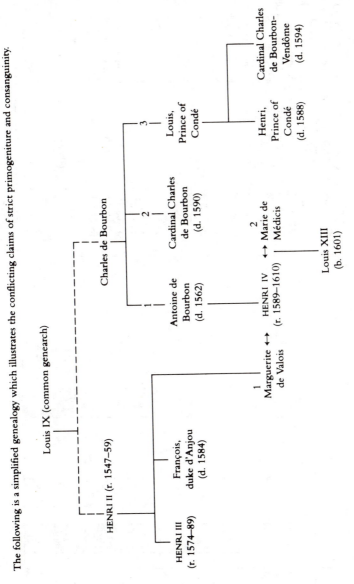

Fig. 2 The Bourbon succession

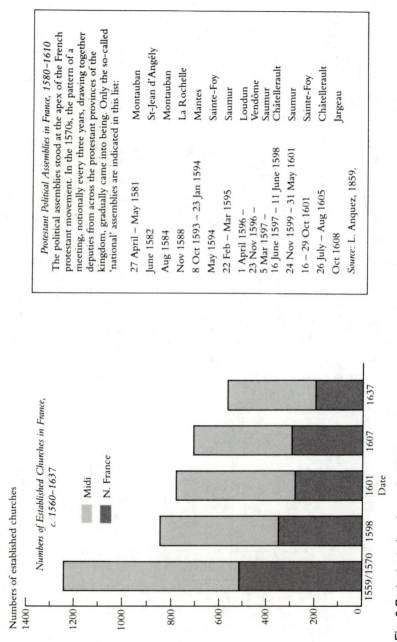

Fig. 3 Protestant church numbers and political assemblies in late sixteenth- and early seventeenth-century France.

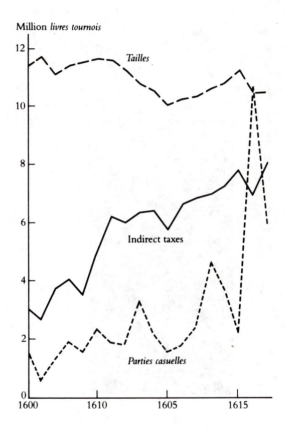

Million *livres tournois*

Tailles

Indirect taxes

Parties casuelles

Note
The basic source for income to the treasury in the reign of Henri IV is: J. R. Malet, *Comptes rendus de l'administration des finances du royaume de France.* London and Paris, 1789.
The figures can be presented in several different ways; I have adopted the method used in J. M. Hayden, 1974.

Fig. 4   Royal income, 1600–1617.

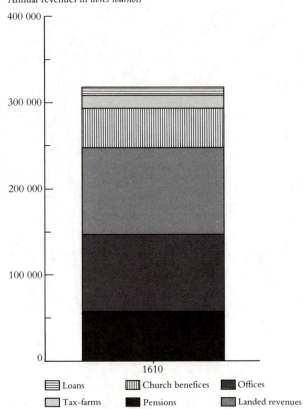

Annual revenues in *livres tournois*

Sully was at the height of his ministerial career in 1610. The analysis of his annual income provided by I. Aristide, 1990, enables us to glimpse the constitution of a ministerial fortune in the first decade of the seventeenth century.

Fig. 5   The fortune of Maximilien de Béthune, duke of Sully.

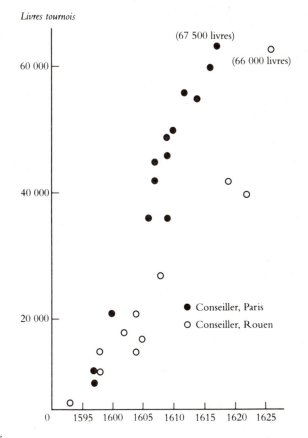

Livres tournois

(67 500 livres)

(66 000 livres)

● Conseiller, Paris
○ Conseiller, Rouen

Note
Office prices can only be calculated with difficulty, generally from notarial archives. Because the market was not completely public, prices could differ for similar offices, sometimes by wide margins. This table overestimates the rise in prices in the early seventeenth century because the market was obviously depressed during and immediately after the League.

Sources used: 1. R. Mousnier, 1971.

          2. R. J. Bonney, *Political change in France under Richelieu and Mazarin*. Oxford, 1978.

          3. R. Mousnier (ed.),*Lettres et mémoires adressés au Chancelier Séguier (1633–49),* 2 vols, 1964.

          4. J. Dewald, 1980.

Fig. 6   Office prices in the parlements of Paris and Rouen, 1590–1620.

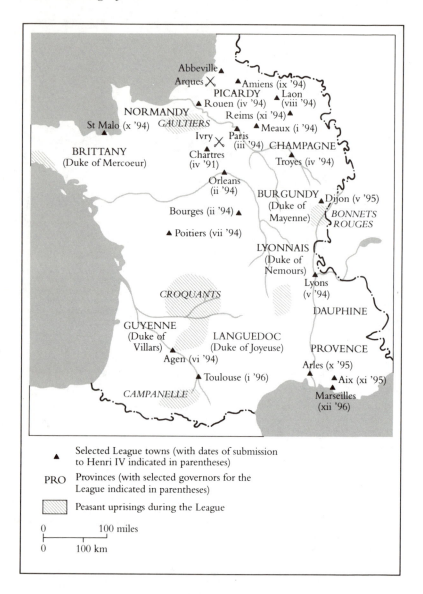

Map 1   France during the Catholic League

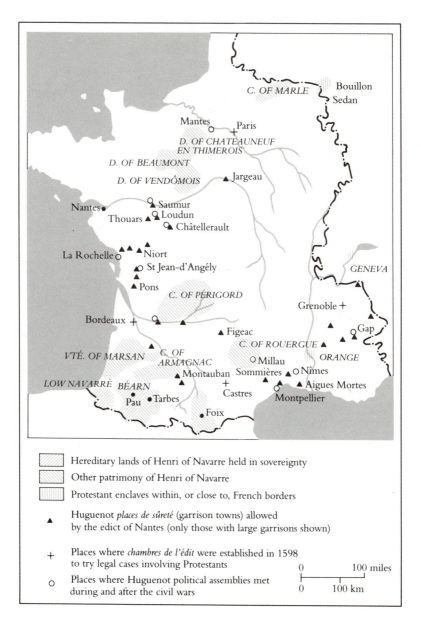

Map 2   *Protestant France, c. 1600.*

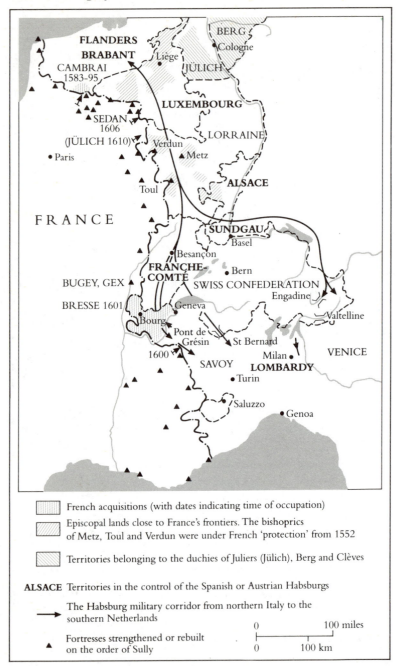

Map 3   France's frontiers, 1589–1610.

Index